THE NEW
AMERICAN TROUT FISHING

To Dad
Christmas 1994

Perhaps a little science
will up the odds.

Nevertheless each year has
its highlights ~ one of which
is casting tales, spinning
ambitions and luring the
elusive trouts with you.

Love to you

Mark

THE NEW
AMERICAN
TROUT FISHING

JOHN MERWIN

Illustrated by Ernest Lussier

MACMILLAN PUBLISHING COMPANY / NEW YORK

MAXWELL MACMILLAN CANADA / TORONTO

MAXWELL MACMILLAN INTERNATIONAL / NEW YORK   OXFORD   SINGAPORE   SYDNEY

Macmillan Publishing Company
866 Third Avenue
New York, NY 10022

Maxwell Macmillan Canada, Inc.
1200 Eglinton Avenue East, Suite 200
Don Mills, Ontario M3C 3N1

Macmillan Publishing Company is part of
the Maxwell Communication Group of Companies.

Library of Congress Cataloging-in-Publication Data

Merwin, John.
The new American trout fishing/by John Merwin.
p.   cm.
Includes index.
ISBN 0-02-584382-6
1. Trout fishing—United States—History.
2. Fly fishing—United States—History.
I. Title.
SH688.U6M47   1994
799.1'755—dc20
92–37213
CIP

Macmillan books are available at special discounts for bulk purchases for sales promotions, premiums, fund-raising, or educational use. For details, contact:

Special Sales Director
Macmillan Publishing Company
866 Third Avenue
New York, NY 10022

Book design by Jennifer Dossin

10 9 8 7 6 5 4 3 2 1

Printed in the United States of America

To Gus Merwin, Sr.,

I dedicate this book with gratitude and affection.

Contents

Acknowledgments

The following people, many of whom are or were in some way associated with the fly-fishing trade, have contributed greatly to this book through years of friendship, discussion, or time shared astream. As such they deserve special thanks. Those indicated in italics are deceased, but still deserve acknowledgment. *Tim Bedford*, Bruce Bowlen, J. Leon Chandler, Doug Cummings, Ralph Daniels, Buzz Eichel, Jim Ellett, Dave Engerbretson, Dick Finlay, Joe Fisher, Charlie Fox, Michael and Susan Fitzgerald, Art Frey, Paul Fuller, Vern Gallup, Keith Gardner, Gardner Grant, Bill Herrick, *Austin Hogan*, Bob Jacklin, Paul Johnson, Larry Kenney, Lefty Kreh, Mel Krieger, Eric Leiser, Greg Lilly, Nick Lyons, *Vince Marinaro*, Darrel Martin, *Al McClane*, Ted Niemeyer, Richard Norman, Don Phillips, George Schlotter, Ernest Schwiebert, Howard Steere, Lou Tabory, *Dwight Webster*, Howard West, Harry Wilson, Phil Wright, Joan Salvato Wulff, *Lee Wulff*, and Ed Zern.

Special thanks, too, for Ernest Lussier, a longtime friend whose drawings add so much to this book. And to Barry and Cathy Beck, the talented fly-tying team from Pennsylvania who tied many of the patterns for this book's color plates. Thanks also to George Schlotter for his streamer flies. Alanna Fisher and the staff of the American Museum of Fly Fishing provided valuable research help, as did Gail Rice and staff at the Mark Skinner Library, Manchester, Vermont. Thanks also to Richard Balkin, my literary agent, for his tenacity and insight, and to Pam Hoenig and Justin Schwartz at Macmillan for their perseverance and help in seeing this book to completion.

Finally, warm thanks to Martha, my wife, and to my children, Emily, Jason, and Sam, all of whom provided immeasurable support during the years this book was in progress.

Preface

Most trout-fishing books these days are either introductory manuals or highly specialized works dealing with a particular group of trout-stream insects, caddisflies, for example, or a particular technique, such as fishing with artificial nymphs. As these specialties have continued to grow since the 1950s, the sheer volume of information available to trout fishermen about their sport has increased enormously. The general views of fly fishing given by onetime popular writers, such as Ray Bergman, Joe Brooks, and Al McClane, are long out of date, and the broad forest that is trout fishing has become almost invisible through its many and distinct trees of technique. It is a confusing picture, even for anglers of some experience.

This book reflects what I've long felt to be the need for a modern overview—one that goes beyond the simple rote instruction in tackle and tactics that every beginner requires. There are, as one reviewer has lamented, almost as many books for beginning fly fishermen as there are beginners themselves. I have thus assumed at least some experience on the reader's part, such as one might get from a weekend fly-fishing school or from any one of many basic texts. Because knowledge of basic definitions and trout-fishing tactics is assumed, we then have the room in this book to explore more advanced topics such as trout-stream ecology, trout behavior, and fly-casting dynamics, among many other things, all of which should be helpful to trout fishermen of all skill levels.

Portions of this book are technical and involved considerable research, although this is not a formal scientific work. I have provided extensive notes to the text as well as a large bibliography for those who wish to further review the topics covered in these pages. Because many of the ideas expressed here are contrary to commonly held beliefs among trout fishermen, the notes and bibliography also indicate the sources of many of these concepts. Enthusiastic trout fishermen often turn into equally enthusiastic researchers into some aspect of their sport, and the bibliography should be especially helpful in this regard. Almost all of the bibliographic entries can be borrowed through your local library's interlibrary loan program, which is how I obtained them myself.

I have been fortunate, first, in having fly fished for trout through more than forty years, and second, in having been professionally involved in fly-fishing for the past eighteen of those years. The latter has allowed extensive exploration of trout rivers in the Midwest, Rockies, West, and beyond that would otherwise have been impossible. In the same interval, my boyhood heroes—men such as Lee Wulff and Al McClane, both recently deceased—became colleagues and, eventually, close friends. I have learned a great deal from men such as these, and I continue to learn from other friends in the fly-fishing trade, for which I am most grateful.

I have tried in the following text and notes to give credit for ideas and concepts where credit is due; I hope that I've made no omissions in that regard.

Beyond a modern overview of fly fishing for trout, this book is based on a deceptively simple premise: Among the myriad fly patterns used by trout fishermen to sometimes fool trout, there is no single artificial fly that fools all of the trout all of the time. Some anglers shrug their shoulders at this, returning to the river another day while hoping for better luck. Other anglers ask why this is so, a seemingly simple inquiry that has produced thousands of volumes of argument over several centuries of trout-fishing. I suppose there are more productive puzzles, such as balancing one's checkbook, but there are none so pleasant as the questions echoed by the spreading rings of rising trout.

JOHN MERWIN
Dorset, Vermont
February, 1994

THE NEW
AMERICAN TROUT FISHING

1
Looking Backward

Starting to fly fish for trout is like falling in love. The early gratifications, be they kisses or rising trout, are heady and decidedly unscientific. They exist of the moment, and for the moment, that's enough. Sooner or later things calm down a little, and as the infatuation continues you want to know more. Where she grew up. What her family was like. What makes her the way she is. So it is with trout fishing, and the questions are many. There are the trout themselves, of course, and what makes them tick. The broad fields of aquatic entomology and ecology are fair and necessary game, in addition to the immediate concerns of tackle and tactics. Fly-fishing has a broad and rich literature that is not only a source of information but for many an appealing subject in itself.

If for no other reason, some knowledge of fly-fishing history is needed just to understand the sport's modern jargon. Some words and phrases that describe modern tackle and tactics have evolved over many years of angling usage and now sometimes have little relation to their original meaning. A "cast," for example, once meant a leader, often with several flies attached, and now refers only to the act of fly casting. Leader-tippet sizes, as another example, are still designated by their "X" size. When silkworm-gut leaders became widely used in the nineteenth century, a size 3X gut leader section was drawn or pulled three times through special dies that

reduced its diameter. A 4X section was drawn four times, and so on, which related the various sections directly to diameter and strength. Modern leaders are made of nylon monofilament on extruding machinery and have no relation either to silkworms or the old drawing process. The X system has been retained by longstanding convention but now relates only to diameter. Because different alloys of nylon are used by different monofilament manufacturers to vary such characteristics as stiffness and stretch, the breaking strength of a particular diameter or X size varies according to its maker.

Leaders are a good example because they also serve to illustrate one of the first things learned by almost anyone delving into angling history: Much of what's purported to be new in fishing at any given time isn't really new at all, at least in concept. Consider Charles Cotton's early yet wonderfully modern admonition that "to fish fine and far off is the first and principal rule for trout angling." This appeared in Cotton's "Instructions how to angle for a trout or grayling in a clear stream," which was appended to the fifth edition of Izaak Walton's *Compleat Angler* in 1676. Like most anglers of his time, Cotton used a fly line made of plaited horsehair that was decreased in diameter toward its smaller end by reducing the number of hairs in intermediate sections. The end of the line, which was effectively the leader, was often only two hairs, because, in Cotton's words, "He that cannot kill a [brown] trout of twenty inches long with two [hairs] . . . deserves not the name of an angler."

As it turns out, Cotton's leader was fine indeed. When I first read this I considered taking a micrometer down to the nearest farm to find a horse willing to help me research some three-hundred-year-old leaders, but a little reading saved me the trouble. The late A. J. McClane once described Cotton's terminal gear as follows:

> The average tensile strength of horse-hair is less than that of raw nylon mon-ofilament. It is somewhat stiffer and has a greater elongation than nylon—stretch-ing about 30 percent. Horsehair diameters run from .010 to .006 [inches], or 1X to 4X, with a tensile strength of 1.7 to 0.9 pounds . . . Charles Cotton probably fished with a tippet testing about 2.5 pounds.

In terms of new leaders and rated breaking strains, which have increased since McClane described them in the early 1970s, Cotton's 2.5-pound-test leader was a modern 6X in strength although larger in diameter. Handling such a large brown trout on a fine leader is a tough test for modern anglers with the best of tackle. Cotton had only his wil-lowy rod of 16 feet or so with a slightly longer length of line tied to its tip, since fishing reels didn't come into general use until well after 1700.

Walton's *Angler* was first published in London in 1653. The written mastery of the pastoral dialogue between Piscator (the mas-ter angler) and Venator (a hunter, and Pis-cator's student in angling) eventually brought the book unceasing critical acclaim far beyond mere fishing circles. Walton him-self was not a fly fisherman, although fly-fishing was relatively well developed by his time, and his early *Angler* editions contained well-described techniques of baitfishing for

a variety of fish, including trout. Eventually, Walton met the much younger Cotton and was obviously taken with the latter's fly-fishing skills. John Waller Hills, in his 1921 book *A History of Fly Fishing for Trout*, of-fered this excellent contrast of the two anglers:

> The affectionate friendship between these two men has always surprised those who do not know the binding force of a common sport: Walton, the retired tradesman, the friend and biographer of good and pious men, and Cotton, the dis-solute aristocrat, the spendthrift courtier, writer of obscene poetry.

Cotton asked Walton's permission to write his fly-fishing addition in Walton's dialogue form for inclusion in some future edition of Walton's own work, and the master happily agreed. Walton was eighty-three years old when the 1676 edition that included Cot-ton's work appeared. He sent the book to Cotton with a letter professing undying love and friendship, a friendship that provided the foundation of modern fly-fishing.[1]

Neither Walton's work nor Cotton's was wholly original, which brings us to a second axiom for the novice in angling history: Be-ware of claims to invention, either stated or implied, and temper your wariness with un-derstanding. Cotton, for example, was pre-ceded in his "fish fine" suggestion by Thomas Barker in his 1651 book *The Art of Angling*, of which Cotton was certainly aware. Walton relied on this book, also, and to an even greater extent on an earlier work with the same title by an unknown author, brought out by a London publisher in 1577, of which only one copy is known to exist, much of which Walton seems to have lifted directly and without attribution.

As a worst case, some find the kindly Wal-ton to be a plagiarizing baitfisherman and his erudite friend Cotton a disorderly drunk, but those judgments are extreme and much too harsh. The two men were both eloquent and accurate in describing the state of angling in their time, and their book has become the most widely recognized work in the English-speaking world after the Bible. It is unfortunately also one of the least read, especially in our current emphasis on ever-newer tackle and techniques. Some of it will seem flowery and difficult going, but the text is mercifully short and the perspective it offers on modern trout fishing is worth your effort. If you choose to read only one book among those of angling ancients, read this one.

It is a relatively short jump from Walton and Cotton to early accounts of American angling, which I'll make quickly for the sake of being able to cover other things in greater detail later. Through the remainder of the seventeenth and eighteenth centuries, British angling authors grew in both numbers and authority, their work culminating in the writings of Charles and Richard Bowlker, father and son, whose highly sophisticated book *The Art of Angling* was first published in the mid-1700s and went through numerous editions for almost one hundred years. By this time, there was already a well-established middle class in American cities such as Boston, New York, and Philadelphia, where fishing for sport was a widespread although poorly documented activity. As yet, there's been no discovery of a contemporary and broad-based account of eighteenth-century American angling. Researchers like Charles Goodspeed and the late Austin Hogan, in his years at the American Museum of Fly Fishing, depended on old diaries, scattered newspaper accounts, and biographies to demonstrate that angling was both widely practiced and little recorded, probably because it was one of the least remarkable things in a very tumultuous time.

Goodspeed quotes an early biographer of patriot Patrick Henry to give some indication of a young American sportsman's life early in the eighteenth century:

> From all quarters the testimony appears to be to this effect,—that he was an indolent, dreamy, frolicsome creature, with a mortal enmity to books, supplemented by a passionate regard for fishing-rods and shotguns; disorderly in dress, slouching, vagrant, unambitious; a roamer in the woods, a loiterer on river banks; having more tastes and aspirations in common with trappers and frontiersmen than with the toilers of civilized life.

There is no evidence that Henry was fly fishing in those early Virginia years, but he was obviously fishing for fun. I am inclined to the admittedly romantic notion that his famous "give me liberty, or give me death" speech delivered about thirty years later owed as much to his early woodland freedoms as his later political ones.

To the north, America's earliest angling club—the Schuylkill Fishing Company—was organized in Philadelphia in 1732. This was a social club more than anything else, and its members gathered often, ladies included, to wine and dine on white perch caught in nearby rivers. This fish was eventually incorporated into the club's flag. In New York, the first recorded angling regulation in America was set in 1734, when Collect Pond on Manhattan Island was restricted to hook-and-line fishing only. Sportfishing was obviously taking place here, but its exact nature remains to this day undefined and elusive. I'm aware of no early sportfishing records in the Dutch settlement of New York, for example, although the Dutch penetrated far up the Hudson and its tributaries to Albany and beyond. There has been revived interest lately in the translation of early Dutch manuscript materials from this period, and I'm hopeful that some fishing-related material will be revealed.

John Rowe was an English-born Boston merchant who kept a detailed diary of his fishing experiences around that city between 1764 and 1774, which included a note to the effect that he imported some fishing rods in 1765. Although there is no indication that he did so, he could just as easily have imported a copy of the Bowlkers' new book, or the 1750 Moses Brown reissue of Walton and Cotton's classic. Rowe's diaries give no account of fly-fishing *per se,* but among his many notes is one mentioning his capture of ten brook trout, "the largest I ever saw, several of them 18 inches in length!"[2] Most of Rowe's fishing was within 25 miles of Boston proper, often in Charles River tributaries and local ponds, and a number of his entries show "poor" or "very poor" fishing on a particular day. Even by this time, the cream of the area's trout fishing was long gone.

There are other contemporary references to sportfishing as one progresses northward, and the British influence in the eighteenth-century settlement of eastern Canada undoubtedly carried the long tradition of English angling as part of its baggage.[3] The most concrete evidence of fly-fishing then, however, is from period newspaper advertising by fishing-tackle suppliers. By 1773, Jeremiah Allen in Boston was advertising fly tackle among other types. Edward Pole was likewise advertising "artificial flies" among other tackle items at his Philadelphia shop during the 1770s. That people were fly fishing at the time is self-evident. There were, however, no American angling books published until well after 1800, nor were there any sporting periodicals. Exactly who was fly fishing in eighteenth-century America and where remains a clouded question.

America in the year 1800 may appear in casual thought as a few small cities separated by vast tracts of wilderness. Because we are flooded these days with news that is electronically immediate, it's easy to assume that the flow of ideas two hundred years ago was primitive, but that's just not true. A commonality of interest in mundane things like fishing or important things like the newly emerging American sciences moved concepts as quickly as commerce between major cities like Philadelphia, New York, and Boston. The exchange of information can often be inferred simply by knowing who knew whom and when, and America in 1800 was a very small world.

In researching the brook-trout section of this book, for example, I followed the life of Samuel Latham Mitchell in New York, who in 1814 published the first uniquely American work in ichthyology. Mitchell was a friend of William Blakewell, a prominent eastern Pennsylvania businessman who also came to be John James Audubon's father-in-law. Audubon himself worked briefly as Mitchell's laboratory clerk in New York during the year 1806. Audubon's early travels took him in 1807 to Louisville, Kentucky, where he became friends with William and Lucy Croghan. Mrs. Croghan's brothers were more widely known: Her maiden name was Clark, and her brother William had just returned from his famous expedition to the Northwest with Meriwether Lewis. Her other brother, General George Rogers Clark, was a Revolutionary War hero and Indian fighter. Dr. William Galt, another Louisville resident, was an enthusiastic botanist and also a friend of Dr. Mitchell's. Galt was said to be especially happy when told that Lucy Blakewell of Pennsylvania would be joining Audubon in Louisville, because of the Blakewell family's friendship in England with the late Dr. Erasmus Darwin, a famous botanist who later became better known as Charles Darwin's grandfather.[4] I haven't exhausted this particular and seemingly incredible chain of coincidence but am using it to point out that such circles were common in this period. Modern biographies of nineteenth-century Americans tend to be exceptionally long simply because it's impossible to review a then-prominent family's relatives and social and business connections in less than several hundred pages. This concept is essential to understanding one man who was an outstanding figure in nineteenth-century American trout fishing: George Washington Bethune.

This stocky Scot was born March 18, 1805. He grew up in Salem, New York, a small village near the Vermont state line, and along the Battenkill and a variety of tributaries that offered excellent brook-trout fishing. He spent his professional life as a minister in the Dutch Reformed Church at various locations, but is best known as the editor of the first (1847) American edition of Walton's *Angler*, to which he appended copious notes on contemporary American angling. Because of his role in the clergy, Bethune consistently asked to remain anonymous as an angler. His *Angler* edition is thus only credited to "an American editor," and acquaintances such as William Porter, whose newly established (1831) periodical *Spirit of the Times* offered wide angling coverage, referred to Bethune in print only by such names as the "Eminent Divine." Bethune is important here not just for what he accomplished in print, but also because he's an exceptional example of just what was possible in American fly-fishing between 1800 and the Civil War.

Bethune got a rigorous classical education at Salem's Washington Academy until he was fourteen years old, and he learned to fish during the same period. Local histories provide a character known only as Fisher Billy, who was apparently doing odd jobs and hanging around this backwoods village to avoid his creditors in Albany and elsewhere. It was Billy whom Bethune later credited with his

George Washington Bethune.

early fishing training, although in searching the records of local historical societies I found no clue as to whether any of this was fly-fishing. White Creek even now is a clear, cold Battenkill tributary that runs within earshot of the old academy building, and it's easy to imagine a young Bethune sitting here with his head buried in a Latin text and his mind on the trout stream he could hear through the open window.

Starting in 1819, Bethune spent two years at New York's Columbia College. Manhattan north of what's now Twenty-third Street was a rural area then, and there were numerous fishing opportunities available, including the once-fabulous brook-trout fishing on Long Island, but I've no evidence that Bethune took advantage of them in that period. In 1821, Bethune went to Dickinson College in Carlisle, Pennsylvania, from which he graduated in 1823. Here such now-famous spring creeks as the Letort and Big Spring were close at hand, although they didn't start to become famous in print until General George Gibson first wrote about them in 1829. Princeton was next on Bethune's list, where he studied religion from 1823 until 1827 when he was ordained by the Second Presbytery of New York. Here again, he might have passed four hard years of theological study without bothering to explore nearby streams in Pennsylvania's eastern Poconos, but I doubt it. Ernest Schwiebert has suggested that Bethune fished the (now) well-known Brodheads Creek after a primitive hostelry was built nearby in 1836, but Bethune's first visits might have been ten years earlier.[5]

Bethune's first parish was in Rhinebeck, New York, in the rolling Hudson River uplands north of Poughkeepsie, where he was in residence between 1827 and 1830. Not far over the eastward hills was what's now Connecticut's best trout river, the Housatonic. Directly across the Hudson were the Catskill Mountains and eastward-draining streams such as Esopus Creek. He moved again in 1830, this time taking a parish in Utica, New York, near the Mohawk River headwaters at the edge of the Adirondacks. This was also not far from the then-wilderness Piseco Lake, which Bethune would later make famous.

Then, as now, it was characteristic of upwardly mobile young Protestant ministers to take a few small parishes while hoping for the luxury of a large and rich one. Bethune got his chance in 1834 when he took a pastorate in Philadelphia, where he served until 1849. He moved back to New York in 1850, serving a parish in Brooklyn Heights until 1859. He then preached at the Twenty-first Street church in Manhattan until his death on April 28, 1862, while traveling in Italy. Pious man that he was, Bethune never made a public connection between his various moves and his trout-fishing passion, but we are left, at the very least, with fifty years of overwhelming coincidence.

In 1841, Bethune became involved in forming the Lake Piseco Trout Club, which, according to the many notes compiled by the late Austin Hogan, was the first such wilderness club in America. At the time of the club's organization, Bethune lived in Philadelphia, but both his travels and his interests were wide ranging. The diversity of the other club members is indicative of both attributes: There were two bankers and an army officer from the Troy area on the upper Hudson; a minister from Medford, Massachusetts; another angler from Philadelphia, and one from Hoboken, New Jersey. They had a large clubhouse built on the remote little lake in 1842 and called it Walton Hall. Here they spent one to two weeks each season for the next eight years, casting or trolling for brook and lake trout, their catches of which were duly entered in the club's journal. Evenings were spent over dinners of fresh trout and considerable wine, with the attendant debates on angling literature often carrying over to the fly-tying and tackle tables. Bethune held services often, both for the members and for the small community at one end of the lake. He eventually recorded some of this activity in one of the several appendices to his 1847 Walton edition.

Like his contemporaries in American angling, Bethune's trout fishing was for brook trout, which were and are much easier to catch than the brown trout of British rivers. Through all of the nineteenth century there were frequent and sometimes violent arguments in the angling press on the efficacy of British tactics and fly patterns on American waters. Almost all of these quarrels ignored obvious differences in the fisheries themselves, although Bethune's observations were unusually acute:

> The trout in our upland streams are more plentiful, and, clearly, less sophisticated than those with whom our transatlantic brethren are conversant. In a virgin stream (such an [sic] one as an artificial fly has never been cast upon, which the American fly-fisher sometimes meets with), the trout, if fairly on the feed, will take anything that is offered to them.

The nineteenth century brought a revolution to British trout fishing that found much of its beginnings in Alfred Ronalds' remarkable 1836 book *A Fly Fisher's Entomology* and its extremes in the work of Frederick Halford in the 1880s. It was a scientific revolution in tactics and aquatic-insect imitations that applied well to brown trout, but which American brook-trout fishermen didn't yet need and thus often ridiculed. That provincial attitude still persists in many areas of this country, and arguments about the need for imitation are widespread here, even more than one hundred years after the introduction of brown trout to American waters.

But even brook trout can react highly selectively to fly pattern at times, something that Bethune acknowledged with a perception that most of his American contemporaries lacked:

> On the other side it is contended, that the non-imitation writers themselves admit, as experience compels them to do, that there must be an adaptation of colors in a fly, and also that certain flies will not be taken at some seasons that are freely taken in others.

He gave lengthy arguments on the need for imitation, pro and con, in long footnotes to his *Angler* edition, and, since Bethune like many others used two or more wet flies on his leader at one time, he finally admitted to hedging his bets: "My practice is to observe the fly on the waters for my tail fly, and experiment with hackles on the drop."

Bethune was well acquainted with the best and newest among British angling books and sometimes quotes Bowlker or Bainbridge or Ronalds at length. By the time of his death, Bethune had collected seven hundred angling-related books and had made several trips to Europe for research and additions to his collection, which led to the long, erudite "bibliographical note" attached to his Walton work. His acquaintances ranged from President Martin Van Buren to the great scientists of Philadelphia and New York, to an assortment of backwoods characters met while fishing between Pennsylvania and

Maine. Other men of his time, like William Henry Herbert and Thaddeus Norris, wrote more widely of American angling in all its forms, but none wrote with greater intellect and insight. It's tempting to call Bethune remarkably modern, but perhaps the reverse is a greater truism; that much of what we call modern isn't really new at all.

As American anglers grew in skills and numbers during the 1800s, their fishing predictably declined. Bethune and his cronies abandoned their beloved Walton Hall at Piseco Lake in the Adirondacks in 1851, when, after several years of killing thousands of pounds of trout, there were simply fewer to be had. It was a pattern that progressed northward through the mountains and into Maine as rushes of fishermen transported by buckboard, steamer, and eventually railroads rapidly depleted what was once wilderness trout fishing. A growing commerce added its own nails to the coffin as northern loggers stripped the riverbanks, warming the streams and suffocating spawning tributaries with slit. Mills farther south spewed their wastes into once-productive trout streams. The combination of increasing fishing pressure in the face of declining trout-stream habitat was a disaster that found its contemporary answer in fish hatcheries.

There were many nineteenth-century American developments in tackle and tactics that affect the way we fish these days—things such as bamboo rods and dry flies—but there were no innovations with so broad a modern effect as the American trout-hatchery movement after the Civil War. This has been explored little in modern angling books, but it defined in many ways both how we fish and the fish we're seeking in the first place. Men like Seth Green and Fred Mather were widely involved in nineteenth-century trout culture and are familiar names even now to some fishermen, but the most im-

Spencer Fullerton Baird.

portant figure—and the man who gave Mather, Green, and others much of their impetus—was Spencer Fullerton Baird.[6]

American trout culture had its start in 1853 with the work of Theodatus Garlick and H. A. Ackley near Cleveland, Ohio, who obtained their brook trout from some tributaries of Lake Superior, but they were first only in this country. The artificial culture of fish dates back at least to the fifteenth century in western Europe and considerably earlier in China. During the 1850s, various northeastern states explored fish culture as a means of restoring not only trout to their widely deteriorating rivers, but also shad and Atlantic salmon to rivers where they had already been exterminated by dams and water pollution. It wasn't, however, until toward the end of the Civil War that trout hatcheries started to proliferate and even then for reasons other than restoring what had been destroyed in the name of progress.

Seth Green was a market fisherman who operated a fish stall in his Rochester, New York, hometown during the 1840s. His sales were declining along with the native-fish populations, and he began experimenting with trout and salmon culture, which led to his famous hatchery at Caledonia, New York, in about 1864. He found a ready market

among sportsmen wanting to buy brook-trout fry for stocking their own depleted waters and an even better market among fish wholesalers, hotels, and restaurants, who would pay as much as $1 a pound for fresh brook trout. This was an astronomical price in the 1860s and, over the next twenty years, fueled a dramatic increase in the number of small private hatcheries throughout the Northeast.

By 1870, all the New England states plus New York, New Jersey, Pennsylvania, Maryland, Alabama, Virginia, and California had established state fish commissions to deal with their respective fisheries problems. In the same year the American Fish Culturists' Association, precursor to the present-day American Fisheries Society, was organized by hatchery men like Seth Green in cooperation with more prominent people such as Green's friend Robert Barnwell Roosevelt, a widely known sportsman and also Theodore's uncle, of the New York commission. There was substantial bickering among the state commissions on many issues, most notably about interstate waterways, and the suggestion was finally made that the federal government get into the fish-hatchery business. After considerable arm-twisting and politicking of the worst pork-barrel sort in Congress, the United States Fish Commission was created in 1872, with Spencer Fullerton Baird, then a widely known naturalist and assistant secretary of the Smithsonian Institution, at the helm.

The new commission's immediate mandates were to create a federal hatchery in California for Pacific salmon and a hatchery somewhere in the Northeast for shad, which were to be restored to their native rivers and also introduced in California and in the Mississippi Valley. Livingston Stone, a private fish culturist in Charlestown, New Hampshire, was promptly sent West, where he established a federal hatchery on California's

McCloud River. Seth Green and Fred Mather were both employed in shad culture in the East. There was at this time a tremendous faith in science, which led to the belief that not only could nature's handiwork be restored, but that it also could be improved. That there were some successes among many failures enabled these ideas to persist. Starting with Seth Green's 1871 efforts under contract to the California Fish Commission, for example, shad became (and are) well established in California's Sacramento River system. But Baird and his commission dumped millions of shad in the Mississippi system without success and spent a small fortune over many years trying to establish California chinook salmon in eastern rivers where Atlantic salmon had been wiped out. Much of the stocking effort was political, used as a means to justify and enlarge the commission's budget. Baird himself once said, in 1877, when it was suggested that shipments of salmon eggs were being wrongly placed:

> It does not make much difference what is done with the salmon eggs. The object is to introduce them into as many states as possible and have credit with Congress accordingly.[7]

His seeming cynicism notwithstanding, Baird apparently did believe that the widespread fish introductions he fostered would in time increase America's food supply. This same belief made him the moving force in the broad introductions of carp in the United States, starting in 1875, an introduction seen a century later as an ecological disaster.

For trout fishermen, the next ten years brought some astounding changes. Eastern brook trout were introduced to California and the Rocky Mountain states, starting in 1872. Rainbow trout, once native only to the Pacific Coast, were introduced in the Rockies, Midwest, and East, starting in 1874.

Brown trout, which were originally not found anywhere in North America, were introduced starting in 1883. While it's true that individual state commissions, especially that of New York, with technicians like Seth Green and Fred Mather backed by the vocal and blustering Roosevelt, might have accomplished all this in time, Baird gave the movement both national and international stature that greatly hastened the process. Many of these introductions are covered at greater length in chapters on the respective trout, but for the moment it's important to note that more than ten thousand years of postglacial evolution in our trout streams was drastically altered in less than a decade, and our trout fishing has been different ever since.

April 1, 1882, was the opening day of the New York trout season and also the opening of the new Fulton Market in lower Manhattan. New York Fish Commissioner Eugene Blackford opened a grand display of trout at his fish stall on the Beekman Street side of the market that was apparently more appealing on this day than the cold streams of the Long Island trout clubs. Rube Wood, then a champion tournament caster and widely published angling writer, was there, along with former governor Myron Clark. The Reverend Henry Ward Beecher, whose immense popularity had somehow survived the widely publicized scandals and recent trial following his seduction of Mrs. Elizabeth Tilton, dropped in to rub elbows with *Forest and Stream* publisher Charles Hallock. There were other guests from as far away as Virginia and Boston; for the socially inclined angler it was an event not to be missed.

There were rows and rows of brook trout on moss and ice, from fish merchants as far away as Bennington, Vermont, and southern

Quebec, as well as many from hatcheries on nearby Long Island. There were other kinds of trout, too, as *Forest and Stream* reported a few days later:

> From the New York state hatchery, Mr. Seth Green sent the following: Brook trout, rainbow trout, hybrid between brook and lake trout, land-locked salmon, lake trout, and the two species of black bass, the latter alive in an aquarium, among which was a small mouth [small-mouth bass] of three pounds weight.
>
> Mr. W. B. Redding, of the California Fish Commission sent rainbow trout . . . dolly varden trout . . . and Humboldt River trout [cutthroat]. One of the rainbow trout, sent by Mr. Livingston Stone, weighed ten pounds; it was from near the United States Hatchery on the McCloud River.

Then, as now, different kinds of trout had their partisans. The resentment of brook-trout anglers toward the later-introduced brown trout has been well publicized in recent years, but such responses certainly weren't unique to brown-trout stockings. Here's the view of one angler who traveled from Boston to see Blackford's 1882 exhibition:

> "The fame of the beautiful rainbow trout had so long sounded in my ears that I felt anxious to behold its beauties. I went to New York . . . to see those which Mr. Blackford was about to exhibit. I have beheld them. I don't want to see any more. The great coarse, black, ugly beasts! A dingy brown with darker spots and a hectic flush along the side as if it had a fever. And to compare this coarse scaled brute with our delicate aquatic gems of *fontinalis* [brook trout]! O, get out! Don't tell me any more about them. I have seen them once and am disgusted. I wouldn't eat one of the fever-flushed looking things unless starved."[8]

Blackford's exhibition shows American trout fishing as both social and contentious, which it still is. The ways of fly-fishing now are well traveled and often highly technical, just as in the life and writings of George Washington Bethune almost one hundred fifty years ago. There are things that are genuinely new these days, most of them pertaining to developments in tackle and the new techniques such developments allow, and our understanding of trout and their behavior has increased dramatically in recent years. But much of what we take for granted as modern, isn't modern at all. That knowledge will not necessarily enable you to catch more fish, but it will enrich your sport every time you cast a fly.

1. Various writers have cited a variety of works as being seminal in fly-fishing, the most commonly mentioned of which is the *Treatise of Fishing with an Angle*, a remarkably complete fishing text often attributed to a prioress, Dame Juliana Berners, and written in England as early as 1450. Some argue that Berners herself was a myth and that the author is unknown. Other manuscripts and fragments that mention fly-fishing date at least back to thirteenth-century Europe, and not only in England. There are probably also Asian antecedents that predate anything of European origin. Literary and not-so-literary arguments about these origins in recent years have occasionally been downright nasty. I have no personal authority to add to this debate and am deliberately begging the question. Walton and Cotton still have my vote, not that they were first, but as fly-fishing's enduring foundation. These questions are discussed to varying degrees in Gingrich (1974), McDonald (1963), Schwiebert (1968), Schullery (1987), and in numerous articles about these topics in the journals and archives of the American Museum of Fly Fishing in Manchester, Vermont.

2. As quoted in Goodspeed (1939).

3. See the detailed account in Schullery (1987).

4. This particular web of acquaintances broadened even more remarkably throughout Audubon's life. See Ford (1964).

5. See Schwiebert (1978).

6. Much of this discussion is based on Dean Allard's doctoral thesis about Baird and also on reports of the U.S. Fish Commission published during Baird's tenure there, both of which are in the library at the American Museum of Fly Fishing.

7. Baird in an 1877 letter to Charles Atkins, as quoted in Allard (1978).

8. From *Forest and Stream*, April 6, 1882, which issue also has an account of Blackford's exhibition.

PART ONE

THE QUARRY

2
The Nature of Trout Streams

Small streams have a friendly, gurgling sound, made more intimate sometimes by shaded alder tunnels. Bigger rivers can have a hiss to them that speaks of power, a promise realized when the river runs a canyon and goes spitting and crashing against the rocks. Spring creeks and meadow streams are the quietest, with only a slight rippling sound against your waders as the water moves evenly between grassy banks. These are trout-stream sounds. And, like trout, they are all dependent upon the nature of flowing water.

Many experienced trout fishermen are also experts on the hydrology of flowing water, although perhaps most would not make such a direct connection between the sport and the science. Flowing water is the creator of trout streams, and the trout themselves have spent thousands of years evolving and adapting to its currents and eddies. The physics and chemistry of rivers and streams have defined the evolution of the fisherman's tactics, too, and those tactics involve much more science than intuition. Understanding water isn't essential to the casual catching of a couple of trout, but it's very necessary to the catching of more than a few.

Of all the inorganic compounds making up the earth's surface, only two occur naturally as liquids: water and mercury. Water is life giving; mercury is lethal. Water has a number of unique physical properties, all of which are in some way germane to trout fishing.[1] For example, if you stand watching a trout stream, you may notice small insects, water striders or water pennies, darting around on the surface. They are living equivalents of the old schoolroom experiment of floating a sewing needle on the surface of water in a dish. The insects and the floating needle both depend not on any inherent buoyancy, but rather on the surface tension of water. Water molecules are loosely bonded to one another in all directions by their dipolar electrical charges. Water molecules at the surface, in contact with both water and air, experience this attraction only to the water at the sides and below, which makes the physical bond stronger. The net result is roughly equivalent to a thin, tough layer—like a thin plastic film—at the water's surface. The surface offers no perceptible barrier to something the size of your poking finger, but for a small aquatic insect trying to emerge at the surface the barrier is substantial. For this reason, emerging insects often collect in great numbers immediately under the surface, where trout feed on them avidly.

If you step into the same trout stream on a hot summer day the water will usually be obviously colder than the air. Water itself is a heat sink, which means that it changes temperature slowly even though its immediate surroundings may be much hotter or colder than the water itself. This is explained by a property called specific heat, which in the case of pure water is 1.0 and is defined as the amount of heat required to raise a unit volume of substance by one centigrade degree. In contrast, the specific heat of most streamside rocks is about 0.2, meaning those rocks will heat up more quickly than the adjacent water when an equivalent amount of heat, usually in the form of sunlight, is applied. This means the temperature regime of a trout stream changes more slowly and less overall than the surrounding air or land. Trout and other aquatic organisms thus have evolved in an environment that is more thermally stable than that of land creatures. The raccoon that frequents the bank of your favorite river may routinely have to survive temperature extremes of 20 or more degrees Fahrenheit below zero in winter to more than 100 degrees in summer. The nearby trout can only survive a temperature range of slightly more than 32 degrees to about 75 degrees Fahrenheit and will usually select temperatures within a much narrower range by moving to cooler areas of the stream in warm weather.

Trout streams acquire heat in a variety of ways, the most important of which is sunlight. Pure water absorbs sunlight selectively, with the blue end of the spectrum being transmitted to the greatest depths. Red and infrared are absorbed quickly, and as much as half of the available solar energy may be absorbed in the first 6 feet of depth. Shaded stream areas are thus important in maintaining the lower water temperatures required by trout, and the wholesale removal of streamside vegetation—whether by livestock grazing, logging, or for the enhancement of a suburban lawn—usually has a deleterious effect on trout habitat for that reason, among others.

All trout streams undergo a daily temperature cycle with a late afternoon peak and an early morning minimum. This cycle coincides with available sunlight, being extreme in the hot sun of midsummer and being minimized on days with heavy cloud cover. In the early season when water temperatures are seasonally low, both insect hatches and peak trout activity often take place during the late afternoon temperature peak. Later in the year, when the river has reached higher summer temperatures, trout and insect activity often (but not always) peak in late evening, when the river has started to cool, and again in early morning, when stream temperatures are at their twenty-four-hour minimum. These events are influenced by many factors, but water temperature is a primary consideration, and its implications in timing a fishing trip should be obvious.

Sunlight or its absence isn't the only source of heat exchange, of course. Heat is simultaneously lost by evaporation and radiation from the stream surface and gained from warm, surrounding air and land. Cold tributaries and springs usually serve to reduce water temperatures, although in rare trout-stream cases, such as the Firehole River at Yellowstone Park, geothermal springs warm the river instead. Surface-water runoff from rainstorms often picks up heat from the ground before flowing into and warming slightly a colder river. The villain in this case, however, is often water that's diverted for irrigation, which—if it's returned to the river at all after baking in a sunlit irrigation ditch—is invariably hotter when returned to the river flow.

Large rivers both heat up and cool off less rapidly than small ones subject to the same conditions, simply because of their greater water volume. The same large rivers, however, are typically warmer than small ones because they are farther removed from the cold headwater sources. Bigger waters typically flow more slowly, too, which exposes their water masses to greater amounts of solar-induced heat in any unit of time. Turbidity has a role here also, since suspended fine particles of silt and organic matter increase the water's rate of solar absorption, and large rivers are often more turbid than small streams. Although there are some notable exceptions, water temperature generally increases as one progresses downstream. Species diversity likewise increases, both among fish and other aquatic organisms, but at some point in the downstream progression trout start to disappear from the mix as the water becomes warmer than the upper limits of their metabolic tolerances.

There are two notable exceptions to the temperature regimes of typical trout streams. Spring creeks that are wholly dependent on the flow of major headwater springs may show relatively little temperature variation either daily or from summer to winter, although the extent of the variation will depend on actual volume of spring flowage and regular factors such as the extent of shading and length of flow. The temperature of emerging spring water is usually about the same as the average annual air temperature in the area of the spring itself. In most temperate-zone trout regions, this means that a water temperature of about 46 to rarely more than 60 degrees Fahrenheit is maintained in the creek all year. For this reason, among others, spring creeks are often ideal trout habitats.

The other exception is man made and increasingly common: tailwater trout fisheries created in major rivers by releases of very cold water from the depths of upstream reserviors. The examples are well known and numerous. Cold-water releases from New York City water supply reservoirs in the Catskill Mountains have produced outstanding trout fishing in the upper Delaware River system since the 1970s, although the releases themselves were and continue to be the result of hard-fought political battles.[2] The Green River in Utah, New Mexico's San Juan, and the Bighorn in Montana are currently the most popular rivers for traveling fly fishermen, and all three are tailwater fisheries below major dams whose trout fishing has either been enhanced or created by cold-water reservoir releases.

The concept is simple, but there's a catch other than trout. Surface water flowing over a dam's spillway is often so warm as to support only a bass or other warm-water fishery in the river below. At the extreme depths of the reservoir water temperatures are often in the mid-40s, so when water is released at the bottom of the dam, as often happens in power generation, the cold water literally creates a trout river that may extend for 10, 20, or even more miles below the dam itself until the water has warmed again to the point of no longer supporting trout. In winter, the reservoir releases increase slightly in temperature because the water in the entire reservoir has both cooled and mixed. This cooler-in-summer, warmer-in-winter downstream environment can be enormously productive of trout.

None of these dams, however, was built with the intention of creating trout streams. They are typically built and managed for power generation or, in the New York case, water supply. In a dry year New York City watershed authorities are understandably reluctant to release sufficient water to maintain downstream trout habitat and have done so only when faced with recurrent public prodding. Dramatic fluctuations in water flow are also implicit in power generation. On Arkansas's White River below Bull Shoals Dam, which by virtue of its tailwater has one of the country's best trophy brown-trout fisheries as well as an extensive fishery for little hatchery rainbows, the water flow may vary from a mere 210 cubic feet per second (cfs) to an astounding 24,000 cfs within the same day.[3]

White River trout guides often start the

day with an early morning telephone call, as mine once did: "How many you runnin' today, Shorty? Three? All day? Yep, fishin'. Thanks." That day Mitch turned and told me we'd start with the boat a few miles downriver to get in some good low-water time before the power flow reached us. Later that morning the placid White turned into a green, boiling ocean with a three-generator discharge, which at Bull Shoals was still far from full bore. It is an odd and vaguely unpleasant fact that in many places these days your fishing will change dramatically when Shorty or whoever he is upstream flicks a couple of switches. Without Shorty, his dam, and his generators, however, there would be no trout here at all.

Water is dense, almost eight hundred times denser then air, and this you can sense readily when wading a trout river. Current velocities of 4 feet per second are common in many trout streams, but the push and friction of the current against your legs can make it difficult to stand up once you're more than knee-deep in such water. On land, the equivalent air speed is about an 8-mile-an-hour breeze, the effect of which is barely noticeable. The force of flowing water, a function of its density, mass, viscosity, and velocity, can obviously be substantial. Not only does it have a major effect on trout, as explored in Chapter 3 and later chapters, it also determines the basic character of trout streams.

Running water sometimes shows laminar, or straight-line flow, but only at very slow speeds and in straight stream channels. Water at more typical current speeds is inherently turbulent and also encounters the friction produced by a rough bottom and stream banks, which increases its turbulent nature. In trout streams, and even in slow spring creeks, turbulent whorls sometimes develop near the bottom and migrate in spin-

ning fashion toward the surface while traveling with the current. When they reach the surface and can no longer go upward, they expand and flatten.[4] This produces a small, flat "window," on an otherwise choppy surface, which travels downstream until its energy dissipates and it disappears. Savvy trout fishermen use these windows to spot fish that are otherwise invisible through the surface currents. When you spot one of these flat whorls coming downstream at the surface, follow it with your eyes as it allows you to scan the bottom.

Friction and turbulence mean that a river's current speeds are unevenly distributed in a cross section of the stream channel, something every fly fisherman discovers when he first tries to make a natural presentation across varied currents that tug his line in every direction but the right one. In general, currents are slower along the banks and bot-

The thread of maximum current velocity (shaded area) typically follows the outside curves of a riverbed and most often is found a foot or so below the surface. Areas to the left and right of maximum velocity are zones of turbulence.

tom because of friction and fastest in mid-stream where the flow is least inhibited. Surface currents are also slowed by surface tension, so the area of greatest velocity is from slightly below the surface to as much as a third of the way to the bottom. This thread of maximum velocity rarely follows the midpoint of a stream channel. At a bend in the river, it's typically closer to the outside of the bend, after which it typically crosses the midstream transition between bends to run along the outside of the downstream and opposite bend. Because of the greater water velocity on outside edges of streambed curves, erosion tends to be greatest at this point; the water is usually deeper and banks typically undercut, providing shelter for trout. The inside curves of bends have the slowest current, and here sand and sediments tend to collect as they're released from suspension by the slowing water.

The extent and force of a river's current is a function of its gradient, which is the amount of its vertical drop over some linear distance, usually expressed as feet per mile or meters per kilometer of stream length. After temperature it's the most important defining character of trout streams because of its relationship to the velocity and force of running water. Water running down a steeper slope is obviously traveling faster than water over a gentle one. The increased velocity and force implicit in high-gradient mountain streams that may drop 100, 200, or even more vertical feet in a mile means the stream bottom will be composed of relatively large rocks and there will be relatively few deep, quiet pools. There is often little spawning gravel, also, and a steep gradient plus high spring runoff may actually define what species of trout survive in the stream. Some steep tributaries of California's Owens River are populated by both rainbow and brown trout. The browns spawn in the fall, using small pockets of gravel from

which the young emerge in March, before the heavy snowmelt. The rainbows spawn in the spring, but their spawning is so close to periods of high flow that their eggs are often washed away, which is believed to account for their reduced numbers in comparison with brown trout in these streams.[5] Conversely, streams along a valley floor with a lesser gradient, say 10 or 20 feet to the mile, will have a gentler flow, more pools, and much of the bottom will be made up of smaller rocks and gravels. The latter case is typically more productive of trout.

Flow velocity is also related to flow volume, an increase in which increases velocity at any given gradient. Some swift-water Ontario trout streams, for example, have measured average velocities ranging from 1.5 feet per second during August low flows to 6 feet per second or more in April when the rivers are bank full.[6] There is a steep mountain stream appropriately called the Roaring Branch a few miles from my home, which in late summer trickles musically around boulders the size of small cars. There are small brook trout scattered in pockets and pools, and it's a welcome refuge from the heat in the big valley below. In April, however, the water roars and churns with mountain snowmelt, and the big rocks are only visible as boils and white water in the flow. At such times you can hear the rocks moving with the water, a grunting and grinding sound with a few sharp clicks when a rock lets go. The sounds coincide with the rolling-rock vibrations I feel through my feet on the stream bank. I am afraid of this water, hold my children tightly, and move a few feet back from the edge. It is this tremendous energy that defines the basic geometry of most trout streams.

Flowing water is erosive, picking up and carrying sediment and sand and rolling larger particles along the bottom, all of which increases the river's ability to alter the streambed. The extent of erosion is largely a function of flow volume and velocity, which in most trout streams across the country peaks with the spring runoff. Riffles and gravel bars may shift in these periods of high water, and where obstructions like ledges or boulders are encountered the high flows may be forced down or sideways, undercutting the opposite bank or digging deep pools in the riverbed. Flood debris such as logs and branches are tossed and carried also, and may be trapped eventually at the edge of a deeply cut back eddy in the bank. When the water level finally drops later in the spring, its erosive effect diminishes and the water clears, leaving broad riffles, deep pools, and sheltered undercuts beneath the edges of jackstraw logs and limbs along the bank. The river looks, again, like a trout stream.

Flooding can be devastating to the trout-stream community. Newly hatched juvenile trout may be unable to escape the high water and be killed. Shifting bottom rocks grind and kill aquatic insects and the algae on which many of them feed. In extreme flooding, even adult trout may be forced into abnormally high backwaters, then left high and dry when the water recedes.

Trout streams of very low gradient, and thus less subject to erosive floods, and those streams dependent primarily on ground water flow are more stable environments and thus are often more productive. Tailwaters also benefit from the mitigation of water-flow extremes by upstream dams, although the dramatic discharge variations characteristic of some power dams can have the same effect as a natural flood. The well-known trout productivity of spring creeks that usually have an almost constant flow year round is as much a function of their thermal and hydrologic stability as it is of their typically rich water chemistries.

Summertime low flows on most trout streams are critical times for trout. This condition may be a seasonal and natural low flow, or it may be artificially created by the removal of irrigation water or reduced releases from upstream dams. Less water volume means the water itself warms more quickly in the sun and may approach lethal temperatures. Reduced water levels have often receded from the bankside cover used by trout in higher flows, and the trout are forced to congregate in deeper pools where they're more vulnerable to predators, including fishermen. On many otherwise productive trout streams, low-flow periods are the most important factor limiting both numbers and size of trout in the stream year round. Some years ago on Montana's well-known Madison River, for example, the water release and storage patterns at Hebgen Reservoir were reducing downstream flows by as much as half during the early spring. This release pattern was modified in 1968 to minimize the dewatering effect, and within three years the number of adult wild brown and rainbow trout in a downstream section had increased by about 80 percent.[7]

The 1970s saw the beginnings of a variety of trout-stream modeling systems that illustrate for our purposes the importance of water's physical characteristics. Such models essentially try to establish by statistical processes the relative importance of trout-stream variables such as current, temperature, or various components of water chemistry, and then incorporate these variables into a formula to predict the numbers of trout[8] in a particular river. It's in many ways an appealing problem, although even now these increasingly sophisticated models among biologists are like fly patterns among fishermen: They argue about them constantly and tinker with them incessantly.

One early such model was the Habitat Quality Index developed by Fred Eiserman and Allen Binns for the Wyoming Fish and Game Department in the late 1970s.[9] In developing a model they measured and tested a wide variety of environmental factors in more than thirty Wyoming trout streams. Among several versions of their mathematical model, one was able to explain more than 90 percent of the variations in trout numbers among the tested rivers. The important factors in their best model were eventually reduced to nine: late summer stream flows, annual stream flow variation, water velocity, trout cover, stream width, eroding stream banks, stream substrate, nitrate nitrogen concentration, and maximum summer stream temperatures. All but one of these factors depend on the physical attributes of water already described in this chapter. That one exception (nitrate nitrogen) is primarily a function of soils chemistry in the watershed and the water's role as a nutrient-bearing medium.

Water is remarkable in being not only a nearly universal solvent, but also in the loosely bonded way it accepts many nitrates, phosphates, sugars, and other compounds in solution. This means that many substances needed for the metabolism of algae and aquatic plants, for example, not only are available, but are easily extracted from the water by plants. As an extreme example, the hydroponic gardening that produces dirt-free supermarket lettuce and tomatoes at a premium price works on the same principles. It is apparently unusual[10] for the basic elements of plant growth—potassium, nitrates, and phosphates—to become limiting factors by virtue of scarcity in a trout stream. It is also true, however, that trout-stream plant growth in agricultural areas can appear noticeably richer as the stream passes through farms where fertilizer is applied to the adjoining land. Water obtains these and other dissolved solids in limited amounts from natural rainfall and in greater quantities from ground and surface water that dissolves these materials from the soils and bedrock as the water flows into the stream.

Gases are soluble in water also, and the two most noteworthy are oxygen and carbon dioxide. Almost all aquatic organisms—including all fish and aquatic insects—extract dissolved oxygen from the water. This is not, by the way, the "O" in H_2O, which is the chemical formula for water, but refers to oxygen in solution. The solubility of oxygen is inversely related to temperature, with concentrations typically increasing as the water temperature drops, a relationship obviously favorable to such cold-water species as trout. Since much of the dissolved oxygen is absorbed from the surrounding air, a process greatly accelerated by water turbulence, its concentration is also dependent on barometric pressure, being higher with a high barometer and vice versa.[11] Trout-stream water is said to be "saturated" with oxygen when it holds the maximum amount allowed in solution by its temperature. Here are a few oxygen solubility values as they relate to temperature:

Solubility of Oxygen as a Function of Water Temperature

TEMPERATURE DEG. C (DEG. F)	DISSOLVED OXYGEN (PARTS PER MILLION)
0 (32)	14.62
5 (41)	12.80
10 (50)	11.33
15 (59)	10.15
20 (68)	9.17
25 (77)	8.38
30 (86)	7.63

(Assumes a standard atmosphere of 20.9 percent oxygen and a sea-level barometric pressure of 760 mm Hg. These figures are for pure water and are usually reduced in the presence of dissolved solids. Trout streams will show somewhat lower values at equivalent temperatures. Adapted from Welch [1952].)

Most trout streams run at or near their oxygen saturation point most of the time. Oxygen content may be modified by the photosynthetic processes of plants and algae, which release oxygen during the day and consume it at night, but this is a minor consideration in most trout streams. Oxygen problems for trout may occur in streams that become dumping grounds for organic waste such as sewage. The decomposing waste consumes oxygen that would otherwise be available to the stream community, and fish and other organisms may be forced to move considerable distances downstream to avoid its effects.

Carbon dioxide is also readily soluble in water and assumes importance in helping to determine the relative acidity or alkalinity of a trout stream. Natural rainfall is very mildly acidic as raindrops absorb carbon dioxide from the air to form dilute carbonic acid. Surface runoff picks up carbon dioxide from decomposing plant material in the soil and becomes slightly acid in similar fashion. Calcium carbonate, a common mineral in many rocks and the principal constituent of limestone, isn't especially soluble in water, but dissolves easily as calcium bicarbonate in weak carbonic acid. Thus groundwater picks up bicarbonate in solution on its way to the river. In the process, the bicarbonate neutralizes, or "buffers," the initially acidic water. Bicarbonates remain in solution in equilibrium with dissolved carbon dioxide. If, for example, some carbon dioxide is removed by plant photosynthesis, some bicarbonates will probably be precipitated as a calcium bicarbonate sediment, which is characteristic of many calcium-rich, alkaline trout streams. Bicarbonate-rich waters are well buffered against acidification because the available bicarbonate neutralizes incoming acids. This has been (and is) especially important in the ability (or lack of it) of some lakes and streams to resist the effects of acid rain in recent years (see the detailed discussion of this problem in Chapter 4).

Moderately alkaline, calcium-rich waters are typically the most productive trout streams. Limestone rivers and spring creeks in America and the chalkstreams of Europe are famous the world over for their trout fishing. Given stable flows and a suitably cold temperature regime, they certainly *look* more productive with their typical abundance of aquatic insects and plants and trout. This is often and incorrectly attributed by trout fishermen to the alkalinity itself, but bicarbonate chemistry alone won't promote this sort of productivity. Implicit in these waters is a rich supply of nitrates, phosphorus, potassium, and other trace elements necessary for plant growth that apparently have their greatest effect in moderately alkaline waters with cool, stable flows.

Trout streams hold a wide spectrum of aquatic life forms that will vary in assortment from spot to spot in the stream depending on its physical characteristics at any given point. A stream's physical characteristics such as temperature and velocity show a general gradient from headwater areas to the stream's lower reaches, and so the stream communities—including various trout foods—also change along the same gradient. A basic knowledge of food production and its distribution in trout streams is intrinsic to understanding and fishing them.

Solar energy and available nutrients are initially used by stream communities in a couple of ways, either one of which may be dominant although they typically occur to varying degrees simultaneously. Streams bordered by trees and bushes receive enormous amounts of leaf litter in the fall, which is broken up by the mechanical action of flowing water and also by certain species of caddis, stoneflies, and other immature aquatic insects that are specifically adapted for feeding on this material after it has been softened by the action of an assortment of bacteria and fungi. In the course of their mechanical and biological breaking down, particles of leaf litter become progressively smaller in a downstream direction and thus become available as food to a greater variety of organisms. Leaf litter from deciduous trees contains as much as 10 percent protein by dry weight and is biologically more productive than needles from coniferous trees, which are also evergreen and shed at a much lower rate. This accounts in part for the relatively low productivity of cold headwater streams that run through heavily shaded pine or spruce forests.

If shade isn't produced by streamside vegetation or the high walls of a canyon or gorge, sunlight can reach much of the stream bottom and enables the growth of algae. These plants derive their nutrients from compounds dissolved in the running water. The mere fact of a current assures a constantly fresh supply of nutrient materials to the extent that they're available in the first place, which ultimately depends on the chemical nature of the watershed. Many species of mayfly nymphs and caddisfly larvae, for ex-

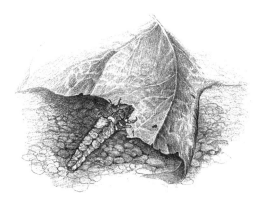

Certain species of aquatic insects, such as this particular caddisfly, are known as shredders, being specifically adapted to breaking down large particles of organic matter such as the thousands of fallen leaves entering many trout streams in autumn.

ample, are specifically adapted for algal feeding, scraping algae from the surface of rocks. Others, notably many caddis types, filter the current by making small, finely constructed nets that capture both free-floating bits of algae and other organic matter, including fine bits of leaves that originated in headwater areas.

Although the importance of aquatic entomology in trout fishing is discussed at length in later chapters, it's important to note here, for example, that the caddis species breaking down leaves in the headwaters are not the same as those grazing on algae and that the filter feeders are different species, also.

In a broad view, this sort of specialization allows maximum use of available food in the stream, and it also allows different species that are generally similar to coexist without competing with one another for food and living space. This is the principal reason why there are so many *different* trout-stream insects that trout use as food at different times and places, which in turn is why trout fishing can be such a complex puzzle.

The same sort of relationship is found among stream fishes, something a trout fisherman may understand more easily because you can see it happening while you're standing in the river. Almost all cold, naturally flowing American trout streams have four kinds of fish in common: a trout species (typically brook, brown, rainbow, or cutthroat), a dace species of the genus *Rhinichthys*, a sculpin of the genus *Cottus*, and a sucker of the genus *Catostomus*. In a given trout pool, where you may be able to see all four kinds of fish simultaneously, each will most likely be doing the following: The trout may be swimming around catching insect larvae at all depths or it may be holding stationary and eating insects carried to it by the current. The sucker will be stationary or moving slowly along the bottom, using its round lips to suck up food from among the rocks. Sculpins are small (almost never more than a few inches long), secretive in daylight, and may be hiding under the rocks; they are adapted only for life on the bottom, where they ambush and gobble down nymphs and larvae. The dace, which are also small, are usually in shallower water near the bottom, darting about actively feeding on a variety of small organisms. Although some of the different kinds of fish are feeding on some of the same things, they are doing so in different ways and in different areas of the stream. The available food resources here are divided among the fish both because of the fish's different physical adaptations to life in different areas of the stream and because of their different behaviors. This is known as *resource partitioning,* an important concept in stream (and other) ecosystems that has much to do with trout behavior as discussed in following chapters.

I have some fishing friends who regard any scientific discussion of their trout streams as an intrusion, as if I were trying to replace their fly rod with a calculator or trying to reduce the joy of their fishing experience to a series of charts and graphs. Still others never bother to learn very much about trout-stream ecology, being able to catch at least a few fish without making the effort required for a broader understanding. But such knowledge can help you to determine how, when, and where to fish more effectively, and for that reason alone is worth your effort. There is some poetry in that knowledge, too, as

answers to simple questions of ecology invariably give rise to even more questions of greater complexity in an endless chain of information and appreciation. Like you, perhaps, I am not fully contented by seeing the rise of a trout. I am compelled to know why.

1. The technical basis for this chapter can be found in most standard works on limnology. I happen to have used Welch (1952), Reid (1961), Ruttner (1963), and Hynes (1970). See also Moyle and Cech (1988), and various portions of Stoltz and Schnell, eds. (1991).

2. There were cold-water releases from some Catskill reservoirs even during the 1950s and 1960s, but these were erratic. State fish and wildlife authorities finally gained partial control over the release patterns by a 1976 state-legislative act. See Sheppard (1983).

3. See Hudy (1990).

4. See Ruttner (1963) for a complete explanation of this phenomenon.

5. See Kondolf, et al. (1991).

6. See Reid (1961).

7. See Vincent (1975).

8. More specifically, the term "standing crop" is often used, usually expressed as total weight of all trout, regardless of size, per unit of stream area; e.g., pounds per acre or kilograms per hectare. I have used "numbers of trout" for the sake of clarity in this case, though this is technically incorrect.

9. See Binns and Eiserman (1979).

10. See Hynes (1970).

11. At an altitude of 2,300 feet with a nominal barometric pressure of 696 mm Hg, oxygen saturation will be about 6 percent less than at sea level for a corresponding temperature. In terms of high-altitude trout streams, the difference is insignificant, partly because of acclimation by the trout. See Reid (1961).

3
The Nature of Trout

A rainbow trout gently sipping midges from the surface of a California stream has a great deal in common with a brown trout rising to caddis in Michigan or New York. A Wyoming cutthroat will take an emerging mayfly in ways identical to those of a Maine brook trout. While these are vastly different fish, they are also similar in many ways, even to the extent that individuals of the different trout species can communicate with one another by underwater signals if they happen to be in the same stream. None of them, in contrast, can communicate as easily with an unrelated sucker or chub in the same river.

People define trout in different ways, usually based on their own inclination or experience. The word "trout" itself is apparently[1] of Greek origin, referring to a "gnawer," becoming *trutta* or *tructa* in Latin, and evolving through such archaic Anglo-Saxon spellings as *trowt* and *troughte* to its present English form. The French *truite* and Spanish *trucha* are corollaries.

Trout are pleasing, colorful fish, and because they require clean, cold water they usually live in places pleasing to us as well. These attributes have led writers into centuries of romantic metaphor, such as this one published by American poet James Russell Lowell in 1866:

And when they come his deeds to weigh,
  And how he used the talents his,
One trout-scale in the scales he'll lay
  (if trout had scales), and t'will outsway
The wrong side of the balances.

Lowell did go trout fishing occasionally but was of no particular note as a trout fisherman and didn't notice, for example, that trout do have scales, albeit small ones. His Adirondack excursions, starting in 1857, so enamored him of angling's pastoral qualities that he edited his own edition of Walton's *Angler*, published at Boston in 1889.

While considerably less romantic, more precise definitions of trout are found with their taxonomists, who have been wrangling with the technical side of the question for centuries. At present, there are almost 22,000 species of fish recognized worldwide, a very minor handful of which are trout. The systematics of fishes, meaning their evolutionary relationships, has become in many ways synonymous with their taxonomy, which names species and describes how they differ from one another. Following the familiar arrangement of order, class, family, genus, species, and so on that you may remember from an old biology class, trout are:

Of the superorder Protacanthopterygii, which includes fish such as trout, salmon, smelt, whitefish, and all the pikes, for about 320 total species. Among their common characteristics are a lack of hard spines. Most have at least a rudimentary adipose fin. Their pelvic fins are situated abdominally and are widely separated from their pectoral fins. These fish have cycloid scales, which means generally smooth-edged and rounded, and their internal swim bladders are connected to their gut by a small duct. These fish are relatively primitive, more so in evolutionary terms than perch or bass, for example. Trout fishermen often resent hearing this and need reminding that evolutionary systematics is not a social register. Primitive in this sense doesn't mean lacking elegance or grace, which trout have in abundance. It does mean, to continue the example, that perch have some characteristics said to be more "derived" or farther up the evolutionary totem pole, such as dorsal spines and a different scale structure.[2]

Within this group, trout are of the order Salmoniformes, suborder Salmonoidae (salmon, trout, whitefish, and smelt), and family Salmonidae. Within this family are three subfamilies: Salmoninae (salmon and trout), Coregoninae (whitefish), and Thymallinae (graylings). Things should now become more familiar, as within the Salmoninae are the fisherman's well-known genera: *Salvelinus*, which includes brook trout, lake trout, Dolly Varden and other charrs; *Salmo*, including brown trout and At-

lantic salmon; and *Oncorhynchus*, which includes all of the Pacific salmon species and within which both rainbow and cutthroat trout have recently been reclassified from their former listings in the *Salmo* genus.

At the species level, things become more openly complex, at least among taxonomists, many of whom are at times unable to agree on whether a particular form of trout is a species, subspecies, strain, or local variation. In general, the arbiter on such matters has been the American Fisheries Society through its periodic publication of a common and scientific name listing.[3] As of its 1991 publication, it recognized ten American trout species: Within the genus *Oncorhynchus*, golden trout *(O. aguabonita)*, Apache trout *(O. apache)*, Gila trout *(O. gilae)*, cutthroat trout *(O. clarki)*, and rainbow trout *(O. mykiss)*; within the genus *Salmo*, brown trout *(S. trutta)*; within the genus *Salvelinus*, brook trout *(S. fontinalis)*, lake trout *(S. namaycush)*, bull trout *(S. confluentus)*, Dolly Varden *(S. malma)*, plus arctic charr *(S. al-*

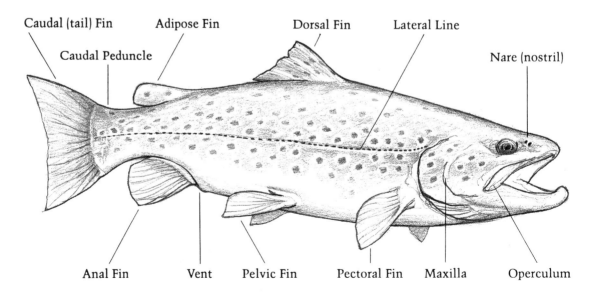

External Anatomy of a Trout

Caudal (tail) Fin   Adipose Fin   Dorsal Fin   Lateral Line
Caudal Peduncle   Nare (nostril)
Anal Fin   Vent   Pelvic Fin   Pectoral Fin   Maxilla   Operculum

pinus), which aren't usually considered as vernacular trout.

In contemporary definitions of species there are almost as many exceptions as rules. A group of individuals is commonly said to constitute a species when its members are phenotypically similar and capable of breeding among themselves, but are reproductively isolated from other such groups. As an example, mountain lions are like other mountain lions (phenotypically similar), produce more of their own kind, and don't interbreed with other animals, such as deer or bear, that are found in the same area (reproductive isolation). The situation with trout is much more complex. Brown and brook trout, fish of different genera, will rarely interbreed in the wild. Rainbow and cutthroat trout, fish of different species in the same genus, occur together in some Pacific northwestern streams, where they don't interbreed. However, when populations of rainbows have been introduced in Rocky Mountain cutthroat waters, the fish have interbred freely, usually to the detriment of pure cutthroat populations since the rainbow is genetically dominant.

Trout systematics and taxonomy are now often based partly on meristic traits, which refers to things that can be counted such as numbers of fin rays or gill rakers, and partly on biochemical protein analyses and chromosome research designed to show evolutionary relationships. Because of this, you may see a much broader listing of trout species and subspecies in other books, and the question is further considered here in the chapters on specific trouts.

The life histories of most stream trout are essentially similar and for our purposes can be considered together, although seasonal spawning times and behavior are different among species and even vary among strains of trout within a single species. As a general case, brown and brook trout are fall-spawning fish, while rainbows and cutthroat spawn in the spring. In all cases the onset of spawning activity appears to be generated by changes in day length and water temperatures.

Female trout dig a nest, or redd, in suitable gravel, usually in a riffle or the tail of a pool or, typically in the case of brook trout, where water is upwelling from the streambed. Digging is accomplished when the female turns on her side and forcefully beats her tail up and down near the gravel. The upward tail motion creates a suction that lifts gravel and other debris from the streambed and allows the current to carry it downstream. This digging process is called cutting. The fish uses its own body depth to gauge the depth of the redd, feeling the bottom with her anal fin periodically during the digging. While the female is digging, male trout are usually nearby and fighting for possession of the female. The dominant and usually largest male remains near the female, chasing other males away through threatening displays of body posture, swimming attitude, and spread fins that usually are recognized by subdominant males without the need for biting and other forms of combat.

At the moment of actual spawning, the female extrudes anywhere from a few dozen to a few hundred eggs at the bottom of the redd, the number usually depending on the female's body size, while the adjacent male simultaneously discharges a cloud of sperm (called milt). The female then moves immediately upstream and repeats the cutting process, both digging another redd and burying the eggs laid in the redd just downstream as the gravel lifted by her tail moves down in the current. The process may continue intermittently over several days until the female is exhausted of eggs. The eggs are fertilized by the milt as they settle into the gravel at the bottom of the redd. Fertilization rates are typically high, often reaching 90 percent, although much lower rates are found in poor spawning habitats or if the male and female are out of synchrony in their spawning act, as somtimes happens.

Spawning trout are easy to catch, especially the males, which tend to be very aggressive at this time. Often under special catch-and-release rules, or even under general regulations, in some states it's technically legal to fish for spawning trout, but I hope you don't do it. The trout's metabolism is geared up for the spawning act and may be severely stressed by the catch-and-release process. These same stresses come at a time when the trout's available food supply—and chances for post-spawning recovery—is at a seasonal low. When you sneak through the streamside brush and find a huge male brown trout guarding a female over the spawning gravel, the temptation to swing a big streamer fly in front of his nose can be overwhelming. You'll make a much better investment in your own future fishing, however, if you just leave them alone. The only exception I make to my own rule is in certain Great Lakes tributaries, where the returns of hatchery steelhead take place in rivers so short in length that the only fishing possible is often for spawning fish.

Once in the redd, trout eggs are sheltered by their gravel covering. Development takes place according to water temperature. Brook-trout eggs, for example, overwinter at low temperatures and may take from 100 to 144 days to develop at water temperatures of from 35.6 to 41 degrees Fahrenheit. The same development happens in only about 35 days at 55.4 degrees Fahrenheit. This temperature dependence is what made the wide-scale transport and introduction of fertilized trout eggs possible in the late nineteenth century. Eggs held under ice in moist, moss-covered trays developed slowly enough for worldwide transport by sail, rail, and horse and wagon.

Juvenile trout emerge from the eggs as yolk-sac fry, miniature trout properly called alevins, with a large yolk sac still attached. As the yolk sac is absorbed, the alevins migrate upward through the gravel and out into the stream. They move to slower currents at the stream margins, where they establish and defend feeding territories and begin to eat zooplankton and the small, immature stages of aquatic insects. Such nursery areas are important to trout-stream populations, and a lack of such suitable areas can be a factor in limiting the eventual numbers of adult trout.

Both eggs and alevins are extremely vulnerable when living in stream gravel. Severe flooding may cause the bottom to shift, killing untold thousands of baby trout. Fine silts may be introduced into the water by poor land-use practices ranging from streamside logging to trail-chewing all-terrain motorcycles. The silt may smother developing eggs or it may fill the spaces between gravel particles and make the upward migration of alevins impossible. Many other alevins starve to death in the natural course of things, as their slightly larger or more aggressive brethren are better able to establish and hold feeding territories in nursery areas of the stream. The natural mathematics of trout survival are both harsh and reasonable. Dr. James McFadden, a former professor of mine, researched such numbers extensively on some midwestern brook-trout streams. I once conned him into writing a popular magazine article, in which he described the numbers this way:

If all the descendants of a single pair of trout were to survive, grow to a length of eight inches, and reproduce, after five years they would stretch all the way to the moon and two-thirds of the way back to earth again. Were it not for a high death rate, trout might quickly crowd even fishermen off the face of the earth. In order for a balance to be maintained, cold, uncompromising mathematics decreed that, of the average 400 progeny each pair of trout had produced, only two would survive two years hence when the little trout themselves were old enough to spawn.[4]

Well-read trout fishermen these days often encounter biologists' technical reports covering some aspect of trout biology or perhaps detailing the trout-population characteristics of a particular stream. It's very important to understand a principal difference between the biologist's point of view and that of a fisherman. The biologist is concerned with the characteristics of a stream-trout population over time. Much of his or her work is based on the statistical treatment of information collected by various means in population studies. One trout is not a good statistical sample, but a large sampling over a period of time can lead to some very worthwhile management conclusions. The fisherman, on the other hand, catches trout one at a time. The encounter and the fisherman's judgments about fishing based on that encounter are instantaneous. The two perspectives are often very different.

Research biologists have demonstrated countless times that trout are opportunistic and generalistic feeders. This means that an average trout will eat whatever is available as food, under certain constraints, at any given time, and that the trout's diet encompasses the range of most food organisms found in or on the stream. This is certainly true when the diet of many trout is analyzed over a relatively long time period and the results of the analysis are compiled. However, if I step into New York's Beaverkill or Colorado's Fryingpan River on a Tuesday afternoon, I might find ninety-nine out of one hundred visible trout eating nothing but small blue-winged olive mayflies and refus-

ing all but the most imitative dry-fly patterns. From my instantaneous fisherman's view, these trout are being anything but generalistic, even though they may return to grubbing around the bottom for caddis, scuds, and midge larvae after the mayfly hatch is over. I have witnessed many red-faced arguments among biologists and anglers that might have been avoided if each had taken into account their differences in viewpoint. Unfortunately, the development of curricula in university fisheries programs continues to emphasize technical training at the expense of communication skills. Although there are some notable exceptions, most biologists aren't as adept at handling the public as they are at handling fish. The other side of the coin was described well by the late humorist Corey Ford, who once wrote that "You can always tell a fisherman . . . but you can't tell him much."

Trout behavior offers another good example of the same disparity in thinking. While at Penn State, Dr. Robert Bachman did a wonderful study of brown-trout behavior in Pennsylvania's Spruce Creek[5] that showed, among other things, his 8- to 12-inch wild brown trout holding the same, shallow stream positions day after day while they fed on insects drifting above the bottom in the current. He described this behavior in a *Trout* magazine article[6] some years ago, which prompted an angry reader's letter to the effect that the reader used big stonefly nymphs on the bottom to catch big trout, and that Bachman's "small trout" analysis therefore was all wet. Bachman's published reply was terrific, saying in part:

Of course weighted nymphs catch fish. And big ones, at that! So does canned yellow corn. But that doesn't mean that trout normally eat canned yellow corn . . . The fact remains that over 95 percent of all trout are less than 12 inches long. The trout that I studied at Spruce Creek were not "small" trout, but were representative of the size of the vast majority of all trout in American trout streams. Might not the constant emphasis in popular angling literature on catching large trout and the use of weighted nymphs to catch these comparatively rare trout be what is misleading? . . . does he [the average angler] realize that if he is fishing for trout 14 inches or larger that he is fishing for less than 5 percent (probably less than one percent) of all trout? I think not!

It is generally true, as McFadden and Bachman among many others have illustrated, that the trout fisherman who inevitably tries to catch larger trout is trying to catch a very small proportion of the trout in any given stream. Easterners, for example, who haven't fished in the Rockies and west commonly assume trout there to be bigger than in eastern streams, which isn't always true. Westerners often make the equally incorrect assumption that trout in eastern waters are universally small. While it is true that some very large, fertile, and well-publicized western rivers may have greater numbers of trout—and consequently a few more of the very large ones—than most eastern rivers, New York's Delaware River system probably offers a better shot at a 20-inch rainbow than Montana's famous Madison, and some of the most recent brown-trout world records have been set in Arkansas. Big trout are rare things in any case and—like gold—are where you find them.

Finding trout is the most important key in catching them. Consistently finding trout means understanding how the trout themselves behave, how they interact with their stream environment, and how they interact with—or, more properly, react

to—fishermen. I am skipping a number of things such as anatomy and trout diseases that are commonly found in full treatments of these fish[7] for the sake of being able to examine trout behavior in greater detail. Behavior is what the fisherman sees and reacts to in his fishing and is usually what determines how and where the fish are found in the first place.

Everything that a trout does, it does for a reason or reasons that may or may not be apparent. In trying to understand trout behavior, both contemporary fishermen and early scientists often ascribe human traits to the trout, but such anthropomorphic explanations are almost always wrong. In 1878, for example, the proceedings of the London Zoological Society described the motivational basis for fish behavior as terror, affection, disgrace, anger, and grief.[8] Even better examples persist in modern fishing.

At Hendrickson's Pool on New York's Beaverkill I once found a group of trout rising at twilight in the shallow side of the pool near the road. At the pool's center is a ledge outcropping with very deep water on its far side, which is a natural hiding and resting place for trout. My first try produced a brown trout of 16 inches or so that I played and released near the tail of the pool to avoid disturbing the other fish. My second try produced a larger brown that measured an even 20 inches along my rod-butt scale when I finally landed and released it. By this time there were only a few trout still rising in the shallow run on the near side of the ledge. I cast to the largest riseform and raised the rod gently when the fly disappeared in a soft swirl. This trout was bigger than the others, although I have no idea how big. I felt only a great weight as it swam very slowly and deliberately over the ledge and down into deep water. I felt my leader sliding over the rocks as the fish dove. The tippet finally sheared on the underwater ledge, and we parted company. Many fishermen and angling writers who should know better would describe the trout as attempting to cut my leader on the rocks. What I and others now know is that the trout, have sensed something mildly wrong, simply left its feeding station and swam to the place where it normally hides when not feeding, breaking my leader in the process. Brown trout are especially oriented to cover, and large ones typically run to a brushpile or undercut bank when hooked. These are places where your leader is apt to tangle, but the trout doesn't "know" this, and it hasn't "decided" to try and break your leader. The trout would show the same reaction if you tried to hit it with a rock and there was no leader attached at all.

This is also a good example of how some knowledge of trout behavior has immediate value for trout fishermen. When I'm home I'm most often fishing the nearby Battenkill in Vermont and New York, which has an excellent population of wild brown trout, including some big ones. There are long, slow-flowing flats lined with overhanging alders and fallen trees on each side that in some areas offer excellent cover for the browns that move out into the flats to feed on a variety of insect hatches. When I locate a larger fish, I can anticipate the fish's behavior on the end of my line. I know even before I start casting that if I hook the trout it's probably going to run hard for some bankside obstruction. When the trout takes, I could hold my rod high, as shown in most fishing-magazine photos, to absorb the shock of the first hard run. This will almost guarantee a broken leader in the brush. After dozens of breakoffs over the years, I finally figured out that I had to hold the rod low and to the side, sometimes even shoving the tip underwater as the trout is running, to keep the leader low and usually underneath whatever obstruction the trout is using as a refuge. This does not work, by the way, in heavily weeded trout streams like spring creeks, where the biggest problem is keeping the leader from picking up gobs of weed and algae, the weight of which can snap your tippet. In this case, you'll want to keep as much of the leader out of the water as possible when playing even large fish.

Behavioral ecology is a relatively new and complex science that offers a great deal to trout fishermen. British ecologist Tony Pritcher, in editing his 1986 book *The Behavior of Teleost Fishes*, defined it as "the study of the ways in which behavior is influenced by natural selection in relation to ecological conditions." It's important to understand that the ultimate payoff or goal in the life-history strategy of an individual trout is successful spawning. If a trout spawns, its particular attributes become part of another trout generation. In a Darwinian sense, that trout is a winner. If a trout fails to spawn and instead falls victim to a heron, that trout is an obvious loser. Behavior among trout is a large part of what determines the winners and losers of this endless contest. Over thousands of years of natural selection, the winners should develop behaviors that better enable them to avoid herons (or fishermen). If this were not the case, by the logic of this admittedly oversimplified example, there would soon be few if any trout.

Trout are constantly making decisions about many things, such as whether or not to dart for cover as our heron flaps its wings and settles into the shallows. Both behavioral scientists and trout fishermen are concerned with what those decisions might be—whether or not to eat a nymph at a particular moment, for example—and how the trout uses its senses to acquire information about its surroundings that enables such decisions to be made in the first place. Please remember that my use of "decision" here implies no humanistic, logical process on the trout's part but rather describes the trout's nearly instantaneous reaction to a variety of sensory inputs that take place simultaneously.

Trout have at least six sensory systems, some of which are analogous to human systems, like smell, taste, or touch, but which may operate in very different ways. Their sense of smell, for example, is extraordinary, capable of detecting some substances in concentrations as low as a few parts per billion and possibly even less. A trout has two small nasal pits, one on each side of the snout forward of the eyes, within which water circulates. As many as 5 to 10 million scent-detecting cells[9] may be found on the highly folded tissues within these nasal pits and are partly responsible for the well-known homing abilities of migratory salmon, which can identify their natal rivers by smell.

Trout have similar abilities, although it has been demonstrated to a much lesser extent in nonmigratory forms, and peak sensitivities to certain amino acids and bile products have been shown in laboratory tests. There are many behavioral implications linked to this ability. A trout may be able to identify another individual trout solely by smell and may also be able to locate specific areas in a stream by their characteristic and unique odors. An upstream predator such as a mink or otter might be detected by its smell in the current. It has been shown that certain ovarian secretions of female rainbow trout will attract males upstream to spawning areas. Finally, and this has not been scientifically demonstrated, I believe that this scenting ability enables trout to anticipate and locate aquatic insect hatches. When hundreds and hundreds of caddisfly pupae emerge from their underwater cases during a hatch in an upstream riffle, for example, there should be a substantial scent released in the current that should in turn attract trout up into the riffle itself. If the

trout don't move in response, and some won't, they will at the very least be alerted to the presence of hatching insects and many will assume a feeding attitude before the insects themselves are brought down to the trout by the current.

The trout's ability to detect minute traces of scent have some other trout-fishing implications. Some salmonids, for example, have been shown to respond negatively to small concentrations of scent left when a human rinses his hand or her hand in the water, an ability that's assumed to exist in all trout. Most artificial flies have some volatile aromatics used in their construction, such as lacquer solvents or the benzene-based compounds used as moth repellents in materials storage, and their scent will remain in the fly for weeks and months after the fly is made. This is probably of little importance with dry flies. But it may sometimes be true that a trout refuses a perfect-looking wet fly or nymph just because it smells bad, especially if the fly is moving slowly in the water, allowing the trout time to detect its scent. I scrub or rub my underwater flies with a little streamside mud or crushed alder leaves after attaching the fly to my leader. This helps, I think, to kill any adverse scent and has the added advantage of wetting the fly to make it sink more quickly. Human saliva, which is probably offensive to trout, is a common but poor choice for achieving a similar result. Fish-attracting compounds have become very popular for many types of fishing in recent years and might solve the problem, but fly fishermen haven't been anointing their flies with them because the act itself is too reminiscent of baitfishing.

Trout also have acute senses of taste and touch. If you watch a naturally feeding trout, the fish may sometimes mistake a drifting bit of bark for a nymph. It only takes slightly less than a second for the fish to eject its mistake, and the same is often true for an artificial nymph that neither tastes nor feels right to the fish. This is the principal reason why dead-drift nymph fishing on a slack line is so difficult, especially when you can't see the fish or the fly.

The fourth sense possessed by trout seems to fall somewhere between touch and hearing, but has no analogy among the human senses. Like most fish, all trout have a lateral-line system that's visible as a very fine line running from head to tail along each side of their bodies. The visible line is a series of hundreds of very small pores containing sensory cells called neuromasts that can detect minute changes in water currents. This has been variously described as a distant sense of touch or a kind of physical sonar, although the sense is not dependent on sound. A trout holding in a slow current next to a sheltering stump can identify its own location precisely by the unique combination of current waves reflected between its body and nearby stationary objects. A slowly swimming trout uses the sense in a similar way, being able to detect nearby objects that reflect the currents created by the trout's own movement.

Among its other behavioral implications, such as communication during the spawning act, the lateral line sense can be important in feeding. There are many stories in fishing books about the sudden appearance of a huge brown trout that circles and attacks a smaller fish being played on the end of a line. This has happened to me half a dozen times over forty years of trout fishing. I have finally become convinced that the large fish's lateral-line sense plays a key role in this event. For example, once while playing a small brook trout that had taken a dry fly in a clear pool about 30 feet long, 12 feet wide, and up to 4 feet deep, I was startled to see a big brown of 4 or 5 pounds start circling the pool and then home in on my fish with extraordinary speed. The larger trout saw me and imme-

diately darted back under a large pile of brush at the end of the pool. From its hiding place, the larger trout could not possibly have seen the underwater struggles of the smaller fish, but it certainly could have detected with its lateral line the underwater commotion that signaled an easy meal in the form of a smaller fish in trouble. The large fish charged from its hiding place, without having actually seen the object of its charge, and searched quickly for a victim until I frightened it off. This is an extreme example, of course, but there's little question that the lateral-line sense could be just as effective in locating a moving crayfish along the bottom of a stream after dark, when larger trout are actively hunting. Large, bulky flies that push water when moved at or under the surface are widely known as effective night-fishing flies, and their effectiveness undoubtedly depends on the lateral-line sense of trout. Finally, a few fishes such as the African butterfly fish show an exceptional lateral-line sensitivity to water-surface waves. These fish can differentiate between a raindrop hitting the water and a moth struggling in the surface tension, determine the direction of the signal source, and attack. Trout are primarily visual feeders and have not been scientifically shown to respond to pressure waves originating at the surface. I do believe they have this capability, although probably not to the extent of other, more specialized fishes, and in this case as in others, visual-feeding cues are the most important.

Hearing is the fifth trout sense we'll consider, which is also something that trout do well. This depends partly on the extreme density of water in comparison to that of air, which means that sound travels both faster and farther underwater. Trout do not have external ears, but do have a pair of internal ears with semicircular canals that enable the fish to maintain its physical equilibrium much as humans do. Within each inner ear are three small, fluid-filled sacs, each containing a small bony object called an otolith. When subjected to the pressure of sound waves, the otoliths move and thereby stimulate sensing cells within the ear, allowing the trout to hear. A trout's hearing occurs within a frequency range less than that of humans; trout are insensitive to sounds above 3,000 cycles per second (hertz), while human sensitivity is retained at 15,000 hertz or higher.

For fishermen, the important consequence is that underwater sounds made while wading, such as banging rocks or the scrape of metal wading sandals on the bottom, will scare trout, even if the trout can't see you. Sounds made above the surface and not in physical contact with the ground or water are reflected from the surface and not heard by trout. Thus you can talk or shout to a fishing companion and not startle the fish. If you stamp around on the stream bank, however, the vibrations may be carried into the water and thence to the trout, which will disappear quickly.

The sixth and last overt sense[10] possessed by trout is vision, which is the most important consideration for both fish and fishermen. A trout's vision has been studied a great deal and still offers many mysteries. Chapter 8, on selective feeding in trout, deals with vision at length. For the moment, and in considering the behavior of trout, remember that within the constraints imposed by the underwater environment trout can see much better than humans. This includes being able to see portions of the ultraviolet spectrum, which are invisible to humans, and also being able to detect polarized light.

The location of a particular trout in a stream at any given time is most often the result of two conflicting factors that are in constant interplay: the need to feed efficiently and the need to avoid predators. A trout that spends all of its time hiding under a stream bank stump may be more successful at avoiding herons or mink, but may also grow relatively little. In contrast, the trout that remains exposed in open water may encounter more food and grow more rapidly, but is also more likely to be eaten by a merganser or to be caught by a fisherman. The ability of most wild trout to adjust their lives accordingly is astonishing.

In order to grow and achieve the Darwinian payoff of successful spawning, a trout has to consume more energy in feeding than it spends in gathering its food. Since much of a trout's food is taken from among items drifting by in the current while the trout remains in one spot, it is correct to suppose that the greater the current, the greater the amount of food passing by the trout's location in any given time interval. Trout are streamlined and capable of swimming in rapid currents. The mucosal covering, or thin layer of slime, over their skin aids in this effort by cutting the friction of water against their bodies by almost half.[11]

Having to maintain position for feeding in a rapid current is wasteful of a trout's energy. The ideal solution, and one that most trout adopt in some way, is to remain in slower water next to a faster current. The trout can often hold its position with very little effort in slowly moving water, which still allows the fish to visually scan the adjacent and faster current into which it can dart to grab a drifting nymph and then return to its customary waiting spot. This movement may be lateral, from behind a streamside rock out into the current and back again, but is more commonly vertical since the trout can hold in the sheltering eddy of a rock on the bottom and simply tip upward to grab a food item from the faster current overhead.

This whole behavioral process is modified by the trout's need to hide, which is why instream cover is so important. Most anglers think of instream cover as physical things such as undercut banks or logjams, but the term also includes deep water and the cover provided by the choppy surface of a rapid current underneath which trout can feel secure in a deep riffle, or where the water tumbles into a pool. The use of instream cover often varies among trout species in characteristic ways. Cutthroat trout, for example, are commonly found under the deep, tumbling chutes at the heads of pools, while rainbows may be spread throughout the deeper pockets of a choppy riffle. Brown trout are especially oriented to overhead cover such as undercut banks and logjams, as are brook trout but to a lesser extent. Please remember that any of these trout might be found at any of these locations at a particular time and that the habitat preferences I've mentioned are no more than a very general rule.

Cover, whatever its form, gives the trout some protection from which it may be reluctant to move. In a wonderful experiment with juvenile coho salmon[12] conducted in a laboratory stream channel, it was found that the little salmon would not move as far to take a drifting food item if a visible predator was nearby. The little fish seemed able to gauge the risks they were taking in feeding. As the predator distance was reduced, the little fish reduced their feeding distance— and risk of predation—accordingly. This reminded me of a brown trout I once spent about half an hour trying to catch in Montana's Armstrong Spring Creek. The fish was rising to a hatch of small mayflies, but its riseforms at the surface were less than an inch from a sheltering streamside log. I kept casting. The fish kept rising and paying no heed to my best efforts. I was finally able to place my dry fly so it floated while literally brushing the edge of the log. The trout finally took the fly. I had built up so much anticipation in thirty minutes of casting that I

overreacted, jerking the rod violently and snapping the leader. My own fumbling aside, the point is that this particular trout had found a location offering both drifting food and shelter, considerations so important and precisely defined by the trout itself that my efforts at catching it had to be measured in fractions of an inch. To be sure, this is an extreme example, but I hope it illustrates that what a few frustrated fishermen may attribute to some undefined and perverse nature of trout can be better explained in terms of a trout's behavioral ecology.

1. For the etymology of "trout" I used *The Compact Edition of the Oxford English Dictionary*; Oxford; 1971.

2. Much of this is based on Moyle and Cech (1988). Their book, *Fishes: An Introduction to Ichthyology*, is a particular favorite of mine because it pointedly puts an ecological spin on what too often is very dry reading. A great deal of this highly recommended book is very accessible to any fisherman.

3. See Robins, C., et al. (1991).

4. McFadden (1976).

5. See Bachman (1984). This study is discussed at greater length in Chapter 5.

6. Bachman (1983).

7. See Willers (1991), or Stoltz and Schnell, eds. (1991) for contemporary coverage of these topics.

8. See Pritcher, ed. (1986).

9. From Pritcher (1986).

10. There are other senses in addition to the six I've mentioned, but these are more indirect. For example, trout have what's called a pineal organ at the dorsal surface of their brains that is light-sensitive. This small organ appears to function in setting the trout's biological clock and may help to regulate such things as spawning that are partly triggered by gradual changes in day length.

11. See Rosen and Cornford (1971).

12. See "Constraints Placed by Predators on Feeding Behavior," by M. Milinski, in Pritcher (1986).

4
Brook Trout

John James Audubon occasionally found diversion from sketching and collecting by playing his violin, a melancholy sound familiar to those who passed his cabin at Henderson, Kentucky, on the banks of the Ohio early in the nineteenth century. On this evening, however, the music was replaced by the waving arms and exclamations of Constantine Samuel Rafinesque, the brilliantly erratic ichthyologist newly arrived from Sicily who had traveled west to pay his respects to the great naturalist. Rafinesque was an enthusiastic part of the explosive growth in American science after 1800, and he was eagerly collecting and describing new species of fish. Late that night he quizzed Audubon about fishes newly encountered in the Midwest until Audubon, his patience exhausted, went to bed.

Rafinesque couldn't sleep, his brain fired by thoughts of new fishes and the scientific acclaim that would be his right. There was a fluttering in the darkened room. A pair of small bats darted above his bed, unable to escape by the same crack they'd entered when darkness fell. He opened the door and then grabbed the nearest object to swing wildly at the bats, shooing them from the room. In his stumbles and waving, the object smashed against the wall. It was Audubon's Cremona violin.

Rafinesque tried to explain in the morning, but the artist was icy, his patience exhausted. The Sicilian left quickly and continued his wanderings along the Ohio. Rafinesque eventually won a professorship at Transylvania University in Lexington, Kentucky, where he received as a gift from Audubon some drawings of Ohio River fishes that Rafinesque immediately saw as new species. Ecstatic, he described them as such in his 1820 book, *Ichthyologia Ohiensis*. The fish, compliments of Audubon, were fictitious, and Rafinesque's scientific reputation plummeted. Even now Rafinesque is known both as a founder of American fisheries science and as as one of its most bizarre practitioners.[1]

Rafinesque was launched on an unsuspecting America by Dr. Samuel Latham Mitchell in New York, who early in 1814 had published his little *Report, in part, on the Fishes of New York*. Rafinesque's ship from Sicily was wrecked in a storm at Fisher's Island at the eastern end of Long Island Sound in 1815, and he arrived penniless on Mitchell's doorstep shortly thereafter. He almost certainly counted on the good doctor's well-

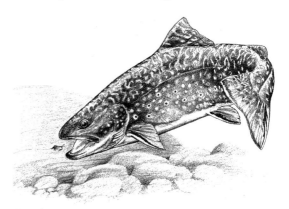

Brook trout.

known and bumbling good nature plus their mutual interest in fish for a free meal and perhaps more. Mitchell accommodated Rafinesque with room, board, and introductions to New York society, where Rafinesque worked briefly as a tutor before heading west in search of new species. On the evening of his arrival, their conversation would certainly have included fish—Rafinesque would talk about little else—and a review of Mitchell's newest book. They probably talked about brook trout that evening, too, for in Mitchell's work was the first formal description of brook trout in the New World.

The *Report* is a small book that Mitchell had privately printed by a D. Carlisle at 301 Broadway in Manhattan on January 1, 1814, in which Mitchell provided the first American descriptions of forty-nine fish species and listed twenty-one others. Among them was what we now call brook trout, which Mitchell described as follows:

Salmo fontinalis—New York Trout
Mouth wide. Teeth sharp. Tongue distinct. Skin without scales. Back a mottled pale and brown. Sides dark brown with yellow and red spots; the yellow larger than the red. The latter appearing like scarlet dots. Lateral line straight. The yellow and red spots both above and below that line. Sides of the abdomen orange red. Lowest part of the belly whitish, with a smutty tinge. First rays of the pectoral, ventral and anal fins white, the second black; the rest purplish red. Dorsal fin mottled [word illegible] yellowish and black. Tail rather concave, but not amounting to a fork, and of a reddish purple, with blackish spots above and below. Eye large, iris pale.

Its characters as derived from the fins and colors, differs [sic] so much from the salmo fario [sic; European brown trout] of the books, that it may be deemed another species; or at any rate a wide variety.

Mitchell's classification of brook trout was mistaken, even given the limited scientific literature of the time. Brook trout remained in the genus *Salmo* (common trout) until properly reclassified as a charr (genus *Salvelinus*) by David Starr Jordan, the eminent Stanford University ichthyologist, in 1878. Jordan retained the specific *fontinalis*, which means living in springs. *Salvelinus* is the generic name given European charrs by Linnaeus in his 1758 *Systema naturae*, to which Mitchell almost certainly had access and which formally established binomial, latinized nomenclature in the natural sciences. The word apparently derives from an ancient Scandinavian term for charr. Other North American members of this genus include arctic charr, Dolly Varden, and lake trout.

Ironically, brook trout populations were already declining in the northeastern United States by the time Mitchell first described them. For one thing, our black history of water pollution was already well entrenched. Water-powered mills of various kinds were commonplace in many areas by the end of the 1700s and were useful dumping grounds for all kinds of waste that conveniently would be carried elsewhere in high water. Also, and although fishing for sport probably didn't start to widely affect brook-trout populations until after 1820 or so, colonials for more than a century before that time were handy with nets to which brook trout are vulnerable. The situation was so bad so early that the first documented fishing regulation in America was enacted in 1734 by the City of New York, which limited Collect Pond to hook-and-line fishing only. By some accounts,[2] the pond continued to produce brook trout until 1816, when it was drained; it's now covered by the Tombs prison.

The first issue of America's first sporting periodical, *American Turf Register and Sporting Magazine*, carried this 1829 note by George Gibson on the decline of brook trout in some western Pennsylvania streams that are famous even now, but not necessarily for brook trout:

> Although I commenced wetting flies in times long ago, my experiences extend only to Cumberland County; but trout were formerly found in all the limestone springs in the state. Owing however to the villainous practice of netting them they are extinct in some streams and scarce in others. . . .
>
> Big Spring, west of Carlisle . . . affords fine sport . . . A law of the state makes it penal to net in this stream and forbids the taking of trout between the months of July and April. It is the only spring branch in the state protected by law, the good effects of which is [sic] apparent.
>
> The Letort [now a world-famous brown-trout stream] which flows past Carlisle is another good stream . . . It formerly offered excellent sport but owing to the infamous practice of netting and setting night lines the fish have been much lessened in numbers and size.

The American trout-hatchery movement (see Chapter 1) responded to declining brook-trout populations with an enormous outpouring of fish after the 1870s. According to the 1895 report of the Pennsylvania Fish Commission, for example, 16 million brook trout fry were hatched and stocked in the state during the eighteen years between 1877 and 1895. Stockings here and elsewhere in the Northeast at the time were often conducted by subscription, through which an individual sportsman could apply for a number of fish to be stocked in a particular section of public waters. Brook-trout stocking was thus more widespread than would otherwise have been possible, which means the naturally reproducing stocks even now present in some northeastern headwater streams and regarded as "wild" probably have hatchery fish among their ancestors.

Perhaps no American brook-trout fishing is as historically well known as the great trout rush to the Rangeley region of Maine after the Civil War. It was a rush in every sense of the word, and modern anglers who bemoan the crowds and popularity of such American rivers as the Bighorn or Beaverkill might have found things even worse on these Maine lakes in the 1880s. The Rangeleys were producing brook trout to as much as 12 pounds at a time when fishing near cities like New York and Philadelphia and even in the wilderness Adirondacks had widely deteriorated. Most contemporary accounts are romantic idylls of encounters with large trout and make no note of either crowds or the blackfly swarms for which the North Woods are notorious. There were a few disgruntled mentions in magazines of boats being crowded from one side of a cove to another, but such complaints were rare and are only a hint of what it must have been like to fish the wilderness in a crowd.

The brook trout were decimated. Overfishing was almost certainly a primary cause but may not have been the only one. The big Rangeley brookies fed partly on local populations of blueback trout, a small and related charr now found only in a few isolated Maine ponds. Both smelt and landlocked salmon were eventually introduced to these waters, where the smelt apparently competed with the bluebacks for food, and the salmon were yet another predator. The bluebacks disappeared and so did the large trout. There is still good brook-trout fishing in the Rangeley region by modern, small-fish standards, but it pales beside its own history.

There is an enormous amount of technical literature on brook-trout biology and at least an equivalent amount of angling folklore and myth. Because brook trout have been widely cultured for more than a century they have been easily available and widely used in laboratory work, which led one researcher to call brook trout the "white rat of aquatic science."

A brook trout can be immediately recognized by the wavy lines, also called vermiculations, on its dark, olive-green back. A similar pattern is created when the sun shines through rippled water to cast shadows on the bottom, and the vermiculations have an obvious camouflage value in helping the trout avoid predators from above such as kingfishers and herons.

Brookies typically have many pale yellow spots plus a lesser number of small red spots surrounded by blue halos on their sides, although the spotting patterns and relative proportions of color are variable among different brook-trout strains. It has often been said that these fish are the only trout with light spots against a dark background, but this is a semantic problem. While cutthroat, brown, and rainbow trout do have the opposite spotting pattern (dark spots on a paler background), other members of the charr genus, such as lake trout, are sometimes referred to as trout and also have the light spot/dark background combination. Sea-run brook trout, also called salters, will retain a silvery sheen over their bodies for a brief period after reentering fresh water, but this disappears quickly. Salters are usually indistinguishable from nonanadromous forms in the same river within a few weeks of their return.

The brook trout's pectoral, ventral, and anal fins are starkly edged in white, which again is unique among other common trouts, but not among charrs. The white is literally a dead giveaway. Often, when trying to spot brookies in a river or stream, the white-edged fins will call your attention to the fish, even if the trout is motionless and otherwise hard to see. The same is true for predators both above and below the surface, and the white-edged fins are probably an evolutionary compromise. Trout, including brook trout, communicate with each other underwater by assuming a variety of body postures and swimming attitudes, which includes a flaring of the body fins (see Chapter 3). This allows the individual trout to defend feeding and resting territories and is important in spawning. Although the highly visible, white-edged fins are a disadvantage to the trout in terms of predator avoidance, this disadvantage is most likely offset by their enhancement of the trouts' ability to communicate with one another by being more visible.[3]

Relatively large heads and mouths are also brook-trout characteristics, and the head may amount to one quarter of the body length on adult fish. This allows for a relatively large mouth size in comparison with other trout, which is probably reflective of the brookie's wide-ranging diet. Along the center of the mouth's roof is the vomerine bone, which in brook trout only carries teeth in a small cluster at its forward end. This is a primary key used by taxonomists in identifying brookies and is easy to feel with your fingertip. If there are teeth all along the roof of the mouth, your fish isn't a brookie.

As brook trout near their fall spawning period, the lower flanks of males become brilliant orange and older males may develop a slightly hooked lower jaw. Contrary to popular belief, this color change may also occur in females, but to a lesser extent. I have handled gravid females in late season northern Labrador whose entire sides were covered by a reddish blush that contrasted strongly with the deep orange flanks of males. In some areas of northeastern Canada, arctic charr and brook trout occupy the same lakes. The fish are often similar in size and color, especially close to spawning time, but the arctic charr can be discerned by the lack of vermiculations on their backs.

It's a long-held belief that the flesh of wild brookies is orange while that of hatchery brook trout is white. Many old-timers will still check for this as they dress their catch from a remote swamp flowage, looking for the orange as proof of having caught some "real natives." Hatchery managers have long been able to induce this color change by adding ground shrimp and crab wastes to the trout's hatchery fare, and wild fish are often white fleshed if their diet lacks small crustaceans. The flesh color of wild fish may also vary with the season, being orange in July and August, when rapid gonadal growth is happening prior to spawning, and pale at other times of the year. It is not clear whether this color change is caused by sexual maturation or by seasonal variations in diet.

Brook trout are typically deep bodied in proportion to their length, more so than other common trout. This robust body form combined with the fish's square tail provides a design adapted more to maneuverability than to long-distance swimming. (For comparison in the world of fishes, tunas are the opposite extreme, with deeply shaped sicklelike tails designed for sustained high-speed swimming. Other trout have more deeply forked tails, although not to the extent of the tuna's, and are better designed for speed than brook trout.) By virtue of their body and tail shapes, brookies can swim efficiently in water as shallow as their body depth. Their maneuverability is an asset in capturing a wide variety of foods in waters of all depths. These attributes help to account for the wide variety of habitats utilized by brookies within their range. The powerful, long run of a large rainbow or brown when first hooked is almost always absent with large brook trout, which tend to a bulldog tugging and twisting fight near the bottom. Such a fight is part of their nature, determined in turn largely by their shape.

Brook trout are creatures of cold, clear streams and lakes and are the most cold tolerant of all common trout. This is the general determinant of both their original range and the extent to which naturalization has been

possible elsewhere.[4] As a general case, brookies are native to the northern half of the eastern United States in addition to eastern Canada. They were introduced widely in the American West during the late nineteenth-century stocking frenzy fostered in part by the U.S. Fish Commission, and I've included a map showing both their original and now naturalized North American ranges.

Their northern endemic range is apparently bounded by Manitoba's Churchill River on the northwest coast of Hudson Bay and by Nain on the northeast coast of Labrador, although there are unconfirmed reports listed in scientific literature of brookies having been found even farther north in areas more typically occupied by their arctic charr cousins. They were originally found west as far as the western tributaries of Lake Superior in Ontario and Minnesota and throughout much of Wisconsin. Pennsylvania, New Jersey, New York, and New England are all original brook-trout areas.

There are some surprises in these distribution patterns, perhaps the greatest of which is in Michigan where, contrary to the assumptions of most anglers, brook trout were not native to much of the lower peninsula. Famous trout rivers there, such as the Pere Marquette, Manistee, and Au Sable, apparently had no brook trout until they were introduced, possibly as late as 1879. Brook trout have been cited by several researchers as being found in Michigan only north of a line extending between Grand Traverse Bay on the west to Thunder Bay on the east, thus including all of the upper peninsula and just the tip of the mitten in the south. The only troutlike fish indigenous to Michigan rivers south of that line was apparently the now-extinct Michigan grayling.

Curiously, and in spite of their absence from lower Michigan, there were once limited native brook-trout populations in northeastern Ohio, northern Illinois, and the hill country of northeastern Iowa. All of these

North American Distribution of Brook Trout
(*Salvelinus fontinalis*)

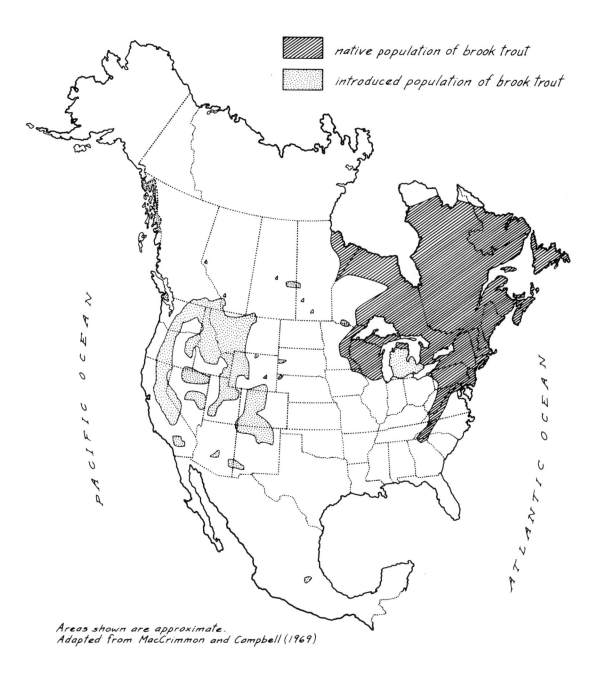

native population of brook trout

introduced population of brook trout

Areas shown are approximate.
Adapted from MacCrimmon and Campbell (1969)

areas are farther south than much of Michigan's lower peninsula, which might lead one to suppose the historical data concerning a lack of brookies there to be wrong. But brook-trout distribution in these areas was spotty, and Milton Trautman, the late fisheries authority at Ohio State University, once noted their original absence from other northern Ohio spring creeks that appeared to offer suitable habitat. One explanation he gave was the dramatic difference in the present landscape from that of about 16,000 years ago, during the retreat of the last great ice sheets that covered most of the brook trout's present range. Much of the region was under large lakes at a time when newly created freshwater streams were being colonized by ancestral brook trout, and some of what we see now as available but empty habitat either didn't exist or wasn't accessible during the time of the trouts' spread westward from the Appalachian highlands.[5]

There are also remnant brook-trout populations as far south as Georgia along the Appalachian spine, but these have been in decline since at least 1900 and probably earlier. Early pressures came from logging that destroyed trout habitat on lower elevation slopes and from overfishing that quickly eliminated brook trout from the more accessible reaches of highland streams. In Great Smoky Mountain National Park on the Tennessee-North Carolina border, where logging was essentially eliminated with the park's establishment in 1936, brook-trout populations have continued to decline.[6] The apparent cause is competition from rainbow trout that were first introduced to this area in 1910 and are slowly displacing the remaining brook trout higher and higher into the region's headwater streams. These headwater areas could be the brook trouts' last refuge here as the rainbows' upstream movement may be finally limited by physical barriers such as waterfalls or by the colder headwater temperatures that are better tolerated by brook trout.

That brook trout are inherently coldwater fish is well known, but the many scientific determinations of their thermal tolerances have produced varied results that can be misleading. Since temperatures must be controlled and the reactions of the trout closely observed, these measurements have long been made in laboratory aquaria. Trout that are stressed in any way often show both metabolic and behavioral differences from fish at rest, and laboratory handling is one source of such stress that can skew results. Then too, brook trout may become acclimated to a certain temperature regime in the wild or in a hatchery, which acclimation may or may not have been taken into account when measuring the brookies' responses to changes in water temperatures. Finally, there may be some differences in thermal response among brook trout of different genetic strains, although I have not as yet seen this demonstrated as fact. It has long been fashionable in the angling press to publish the preferred water temperatures of a variety of gamefishes, and fishermen too often take these figures as absolutes. Such information can be valuable as an aid in finding fish but should always be taken as indicating a probable range of values.

Given those caveats, it's been generally found that brook trout can perform reasonably well within a temperature range of 41 to 68 degrees Fahrenheit. If it's available within a particular stream or lake, trout will usually themselves select a narrower range, with 60.8 degrees having been shown in one series of tests to be a statistical optimum. Temperature preferences and effects also change with the seasons. For example, one researcher demonstrated that spawning wouldn't take place in waters of 66.2 degrees or warmer and that both the extent of spawning and the number of viable eggs in female fish increased as water temperatures were reduced to 50 degrees.

Brook trout have been shown to feed at temperatures as low as 33.8 degrees. The winter water temperatures of many trout streams may be as low as 32.2 degrees, or almost freezing, which the trout can survive, but water a few degrees warmer is usually available to fish at the bottoms of pools and near seepages of underground water into the streambed. The lower lethal temperature limit of these fish appears to be around 30.8 degrees, a temperature the fish might encounter in saline estuaries at the northern extremes of its range.

The upper limit of a brook trout's thermal tolerance is more important, since many trout streams in the middle and southern portions of its range approach these temperatures in late summer. The figure is usually given as somewhere between 72 and 77 degrees, but even this doesn't mean instantaneous death. One technical definition of "lethal" for purposes of such thermal testing is a 50 percent mortality rate within a group of trout after ninety-six hours of exposure to a particular temperature. Obviously, still higher temperatures will produce death more quickly until at some point close to 86 degrees, death will be immediate. In the real world this means that a brook trout might venture briefly into relatively warm water to feed on a hatch of mayflies, for example, or perhaps to avoid a predator, but will otherwise remain in or near a cold-water refuge such as the mouth of a cooler tributary or an underwater spring. If there is no cold-water refuge there will be no naturally reproducing brook trout.

Of particular concern to both anglers and biologists is the brook trout's relative tolerance of acidity, especially since during the past twenty years or so it's been shown that acidic precipitation, meaning snow as well as rain, is impacting trout populations in the United States and Canada.[7] This acidity is described in terms of pH, which is a relative measure of both acidity and alkalinity where a pH of 7 is neutral, lesser values are increasingly acidic to a minimum scale value of 0, and values increasing from 7 to a maximum of pH 14 at the other end of the scale are alkaline. The scale is logarithmic, which means pH 5 is ten times more acid than pH 6, pH 4 is one hundred times more acid than pH 6, and so on. By way of perspective, the McIntosh apple that makes your cheeks pucker is acidic, having a pH of about 3, and the milk of magnesia you might take to soothe or neutralize an acid stomach is alkaline, with a pH of about 12. Most trout streams are relatively neutral in a natural state, with pH values ranging from 6 to 8.

Oxides of sulfur and nitrogen are common components of industrial, power plant, and automotive emissions sent upward and carried generally east across the United States and Canada by prevailing winds. By some estimates in the 1980s, United States sources were pumping 26 million tons of sulfur dioxide and 23 million tons of nitrogen oxide into our atmosphere annually. Once airborne, and while being carried downwind hundreds of miles from their sources, these compounds undergo chemical change into sulfuric and nitric acids, which are then captured in rain or snow and deposited on the landscape. For many organisms, including trout, the combination can be lethal.

By virtue of prevailing air flows from southwest to northeast, almost all of the brook trout's native range is subject to increasingly acidified precipitation. Emissions and air currents have no regard for political boundaries, and even the remote pristine trout waters of the Canadian north are subject to this effect. Some trout waters are slightly alkaline, having calcareous rock such as limestone in their watersheds, the buffering character of which can neutralize some effects of increasing acidity much as an antacid tablet soothes an irate stomach. Much of brook-trout country, however, is granitic, with thin soils and sparse vegetation. This means its streams and lakes are slightly and naturally acidic to begin with and have limited buffering capacity. Acidic precipitation not only lowers the pH of the groundwater and surface water, an effect deleterious to the trout, but also dissolves increased amounts of chemically active and naturally occurring metals—notably aluminum—from the bedrock and soils. The metals are carried in solution into trout water, and their presence reduces the trout's metabolic ability to survive in the face of the falling pH. Brook trout have demonstrated survival at a pH as low as 3.5, but pH 5 is a more realistic lower limit. Spawning females have been shown to avoid spawning sites of pH 5 or lower, values at which young trout emerging from the spawning gravel are especially affected. Some recent studies have shown the presence of acid-soluble aluminum may amplify the adverse effect of a reduced pH by a factor of ten and possibly more.[8]

Not all brook-trout waters are adversely affected, of course. Some have demonstrated adequate buffering capacity. Others by virtue of their lower altitides or location out of the path of pollutant-laden air streams will be less affected or affected more slowly. Unfortunately, such waters are in the minority in brook-trout country. New York's Adirondack Mountains are the heart of the brook trout's range and are also the first mountains hit by eastward flowing air masses that pick up pollutants in the Midwest. In the 1930s, which is when New York conducted its first modern surveys for baseline fisheries data, the average pH of Adirondack lakes was between pH 6 and pH 7. By 1975, that figure had dropped to an average of about 4.5, an astonishing thousandfold increase in relative acidity. By the early 1980s some 212 lakes and ponds, mostly on the Adirondack west slope, were documented as being without any fish, acidified to the point of sterility.

In much of brook-trout country acid precipitation accumulates as snow during the winter, being suddenly and massively released into rivers and lakes when the snow melts in April and early May. In his powerful book *Acid Rain* (1983), Bob Boyle included this description from a New York geologist of the snow-storage phenomenon: "The snow and ice store acids for three or four months and then when the spring melt comes, lakes and streams get one hell of a slug of acids. It's as though a pack-a-day smoker gave up cigarettes for four months and then tried to make up for what he had missed by smoking 120 packs in ten days."

This acid jolt hits the rivers when vulnerable young trout are first emerging from the spawning gravels, and it can be strong enough to kill adult trout outright. The late Dwight Webster was famous worldwide as a Cornell University fisheries professor and brook-trout authority, a fascinating companion with whom I shared several Adirondack trout ponds and many evening discussions. He once told me that when acting as a consultant to one of the west-slope Adirondack trout clubs he was in charge of timing the annual spring stockings of club waters. "It was easy to figure when to do it," he said with a wry smile. "I just put a caged hatchery rainbow in the river overnight. If the trout was dead in the morning it was still too early in the spring runoff to stock. If the rainbow was alive, I told 'em to go ahead."

Water pollution is stereotypically seen as garbage in a river from a nearby mill, or sewage effluent that's linked closely to its local source. Public outcry is immediate, and many of these problems were widely publicized in the 1960s and cleaned up during the 1970s. Acid precipitation is more insidious.

You can't see it. Its effects are often geographically far removed from its sources. Jobs at an inefficient midwestern power plant will almost inevitably be seen as more important in domestic politics than a dwindling population of wilderness Canadian brook trout some thousand miles away. It is a bleak—and unresolved—picture.

Brook trout are generally described as opportunistic feeders, eating whatever happens to be close by and easily caught. At any given time and depending on fish size and habitat, brook trout foods will range from plankton and midge larvae to frogs and meadow mice. The maneuverability brook trout gain from their body and tail shapes allows them to catch a variety of foods but usually not those involving a high-speed aquatic chase, such as minnows in open water. Like rainbow trout (see Chapter 6), individual brook trout within a group have been scientifically shown to have food preferences different from the group taken as a whole.

In his 1938 book *Trout Streams*, the late Paul Needham presented a list of natural brook-trout foods ranked by their frequency of occurrence in the stomachs of 251 brook trout that he captured and autopsied during a twelve-month period ending in March of 1929. He noted correctly that his data reflected the general bottom-oriented feeding of brook trout. Since the average trout in his sample was only 5.5 inches long, he also advised that a sampling of larger trout might give different results and that samples might also vary on a river-by-river basis. Caddisflies predominated as diet forms in Needham's data (30 percent of total), which has been taken by many anglers for more than fifty years to mean that brook trout have an innate preference for caddisflies. This simply isn't true, and such assumptions not only ignore the caveats Needham gave with his own data

but have since been shown to neglect the many factors that influence a brook trout's diet at any particular time and place.

Foods taken by brook trout may vary widely among different habitats, and such differences generally reflect differences among the habitats themselves. A brook trout caught on a July afternoon from a small pond in Yellowstone Park may be full of snails to the extent of feeling like a beanbag when you handle and release the fish. A brook trout taken below thundering Ripogenus Dam on Maine's Penobscot River in late May will probably be stuffed with the spring-run smelt that flutter weakly in the giant river eddies here after passing through the turbines. These are extreme examples, but the stomach sampling of large numbers of trout in either case would obviously be misleading if the data were presented without qualification as to place and time.

Seasonal variations also have to be taken into account, even in the case of a single stream or pond. For example, terrestrial insects are rare along stream margins in winter, and one Vermont stream study[9] showed terrestrials comprising less than 2 percent of brook-trout diet in winter. The same component rose to 60 percent by late summer. Not only are terrestrial insects more available at that season but the available biomass of aquatic insects is at a seasonal low, since the mature nymphs and larvae have already emerged during the spring and summer hatches. In this case a seasonal increase of one food and the seasonal decrease of another have combined to produce a temporal "preference" in the trouts' diet that has little to do with the inclinations of the trout themselves.

A similar situation exists in many brook-trout lakes, where larger trout may feed heavily on schools of smelt in early spring when the smelt are schooled in shallow water preparatory to spawning. In the summer, however, smelt are in the deep, open waters of the lake and are often in deeper water than that frequented by brook trout, which instead feed on insects in the shallows. The fabled brook trout of northern Quebec and Labrador apparently reach their prodigious size largely on an insect diet. Northern brookies of more than 3 pounds are most abundant in large lake and river systems in which the lakes offer vast expanses of insect-rich shallow water. Lakes Albanel and Mistassini in northern Quebec offer both shallow and deep-water habitats, and brook-trout biologist Bill Flick once found in summer sampling[10] that the 2- to 5-pound brookies here were almost exclusively insect-feeders, at least at that season. The same has been found true in the famous Minipi Region of Labrador, where the wide, sunlit shallows of such lakes as Anne Marie still yield trout to 8 pounds or more, often to a dry fly. It's worth noting that the cisco, or lake herring, is a primary forage fish of deeper lakes in the far north but, like summertime smelt farther south, are in deep water not frequented by brookies. The cisco enter the shallows late to spawn, as late as December in some areas, so their run is of little importance to anglers. It may, however, be of vital importance to lake-dwelling brook trout in that same early-winter period when aquatic-insect activity is reduced and the trout themselves have recently completed spawning.

A brook trout's diet may also depend on what, if any, other sorts of trout occupy the same environment. In studies on tributaries of Idaho's Clearwater River populated by both brook and cutthroat trout,[11] it was shown that adults of the two species tended to occupy different habitats in the same stream and to specialize in different insect foods. Brook trout lived in slower water and tended to eat the caddisfly larvae typically found in slower currents. Cutthroats occupied areas of higher water velocity, and their diet was dominated by diptera larvae and

pupae. Local streams containing only one or the other of these species were also studied and the same differences were found to exist, although where the two trouts lived sympatrically (sharing the same reaches of stream), the differences in habitat and food choices were more pronounced.

Such resource partitioning among different species, and even among different strains of the same species, is common in the world of fishes and is successful as an adaptive mechanism to the extent that available forage allows. A similar situation was noted in some lakes holding both rainbow and brook trout. Rainbows are more open-water oriented than brookies and depended more on terrestrial insects taken in wide-ranging fashion at or near the lake's surface. Brook trout are more bottom oriented in feeding and depended heavily on dragonfly nymphs. Brook trout and Atlantic salmon parr diets were also found to be partitioned in far northeastern rivers where the two fish are commonly in association. Here, however, the salmon parr and trout of similar size both held in faster water and ate caddis and mayfly nymphs in the spring when the insects are abundant. In summer, when the abundance of mature nymphs had declined, the more aggressive salmon apparently forced the trout away from the fast water reaches and into quieter backwaters. At this season, the trout's diet was dominated by slow-water caddis larvae and that of the salmon parr by caddis types characteristic of rapid flows. In other reaches of the same rivers without salmon, the brook trout occupied fast-water stretches all summer and ate insect foods there typical of a salmon-parr diet elsewhere.[12]

Most brook trout rarely survive to age four in the wild and, as such, are generally the shortest lived of all trout and charr. The much-studied brook trout of Lawrence Creek, Wisconsin,[13] almost never exceed three years old, a population attribute that may have been produced in part by a long history of angling pressure that characteristically selects for early-maturing, short-lived fish by systematically removing both faster-growing and longer-lived individuals. The removal of other predatory fish and a reduction in angling pressure were shown to extend the longevity of some brook trout in a California lake from four years or less to as much as seven years.[14] The short life span of most southern (meaning Maine and south) brook-trout stocks is also attributable to more than 150 years of genetic meddling, as the development of hatchery programs concentrated on breeding early-maturing fish that were eventually mixed by the untold millions with wild stocks. As a general case, the farther north one travels in the brookie's original range, the larger and older the fish. Some strains of brook trout in northern Quebec and Labrador may produce twelve-year-old fish, although eight or nine years is a more typical maximum. These fish even now are subject to relatively little angling pressure and have not been subjected to dilution of their gene pool by the introduction of hatchery stocks. The oldest recorded brook trout are apparently from Bunny Lake in California, an infertile, high-altitude lake where stocked brook trout have grown poorly but have lived to an astounding twenty years old,[15] which is a noteworthy exception to the typically short life spans of hatchery fish.

The longevity of northern brook trout strains was found to persist when the same fish were introduced into more southern Adirondack habitats. Dwight Webster, Bill Flick, and other Cornell University researchers worked for almost thirty years, starting in the 1950s, on the relative performance of wild Canadian, New York, and domesticated (hatchery) brook trout. One result of their hybridization experiments was new hatchery strains that show both better survival in the wild *and* increased longevity. New York State also now manages many of its brook-

trout waters based on the strains of brook trout they contain rather than the willy-nilly stocking of hatchery fish that characterized the past 150 years of trout management in this and other areas.

Growth of brook trout is extremely variable, depending on such things as the productivity of a particular habitat, water temperatures, competition from other brook trout and other fish species, and, perhaps most of all, longevity. Other things being equal—which they rarely are—old brook trout are big brook trout. In productive and unpressured waters, brookies may weigh 3 pounds or more by the end of their third year, but such situations are increasingly rare. Even with no angling pressure and in the absence of major predators, brook trout will sometimes overpopulate their habitat. This happens especially in closed systems such as ponds without tributaries, where competition among themselves may produce hundreds of trout that never exceed 8 or 9 inches. This can be true wherever brook trout are found, but is especially true in many western ponds that have been stocked with brook trout. The brookies can often reproduce in the ponds themselves and quickly create a stunted population that usually seems unaffected by fishing pressure. The management answer in recent years has been to eliminate the brook trout entirely from such waters and to stock with rainbows or other trout that can't reproduce in the pond itself.

Such slow growth is also characteristic of the cold, nutrient-poor headwaters of many streams in the eastern United States and elsewhere, to which brook trout have become limited by loss of other habitat, overfishing elsewhere, or both. In the frigid headwater cascades of New Hampshire's White Mountains, a one-year-old brookie will be about 3.5 inches long, and the rare three-year-old fish in the same water will only average 5.5 inches.[16] This growth attribute, however, is not totally genetic, as the same fish will show increased growth rates when moved to a more productive habitat. The genetic component of brook-trout growth finds most of its expression through longevity in the absence of competition in a productive environment; the 8- to 10-pound brookies of northern Canada get that big by virtue of having more food over a longer, un-molested life span. The world-record brookie was certainly such a fish and was the product of a large lake and river system. It weighed 14 pounds 9 ounces and was 31.5 inches long, taken in 1916 from Ontario's Nipigon River, which flows between lakes Nipigon and Su-perior. This race of brook trout is apparently now extinct, the victim of overfishing and dams.

Brook trout are fall-spawning trout; the time of spawning is apparently determined both by falling water temperatures and by decreasing day length. Spawning time may thus vary from November or even December in southern, warmer areas to as early as Sep-tember in the far north. The spawning act itself is similar to that of other trout species (see Chapter 3), so I won't repeat the descrip-tion here. Brook trout appear to be unique in their selection of gravel beds with upwelling water as spawning sites, which, unlike other trout, allows them to spawn in lakes and ponds without spawning tributaries.

Brook trout at spawning time appear to be severely stressed by the catch-and-release process. I've had to work for as much as half an hour reviving some big Labrador males after a five-minute battle on the end of a line late in the season. Some studies have shown the oxygen metabolism of large brookies al-most doubles in the fall as spawning ap-proaches, which leaves less of a metabolic reserve for recovery from such stressful things as being caught and released. The im-plication is that they should be left unmo-lested at this season, even though catch-and-

release rules on some brook-trout waters per-mit year-round fishing.

1. There are many versions of this story and even Audubon's own journals are notoriously un-reliable on many matters of fact. This account is based on one given by Professor George Myers in his history of American ichthyology before 1850. See Myers (1964).
2. See Merwin, ed. (1988).
3. I have never seen what I felt was an ade-quate explanation of this fin coloration. Because it's also characteristic of some migratory charrs, e.g., arctic charr that aggregate in loose schools, it may have evolved as a means of enhancing the fish's schooling ability. In most fishes that form distinct schools, however, the schooling ability is based on their lateral-line sense. Brook trout in general are not schooling fish, and the best ex-planation still seems to be a means of commu-nication enhancement among individual fish.
4. Much of this discussion is based on the published papers of Hugh MacCrimmon and Campbell (1969) at the University of Guelph, On-tario, as cited in the Bibliography, which offer an excellent review of brook-trout introductions worldwide.
5. See Trautman (1957) and (1971).
6. See Larson and Moore (1985).
7. The problem, of course, is worldwide. For a full discussion see Boyle and Boyle (1983), also Stoltz and Schnell, eds. (1991).
8. See Woodward, et al. (1991). Although their recent experiments involved greenback cut-throat trout in Colorado, the net effects on brook trout of soluble aluminum in a low pH back-ground are essentially similar.
9. See Lord (1933), as quoted in Power (1980).
10. See Flick (1991).
11. See Griffith (1972) and (1974).
12. See Power (1980).
13. See the many papers by Robert L. Hunt on this topic, such as Hunt (1984), and also Mc-Fadden (1961).
14. See Wales and German (1956), as cited in Power (1980).
15. See Moyle (1976).
16. See Scarola (1987).

5
Brown Trout

Reuben Wood was a hearty, back-slapping character who became well known as a fisherman and tournament fly caster in America after the Civil War. His measured casts with relatively primitive lancewood fly rods exceeded 60 feet, and by the time split-bamboo rods became popular in the 1880s, Wood was able to reach slightly more than 100 feet, using salmon tackle. His widely publicized skills were developed on northeastern trout rivers and in fishing for brook trout, which in his time and place were the only trout available. Brown trout were first successfully introduced to American waters in 1883 through the efforts of Wood's friends Fred Mather, Seth Green, and U.S. Fish Commissioner Spencer Baird. In that same year, Wood had what was probably the greatest shock of his angling life.

Wood was in charge of the American display at the 1883 International Fisheries Exposition in London, a position he quickly parlayed into a casting competition with the best of the British casters. He beat his competitors in salmon-tackle distance casting with a 108-foot toss and also took top honors with single-handed trout tackle. He was finally invited to fish by R. B. Marston, editor of the English *Fishing Gazette*, on the Kennet, a lovely little trout stream at Hungerford south of London. Then, as now, the Kennet was well known for its difficult brown-trout fishing. For Wood, the highly skilled brook-trout man, it was a sucker bet that he didn't

know enough to pass up. Some years later, Marston wrote this account of their brown-trout fishing:

> Our trout are so well educated that the angler who can kill with a fly a few brace of them in a day must be good handed. I remember taking that very jolly, genial and skillful American angler, the late Reuben Wood [Wood died in 1884], to fish for trout in the Kennet at Hungerford. There is a long and broad shallow below the bridge which was then alive with rising trout, fish from a half a pound up to two pounds. I could see he was putting his split-cane Leonard rod together and looked at the river, that he had made quite certain he was going to pull those fish out, one after another. I offered him what I

Brown trout.

thought was the artificial copy of the fly on the water but he guessed he would use the one he had shown me in the train as we traveled down. He threw a splendid line and in half an hour had cast over every bit of water. Not a rise could he get, nor could he find words enough to express his astonishment. I introduced him to some members of the club and they took such a liking to him they invited him to stay two days longer as the May fly was just coming on, and although many splendid trout were killed, he only got one half pounder. But he assured me he had never spent a more delightful time in his life. It was quite in vain that we told him his reel line and gut cast [line and leader] were far too heavy, but he admitted our trout were far more difficult to catch than those of any water he had fished in America.[1]

Reuben Wood's comeuppance on the Kennet is generally reflective of what happened to much of American trout fishing with the introduction of brown trout. By the 1880s, populations of the more gullible brook trout had been eliminated or severely reduced in many American waters by overfishing and water pollution. Brook and rainbow trout were both being cultured in American hatcheries before brown trout were first brought here in 1883, and the brown trout's introduction was probably more a matter of environmental fiddling and experimentation than of the necessity to rescue declining American trout streams. Between 1883 and 1900, however, brown trout were introduced in thirty-seven states from California to Maine.[2] The fish were not always popular and were universally regarded as harder to catch than other trout, but their introductions coincided with—and probably helped to bring about—radical changes in American trout tactics and tackle. Such things as dry-fly fishing and shorter, faster-actioned bamboo rods didn't

become popular until after 1900, by which time brown trout were becoming widely established.

Although the introduction of brown trout here is widely attributed to Fred Mather, the nineteenth-century New York fish culturist, it was from Spencer F. Baird, then-head of the U.S. Fish Commission in Washington, D.C., that Mather got much of his impetus. Lucius von Behr, more commonly referred to as "Herr von Behr," at the time headed the Deutscher Fischerei Verein (German Fishery Association) in Berlin, and between 1877 and 1882 Baird sent Von Behr five different American fish species for introduction into German waters.[3] By the time Baird sent Mather to Berlin in 1880 as his representative to that year's International Fisheries Congress, Von Behr was already in Baird's debt and eager to make a contribution. Von Behr took Mather brown-trout fishing in some Black Forest streams, and Mather, impressed with the gameness of these fish, arranged with Von Behr for a later shipment of brown-trout eggs.

The first shipment of German brown-trout eggs that arrived in New York harbor in February 1883 apparently contained those of two different brown-trout types: "One kind, the larger eggs, were from trout inhabiting deep lakes, while the smaller kind were from mountain streams," according to a description Mather wrote in 1887.[4] Mather retained a few of the 1883 eggs for rearing at the Cold Spring, New York, state hatchery, but sent most of them to the federal hatchery at Northville, Michigan, and the balance to his colleague Seth Green at another state hatchery on Spring Creek in northern New York. Most of these fish were apparently retained as brood stock, but some either escaped the hatchery or were deliberately stocked in Spring Creek near Caledonia, since there are records of a Mr. Amsden catching a 3-pound brown trout near there in 1886. The first formally recorded brown-

North American Distribution of Brown Trout
(Salmo trutta)

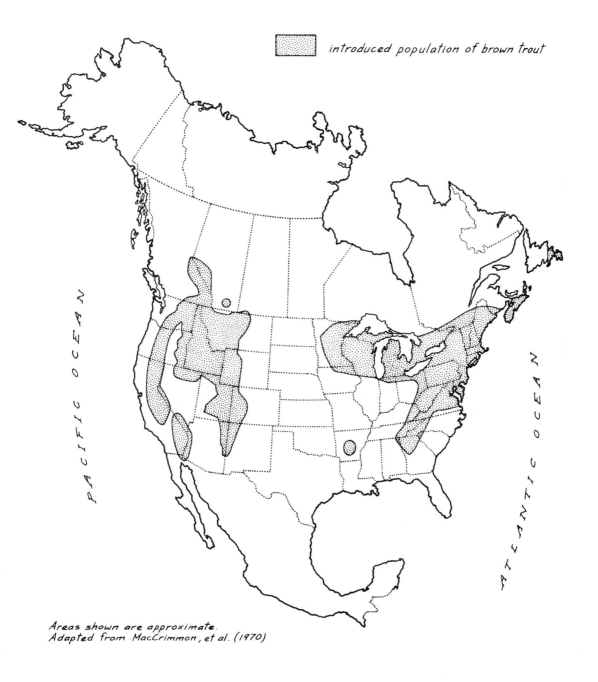

introduced population of brown trout

Areas shown are approximate.
Adapted from MacCrimmon, et al. (1970)

trout stocking in this country was on April 11, 1884, in Michigan's Pere Marquette River. The stock came from a second Von Behr shipment of eggs, some of which were again hatched in Northville. On January 1, 1885, yet another brown-trout egg shipment arrived for Mather in New York, this time from a Scottish hatchery that was forwarding Loch Leven trout. Mather sent most of these to Northville within a few days, many of which were further distributed to hatcheries in New Hampshire, Iowa, Minnesota, and Maine. Others were retained at Northville for stocking in Michigan waters that spring.

Mather was a descendant of the Dorchester, Massachusetts, Mathers, a family that earlier included such prominent New England clergymen as Increase Mather and his fire-breathing son Cotton, but Fred Mather seemed to find his own religion in angling. He grew up hunting and fishing in upstate New York and, after being discharged as a captain from the 7th N.Y. Artillery at the end of the Civil War, started his experiments in fish culture at Albany in the late 1860s. He was involved in various activities with Baird's U.S. Fish Commission from the time of its start in 1872, and was in charge of the state hatchery at Cold Spring from 1883 until a few years before his death in 1900. Brown trout were a relatively minor part of his work. He experimented widely with shad culture, for example, and also the culture of perch, cod, lobsters, and smelt. Mather wrote widely in various periodicals, including *Forest and Stream*, at which he was an editorial staff member. Of brown trout themselves, Mather wrote in April 1887:

> From my experience I think that the brown trout, as it is called in England, and which is the common brook trout of Europe (*Salmo fario*), is a quick-growing fish, which is destined to become a favorite in America when it is thoroughly known. I have taken this fish with a fly,

and consider it one of the gamiest, in fact, *the* gamiest, trout that I ever handled with a rod. I will state, however, that angling friends who have had more extended experience in European fishing than I have say that the Loch Leven trout is a gamier and better fish than the brown trout, but I have had no experience with the Loch Leven fish further than to hatch it. I believe that the brown trout will be found to be a better fish, taking it all around, than our own native *fontinalis*. The reasons for this belief are: (1) It is of quicker growth; (2) it is gamier; (3) except in the breeding season, when the males of *fontinalis* are brilliantly colored, it is fully as handsome; (4) from what I can learn I incline to think it will bear water several degrees warmer than *fontinalis*, and therefore it is adapted to a wider range.[5]

Although some hatcheries continued to maintain the distinction between the Von Behr, or German, brown trout and the Loch Leven variety as late as the 1920s, for the most part these and other European brown-trout strains appear to have been quickly mingled and were soon simply called brown trout. This homogenization of brown-trout strains is undoubtedly part of the reason for the wide success of brown trout in American waters because of the genetic diversity implicit in the widespread mixing of brown-trout stocks. More than a century later, many brown trout stocks that are now naturally reproducing but which were derived from hatchery plantings here seem to be slowly reverting to their original, European attributes.

Brown trout are the true trout. They are native to Europe, western Asia, and the extreme northeastern edge of Africa and have been introduced to many waters suited to them around the globe. Fishing for sport—including fly-fishing—evolved within the native range of brown trout. The word "trout" itself apparently evolved with specific reference to these fish and was later applied to such fish as rainbow, cutthroat, and brook trout simply because of their resemblance to brown trout. The genus *Salmo* in North America includes only two fish: brown trout and the closely related Atlantic salmon. Brown trout are known specifically as *trutta*, an old Latin form meaning "trout." Classical European angling writers like Izaak Walton were describing brown-trout fishing whenever they mentioned trout. Interestingly, Walton himself described several kinds of brown trout, which leads us to a modern paradox.

Although contemporary taxonomists classify all brown trout as a single species (*Salmo trutta*), the fish themselves may show wide variation in color and spotting patterns, age at sexual maturity, habitual foods, and behavior, among other attributes. These traits are often genetic, breeding true within discrete populations, but may be lost or, more commonly, modified as genetic stocks of brown trout are mixed in hatchery operations as happened around the turn of the century. Some brown-trout strains may also coexist in the same habitat, maintaining their uniqueness through some form of reproductive isolation such as different spawning times or the consistent selection of different spawning areas. For example, four forms of brown trout have been recently reported from the same Irish loch, at least two of which are genetically distinct.[6] This sort of differentiation has led to subspecies designations for some forms of cutthroat trout, for example, although the acknowledgment of such differences in brown trout has yet to be made in formal nomenclature. Any angler who fishes a variety of rivers may eventually encounter brown trout that somehow look different from those he's used to catching and may even encounter two different-look-

ing brown trout in the same stream. I have, for example, caught both Von Behr and Loch Leven brown trout in Montana's Madison River, and although I made no formal analysis of their characteristics, the dramatic difference in their appearance was convincing.

The original Von Behr browns were called *Bachforellen* ("brook trout") in Germany, not to be confused with the unrelated brook trout of North America, and are a brightly colored fish common to small streams. Color along the dorsal surface (back) varies from olive-brown through yellowish brown, becoming lighter toward the whitish belly area. There are usually greater amounts of an overall yellow tint along the flanks. Black spots are present on the back and in diminishing numbers down the sides. Bright red spots are found in lesser numbers along the sides and sometimes on the adipose fin, which may be tinged with bright red. There are few, if any, spots on the tail in contrast with rainbow and cutthroat trout, the tails of which are heavily spotted. Unlike brook trout, brown trout have no vermiculations, or wavy lines, on their backs and have teeth along the full length of the vomerine bone on the roof of their mouths. Brown-trout coloration is much subdued in hatchery fish, the overall appearance of which is often grayish brown, although hatchery brown trout often assume the brighter colors of wild fish after several months in the stream.

The Loch Leven form is characterized by a much heavier pattern of black spots and the general absence of red spots. There is also, at least in my own experience, less yellow and more olive-brown in the overall background color along the fish's back and sides. In at least a few cases, European strains of brown trout may persist in this country if the original late-nineteenth-century stockings remain genetically undiluted by subsequent plantings of trout. For example, the Lewis River system in Yellowstone National Park apparently still contains pure-strain

Loch Leven browns derived from a single stocking in 1890.[7]

Although color may be indicative of a particular form of brown trout, it can also be highly variable among individual fish. Brown trout are also apparently unique among trout in being able to change their color quite rapidly as a means of concealment. This sort of color change in fish has been perhaps most studied in certain bottom-living saltwater flatfish that will quickly turn dark against a dark bottom and vice versa, an ability that extends to the fish's trying to match a checkerboard pattern when placed on an artificial bottom of that design. Over many years of trout fishing I have occasionally seen brown trout with a startling, zebralike banding that I, out of ignorance, attributed to some sort of disease. I recently encountered a brief report describing this pattern published in 1969 by biologist Thomas Jenkins[8] that was based on more than 1,300 hours of direct observation of brown and rainbow trout in certain northern California streams. After observing both rainbow and brown trout, Jenkins reported:

> General lightening and darkening of [skin] background color in response to varying bottom colors and light intensities was observed in both species, but the change was slower and less extensive in rainbow trout. In addition to lightening and darkening, the ability to produce variable mottled patterns has been ascribed to stream-living trout . . . I observed this type of response of pattern to background in many brown trout, but never in rainbow trout. However, even in areas of stream with complex patterns of light or bottom color, mottling was observed only in fish holding positions close to or on the bottom.

Jenkins went on to describe the zebra-striped banding I mentioned previously and noted that the appearance of mottling or banding seemed to take place within about thirty seconds of the time the brown trout went to rest at the bottom or took other shelter. He further noted that the mottling or banding disappeared quickly when the trout resumed normal feeding activity or was captured by angling, which probably is why these color changes have rarely, if ever, been mentioned in popular works about brown trout. Please note that I'm not suggesting this color transformation is something that all brown trout do all the time, although I do believe it happens more often than anyone has heretofore suspected.

Jenkins closed his short paper with this excellent contrast between the many brown and rainbow trout he observed:

> The color change differences between the two species [rainbow and brown] are closely related to differences in their cover-related behavior. For example, in the same section of stream, groups of brown trout utilize cover much more frequently than rainbow trout groups of the same size. Brown trout are also the only fish ever to rest on the stream bottom [within the scope of his study]. . . . It would be interesting to find the adaptive reasons for the two species being so similar in their social and feeding behaviors, but so dissimilar in their color change and cover-related behaviors.

Jenkins' question of more than twenty years ago is a good one, and one for which I don't even have the suggestion of an answer. The foregoing does explain in part the relative success of brown trout in many waters: They are often just plain hard to spot by predators and fishermen alike. Remember that the color changes discussed here refer to changes in the background color of the trout's skin. Individual brown trout are like leopards in that they can't change their spots either.

As with other kinds of trout, the growth of brown trout is extremely variable, depending primarily on the productivity of a particular stream or river and apparently also on the strain of brown trout under consideration. One-year-old fish may range from 1.2 to 3.3 inches long, reaching 2.8 to 8.8 inches in their second year, 5.2 to 14.4 inches in their third year, and 9.2 to 18 inches in their fourth year.[9] The maximum recorded longevity is eighteen years, but seven to nine years is a more typical maximum. (In some productive eastern trout streams, some drift-feeding brown trout have been found not to exceed 12 inches or so, even at ages of five years and greater. The reasons for this are explored later in this chapter.) Brown trout can grow to extraordinary sizes, and there are authenticated reports of lake-dwelling browns to almost 70 pounds having been caught in certain Bavarian lakes. This strain—called *Seeforellen* ("lake trout")—has been introduced to the American Great Lakes and may offer the potential for truly enormous brown trout. The present all-tackle world record is a 35-pound 15-ounce monster caught in Argentina in the 1950s. Tailwater fisheries—those big, productive rivers below large dams—in the American Ozarks have been prime spots for trophy browns in the last two decades, having produced a number of browns from 20 to one a shade over 40 pounds caught in 1992 in Arkansas.

It's been said often that brown trout can survive in stream habitats that have deteriorated to the point of no longer supporting brook trout. This was the rationale for much of the brown-trout stocking that has been done since the 1890s, but is somewhat misleading and only partly true. Brown trout don't survive well in warm, polluted water either. These fish may survive for a short period in 81 degree Fahrenheit water, but the upper lethal limit for brown trout is usually cited as 77 degrees. Brown trout show a preference for and are typically most active in water ranging from 54 to 67 degrees.[10] These figures are only slightly higher than those cited for brook trout in the previous chapter.

The principal reason for the success of brown trout in streams depleted of brook trout is almost certainly because brown trout are harder to catch. Overfishing, sometimes in conjunction with habitat degradation, was a primary cause of brook-trout declines since before the American Civil War. It has been widely demonstrated that brown trout are harder to catch than brookies, something that holds true for both hatchery and wild stocks, although wild trout of any kind are usually harder to catch than those fresh from the stocking truck. For example, a detailed survey of one lightly fished Wisconsin stream in which legal-size brown trout outnumbered legal-size brook trout by almost four to one showed brook trout making up about half of the total catch.[11]

Brown trout are competitive with brook trout in the same stream to a degree, although this question has been hotly argued by trout fishermen ever since brown trout stockings became common by the turn of the century. It is a fundamental ecological principle that complete competitors (meaning different species with identical life histories and behaviors) can't coexist in the same habitat, and the existence of naturally reproducing populations of the two trout in the same streams has continued to fuel the argument. The two kinds of trout are usually able to partition the available stream resources to the extent that they usually hold feeding stations in currents of different speeds, with the brook trout most often using areas of slower water. In an elegant experiment done around 1980, Kurt Fausch and Ray White[12] removed the brown trout from a test stretch of Michigan's Au Sable River and made underwater observations to measure the changes in habitat utilization by the remaining brook trout. Their results showed clearly that the dominant brown trout were excluding brook trout from favorable resting (not feeding) positions in the stream, which I further take to mean that brook trout were made increasingly vulnerable to predation. This competition for space in combination with the brook trout's greater vulnerability to angling clearly puts brook trout at a disadvantage when coexisting with brown trout. This creates a situation that's often aggravated by many general angling regulations that allow the capture of a certain number of trout per day without regard to species, thus encouraging the removal of brook trout at a faster rate than brown trout.

Brown trout have often been accused of cannibalism, too, and of reducing overall trout populations by feeding heavily on young trout. On some extensively managed European streams, it has long been the practice to remove large brown trout by any means possible, including shotguns, as a means of enhancing the overall trout population. The brown trout's defenders have correctly pointed out that large brook trout can also be highly piscivorous, likewise eating large numbers of small trout. This is certainly true, but in most American trout streams brook trout rarely exceed a pound in weight and the extent to which they're fish-eaters below this size is insignificant. Brown trout, in contrast, commonly reach much larger sizes, at which their diets may be comprised almost exclusively of other fish.

The only extensive study of which I'm aware concerning trout predation was done by veteran Michigan biologist Gaylord Alexander and his associates on the North Branch of Michigan's Au Sable River, starting in the 1960s.[13] Alexander measured the overall trout mortality caused by American mergansers (a fish-eating duck), great blue herons, kingfishers, brown trout, mink, otter, and anglers—all of which prey on trout. Brown trout were found to cause as much as 58 percent of the annual mortality of juvenile (age up to one year) brook trout and as much as 16 percent of the annual mortality of juvenile brown trout of the same age and size. Apparently, in common with human fishermen, browns find brookies easier to catch. Great blue herons were a distant second, accounting for about 8 percent of the brook trout mortality and about 7 percent of the brown trout mortality, again for juvenile trout up to one year. Some knowledgeable readers will quickly point out that predatory brown trout also eat large quantities of nongame fish such as chubs, sculpins, suckers, and dace. This is quite true and was also shown by Alexander's data. During the May through October period, when brown-trout predation was most extensive, the predatory brown trout sampled were eating about 178 pounds of nongame fish per mile *in addition to* about 119 pounds of smaller trout consumed per mile of stream. Obviously, predatory brown trout eat other kinds of fish in addition to trout, but this clearly doesn't negate the fact that they're eating a substantial quantity of small trout. Given the choice, larger brown trout eat both.

I won't take the space here to describe Alexander's study in full detail, but his information is important in understanding trout-stream dynamics, so I've summarized some of his data in the graph on the next page. It's worth noting that brown-trout predation is most significant on juvenile trout less than one year old. Both herons and mergansers, in contrast, feed most heavily on larger trout, with herons selectively catching trout from 7 to 12 inches long, according to Alexander's data. For that reason, our statistical herons outfished brown trout in pounds of trout consumed in one study section during the May-October period, eating 151 pounds of trout per mile against the brown trouts' consumption of 119 pounds. It's tempting to conclude that one way to produce more stream trout in the short run would be with the (presently illegal) shotgun management of predatory birds, but the response of local Audubon Societies would probably be even more violent.

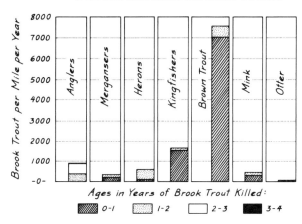

Predators and Brook Trout

Brook Trout per Mile per Year

Anglers · Mergansers · Herons · Kingfishers · Brown Trout · Mink · Otter

Ages in Years of Brook Trout Killed:
0-1   1-2   2-3   3-4

There are two general areas of brown-trout behavior that have only been explored in recent years and that are of immediate pertinence to trout fishermen. These areas can generally be divided according to the size of the fish in question, because most large brown trout apparently behave very differently from small ones. Brown trout up to a length of about 12 inches—and this includes the vast majority of stream-dwelling brown trout—are so-called "drift feeders." They feed primarily on insects and other food items drifting in the current. Such trout typically hold a stationary feeding position and move only to intercept food items in adjacent and faster currents to the side or overhead. Much of their lifestyle and behavior is based on this drift-feeding strategy.

As brown trout grow beyond 12 inches or so, some of them start to feed on larger items such as crayfish, baitfish, and smaller trout. The individual trout that adopt this feeding strategy almost always grow much larger than the drift feeders; these are the rare trophy-size browns found in relatively small numbers in almost all brown-trout streams. Most of the food items that enable this sort of growth are *not* brought to the trout by the current. To acquire these foods, the brown trout must become—and does indeed become—an active hunter. The differences in behavior between the smaller drift feeders and the larger hunters are radical differences,

and understanding them is vital to your fishing.

Certainly the most important recent study of drift-feeding brown trout was that done in the 1980s by Robert Bachman, which I described briefly in Chapter 3.[14] He spent three years in streamside towers observing and filming undisturbed wild brown trout in a long, shallow pool in Spruce Creek, a productive western Pennsylvania trout stream. A few years later, I watched him give a presentation based on his work to a group of trout fishermen and offered the caution afterward that he not extend his conclusions about Spruce Creek brown trout to all brown trout. To his credit, he has almost always made this qualification in discussing his results. I have since concluded, however, that Bachman's observations pertain in some ways to all drift-feeding brown trout in all streams. But it's important to note once again that his trout were undisturbed; fishing was prohibited in his research area during the time of his observations. If these same fish had been subject to the constant parade of anglers, canoeists, and other recreational users who characteristically frequent many trout rivers, his results would probably have been very different.

The trout observed in this study ranged in age up to seven years old; most were from about 4.8 inches to about 12 inches long. They spent most of their time in the spring, summer, and fall holding in feeding positions near the bottom in relatively shallow—less than 2 feet to only a few inches—water where they could intercept food carried by the current to their stations. Most of these feeding stations were defined by a rock or rocks on the bottom that broke the current flow, and the way in which these stations were used by trout was remarkably precise. One trout was photographed at its station in three successive years, during which time span the position of the trout's eye with respect to the sheltering rock at its head didn't vary by more than 1.6 inches. That a rising trout in flowing water usually keeps rising in the same spot is well known among anglers, but what's equally important is that—assuming the continued availability of suitable surface food—an undisturbed trout will usually rise in the same spot on the next day and the next and so on as long as the physical configuration of the stream's currents and bottom remain the same. Trout fishermen can learn these locations, also, just by paying attention when they're fishing and remembering precisely the locations of rising fish. Gaining this knowledge is one of many ways in which experienced anglers "learn" trout streams, and obviously has a lot to do with fishing success.

As Bachman explained, the brown trout he observed were using these feeding stations for the sake of energy efficiency. They could hold these positions with relatively little effort and tip upward or to the side to intercept food in the faster currents. These undisturbed fish remained in their open-water feeding positions most of the time, averaging 86 percent of the daylight hours over a three-year period. Contrary to popular belief, they didn't spend most of their time hiding under rocks or near the bank and did not feed only at dawn and dusk; they fed actively all day as long as they were undisturbed. Disturbances, when they occurred, were of two different forms that elicited different responses from the trout. A fleeting shadow, such as that caused by a bird flying overhead, caused the trout to dart to the bottom, where it remained motionless and then, after a few minutes, resumed feeding. A stronger alarm, such as a landing duck, caused the trout to dash for shelter—either deep water or overhead cover—where it remained motionless for up to half an hour before returning to its feeding position. This is why most anglers have never seen the sort of behavior Bachman described; by the time the fisherman gets into a position of being able to view the trout, the trout themselves are long gone into hiding.

As I described in a previous chapter on the general nature of trout, successful spawning is the Darwinian payoff in a trout's life history, and the trout's ability to get to that point is described by a gospel of efficiency in the stream. This dictates not only the feeding positions chosen by trout, but also the social interactions among the trout themselves. From the standpoint of the trout's own energetics and growth, the greatest efficiency is gained if an individual trout doesn't have to compete with other trout for drifting food at the same location. The physical combat that might take place to resolve such competitive differences among individual trout is wasteful of energy, too, and trout (all trout) have evolved a signaling system that usually means physical combat is avoided. Trout interact through a series of aggressive displays characterized by distinct swimming attitudes and a flaring of the body fins that are collectively called agonistic behavior. The larger trout will usually "win" such a contest without having to resort to the ramming and biting that trout use as a last resort in such cases when agonistic displays fail to resolve things. It's interesting to note that such displays work between trout species—brook trout and brown trout interact in this manner, for example—while trout and nontrout species such as suckers don't interact this way; probably because suckers and trout aren't competitive for feeding positions.

This behavioral mechanism produces a dominance hierarchy within a group of trout in a pool, for example, which is why smaller trout are almost invariably seen feeding to the rear of larger ones if both are in the same proximity. Many writers of both popular and technical works have described trout as being territorial based on this behavior, but this isn't really true. The so-called territories established by this behavior are collapsible under various circumstances. In very low water trout will congregate in the depths of deeper pools without conflict, and brown trout specifically have been shown to share hiding spots, such as under a rock or streamside stump, without conflict. A dominant trout's influence is portable, too, being carried with it as it sometimes moves from one feeding station to another. Robert Butler at Penn State, who instigated Bachman's study based on his own earlier observations, has called this characteristic a "social force field," which is a much better description. Trout in the Spruce Creek pool Bachman observed separated their feeding stations by at least 18 inches (45 cm) by this mechanism. This distance, I believe, may be greatly reduced in a temporary abundance of food—a heavy hatch or spinner fall, for example, during which I've observed wild fish feeding literally side by side within inches of one another, though not one upstream of another.

Although the behavior that Bachman described so well may be prototypical of brown trout in streams, it's often modified by other circumstances, and these are the cases often encountered by anglers. In some cases, and this is especially true of the popular catch-and-release areas on some streams, the trout may become acclimated to the presence of anglers and tolerate their presence without hiding. The most dramatic instance of this I've ever seen was shown to me by Charlie Fox on the Letort, a small and widely famous spring creek in southwestern Pennsylvania. Fox some years ago had built a series of benches along the stream bank behind his house where he could sit and watch trout in the creek for hours on end. During the years when I traveled there to fish and to watch from Charlie's benches, the Letort brown trout faced a nearly constant parade of anglers to which at least some of the trout became accustomed. The slow, clear water also made the fish notoriously cagey and hard to catch, a difficulty compounded by the fish's often feeding in spots where it was hard to drift a fly properly. A small brown trout of a foot or so was feeding at the edge of a weedbed, and I was having a hard time getting a good dry-fly drift in its feeding lane. Fox asked me to wait a minute and then took a short, slow step toward the trout. The trout moved an equal distance farther away from Fox, into a current lane more accessible to my casting, and I caught it a few minutes later. I have since used this little trick on other hard-fished trout waters from New York to California, but only as a last resort. Too often I've overdone my attempt to move the fish gently, and the trout has simply swum out of sight.

A more common example is any trout stream that gets intensive recreational use from trout fisherman and others such as canoeists and inner-tube floaters, on summer days. The Battenkill in Vermont and New York, with its excellent population of wild brown and brook trout, is a good example of this sort of usage, which is becoming increasingly common in many areas. The traffic caused by waders, floaters, and swimmers is such that there's a major disturbance in most pools at least every half hour. Broad, gently flowing flats that might otherwise be dotted with rising trout are almost empty of fish. The trout are all hiding under the bankside alder bushes or other cover. At best, you may see a few small brook trout rising in open water or the more subtle rise of a brown trout near a bankside bush. The trout do move out into the flats to feed in a more typical fashion in the late evening, well after most of the river traffic is gone, at which time the greatest numbers are caught by those few fly fishermen who know how to move in the water with the least disturbance. It is, I think, impossible for trout to become acclimated to the clunking passage of tourists in 16-foot canoes, and the fishing is altered accordingly. The message in this case is simple: fish early and late.

On a calm and hot June afternoon a dozen years ago I was sitting on a log at the end of a long, still flat. The fishing had been terrible along the upper reaches of New York's Ausable River that day, and at the moment I was mostly annoyed at frying inside my waders, ready to take them off and to sit in the water instead. A school of shiners played back and forth over a shallow gravel bar a few feet in front of me. I glanced up and saw a large wake about a hundred feet distant and heading in my direction. The wake moved faster and faster as I watched, accelerating in a straight line toward me. It finally materialized as a big brown trout, weighing perhaps 3 or 4 pounds, in a slashing attack on the minnows a few feet away. In the splashing swirls I couldn't see if the trout caught anything, but I did see the minnows

scatter in all directions and watched awestruck as the big fish swam slowly back to the upstream depths of the pool.

It was an exciting moment that I've mentally replayed often over the years. I have since decided that the trout's behavior wasn't accidental; in other words, the big brown knew exactly what it was doing. It had learned the location of the gravel bar exactly, even though it was far enough away initially so the bar was out of sight. It had learned that minnows frequent the gravel bar. And it had learned that the best way to catch one of those shiners was by a high-speed attack launched from a considerable distance. In writing this, I'm reminded of films I've watched of cheetahs hunting antelope on open plains, in which the big cats' attack comes at high speed and from a considerable distance. Also, in describing this trout's behavior, I know that "high-speed attack" is far removed from the vocabulary of most genteel trout fishermen. Big brown trout, however, are a world apart.

Big is relative, of course, and I use the term to mean a couple of things. First, I refer to those relatively few brown trout that make the transition from more-or-less stationary drift feeding to active hunting of larger prey. If it occurs—and it doesn't always—the timing of this switch in a particular trout's life history, again, varies possibly with the particular strain and certainly with habitat; a fat spring-creek brown may grow to several pounds as a drift feeder in its rich environment, while a brown trout in a relatively infertile freestone stream may become a more active predator at 12 inches or so. Second, and because of the foregoing, a "big" brown trout in a smaller creek might measure 16 to 20 inches or more, while a "big" brown from Montana's huge Missouri River might weight 10 or even 20 pounds. Such trout are obviously in the minority in all trout rivers, probably accounting for well under 1 percent of the overall trout population. Because of this scarcity, these fish are statistically insignificant and have been subject to little formal study. They are, however, the brown trout that fishermen most hope to catch and as such are extremely important.

At this writing I've seen only one behavioral study directed at large brown trout. This was recently conducted on Michigan's Au Sable.[15] In this case eight large wild brown trout between 17.5 and 25.5 inches long were surgically implanted with small radio transmitters, each with a discrete frequency, and tracked for as long as 346 days. These trout were close to the maximum size achieved by wild browns in this river system and had made the transition from being primarily drift feeders to the active-predator stage. What was found in this study was in some ways dramatically different from much of the common angling wisdom about big browns.

The large brown trout tracked by this telemetry process moved considerably up and down the stream over time, and their movement was by no means random. During the spring and summer, the fish hid in deep, slow water under overhead cover—usually a logjam—during the daylight hours and usually didn't move around. At night, the fish sometimes ranged almost a mile away from their daytime hiding spot, returning to that spot by dawn. This behavior seemed to persist for two or three days in a row, with the trout returning to its daytime lair each morning. After that period, the trout used a *different* and distant hiding spot for the next two or three days. Several of the trout in this study were each found to rotate among four different daytime refuges that were separated by an average stream distance of about 1,270 feet. For decades the conventional wisdom on big browns in most trout streams has been that once you locate one in a particular pool

it will be there until someone catches it or it dies of old age. Sometimes this is true, but it should now be obvious that this is not always the case. I should also point out that much of the Au Sable system where this study was done is relatively flat water without steep rapids or falls that would in any way impede the nighttime hunting expeditions of its brown trout. On the other hand, there has been no study at all as to how much of a rapid *would* impede this acitivity. I have a number of times seen browns of several pounds moving at last light, coming slowly up a riffle and sliding through the tail of a pool I happened to be fishing. This activity is not related to a spawning migration, by the way, which happens in the fall and is often even more extensive.

Among the many other things demonstrated by this study were variations in foraging activity by month and time of day. In June, activity showed four daily peaks: 10 P.M. (right after the last light of sunset), 1 A.M., 5 A.M., and the fourth at 2:30 in the afternoon. During this month, the 10 P.M. activity period was the most intense. In July, there were only two activity peaks: one at midnight and a second at 5 A.M., with the latter being the highest peak of foraging activity measured at any time in any month. In August, there was yet another change, with the fish seeming to alternate periods of foraging activity with periods of relative quiet every three or four hours. I'm reluctant to say this data offers every fisherman a timetable by which to seek big brown trout everywhere. On the other hand, if I had to bet on my catching a big brown, I would very cheerfully place that bet at 5 A.M. on a July morning on just about any of this country's brown-trout rivers, excepting, of course, those in snowmelt or flood.

The behavior of large brown trout always seems remarkable, perhaps most of all because we see it so seldom. Perhaps it's perfectly ordinary but something we simply don't yet understand. Bob Butler at Penn State has written about seeing trophy-size brown trout literally bury themselves in stream-bottom gravel as a means of concealment until the dark hours, at which time they burst forth to start prowling.[16] It would seem farfetched to describe this as ordinary behavior, but perhaps for brown trout of this size it is. Butler, by the way, was also (in the same article) critical of the Au Sable study I just discussed, because the individual trout had to be handled and put through surgery before the study was undertaken, possibly affecting the subsequent behavior of the fish. I would never disagree with Butler lightly, for I know him to be an exceptional scientist, but in this case much of the Au Sable work matches my own, more casual observations over the years.

Finally, and before ending this brown-trout section, we should explore just a little why large brown trout are often nocturnal in the first place. Contrary to what many suppose, this nocturnal habit is not simply a means of predator avoidance by older fish that are both larger and wiser. The same trout are perfectly capable of hunting in the daytime and sometimes do just that. If you shine a flashlight along the bottom of a trout stream in the middle of the night, you'll often see crayfish, sculpins, and large predatory insects such as dragonfly nymphs out crawling the stream bottom in darkness as they search for food. All of these animals are hiding under rocks and elsewhere during the day. All of these animals are also prime foods for larger brown trout. The dark hours are often the time when the most food is available to large trout, so that's when they feed; it's as simple as that.

1. As quoted in the 1895 report of the New York State Fisheries, Game and Forest Commission.

2. See MacCrimmon (1970 a and b).

3. Chinook salmon in 1877, brook trout in 1879, whitefish in 1880, landlocked salmon in 1881, and rainbow trout in 1882. See "Five American Salmonidae in Germany," by Von Behr, as quoted in the 1882 *Bulletin* of the U.S. Fish Commission.

4. See "Brown Trout in America," by Fred Mather, in the 1887 *Bulletin* of the U.S. Fish Commission.

5. *Bulletin* of the U.S. Fish Commission, 1887.

6. See Ferguson and Mason (1981).

7. See Jones (1990).

8. See Jenkins (1969b).

9. See Moyle (1976).

10. See McClane (1974).

11. See Avery (1983).

12. See Fausch and White (1981).

13. See Alexander (1979).

14. Bachman (1984).

15. See Clapp, D., et al. (1990).

16. See Butler, R., "Rogue Trout," appearing in Stoltz and Schnell, eds. (1991).

6
Rainbow Trout

There were cries of sea gulls and the noises of loose hardware on sailboats that clanked rhythmically as the boats rocked at their moorings. The sounds of traffic heading over the bridge toward Marin and points north were almost drowned out by the more immediate, closer sounds of moving water, tide rips forcing their way out through the narrow cut against a stiff onshore wind. The still closer sound of a popping cork got my attention, and I turned back to the dinner table. We were celebrating that night, having just finished the museum installation of a large traveling flyfishing exhibit, and one of our hosts had thoughtfully provided an evening table at a yacht club almost directly underneath San Francisco's Golden Gate Bridge.

I guess it was the moving water outside that got me into trouble, because I can't look at any water without thinking of fish. At any rate, I ventured some idle remark about how eastern brook trout were the true trout, native to America, and was immediately taken to task by John McCosker, a dinner companion and the talented director of San Francisco's well-known Steinhart Aquarium. McCosker is a knowledgeable fly fisherman and ichthyologist whose professional expertise ranges from coelacanths to a more recent passion for great white sharks.

"Rainbow trout are the true American trout," he said, throwing down the gauntlet while cocking an eyebrow at me. "And they are native to California."

"But brook trout are—" I started what would have been a long-winded explanation.

"—charr. They aren't even trout." He lowered his eyebrow and smiled as yet another eastern dude bit the dust. We had to agree that brown trout were out of the running because there weren't any brown trout in America until imported from Europe in the late nineteenth century. As I recall, we disposed of cutthroat trout in the same discussion because of their limited geographic range. Rainbow trout are now found in forty-seven of our fifty states and are indigenous

Rainbow trout.

to the Pacific Coast. If it's essential that the term "true American trout" be defined, which I doubt, then the rainbow is it.

Or at least it was. At the time of our admittedly silly argument, rainbow trout were classified within the genus *Salmo*, which then also included both brown and cutthroat trout. Since then, rainbows, cutthroats, and other native western trout have been reclassified within the genus *Oncorhynchus* by modern taxonomists, which genus also includes all five species of Pacific salmon. By this semantic twist, the only true trout in America (genus *Salmo*) is the brown trout, which by virtue of its foreign origins isn't a true American trout either. Ever since the nomenclature committee for the American Fisheries Society switched trout names in 1988 and diminished McCosker's argument, I've been tempted to send him a snotty letter. But I haven't bothered because a trout by any other name is just as much fun to catch.

In recent times and until 1988, rainbow trout were known as *Salmo gairdneri*, a name provided by John Richardson in 1836 when he described rainbows and a variety of other salmonids from the Pacific Northwest. The genus *Salmo* was established first by Linnaeus in 1758 in describing Atlantic salmon and European brown trout. The specific name *gairdneri* referred to a young man named Gairdner who originally provided Richardson with specimens. Forty-four years earlier, in 1792, many of the same fishes described by Richardson had been described and named differently by Joseph Walbaum, based on specimens collected from the Kamchatka Peninsula in far-eastern Asia, across the Bering Sea from Alaska and British Columbia. Walbaum also used the *Salmo* genus for rainbow trout, but used the specific name *mykiss*, which was apparently derived from the local (Kamchatkan) named for these fish. For almost two centuries, *gairdneri* and *mykiss* were assumed to be different species de-

spite their obvious similarities. Adding further confusion was the habit of Victorian ichthyologists of describing different strains of trout, including rainbows, by different species names if the trout in one location varied in appearance from those in another, as is commonly the case. Thus the assorted strains of rainbow trout have at one time or another been known by as many as fifteen different species names.[1]

Modern taxonomy and classification attempt to have scientific names reflect evolutionary relationships. They further observe a right of historical precedent; that is, if the first name historically applied to an organism is biologically valid, it takes precedence over all subsequent names. The rainbow trout's generic name—*Oncorhynchus* (literally, "hook-nose," referring to a physical characteristic of sexually mature Pacific salmon)—is reflective of the fishes' recently described evolutionary origins, which are largely shared with other salmonids around the north Pacific. Further, the rainbow trout of Kamchatka and those of western North America have been determined to be the same species, so the specific name *mykiss* is now used instead of *gairdneri* because *mykiss* has historical precedence. Rainbow trout is still the officially accepted common name, by the way, just as certain members of the charr group, such as brook trout, are also called trout. The *Salmo* genus is now reserved for those salmonids that evolved around the North Atlantic, the best known of which are Atlantic salmon and brown trout. The scientific distinction is obviously more important to taxonomists than it is to fishermen.

Thoughts of trout often bring moods to mind that are reflective of the trout themselves. Brook trout remind me of relaxing in bankside wildflowers, of the smells of wood smoke and the spruce forests of northern Maine. Thoughts of brown trout are more intense, with memories of chess-like games played out on clear, smooth water, changing from one fly pattern to another for these often fussy fish. Cutthroats are a western wilderness in my thoughts, fish rising freely in clear water under the highest of mountains. Thoughts of rainbows are thoughts of adventure.

I have endured more hours of discomfort and occasional danger in pursuit of rainbow trout than of any other fish. Such encounters have ranged from a scary near-handshake with a giant brown bear along an Alaskan creek to the threat of arrest by a drunken officer in the Bolivian Army after fishing a rainbow stream high in the Andes. I have nearly drowned while trying to reach a distant rising rainbow in New Hampshire's big Androscoggin, which I survived only to become nearly hypothermic while trying for the big midwinter rainbows of Michigan's Pere Marquette. There was a long, white-knuckled ride in a twin-engined Beechcraft through a British Columbia canyon under a *very* low ceiling when it seemed as if I could count the very pebbles on the stream bank below, a memory just as strong as the huge rainbows that twisted powerfully in the green water when I hooked them on that trip, fish that were gunmetal bright and freshly run from the Bering Sea.

There have been quieter moments, too, with groups of gently rising rainbows in the soft currents of California's Fall River, for example. They rise like that in Armstrong's, too, and in the other Montana spring creeks, and in the Henrys Fork and Silver Creek in Idaho, where you'll see their broad green backs in the easy, quiet rolls of confidently feeding fish, the kind that give you the buck-fever shakes as you try to tie on what might be the right fly. There are rainbows, also, in New York's big Delaware that have driven

me absolutely nuts. I once waded in to my wader tops in one of its huge pools while trying to reach an especially large and distant fish. My casting was still short, but the apparent size of the fish was so compelling that I said to hell with it and kept wading out up to my shoulders, filling my waders and soaking everything in the process for a fish that I never did manage to hook.

The rainbow has character. It hasn't the jewel-like quality of brook trout nor the subtle guile of the brown. Rainbows are more like the battery salesman with a chip on his shoulder, daring you to knock it off. They don't associate with the river bottom like brown trout, nor hide in quiet backwaters like brookies. Rainbows are creatures of open, faster waters, where they tend to feed at the surface more often than other trout. Their behavior is often in the open, up front and honest, and for that reason fishing for them often is the most fun.

In North America rainbow trout are native to westward flowing Pacific Coast rivers from Alaska's Kuskokwim, north of the Aleutian Peninsula, south to northwestern Mexico, plus some isolated populations in a few western-interior basins as shown on the accompanying map. They have subsequently been introduced into almost all suitable lake and river habitats worldwide. Some anadromous populations exist from California north to Alaska and are called steelhead after the cold, gray-blue color of adults freshly returned from the sea. Resident, nonmigratory populations are just called rainbows, although both steelhead and rainbows share the same scientific name. Rainbows are perhaps the most easily cultured of all trout and are thus a favorite of hatchery managers and a common component of stocking programs. This attribute has also led to widespread commercial trout farming in the western United States, notably Idaho, and in Europe, and the annual production of rainbow trout for supermarket shelves and restaurants is measured in the tens of thousands of tons. Unfortunately, a long hatchery history of interbreeding and mixing of rainbow stocks has produced a genetic bouillabaisse within which pure-strain rainbow populations are few and far between.

The first hatchery rainbows apparently didn't come from California's McCloud River near Mount Shasta as commonly believed. Based on his review of both federal and early California Fish Commission records, ichthyologist Robert Behnke has written that hatchery rainbow stocks were first cultured by the California Acclimatization Society in the San Francisco area around 1870.[2] These fish were obtained from wild populations in the immediate San Francisco Bay area in such places as San Mateo Creek. Eggs were hatched in the basement of San Francisco's city hall and also cultivated at Berkeley at the University of California. Further, and again from Behnke's review: "The first recorded shipment of rainbow trout eggs out of California was made in 1875 to Seth Green in New York (500 eggs of what Green called 'California mountain trout')." The first McCloud River rainbow eggs received by Green in New York came in 1878, the result of hatchery work conducted privately on the McCloud by J. B. Campbell. This was taking place at about the same time that Livingston Stone was developing a salmon hatchery on the McCloud and shipping the eggs East on behalf of the U.S. Fish Commission. That commission also got in the rainbow-trout business on the McCloud by 1880, haphazardly mixing the eggs of both McCloud's stream-resident rainbows and its migratory steelhead for the next eight years until other rainbow populations elsewhere in California and in Oregon began to be used as sources for eggs.

Hatchery rainbow trout stocked in major river systems have a disconcerting tendency to migrate downstream and ultimately disappear as the individuals grow larger. Apparently many of the rainbow eggs taken in the early California hatchery operations were from migratory steelhead, specifically steelhead from the McCloud River. In some cases, it seems the migratory urge has persisted though hundreds of trout generations in a variety of hatcheries since the 1870s, and the wanderlust characteristic of some hatchery rainbows may simply be a product of their seagoing ancestry. Rainbows were introduced to Michigan's Au Sable as early as 1876, and by 1878 their general introduction to waters of New York and New Hampshire was well underway.[3] By 1900, rainbows had been introduced in forty-one states, a remarkable record spanning only twenty-five years that has probably never been equaled before or since.

Stream-resident rainbows are usually easy to identify. Their upper bodies are heavily covered with black spots, a pattern that extends over the tail. Their backs range from light to dark olive, the abdomen is white, and there's a characteristic reddish pink band along the lateral line, a color that usually extends forward over the central portion of the fish's gill covers. There are no red or yellow spots. Juvenile fish of less than a few inches usually have a series of parr marks, large eliptical, dark spots occurring along their sides that disappear in most varieties as the fish grow larger. Lake-dwelling fish and steelhead freshly returned from the sea have an overall silvery gray color that partly masks the brighter colors underneath, colors that return to prominence as the fish approaches its spawning period.

Other than the rainbows from Kamchatka and those central to California's Eagle Lake, both of which may soon formally be considered subspecies, there are two basic forms native to the far West. Redband rainbows are the most colorful type, showing some gra-

North American Distribution of Rainbow Trout
(Oncorhynchus mykiss)

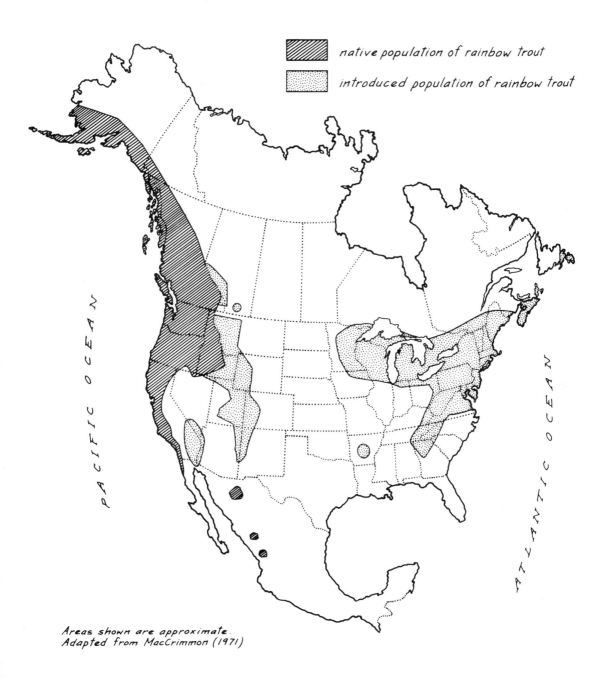

native population of rainbow trout

introduced population of rainbow trout

PACIFIC OCEAN

ATLANTIC OCEAN

Areas shown are approximate.
Adapted from MacCrimmon (1971)

dations of orange and yellow along their sides in addition to a bright red stripe. Parr marks are commonly retained even by large fish, rearward fins on the lower body are tipped with white, and the heavily spotted dorsal fin is also tipped with either white or yellowish white. These are the so-called interior rainbows that exist as a variety of forms, some of which may wind up as subspecies themselves if the apparent present trend in taxonomic splitting continues. Coastal rainbows are in general more drab, lacking the orange and yellow side shading and a white or yellow dorsal-fin tip. Most of these color patterns have undergone considerable modification through many years of interbreeding and hatchery manipulation around the country. Outside of the native range of these fish, it's safest to say a rainbow is a rainbow and to let things go at that.

Rainbows are perhaps the most adaptable of all trout and both native and introduced populations are successful in a wide range of habitats.[4] The major exception to this adaptability seems to be a relative intolerance of low pH (acidic) waters; pH values of 6.0 and less deter spawning. This is in contrast to brook trout, for example, some of which may spawn successfully in waters with a pH as low as 5.0, and is sometimes cited as a limiting factor governing the success of rainbow-trout introductions. Rainbows apparently do best in waters of moderate alkalinity, with a pH ranging from 7.0 to 8.0, although the well-known rainbow strain of Eagle Lake, California, has adapted to waters with a pH as high as 9.6.

Water temperatures tolerated by rainbows are likewise quite variable, probably more so than those tolerated by brown trout, which are better—and incorrectly—known for their wide-ranging temperature tolerances. Rainbows can survive temperatures approaching 32 degrees Fahrenheit and some can survive in water as high as 83 degrees, although survival at high temperatures depends largely on acclimation over time, as is the case with all trout. Their optimal temperature range, as cited by ichthyologist Peter Moyle at the University of California, is apparently 55 degrees to 70 degrees. Given a choice, meaning access to streambed springs or cooler tributaries, most stream rainbows will probably avoid water above 71.6 degrees. In Wyoming's Firehole River, a geothermally heated stream with a naturalized population of rainbows acclimated to elevated water temperatures, the rainbows have been shown to consistently seek a cooler tributary on summer days when the maximum water temperature in the main stream reached 77 degrees.[5] As with other kinds of trout, the implication for fishermen trying to find rainbows in summer is obvious. What's not so obvious is that trout are extremely vulnerable when concentrated in this fashion. Not only is catching them when concentrated by a cooler tributary mouth unsporting to a degree, they are also vulnerable to poachers. A gallon of liquid bleach dumped a short way upstream in a tributary has killed untold numbers of summer trout concentrated downstream, and finding such an empty container on the stream bank may represent much more than simple and unpleasant litter. Such areas deserve special protection at certain times of the year, from anglers and poachers both, a fact that most state regulatory agencies have been slow to recognize.

As a general case, rainbows are spring-spawning fish. Through the artificial manipulation of such things as photoperiod (day length) in hatcheries, some rainbow strains have been developed to spawn in every month of the year, and spawning has even been recorded for the same fish twice in the same twelve-month period. The extent to which rainbows have undergone hatchery manipulation is made most apparent by a recent inventory[6] of rainbow-trout strains held in federal and state hatcheries that showed more than fifty *different* brood stocks. Differences extend from such things as a strain's relative vulnerability to angling to growth rates and food-conversion efficiencies and spawning times. Perhaps the extreme example is the so-called palomino rainbow developed some years ago in West Virginia. These fish are a bright yellow color overall and enjoyed a thankfully brief popularity in some stocking programs because they were supposedly easier for fishermen to see in the water. The few that I have seen were ugly things, looking more than anything like a hunk of bright-yellow Velveeta cheese hanging in the current, a clear case of genetic manipulation being carried to an absurd level. Not all such changes are directly man made, however. The naturalized Firehole rainbows have adapted as fall spawners, which is apparently a long-term response to that river's relatively high water temperatures.[7] In general, however, most rainbows spawn between February and June or even later in very cold, high-altitude streams. The spawning act is generally similar to that of other trout as described in Chapter 3. The eggs hatch in twenty-one to twenty-eight days at typical spring water temperatures of 50 to 59 degrees Fahrenheit, although the time to hatching will be increased by depressed temperatures. This is what enabled the widespread transport of fertile rainbow eggs on ice in the late nineteenth century.

Again, as with other trout, growth rates in rainbows are extremely variable, depending on habitat and available food supply as well as the age of the fish at sexual maturity and its particular genetic strain. In certain California mountain lakes and streams, for example, one-year-old rainbows will be 4.4 to 6.8 inches long; they'll be 5.6 to 8.4 inches long at two years, and 8 to 9.2 inches long at three years, by which time the fish are sexually mature. In contrast, rainbows in California's Eagle Lake have been shown to reach 18.4 to 22.4 inches in three years, by which time they are feeding heavily on other fish, mostly tui chubs. Stream-resident rainbows are usually drift feeders like most other trout in similar situations, a factor that largely determines and usually limits their rate of growth. There's a stream with a naturalized population of rainbows near my Vermont home in which most of the larger rainbows are 10 inches long or less and are as much as six or seven years old. Stream-resident rainbows can reach large sizes feeding on drift, as much as 8 pounds or even more, but only in extremely fertile habitats.

The real giants among nonmigratory rainbows are lake-dwelling strains that feed heavily on fish, typically kokanee, which are a small form of landlocked sockeye salmon introduced in numerous areas but most common to many large western lakes. A so-called Kamloops strain of rainbow is indigenous to lakes in southern British Columbia, and one of its varieties has been documented at more than 50 pounds in that province's Kootenay Lake.[8] I refer to the Kamloops fish as "so-called" because, while it persists largely unaltered in some of its original range, the strain has been widely used as a hatchery stock all over the country and subjected to substantial genetic mixing. The present all-tackle record rainbow as recognized by the International Game Fish Association (IGFA) is a 42-pound 2-ounce fish taken at Bell Island, Alaska, in 1970. The IGFA doesn't differentiate between migratory and stream- or lake-resident fish in terms of its rainbow records since the fish are all the same species, so almost all of the IGFA rainbow records are held either by large, ocean-run steelhead or by fish from large lakes, such as Kootenay or Idaho's Pend Oreille, where they reach record size on a kokanee diet.

The maximum age reached by most non-migratory rainbows is about seven years, and for many years the upper limit was thought to be the eleven years attained by some of California's Eagle Lake rainbows. Recent Alaskan studies have shown the outsize rainbows in the Lake Iliamna region to reach as much as fourteen years old, although eleven years is a more common maximum for them also. The large old Alaskan rainbows, especially the Talarik strain found in the Iliamna region, are interesting because their life histories have certain parallels with the large and equally old brook trout found in northern Labrador and Quebec. In both cases, the trout are five or six years old before their first spawning. Some individuals within each population spawn more than once over a period of years. In both cases some individuals are more than ten years old and quite large by virtue of their longevity and food supply. Both of these populations are found near the extreme northern limit of their geographic ranges.

For brook trout this has been explained in terms of an adaptation that minimizes the impact of a poor spawning season on the overall population over time.[9] The same is probably true of the Alaskan rainbows, although I've never seen it explained as such. If most of the reproductive capacity of a trout population is found in two- and three-year-old fish, as is common in many trout populations, a single event such as a major flood that ruins a season's worth of spawning activity can devastate the population. In this case, most of the potential spawners that would replace (by spawning again) the flood-lost fish will die of old age before they can spawn again. Two floods in successive years could eliminate the population entirely. The near-Arctic populations of resident rainbows in the Northwest and brook trout in the Northeast, by having their reproductive capacity spread through a greater number of fish of different ages, have simply avoided the liability of having all of their eggs in one season's basket. This may also be reflective of the Alaskan rainbows' dependence on migrating salmon as a food supply. These northern rainbows feed heavily on emerging salmon fry in the spring and on both the eggs and rotting flesh of adult salmon migrating in the fall. A year or two of poor salmon runs shows up directly in the reduced physical condition[10]—and spawning capability—of the resident rainbows, and here again, the Alaskan rainbows' longevity and the multiple spawning ability of at least some individuals is apparently an adaptive hedge against such environmental events.

The behavior of most stream-resident rainbows as encountered by most anglers most of the time is generally similar to that described for brown trout in Chapter 5. These fish are drift feeders that hold stationary positions in the current, usually in relation to a rock or other current-breaking object.[11] Like brown trout, the interactions and spatial organization among individual rainbows are governed by a dominance hierarchy. This is established through similar agonistic behavior that includes fin flaring, mouth opening, and swimming attitudes in a contest usually won by the largest fish. As with other kinds of trout, this dominance is both portable and collapsible, depending on the needs of the trout. A dominant trout will probably remain dominant if it moves a few feet to another feeding station, for example. This hierarchy usually isn't evident when fish are crowded into deeper pools during low water, at which times safety, rather than feeding, is the primary consideration for the trout.

There are some characteristic behavioral differences between stream rainbows and other trout, however, that can help a great deal in finding them. Rainbows usually prefer faster water than other trout, which is partly why tumbling rivers such as California's McCloud, Montana's Madison, and New Hampshire's Androscoggin and upper Connecticut are such good rainbow fisheries. Although rainbows don't hold feeding stations in a torrent, which would be wasteful of their energy, there is some research data indicating that they will hold feeding positions in slightly faster water than that used by brown trout. Rainbows also often hold themselves higher in the water column than brown trout, which usually orient themselves close to a rock or other bottom object. The entire expanse of a big, fast Delaware River riffle may hold a large number of rainbows, for example, while brown trout occupy slower areas along the bank or are farther downstream in the slower currents of the pool. This does not mean, by the way, that rainbows are never found in slow water, as anyone who has hunted for big fish in the slow currents of Silver Creek or Fall River will attest. Holding in faster water is a rainbow characteristic, however, the notable spring-creek exceptions notwithstanding.

Rainbows apparently find the same sort of security under a choppy, broken surface that a brown trout finds by hiding under a stump. Rainbows are much less oriented to physical, overhead cover than browns. When hooked, larger rainbows don't usually run for overhead cover as larger browns do, but rather just run and run and run in their attempt to evade the difficulty of being hooked. These trout are also almost unique among trout in usually jumping one or more times when hooked, a characteristic that seems to be just as prevalent among large rainbows as among small ones. I have qualified this slightly because I've hooked many brown trout that also jumped, although rarely more than once, and the jumps I've gotten from browns have been most frequently with fish between 6 and 15 inches and rarely with larger fish. I

have never seen a hooked cutthroat jump and have so far only encountered one brook-trout strain that jumped regularly when hooked, that being the Temescamie strain from Quebec that formed the basis for some of the late Dwight Webster's brook-trout experiments in New York's Adirondack Mountains.

Because rainbows have been so widely cultured, they have and continue to be widely available for laboratory experiments. One of the most notable was performed in Scotland during the 1970s and demonstrated an extraordinary learning ability on the part of some hatchery fish.[12] Some 3- to 4-inch-long hatchery rainbows—domesticated trout that most fishermen regard as village idiots—were placed in a tank with a small trigger mechanism at the water's surface. If a fish hit the trigger, a few food pellets were automatically dropped into the water. Early on, trout accidentally hit the trigger and thus found a food reward. Soon trout were attacking the trigger itself. But within ten days the trout learned to gently hit the trigger and to allow their forward momentum to carry them to the exact spot where the food fell to the water. After training, the trigger mechanism was removed, and the trout were fed by hand for three months. When the trigger was installed again, the trout responded immediately as before and without the need of any relearning.

The trout had not only learned, but had remembered as well, demonstrating two attributes that many fishermen are reluctant to recognize in an ostensibly dumb, cold-blooded fish. Lacking any power of reason, trout *are* dumb, but they aren't stupid. Among its many fishing implications, this means that the same trout is probably not going to be caught and released over and over again with the same Adams dry fly until the fish dies of old age. A common characteristic of many very popular catch-and-release trout fisheries is an increase over time in the general difficulty of catching fish. This is just as true of Montana's famous Madison River as it is of New York's Beaverkill. "There's no question about it. The trout are just plain getting harder to catch," Bob Jacklin told me one day as we talked about the Madison, where Jacklin has guided fishermen for more years than he'd care to admit. In recent years, these Madison trout have seen two hundred or more passing drift boats, each usually containing two fly fishermen, *every day* in season. While the trout are not necessarily smarter, they are certainly becoming more experienced in a hurry. Even hatchery trout can quickly learn to ignore both the fisherman *and* his fly patterns. I have watched smaller brown trout in the equally crowded Beaverkill that were stocked only a month or two before swim placidly around my waders and ignore my best efforts at catching them while they calmly took floating insects a few feet away.

Not only can trout learn and remember, but individual trout can be idiosyncratic, even eccentric. This will strain the imaginations of many anglers, even those with considerable experience, but it's true and has been scientifically demonstrated in at least one study of rainbow trout. Part of the conceptual problem relates to an earlier observation I made on the difference between the observations of trout biologists and those of trout fisherman. The biologist seeks an understanding of a large group of fish and extends that understanding to fish in general. The fisherman catches his fish one at a time and may be confounded if the behavior of the fish in question doesn't conform to what the fisherman understands to be "normal." The fact that all of the trout in a stream don't necessarily behave in the same way at the same time is one of the delights of trout fishing that continues to make it an unpredictable game.

More than twenty years ago, veteran bi-

ologists James Bryan and Peter Larkin at the University of British Columbia did a study of rainbow, brook, and cutthroat trout in a small stream and in ponds to investigate differences in feeding preferences among individual trout.[13] Other things being equal (such as feeding opportunities, location in the stream, etc.), individual trout showed specialization in the amounts and kinds of prey consumed when compared to other individuals of the same trout species and size. The most dramatic example was that one of several rainbows in the test pond developed a unique preference for salamanders, a preference that the fish retained when placed in an aquarium. Bryan and Larkin further showed that such individual specialization by trout could be persistent, lasting for as long as six months before undergoing a gradual change.

There are several possible explanations for this sort of behavior, and those same explanations probably all apply in some combination at the same time. Some of these reasons relate to pure chance. If a trout that's swimming at a particular depth in the pond happens to encounter and eat several damselfly nymphs, the trout may thus have learned several things: where damselfly nymphs are sometimes encountered, how to catch damselfly nymphs, and that damselfly nymphs taste good. The trout's subsequent searches for food may become conditioned by this learning experience, and eventually the trout becomes specialized, for a time at least, at feeding on damselfly nymphs. A different trout of the same species and size may have had a different series of experiences with a different food organism—say salamanders, to continue the example used in the experiment—and thus becomes specialized at feeding on salamanders. It's important to note that the trout in question were not pursuing their food specialties to the exclusion of all other food organisms, but did demonstrate a tendency to specialize within the food forms available—just as you might eat ten cashews but only two pecans from a bowl of mixed nuts.

The demonstrated ability of rainbow and other trout to learn, remember, and to act as individuals different from the norm is central to the whole sport of fly fishing for trout. These abilities have much to do with why trout are selective in the first place and why, as a result, there is no one trout fly that works for all of the trout all of the time.

1. The most helpful paper on the reclassification question is that by Smith and Stearley (1989), who did much of the research leading to the change. See also Robert Behnke's account on the same topic (Behnke, 1990a). This discussion is based largely on their published work.

2. See Behnke (1990). Most sources, both popular and technical, have given the origin of hatchery rainbows as the McCloud River, following a mistaken description by J. H. Wales that was published in 1939 in the *California Journal of Fish and Game*. Rainbows from early stockings have

thus been called "McCloud" or "Shasta" strain rainbows, which is not necessarily true.

3. See MacCrimmon (1971).

4. Much of this discussion is based on Peter Moyle's excellent book *Inland Fishes of California* (1976). See also Robert Henry Smith's chapter on rainbows, appearing in Stoltz and Schnell, eds. (1991).

5. See Kaya, et al. (1977).

6. See Kincaid and Berry (1986).

7. See Kaya (1976).

8. See Raymond (1980).

9. See Balon (1980).

10. See Russell (1977).

11. While the prototypical behavior of stream-resident rainbows is generally similar to that shown by Bachman (1984) for brown trout in a Pennsylvania stream, Bachman was observing only brown trout. The classic study of stream rainbows is the long monograph by Thomas Jenkins, who recorded his observations of rainbows and browns together in two California streams. Jenkins noted that most aspects of the two species' behavior were essentially similar. See Jenkins (1969a).

12. See Adron, et al. (1973).

13. See Bryan and Larkin (1972).

7
Cutthroat Trout

The little creek tumbled brightly down through the pines, then under the road and into Yellowstone Lake. It was an unusual time of low water for late spring, and the creek broke into shallow braids over a sand flat at the edge of the lake in an area that would normally have been underwater. Large signs on stakes at the creek mouth prohibited fishing at its immediate junction with the lake. As we watched, a man stood knee-deep in water between the signs, illegally catching and releasing cutthroat trout as fast as they could be unhooked. We could see the occasional roll of a trout at the surface some distance down the shoreline where fishing was apparently legal, so we walked down with fly rods in hand.

The man stopped casting, turning toward us and shouting a command: "There's no fishing here!"

I started openmouthed at both him and the signs. Dave Engerbretson, my fishing companion, shouted back at him, "So what the hell are *you* doing?" The man turned and resumed his fishing without further comment. We walked down the lake shore past the signs and waded knee-deep in the lake.

Small groups of cutthroat were swimming back and forth in front of us in every direction. It was their spawning time, but low water had blocked their access to the creek. So they hung there, waiting for rain and rising water. The fishing was absurd. I caught three or four immediately on a small WoollyWorm, and it was soon obvious that the choice of fly pattern was of little consequence. As an experiment, I flipped out a cigarette butt, which was likewise taken immediately by one of the trout.

I turned to Engerbretson as he was releasing a fish. "Are you embarrassed yet?" I asked loudly, hoping the other man would hear and pointing to the car.

"For God's sake, yes!" Engerbretson turned and waded to shore. "Let's get out of here before somebody sees us." So we left as the other man continued to fish, having perhaps found his own heaven on earth, the law notwithstanding.

I would have called it hell. G. E. M. Skues, the late and wonderfully perceptive British angling writer, once defined hell through Mr. Castwell, a fictional fly fisherman who was

Cutthroat trout.

doomed for eternity to catch the same trout in the same bend of the same river. The monotony of Castwell's fate removed any aspect of sport, and even the wonderful act of fly-fishing became itself a personal torture. So it was with our brief cutthroat experience that day; there was just no sport in it. It was embarrassing, too, as if we were taking unfair advantage of fish that had become unnaturally vulnerable.

Cutthroat are the trout of the American frontier, or rather what's left of it. Until the 1870s, when introductions of other species began, they were the *only* trout in the vast area from the east slope of the California Sierra eastward through the east slope of the Rockies and including almost all of the rivers there that are now famous for rainbow or brown trout. They were—and still often are—easily caught fish that live in fragile habitats. In the white man's nineteenth-century rape of the American West, cutthroat populations declined along with almost everything else. They remind me of our once-vast buffalo herds; dumb beasts that would stand still as distant men with powerful Sharps rifles picked them off one by one. One by one multiplied quickly into hundreds of thousands, and the big herds were gone. So it has been with cutthroat trout, which have fallen victim to dams, pollution, and overfishing. Like our modern-day buffalo, they have responded in some areas to conservation and management, but their numbers and present range are only shadows of what used to be.

Meriwether Lewis was eighteen years old when his stepfather died in 1792, forcing Lewis to forgo his planned studies at Virginia's William and Mary College for the sake of managing the family estate. Lewis, chafing in those ties, began in that same year to badger his Virginia neighbor and friend Thomas Jefferson, then U.S. Secretary of State, about the need for an overland exploration of the far West. Jefferson turned him down, feeling the time wasn't right, but kept both Lewis and the proposed expedition in mind. When Jefferson entered the White House as president in 1801, one of his first acts was to appoint Lewis as his personal secretary, bringing Lewis, now a captain, back from a frontier army posting in Detroit. Lewis served Jefferson for two years in the White House, where the idea of a western expedition was discussed often. In January of 1803, Jefferson finally requested and got $2,500 from Congress to fund the search for an overland route to the Pacific and named Lewis to head the expedition. On instructions from Jefferson, Lewis was to name a coleader. He chose William Clark of Louisville, a retired army officer and Indian fighter with whom Lewis had served briefly in 1794. The names of Lewis and Clark are probably even better known than the details of the expedition west they began from near St. Louis on May 14, 1804, much of which has become part of American folklore. Almost incidental in their two years of struggle to the Pacific and back was their being the first white Americans to describe cutthroat trout.

By July 1805 the group was heading up the Missouri River near what's now Great Falls, Montana. When their fabled female Indian guide, Sacajawea, became sick, Clark and most of the party remained in camp while Lewis led a group of four men up a river fork, hoping to find a large rapid they had been told would indicate their route. What they found was the great falls of the Missouri, where one of the four, Silas Goodrich, caught a number of whitefish and several unusual trout.[1] The trout were sufficiently novel to warrant description in Lewis' journal:

> The trout are from 16 to 23 inches in length, precisely resemble our mountain

or speckled trout [eastern brook trout] in form and the position of their fins, but the specks on these are of a deep black instead of the red or goald [*sic*] of those common in the U' States. These are furnished with long teeth on the pallet [*sic*] and tongue and have generally a small dash of red on each side behind the front ventral fins; the flesh is of a pale yellowish red, or when in good order, of a rose red.[2]

William Clark, who was apparently more of a naturalist than Lewis, later wrote more detailed descriptions of cutthroat trout the party encountered along the Columbia River.

While their early accounts are perhaps the best known, Lewis and Clark were not the first explorers to encounter cutthroat trout. That distinction apparently belongs to members of Coronado's army who searched for treasure in the southwestern United States in the early 1540s. According to some recently published historical research by Pat Trotter,[3] members of Coronado's group encountered cutthroat trout in what's now called Glorieta Creek near the headwaters of the Pecos River in northern New Mexico. The published narratives of that expedition mention the "excellent trout" encountered in a small stream there during 1541. This date is by far the earliest known mention of a native trout in the exploration of North America.

Cutthroat trout were included along with rainbow trout and other fish samples sent by Meredith Gairdner to John Richardson, the Scottish naturalist who named cutthroats *Salmo clarki* (after William Clark) in 1836. Prior to the late 1880s, cutthroats weren't called cutthroats but went by an assortment of other names such as Rocky Mountain trout or salmon trout, the latter being a reference to their often large size. As Trotter has noted, the name "cutthroat," which refers to the red slashes of pigment on the fish's

lower jaw, was given by Charles Hallock when he described a Montana fishing trip in an 1884 issue of *The American Angler*:

It resembles the iridea [the scientific name of rainbow trout at the time, which were first introduced to Colorado in 1882] of Colorado in respect to the metallic black markings scattered like lustrous grains of coarse black powder over its shoulders and body; but it lacked the rainbow lateral stripe. Its distinctive feature, however, was a slash of intense carmine across each gill cover, as large as my little finger. It was most striking. For lack of a better description we called them cutthroat trout.

Hallock was a veteran journalist, sportsman, and conservationist best known as the New York founder of *Forest and Stream*, a widely read periodical that he published from 1873 until 1880. He was also the well-traveled author of several popular angling books, and his wide audience quickly accepted the name cutthroat even though he obviously misplaced the location of the trout's colored slashes in his description, putting them on the gill covers instead of under the jaw.

All of the major kinds of trout we've examined in this book show degrees of variation within each single species that may be described as strains or varieties or simply local variations. Some of these either have been or probably will be given formal status as subspecies by at least some modern taxonomists. Cutthroat trout are the extreme example of this sort of variation, and at least one prominent taxonomist, Robert Behnke, recognizes fourteen distinct cutthroat subspecies. Behnke has written widely in both scientific and popular print on this topic, and almost all other modern descriptions of cutthroat variations, including my own, are derived from his work. Before describing some of them, I'll note that cutthroat trout, along with rainbows, were reclassified in 1988 from the genus *Salmo* to the genus *Oncorhynchus*, which is indicative of their close evolutionary ties to the five species of Pacific salmon that share the same generic name. All cutthroat trout are now known as *Oncorhynchus clarki*, plus a subspecies designation if appropriate.

While some of this taxonomic tangle may seem a little tedious to some trout fishermen, it's important even to casual anglers. For one thing, the cutthroat you catch in Yellowstone will look very different from the cutthroat you catch not too far away in Jackson Hole, so much so as to almost seem a different trout. The cutthroat you'll see in Oregon's Cascade Mountains will likewise seem very different from those you might find along the California-Nevada border. For another, some cutthroat subspecies are federally listed as threatened or endangered, and large amounts of money derived from excise taxes on fishing tackle, plus fishing-license fees and general federal and state revenues are being spent on their management and, hopefully, recovery. The payoff for fisherman, in addition to the somewhat abstract benefits of basic conservation, is the opportunity to catch and release some exceedingly rare forms of trout. Although I have not as yet done so, for example, traveling to the mountains around Denver to catch and release some small and very rare greenback cutthroats is high on my list of future trips. Measured in terms of dollars spent for inches of trout caught it will be an expensive trip; greenback cutthroat aren't very big, but their rarity gives them importance out of all proportion to their size.

Like the brook trout, which entered eastern North America from the Atlantic, cutthroats penetrated the West from the Pacific Ocean in the prehistoric times of the advances and retreats of the great ice sheets.

Over thousands of years, inland populations were established, wiped out, and then reestablished through the ebb and flow of glacial activity. In the intervening millennia, habitats changed; new lakes and rivers were formed, others shrank or dried up. The end result was discrete populations of cutthroat trout that were maintained through geographic isolation until generally—but still not completely—disrupted by the genetic vandalism of the widespread trout introductions begun in the 1870s.

The trout's most distinctive feature is the "cut-throat" slashes of color under its jaw, one on each side, which is also the most discernable characteristic for anglers unfamiliar with these fish. There are reportedly a very few native rainbow-trout populations that also display this coloration, and it's also common to many rainbow-cutthroat hybrids, so don't take these marks as being indicative of pure-strain cutthroats. Another way of identifying your fish is to check the rearward portion of the fish's tongue (toward the throat) for what are called basibranchial teeth. Cutthroats have these teeth; almost all rainbows do not. These teeth are also commonly (but not always) missing or reduced in cutthroat-rainbow hybrids. Like rainbows and unlike brook or brown trout, all of the cutthroat's spots are very dark gray or black. The spotting patterns, meaning the distribution of the spots over the fish's body, are one way of making a casual but still uncertain identification of a particular cutthroat subspecies. A positive identification often depends on the chromosome counts and protein analysis only possible in a sophisticated laboratory.

There are presently four major cutthroat groups, the original distributions of which are shown on the accompanying map. I'll be using both common and technical (subspecies) names here, the latter of which are conventionally represented as *G.(enus) species subspecies*. Coastal cutthroats (*Oncorhynchus clarki clarki*) are found from the Eel River in northwestern California north to Seward in the Kenai region of southwestern Alaska. They are not found more than one hundred miles inland within that range, a distance that generally represents the highest point of the coastal mountains as one progresses eastward from the ocean. These fish are heavily covered with fine black or gray spots on a background color of dull brass or copper. Spotting patterns are even over the entire body, dorsal and tail fins, and may even extend to the belly of some fish. Some populations are anadromous, but remain close to shore rather than going far to sea like steelhead and salmon. The characteristic red slashes will be present on the lower jaws of most fish, although they may be almost indiscernible or even nonexistent on sea-run individuals.

The westslope cutthroat subspecies (*O. clarki lewisi*, which designation is a tribute to both the explorers) is found in parts of southern Alberta and British Columbia as well as parts of Washington, Idaho, and Montana. There are relatively few pure strains of these fish remaining, although a number may still be found in the Flathead headwaters of Glacier National Park; most cutthroats found within this region are apparently hybrids either with rainbows or other cutthroat strains or both. Westslope cutthroats are finely spotted like the coastal subspecies, but in the case of westslope fish the spotting pattern is concentrated on the fish's body to the rear of the dorsal fin and there are few, if any, spots along the forward half of the fish's sides.

Lake Lahontan was a huge prehistoric lake that once covered most of northwestern Nevada and a small area of adjacent California. Its drainage area included what's now called Lake Tahoe on the California-Nevada border. The giant lake eventually receded, leaving a number of modern lakes, of which Nevada's Pyramid Lake is the largest. Of the four subspecies of cutthroat that are—or were, since there's still some question—endemic to this region, the best known is the Lahontan cutthroat (*O. clarki henshawi*), which at one time was both big and abundant in Pyramid Lake. The official (IGFA) world-record cutthroat of 41 pounds was taken here in 1925, and there are unconfirmed accounts of cutthroat exceeding 60 pounds having been taken commercially here around 1900.[4] An extensive commercial fishery that annually removed as much as 264,000 pounds of trout from the lake in the same period helped decimate the fish, and the construction of a dam on the Truckee River in the early 1900s eliminated most of the fish's spawning habitat. By 1944, this race of giant cutthroat was finally deemed extinct. Restoration programs were begun in the 1950s, and the lake was periodically stocked with a variety of trout, including various cutthroat strains, none of which performed as well as the original natives. Biologists are still experimenting with various remnant populations of pure-strain Lahontans that are found in remote headwaters, trying to find some that will reach the same astonishing sizes as the old Pyramid Lake fish. Identifying a pure-strain Lahontan cutthroat is a job for an expert, but the fish are in part characterized by medium to large spots distributed evenly over the body, against a dull-brass-colored background.

The fourth and last major cutthroat group is represented by the Yellowstone cutthroat (*O. clarki bouvieri*) and six other subspecies as shown in the accompanying chart. These are the cutthroats of the interior Rocky Mountains extending from Montana south to New Mexico. Within this group, the Snake River cutthroat, which is widely thought to be a cutthroat subspecies but still lacks a formal subspecific name, is well known to fly fishermen who frequent Jackson Hole and

North American Distribution of Cutthroat Trout
(*Oncorhynchus clarki*)

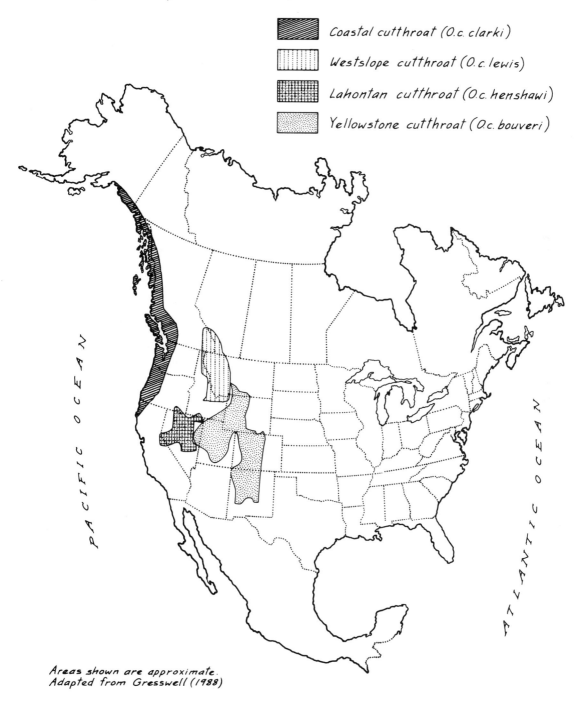

Coastal cutthroat (*O.c. clarki*)

Westslope cutthroat (*O.c. lewis*)

Lahontan cutthroat (*O.c. henshawi*)

Yellowstone cutthroat (*O.c. bouveri*)

PACIFIC OCEAN

ATLANTIC OCEAN

Areas shown are approximate.
Adapted from Gresswell (1988)

Subspecies of Cutthroat Trout
(Oncorhynchus clarki)
(adapted from Behnke [1991])

COASTAL FORM
Coastal cutthroat (O. c. clarki)

UPPER COLUMBIA RIVER FORM
Westslope cutthroat (O. c. lewisi)

LAHONTAN BASIN FORMS
Lahontan cutthroat (O. c. henshawi)
Paiute cutthroat (O. c. seleniris)
Humboldt cutthroat (O. c. unnamed)
Alvord cutthroat (O. c. unnamed)
Willow/whitehorse cutthroat
   (O. c. unnamed)

SNAKE RIVER
(YELLOWSTONE) FORMS
Yellowstone cutthroat (O. c. bouvieri)
Bonneville cutthroat (O. c. utah)
Colorado River cutthroat
   (O. c. pleuriticus)
Greenback cutthroat (O. c. stomias)
Rio Grande cutthroat (O. c. virginalis)
Yellow Fin cutthroat (extinct) (O. c.
   macdonaldi)
Snake River cutthroat (O. c. unnamed)

inland population of cutthroat trout.[5] These fish are relatively drab in color, with medium to large black spots concentrated just forward of the tail, against an overall dull yellow background. Even within the Yellowstone system, however, there are several discrete populations of this subspecies whose spotting patterns vary slightly from my description. Larger fish often show a rose-colored blush over their gill covers and the forward half of their bodies.

When catch-and-release fishing for trout began to assume wide popularity among fly fishermen in the 1970s, the Yellowstone River and its cutthroats were—and still often are—the concept's most widely cited success story. Before 1973, when 9 miles of the river below Yellowstone Lake were dedicated to catch-and-release fishing only, the capture by anglers of large numbers of trout had effectively reduced the numbers of fish longer than 16 inches to zero. Within a couple of years under the new regulations, the average angler catch rate per hour of Yellowstone cutthroats tripled, and the average trout size increased to about 16 inches.[6] According to one study made on the popular Buffalo Ford section of the river in 1981, each trout in this stretch was caught and released an *average* of 9.7 times in a six-week summer interval. Some were even caught two or three times on the same day.[7] Before you run off to Yellowstone expecting to catch and release bushels of big cutthroats, I should add that the fishing there is not always easy and is probably getting more difficult with time. While cutthroats are the most gullible of all trout, even they are capable of learning eventually. I have stood in the Yellowstone's broad, green currents and gnashed my teeth while big cutthroats inspected and refused my small flies on the lightest of leaders. It's worth noting, too, as Bob Behnke has pointed out, that the gullibility of cutthroats—meaning the relatively high likelihood of multiple recaptures by fishermen—has

the Snake River country of western Wyoming. These fish are unique in that their spots are extremely small and fine, the smallest spots found on any American trout. The cutthroats of Yellowstone National Park are even better known. They are abundant in the park, where one can find what's arguably the world's best fishing for cutthroat trout in waters such as Slough Creek and the Yellowstone River. Yellowstone Lake itself is said to presently hold the world's largest much to do with the success of catch-and-release rules instituted on that fish's behalf. It would be virtually impossible to catch the same large, wild brown trout nine or ten time in six weeks, unless it was one of the rare village idiots whose ancestors flunked out of European brown trout school a century ago. I don't mean by this that catch-and-release doesn't work for other kinds of trout. It does work, at least sometimes, and that's a management question we'll argue in the last chapter of this book.

As one would expect of a fish with so many subspecies and diverse populations, the life histories and growth characteristics of cutthroats are widely variable.[8] In general, cutthroats are spring-spawning fish, the exact time ranging from April to as late as August in some waters, and spawn only in flowing water. Spawning may take place in the area where the trout has spent much of its river life if the stream is small and conditions suitable. Other populations may undergo spawning migrations of varying length. Peter Moyle has noted reports of spawning migrations as long as 93 miles in certain rivers. The spawning act itself is essentially similar to that of other common stream trout as described in Chapter 3.

Growth is likewise variable, depending perhaps on the particular strain of fish and certainly on the productivity and temperature of its habitat. Thus high, cold, and typically infertile mountain streams may have fish that are sexually mature at only 4 inches in length and three or four years of age. The following figures are more typical, however: One-year-olds at 4 inches, two-year-olds at 7.2 inches, three-year-olds at 9.6 inches, extending upward to six-year-olds at 16.4 inches. The maximum age reached by these fish has been cited as eleven years, although seven to nine years is probably a more usual maximum.

Cutthroat populations suffered widely because of introductions of other trout within their native range, which until recent years was often done with little or no regard for the competitive and genetic consequences. Rainbows have and continue to interbreed freely with the closely related cutthroats, and most of the rainbows' traits—including coloration—have proved to be genetically dominant. This has effectively eradicated pure-strain cutthroats in watersheds all over the West. Although I've seen no records of brookies or browns interbreeding with cutthroats—they are of different genera—brooks, browns, and rainbows all put the cutthroat at a competitive disadvantage in most rivers. Cutthroats are like other stream trout in being largely drift feeders, holding their feeding positions in the currents of a stream and maintaining those positions through aggressive interactions with other trout. But unless a particular cutthroat has a large size advantage, it usually loses such contests with other kinds of trout. Further, because cutthroats are in general much more easily caught than other kinds of trout, most angling limits that don't differentiate among trout species encourage the removal of cutthroats at a disproportionately faster rate. While there are still many places where cutthroats coexist with browns, rainbows, or brook trout, in almost all such cases the cutthroats are declining in numbers while the numbers of other kinds of trout are either comparatively constant or increasing.

That cutthroats are generally gullible is well known, but now it's possible to measure that gullibility, at least in a relative way. In comparing brook and brown trout in some previous chapters, I noted that in streams where they coexist the more easily caught brookies may be removed from the stream by anglers at a rate four or even more times faster than browns. In some cases where cutthroats and brook trout coexist, it's been likewise noted that cutthroats are at least twice as likely to be caught as brookies. In comparing the vulnerability of cutthroats and brown trout, Bob Behnke noted that some catch rates for the two fish differed by a remarkable factor of 95; that is, it took ninety-five times longer to catch an equivalent number of brown trout.[9] This is certainly not true of all trout everywhere, but is indicative of the differences between the two fish. Some fly fishermen partial to cutthroats will be insulted by this and may correctly note that "their" cutthroats are harder to catch and are thereby "better" fish. I've already noted that cutthroats don't always come easily to the fly. They may become temporarily locked on a particular hatch of insects, requiring the best of imitative fly patterns, and certainly they require some stealth on the angler's part when the fish are found in low, clear water. It remains generally true, however, that cutthroats are the most easily caught of all trout, and that innocence is a large part of their charm.

Cutthroat trout populations are sensitive not only to fishing pressure but also to all sorts of environmental degradation. David Starr Jordan, the eminent Stanford University ichthyologist, surveyed the waters of Colorado and Utah in 1889 on behalf of the U.S. Fish Commission.[10] By the time of his trip, many local trout populations had already become extinct or were well on their way as silt from mining operations had made much of the upper Arkansas and Colorado rivers' watersheds unfit for trout. Jordan also wrote:

> In the progress of settlement of the valleys of Colorado the streams have become more and more largely used for irrigation. Below the mouths of the canyons dam after dam and ditch after ditch turn off the water. In summer the beds of even large rivers are left wholly dry, all the water being turned into these ditches. . . .
>
> Great numbers of trout, in many cases thousands of them, pass into these irrigating ditches and are left to perish in the fields. The destruction of trout by this agency is far greater than that due to all others combined, and it is going on in almost every irrigating ditch in Colorado.

The area Jordan described included the native range of yet another cutthroat subspecies, the greenback cutthroat (*Oncorhynchus clarki stomias*), one of the interior Rocky Mountain group and characterized by the largest spots of any cutthroat (typically concentrated near the tail). By 1937, greenbacks had been formally described as being extinct.

In the early 1970s, small remnant populations of greenbacks were known to exist in two small tributaries of Colorado's South Platte River not far from Denver. According to one report,[11] there were about two thousand individual trout left in slightly more than 3.5 miles of stream. The species was listed as "endangered" under the 1973 U.S. Endangered Species Act, a designation that was lowered to "threatened" in 1978 when three more small populations were discovered. In 1977 an ongoing recovery program was started by federal and state fisheries authorities that entailed breeding captured greenbacks in hatcheries, using sperm taken from wild males to guard against domestication of the strain. As of 1988, pure-strain greenbacks had been reintroduced into about 50 miles of streams and five small lakes and ponds in Colorado, such as Ouzel and Fern lakes in Rocky Mountain National Park.

Ironically, and despite the biological successes of the greenback recovery efforts, the same fish face yet another environmental threat, even in their now relatively pristine environments. Although acid rain is commonly viewed as an eastern problem—the result of pollutant-laden air traveling from the American Midwest over the Northeast—it also occurs in the Rockies. The relative acidity of rain and snow along the Colorado Front Range has been increasing at least since 1975, a trend that is expected to continue especially near high-altitude urban and industrial areas such as that extending from Denver north to Fort Collins. Greenback cutthroats are typically found at relatively high altitudes and in areas of thin soils over granitic bedrock. These are areas of limited buffering capacity where the soils chemistry is unable to mitigate the effects of incoming acids, very much like those eastern areas where some brook-trout populations have already been seriously affected. While acid rain is a much more serious problem in the northeastern United States, greenbacks have shown the same sort of vulnerability as eastern brook trout to increasingly acid waters.[12] While there's no reason to suppose that the recovery effort is immediately endangered by acid rain, laboratory tests with these fish have already demonstrated the potential for long-term adverse effects.

Much of the concern about the various cutthroat subspecies reflects in a small way the much larger concerns about biodiversity in general, a concept that makes headlines these days in the face of rapidly disappearing rainforests. As genetic diversity decreases, so does the ability of any particular species to adapt to a changing environment. As populations of trout decline, their adaptability as a species likewise shrinks. The world wouldn't change a great deal overnight if the little greenback cutthroats were to become extinct. For fishermen, there would be other trout. But the greenbacks can be seen as environmental indicators much like the miner's caged canary. The long-term implications of their possible extinction are frightening.

1. According to copies of some original documents on file at the American Museum of Fly Fishing, in 1803 Lewis had bought fishing tackle for the trip from George Lawton in Philadelphia. Lawton was a tackle merchant who succeeded Edward Pole, whose early business in the same city was described in the first chapter of this book. Unfortunately, I've never encountered any biographical information concerning Silas Goodrich, who was by all scant accounts the fisherman within Lewis and Clark's group.

2. From Thwaites (1904), as quoted in Trotter and Bisson (1988).

3. There are three excellent recent works dealing with cutthroat trout. Pat Trotter's 1987 book *Cutthroat: Native Trout of the West* is a very readable review that will be useful to all interested anglers. In a more technical vein, but equally useful, are Gresswell, R., ed., *Status and Management of Interior Stocks of Cutthroat Trout*, a 1988 publication that contains the proceedings of an American Fisheries Society symposium on that topic, and Trotter's chapter on cutthroat trout in Stoltz and Schnell, eds. (1991). Complete citations for these works appear in the Bibliography.

4. See Coleman and Johnson's chapter in Gresswell, ed. (1988) for an excellent account of the past and present cutthroat fishery in this region.

5. See Varley and Gresswell (1988).

6. See Behnke (1988).

7. See Varley and Gresswell (1988).

8. See Moyle (1976) for a general account; also Varley and Gresswell (1988) for life-history information specific to Yellowstone cutthroats.

9. See Behnke (1988).

10. See Jordan (1891). Jordan's comments on the destruction of western habitat have been quoted often. For this and also information on greenback cutthroat trout, see particularly Stuber, et al. (1988), also Dwyer and Rosenlund (1988).

11. See Dwyer and Rosenlund (1988).

12. See Woodward, et al. (1991).

8
Selective Trout

Willie Gunner grunted, then heaved and slid the big duffle box and outboard motor off his back to the ground at the edge of the river. He untied the tump line and stuck it in his pocket, ready for the next portage. The leather strap over his forehead had rubbed the skin red, but the tump tied to the load on his back enabled him to use his neck muscles as a help on long carries. Once he had told me, bragging, about carrying 500 pounds on his back with a tump line between the load and his forehead, making it all the way around the local ice-hockey arena before collapsing and winning his bet. He hiked back up along the riverbank to bring our now-empty boat down through the rapids on a rope.

We had been mucking around the head-waters of La Grande River in far northern Quebec for several days, trying to find a motherlode of big brook trout. My Cree hosts hoped that such a fishery might form the basis for a new sporting camp operated as a tribal enterprise, but—even though such fishing might still be discovered in that region—we couldn't find it. While we saw many miles of unblemished wilderness, we also saw very few brookies over 3 pounds and none of the 8- to 10-pound fish that had lured me north on a slim rumor. There were no other human tracks, no aircraft other than our own floatplane, and no real trails. The area had been fished only a little by occasional trappers, one of whom had marked river routes and portages on our map.

I waded into the pool below the rapid while waiting for Willie and the boat. There were a number of trout rising in the big black-water eddy between the main current and the huge blocks of granite that sat like odd prehistoric sculptures along the shore. These were large wild brook trout that had in all probability never seen an artificial fly of any kind. They would certainly strike anything I happened to use, so I tied on a big Irresistible dry whose deerhair body I figured would survive the chewings of many trout. I cast between two rolling fish and quickly made ready for a strike that never came. My fly bobbed on the surface, bouncing up and down in the waves made by rising trout only inches away, and I was confounded.

I slid the line off the water and into my hand, snipped off the fly, and stood to watch for a minute. Little tan caddisflies scuttered across the water's surface before taking off, and I saw one of the flies disappear in a splash. A small, tan Elkhair Caddis dry was the answer. Changing to a finer leader and tying on the little fly were made difficult as I developed a case of buck-fever shakes in watching the fish. Finally I could cast, and the difficult fish became suddenly easy. I spent half an hour catching and releasing them until I noticed smoke from Willie's fire. He had water boiling by the time I got out of the river, and we had afternoon tea by the rapids; black, bitter tea loaded with sugar, which I drank slowly while I watched the still-rising fish. They had certainly been selective. Yet they were wilderness trout that had never seen a fly; brook trout that by all angling accounts should have shown no selectivity whatsoever.

In terms of trout streams and human traffic, among the many and much more common opposite extremes is the spring creek on Montana's Armstrong Ranch near Livingston. Here the rainbow and brown trout of its clear, slow-flowing waters are confronted with a parade of fly fishermen every day in season. The creek is so popular that for many years access has been restricted through a limit on the number of anglers, who are also charged a daily rod fee, a system that protects the creek from overuse and also means that it's fished mostly by highly skilled enthusiasts willing to pay a premium to confront its selective trout. Armstrong's is a particular favorite of mine because it's usually possible, given reasonable stealth on my part, to watch the abundant trout as I fish for them in the clear water and to see how they respond to whatever fly I happen to be using. The trout, of course, are experienced and can be exceptionally fussy as to fly pattern.

I had spent the past several hours of a sunny afternoon sitting low on the bank while fishing over a group of twenty or so rainbows that were feeding on intermittent hatches of small mayflies, midges, and caddis. I was changing flies often to match the hatch of the moment, which seemed to change every half hour or so. A very small cream dry fly worked for a little while as the fish were taking the corresponding mayflies, but then I'd have to switch to a small emerging midge pattern when the hatch changed and the fish likewise switched. By all this maneuvering I was sometimes able to hook one of the trout, which would flip around a little and then be hurriedly released so I could get back to my hatch-matching games.

After a while I stopped working over the rainbows that I could see and started fishing to a small riseform against the far bank. I couldn't see the fish through the reflections on the water's surface, but the gentle ripples made by its feeding appeared regularly in the slow current. There were small, olive mayflies emerging and riding the gentle currents as the flies gathered enough warmth for flight, but I could see the adults floating over the fish's position unmolested. I decided to try a small floating nymph; a minuscule fly that matched the mayflies in size but which would float low in the surface tension to imitate a partly emerged dun. The fly disappeared in a small dimple, and I raised the rod gently to set the hook without breaking the necessarily fine leader.

The trout shook its head without otherwise moving, a characteristic of large trout when first hooked gently with fine tackle. Then the fish, still unseen, started to swim slowly up the middle of the creek. There was no line-scorching, reel-screaming run; just a slow *click-click-click* of the reel as the trout pulled line deliberately upstream. It was obviously a very large trout that had sensed something wrong but had not yet panicked into a hard fight. I waded to the middle of the stream and pointed the rod directly at the fish, hoping thereby to reduce the moving line's friction against the rod guides and to prevent the leader from snapping. Line was continuing to disappear from the reel in a seeming eternity of slow, steady clicks.

Larry Auippy, a widely published photographer from Wyoming, was fishing with me that day and stood in the creek about 75 feet upstream. "Watch out!" I hollered and pointed at my rod. "Fish coming up!"

He stopped casting and watched. In a few seconds, the end of my yellow fly line slowly passed him, still heading upstream. "Oh, wow!" I heard him whisper.

By this time, the fish had slowly pulled 90 feet of fly line through the rod guides, and I was wondering why the leader tippet, which only had a breaking strength of about 16 ounces, was still intact. I didn't have to wonder for too long, however, as everything soon went slack. Yards of yellow line came drifting back in the current. The fly was still attached. The trout, which neither of us ever did see, had simply swum slowly away until the little hook pulled free. I was left marveling, not about the loss of a big trout—I don't think I had a prayer of landing such a fish in that weedy creek—but about the fussiness of trout in general and how such a large fish could be so particular about such small flies.

Because almost any trout fly will catch at least some trout at certain times and places, there is still considerable controversy among trout fishermen as to whether or not trout are selective and even what selectivity means in the first place. For a behavioral scientist, selective feeding in trout means the fish is deliberately choosing and eating—or rejecting and not eating—a food organism, such as a particular kind of caddisfly larva, in numbers that are disproportionate to the numbers and kinds of all food organisms available in the stream. In other words, and to oversimplify things, assume that little tan caddisflies and large yellow mayflies are drifting by the trout in a ratio of ten caddis for every mayfly within a certain time interval. At the same time, this trout's stomach contains nine of the mayflies and only one caddis. The fish is thus said to be feeding selectively on mayflies. If the trout's stomach contained ten caddis and only one of the mayflies—the same proportion as available in the trout's environment—the trout would not have been feeding selectively in a behavioral sense.

A fishman's view is more immediate: A trout that is feeding but refuses to strike a well-presented fly pattern thought plausible by the fisherman is said to be selective. In either definition, selectivity depends on the trout's making active choices in a way that is consistent over at least a brief time interval. If a trout isn't feeding, but is hiding under a rock, the trout isn't being selective—at least not about food or flies. Finally, trout in certain streams acquire reputations among fishermen for being difficult or selective in general. This is particularly true in catch-and-release or "no-kill" areas where the trout gain considerable experience with anglers. In other locations, most commonly in wilderness areas, trout have a sometimes undeserved reputation for being unselective and easily caught.

The basic answer to the often-argued selectivity question is simple: All trout are selective. If they weren't, they'd starve to death. Picture the trout holding its feeding position in the stream, scanning the current for insects and other food items as they drift by. Also floating by are numerous bits of leaves, bark, twigs, and other debris, many of which look superficially like small insects. A trout that can't tell the difference and spends much of its time eating bits of debris is obviously not going to be a survivor. Many of the trout's acute senses—most especially vision—have evolved over thousands of years to enable the trout to make such distinctions. That remarkable sensory capability is what enables newborn trout to quickly learn about what's edible and what's not, starting from the first day they begin feeding, a learning process that continues throughout the trout's life.[1] Thus selectivity in feeding is an innate characteristic of *all* trout everywhere. For fishermen, the question isn't whether or not trout are selective, but rather how selective they happen to be at a particular moment. Degrees of selectivity can vary enormously in different circumstances and at different times, even when considering a single fish.

Although the trout's various senses, such as taste, smell, hearing, and lateral-line sensitivity, all play various roles in feeding at times, trout are predominately visual predators. Any discussion of selectivity in trout necessarily includes a description of their visual capabilities.[2] As a general case, trout see both differently and much better than humans do. Also, certain aspects of trout vision are hard for humans to grasp because there's no human counterpart. Some of the more significant attributes of trout vision are:

Trout live underwater, so their vision is specifically adapted to that environment. Humans see poorly underwater without the supplementary air/water interface provided by a diving mask.

Trout can see and differentiate among colors, not only all of the colors visible to humans but also those in the shortwave, ultraviolet part of the spectrum that humans can't see.

A trout eye has a movable lens, enabling the trout to focus carefully on close objects.

When at rest—that is, not closely focused—the configuration of the trout's lens and retinal system allows the trout to see both near (as close as 2 feet) and far objects in sharp focus simultaneously through the fish's entire field of view.

Because the fish has an eye at each side of its head, each eye can work independently. The fish is literally looking left and right at the same time. Binocular vision, such as humans have, is only obtained in forward and upward directions, in which case both eyes can bear on the same object.

Again because of the placement of the trout's eyes, the fish has a blind spot to its immediate rear. This is why you can sometimes carefully sneak very close to a rising trout from behind, although if you splash or scrape a rock, the trout's acute hearing will give it ample warning.

In very dim light—late evening, for example—the color-sensitive cone cells in the trout's retina retract into the retinal tissue, and the fish's color sensitivity is diminished. At the same time, the trout's black-and-white- (and gray-) sensitive rod cells become visually paramount. Brown trout—and probably all trout—can thus feed accurately even in starlight on a night with no moon. The process is reversed with the growing light of dawn.

Trout are more sensitive to motion than any other possible visual input. They may even have some retinal cells specifically adapted to detect moving objects in their environment.

Trout can apparently detect polarized light, a capability lacking in humans. I have seen no research that makes clear whether this is an active, visual capability with a result analogous to what a fisherman sees with polarized glasses—namely a reduction in glare and a greater purity of color—or if this simply is a means whereby the trout can determine the direction of sunlight as a means of orienting itself, an ability that may play a role in the migrations of its close relation, the salmon.

The physical characteristics of the trout's environment exist as corollaries to the trout's own diverse visual capabilities to further define what trout can and cannot see. As noted in Chapter 2, water absorbs different colors of light at different rates, with the shorter wavelengths in the blue end of the spectrum penetrating to the greatest depths. In clear streams, however, where most trout are caught at depths of 3 feet or less, the rate of color attenuation is insignificant, and fishermen should assume that trout can see all colors most of the time.

Off-color or turbid water is another problem that will obviously alter color perception. In northeastern rivers and lakes, for example, the water is often naturally stained to a slight rust or tea color, the result of dissolved humic matter. Successful underwater fly patterns that have evolved over the past century for brook trout and landlocked salmon in New England and eastern Canada often show varying amounts of yellow in the body or wing. This is a remarkably common characteristic of these flies; one that I think accidentally but accurately points to yellow as an effective fly color in tea-colored water anywhere.

Black is also important in underwater flies. This color—or more properly a complete lack of color, which is the definition of black—will most of the time offer the greatest contrast between the fly and almost any natural background. It is probably the color most visible to trout because of this contrast. In turbid, muddy water a Black Marabou streamer is almost always my fly of choice if the fish aren't rising. Here again, the evolution of a fly pattern offers a key. The Esopus Bucktail is a conventional bucktail tied with a stark black-over-white wing that would appear to offer the maximum contrast in dirty water. It evolved, according to my friend Eric Leiser, on the Catskills' Esopus Creek, which invariably has a slightly turbid flow because of water introduced through a reservoir storage system.

Remember in tying or buying flies that there's black and there's black. A primary feather from a common crow's wing, for example, looks black and is commonly used for wet-fly wings among other things. Although the bird looks black, its feathers have a greenish tint. The primary feathers from a raven's wing, in contrast, are a beautiful dead-flat, pure black. Veteran Atlantic-salmon fishermen years ago, men like the late Charles DeFeo, deliberately sought raven feathers for certain black-winged wet flies. After learning this, I almost killed myself on a long stretch of the Maine Turnpike at dawn, where ravens could be found every few miles, feeding on the previous night's crops of road-killed porcupines. I tried hard—and with no success—to nip a raven with my fender at 70 miles an hour so as to collect some feathers. I finally gave up in the interest of my own safety; the birds were much too clever at getting out of the way. Ravens, of course, are now protected in most areas, and I'm not encouraging you to collect fly materials illegally. The point is that in selecting black flies or materials, try to make sure they are indeed black.

Rays of light passing from the air through the water's surface (and vice versa) are bent, a phenomenon called refraction. This is why a soda straw appears bent when standing in a glass of clear water. This gives rise in part to a complex physical phenomenon that's often called the trout's window, although it certainly isn't unique to trout, since it depends solely on the refraction and reflection of light. A better but seldom-used name (among fishermen, at least) is Snel's Circle, after the Dutch physicist who first described it some three hundred years ago. The net result of this phenomenon is that a trout looking upward sees the world above the water's surface through a circle overhead. Outside the circle, all that the fish—or a human diver, for example—can see is a reflection of the stream bottom on the undersurface of the air/water interface. The effect is a little like looking up through a mirror with a round hole in its middle. This is very odd in human terms, being outside the realm of our everyday experience. It's important to realize, however, that for trout it's perfectly normal since no trout has ever experienced anything else.

This phenomenon was first introduced to anglers by Alfred Ronalds in his 1836 classic *Fly Fisherman's Entomology*, in which Ronalds presented some remarkably elegant drawings to illustrate how trout must (at least in part) view things above the surface, such as nearby fishermen. Snel's Circle has subsequently intrigued other fishing writers, too, such as the late Edward Hewitt and Vince Marinaro, both of whom built special aquaria with slanted sides that enabled them to view this phenomenon directly. I've duplicated their experiments with my own tanks, as have a number of other amateur researchers.[3] Since both Hewitt and Marinaro lacked the small computers and sophisticated mathematics needed to fully explore Snel's Circle, a number of questions they raised about its effects on the perceptions of trout have only been answered recently. I'll get into these shortly, but first we need to examine the basics behind the phenomenon.

Assume for this discussion that the water's surface is calm and perfectly flat. Obviously this isn't always the case, and Snel's Circle also applies to a ruffled or choppy surface, but the matter becomes even more complex. The principles in any event are the same. Light rays entering the surface from directly overhead, meaning at 90 degrees above horizontal, are not refracted or bent at all. Relatively little (only about 2 percent) of the light is reflected and most penetrates the surface. As the angle of incident light inclines toward the horizontal, both refraction and reflection increase dramatically; the incoming light is bent at an ever-increasing angle, and less and less light actually penetrates the surface.[4] Although it may be difficult to visualize, the fish's upward vision of objects above the water takes place within a cone-shaped field defined by the refraction and partial reflection of light passing through the surface. The sharp point of this hypothetical cone is located at the fish's eyes, and its internal angle is about 97 degrees. The cone expands upward until it intersects the surface as a circle. Since the internal angle of the cone is constant, the diameter of Snel's

Circle where the cone intersects the surface depends on the depth of the fish. The diameter of the circle—or trout's window—for a fish 3 inches below the surface is a little less than 7 inches, for example. If the fish were deeper, the diameter would be correspondingly greater. The trout's window, by the way, travels with the trout wherever it goes in the stream, unless, of course, the fish is hiding under some object and can't see upward at all.

For anglers not familiar with the concept, it might seem logical to assume the trout can see everything that anyone might see while looking straight through a hole in a mirror from some distance away. It's not that simple. A tall pine tree on the shore, for example, will appear to the trout to be suspended in air near the inside edge of Snel's Circle. This is because light passing from the tree through the air and water to the fish is bent, or refracted, changing the apparent position of the tree. The size of the tree is also distorted because light from the top of the tree is hitting the water at a different angle

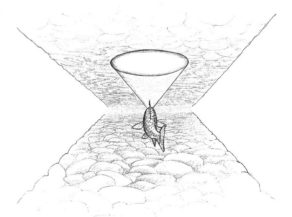

An upward-looking trout sees only the streambed reflected at the surface except for a small area—known as Snel's Circle—directly overhead through which objects above the surface are visible, a phenomenon caused by the refraction and reflection of light.

than light from the much lower bottom of the tree, which means the light rays are both refracted and reflected by different amounts. I'll add once again that when I say "distorted," I mean in human terms, because what's distorted for us is the trout's undistorted view of reality; the trout has never seen things any other way.

Let's go from the pine tree example to the more pertinent case of a mayfly drifting on the surface toward a ready trout. This was the example used by the late Vince Marinaro[5] in his studies along Pennsylvania's Letort Spring Run. For purposes of the rest of this discussion, I'm assuming the trout is 3 inches deep, which by various trigonometric functions determines the other numbers I'll be using. When the fly is 2 feet or more away from the trout, all the trout can see is those parts of the fly in contact with the surface. Usually this is a small, sparkling area created as the fly's legs and abdomen indent the surface tension, which creates a pattern of light reflection and refraction. As the fly drifts closer, the first things visible within the trout's window are those highest above the water—the fly's wingtips. These wingtips appear within the window while the fly itself is still several inches away and seem to be detached from the also visible indentations of the fly's legs on the surface. As the fly drifts still closer, more and more of the wings become visible and they appear closer and closer to the surface indentations of the fly's legs. Finally the fly arrives at the edge of the window, where the fish can see the entire fly. At this point the fly will usually be eaten or rejected, although a fussy trout may drift back with the fly in the current to hold the fly's image at the window's edge for further inspection.

Marinaro correctly noted the importance of dry-fly wings based on his observations, since these together with the light pattern of the insect on the surface are the first things the trout sees. He further demon-

strated that the absence of wings on both natural and artificial mayflies could at least sometimes result in the rejection of both by selective trout. Finally, Marinaro also pointed out that because of light refraction, the trout can see the top and sides of an upright dry fly or a floating natural even though looking at the fly from below.

Marinaro, Hewitt, Ronalds, and others all contributed greatly to an angler's understanding of Snel's Circle, but they all missed the most important factor relating it to selectivity in trout. Marinaro noted, for example, that a trout moves with a drifting fly to keep that fly at the edge of the trout's window during inspection. He explained this by the position of the trout's eyes, noting that the fish can neither see nor eat the fly if it's directly overhead instead of 2 or 3 inches in front of the fish. Marinaro also wrote in 1976:

> The dun [mayfly], riding lightly above the surface film, is never clearly defined at the point where the trout see, inspects, and takes the insect.

With all due respect to his many important fly-fishing contributions, Marinaro was in this case wrong. The trout can see the floating fly with exceptional clarity. Because of the distortion produced by light refraction, a fly floating at the edge of the window is *magnified* in the trout's view. An upright natural fly or an artificial dry fly may appear to the trout two or three times life size! This is truly extraordinary and was discovered only recently.

In the late 1970s, when I was publishing the magazine now called *Fly Rod & Reel*, I received a manuscript describing the magnification phenomenon from Bob Harmon and John Cline, two Chicago-area attorneys with engineering backgrounds who had used intensive mathematical analysis—rather than the intuition that had guided Marinaro—to explore many aspects of the trout's

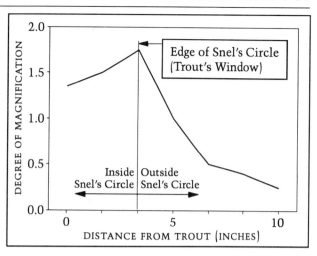

Magnification of a #4 Dry Fly

Apparent—to the trout—magnification of a Size 4 dry fly that's one inch in diameter. Assumes a trout holding 3 inches below the surface, and that the fly is floating upright. Graph adapted from Harmon and Cline (1980). Graph copyright © 1992 by John Merwin.

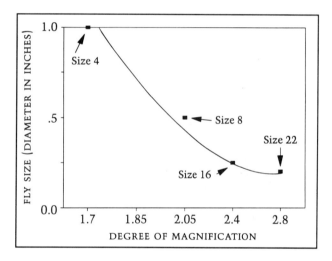

Magnification a Function of Fly Size

Apparent—to the trout—magnification of dry flies at the edge of Snel's Circle (trout's window) varies with fly size as shown. The smaller the fly, the greater the apparent magnification. Assumes conventional-style drys being viewed by a trout holding 3 inches below the surface, and that the fly is floating upright. Graph adapted from Harmon and Cline (1980). Graph copyright © 1992 by John Merwin.

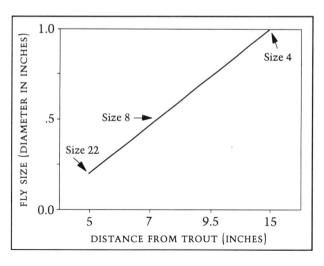

Wing-Tip Visibility Distance

The maximum distance from a trout holding 3 inches deep at which the trout can perceive the wing tips of various size conventional dry flies, assuming the flies are floating upright. Trout, of course, can see the wing tips of any dry fly before the fly itself appears fully within or at the edge of Snel's Circle. Graph adapted from Harmon and Cline (1980.) Graph copyright © 1992 by John Merwin.

window.[6] After more than two years of questions back and forth in the mail, during which time I also had their calculations verified at a local university, I was finally convinced they were right and so published their article describing edge-of-the-window magnification and related phenomena.

Although the article was later picked up and elaborated upon by *Scientific American*, it never really captured the attention of the fly-fishing community, in spite of its obvious importance. Harmon and Cline were able to demonstrate that peak magnification of an upright dry fly occurs precisely at the edge of the trout's window. This is without question the reason why trout are so often seen to inspect a dry fly within a few inches of their nose. Not only does the trout have a binocular view (with both eyes) of the fly at this point, but the fly is also at its largest apparent size. Interestingly, and again because of refraction phenomena, smaller flies are magnified more than large ones. A size 22 dry fly, which is usually less than a quarter of an inch in diameter, appears almost three times life size to a trout 3 inches under the surface when the trout views such a fly at the edge of Snel's Circle. Fishermen are often puzzled by the trout's obvious ability to scrutinize and refuse such small artificial drys, but a large part of the reason should now be apparent. Remember in considering all of this that the trout doesn't know the fly is magnified, and that all upright surface flies—natural or artificial—appear thus to a trout.

Also remember that this whole discussion has nothing to do with what goes on inside a trout's brain, but rather with how the laws of physics affect the visual image that's available to the trout. That portion, if any, of a dry fly that's under the surface isn't affected by the refraction phenomena of Snel's Circle, of course, and as with all subsurface flies we can assume the trout has the same literal view that we do. I have summarized some of

Harmon and Cline's information in three accompanying graphs, which were originally developed with their assistance. Their observations were and are remarkable, for which I hope they get the future credit that's their due.

Dozens of authors have speculated in print about trout selectivity for many years, usually ending their discussion with some sort of qualification to this effect: "Of course, it's actually impossible to see into the mind of a trout." Such qualifications are only partly true. In some respects, it *is* possible to see into the mind of a trout, and sometimes this is done quite literally. It's fairly common, for example, for laboratory researchers to immobilize a living fish and to then insert microelectrodes into a desired area of the fish's brain. An external stimulus is provided, and the response of the brain, if any, can be measured electrochemically in both absolute terms and also in relation to responses to other stimuli. This gives some indication of whether there's any response at all and, if so, how much. It does not, however, describe how the trout deals with the stimulus by taking or not taking some sort of action, which is of more importance to fishermen in trying to understand—and thus predict—the actions of trout.

Behavioral scientists and fishermen both gain their insights into trout behavior and selectivity by their observations of trout in particular circumstances over time. The scientist may use an artificial stream in a laboratory, varying the amounts and proportions of different food items and noting the trouts' response. This has been the approach of Neil Ringler, now of Syracuse University, who has studied and written since the 1970s about selective predation in brown trout.[7] The fisherman confronts the same thing in the wild, as a visible trout is often feeding selectively on one of a number of available food organisms, many of which are often also visible to the fisherman. The fisherman, rather than making the scientist's counts of which trout eats how much of what, finds a fly the trout will accept; usually by the trial-and-error process of changing flies until a particular pattern is found to work, although the trial-and-error process can be greatly reduced by accurate observation and experience. Interestingly, the scientists and the fishermen have in recent years started arriving at the some of the same conclusions.

In many of the numerous studies of natural predation, reference is usually made to something called Optimal Foraging Theory. As a simplified case, this means that a predator—including all trout—will tend to feed in ways that maximize the animal's energetic benefit. This is why, for example, stream trout often hold in slow currents while taking food items from adjacent faster currents. By this mechanism, which you may recall from previous chapters, the trout conserves energy while still obtaining ample food.

Further, the trout should feed in such a way as to get the maximum caloric intake for its effort expended in feeding. This would seem to mean that if large insects and small insects are hatching simultaneously in a particular section of stream and are equally available to the trout, the trout in turn should be feeding primarily on the large ones. This is not always the case, and the examples are legion. In recent weeks, large Hendrickson mayflies have been drifting on the Battenkill's placid currents, unmolested by trout that were feeding avidly on concurrent hatches of much smaller *Paraleptophlebia* duns. Fishermen who had made the trip north specifically for the well-known Hendrickson hatch were moaning about fussy fish, while those few who noted what was happening on the river were scoring consistently with small Blue Quill drys. This

illustrates the so-called masking-hatch[8] phenomenon, in which trout are feeding selectively on smaller, less-apparent flies in the presence of larger ones. This is common on many waters, and the fisherman's response is often confounded by his seeing a trout occasionally taking one of the larger flies, even though most of the fish are feeding on smaller ones. By the angler's stubborn logic—and seemingly by Optimal Foraging Theory—the trout *will* eat the bigger bug. So the fisherman beats the water to a froth in casting a perfect imitation of the larger fly and catches little or nothing. Our fisherman leaves, frustrated, and at the local bar and grill that evening the tale expands, jacking up by yet another notch the trout's reputation for difficulty.

The trout, however, is not so much difficult as misunderstood. Optimal Foraging Theory, which our fisherman has apparently just seen refuted, is generally valid, but like most such theories is considerably modified in practice by the innate behavioral characteristics of the trout themselves. As seen in previous chapters, trout can both learn and remember what they've learned. This faculty combines with the trout's acute sensory capabilities to form the basis for selectivity. In the previous case of a masking hatch, this usually means that a trout that has gained experience in feeding on the smaller fly first is mostly likely to continue doing so and is not likely to switch to the larger fly in the short term. Laboratory experiments have confirmed that it may take a thousand or more exposures over several days to a new, drifting food form before a trout will switch from a familiar item to the new one, even if the new one is more palatable, of greater caloric value, and is present in greater numbers.[9]

Trout fishermen will encounter other reasons that don't exist in laboratories that compound or reinforce such behavior in trout. Variations in habitat from one trout's holding position to another may alter the trout's likelihood of encountering a particular insect in the first place. The trout in a slow-water eddy may not encounter the caddis on which trout are feeding avidly in an upstream riffle, for example. Then, too, some attributes of selectivity may simply be a function of our crowded waters. When you wade into a good-looking pool on a popular trout stream and start fishing with the dry fly recommended at the fly shop down the road, you are generally ignoring what the rising trout have been looking at for the past several days: dozens of fishermen casting with the same fly over the same fish, many of which have been caught and released. If you got hit in the head with a brick every time you reached for a hamburger, after a while you'd become cautious about reaching for hamburgers. So it is with trout. They gain experience, and they learn. The trout may thus feed selectively on the smaller flies in a masking-hatch situation partly because fewer of them have been caught and released during the past few days on imitations of the smaller flies.

A trout's selectivity, then, is a fact of trout-fishing life. It is common to all trout, but will vary considerably in degree according to a wide variety of circumstances. Selectivity is what ultimately confronts the angler who has mastered casting and all the other mechanical aspects of fly fishing for trout. The challenges it produces are central to the sport, and many of these are considered in the remaining chapters of this book.

1. Some readers may recognize this statement as being the old argument about phylogeny versus ontogeny; nature versus nurture commonly expresses the same idea. My contention is that the trout's sensory capabilities that enable selectivity are phylogenetic; trout are born with them. Trout then use those senses in learning to become selective when they start feeding, which makes selectivity *per se* ontogenetic, an acquired

characteristic of the individual, but common within the population. At some point in the ongoing evolution of trout, some aspects of ontogeny may *become* phylogeny. It's been shown that some strains of trout always migrate upstream from a particular waterfall to spawn, for example, and this characteristic has been shown to be phylogenetic; that is, hereditary. Whether or not selectivity has yet become phylogenetic in at least some trout is an interesting concept that I've enjoyed arguing with people like friend Ernest Schwiebert, who has suggested that centuries of angling for brown trout in Europe has made this fish inherently selective as a matter of heredity; more so than other kinds of North American trout that have only been fished over for two hundred years or so. Maybe; and then again, maybe not. I happen to think that selectivity as a trait is too widely variable among individual trout to become itself an inherited characteristic.

2. There are many recent technical references on the physiology of vision in fishes and a few that deal specifically with trout. For simplicity's sake, I've described many characteristics of trout vision in this chapter without heavily end-noting the main text. There are numerous references on fish vision listed in the Bibliography, and interested readers might start with the excellent article "Angling Optics," by J. H. Fenner (1990).

3. See Merwin (1978).

4. Fenner (1990) gives an excellent chart detailing this information in 5-degree increments and based on Snel's Law, by which the relationship between angles of incidence and angles of reflection/refraction can be calculated. Also see any modern text on general physics.

5. See Marinaro (1976).

6. See Harmon and Cline (1980).

7. See the various papers by Ringler cited in the Bibliography. These, in addition to the earlier works by Ware, are the most important modern technical studies describing selective feeding in trout.

8. A term made popular by Doug Swisher and Carl Richards in their 1971 book *Selective Trout*, although the phenomenon has been known by angling writers for more than a century.

9. See Ringler's various papers, most especially Ringler (1975).

PART TWO

THE TOOLS

9
The Modern Fly Rod

I was thinking about whether or not my head hurt worse than my feet, and finally decided it was toss-up. It had been a long day in Denver, trudging up and down the aisles of a fishing-tackle show where manufacturers were displaying the best and brightest of their products for the new season, hoping not only to attract new dealer orders but also to inform the angling press about their wares. The day was ending like many such days over the years, late at night over drinks with friends from distant points, people whose company I've enjoyed for years but seldom see these days except at such national events. There were three of us at the table when the conversation turned to fly rods.

That conversation is worth reporting, but requires anonymity. In the interest of keeping the friendship of my companions, I'll refer to the man who runs a major fly-fishing magazine as "the Editor"; the man who's a nationally known casting instructor as "the Caster"; and myself as "the Writer" for the sake of continuity. The Editor and the Caster were going on at great lengths about how the introduction of graphite as a rod material in the early 1970s had changed fly casting and fly-fishing dramatically. The Writer was tired, had not only heard but had also written about all this more than once, and was mostly just listening.

"The remarkable thing about most graphite fly rods these days is that they can handle a whole range of different line sizes," the Caster said. The Editor nodded sagely. The Caster went on to explain his feeling that some modern graphite fly rods could be made to perform equally well with a variety of line weights rather than only with the single weight for which the rod was specifically designed and rated. The Writer, disagreeing with this, pricked up his ears but kept silent. The argument at the moment didn't seem worth the effort.

The topic quickly changed to modern fly lines as the Editor asked the Caster if he didn't agree that the weight-range tolerances used by line manufacturers were too broad. "Oh, yeah. Those guys [line makers] are really screwing around with the weight of a given size line. You know a five-weight line is supposed to fall within a certain weight range, but those guys miss it sometimes. They really need better quality control," the Caster answered.

At this the Writer quit listening and rose much like B'rer Rabbit from the briar patch as he confronted Fox and Bear. "C'mon, you guys! You can't have it both ways. If your graphite rod can handle a wide range of line weights equally well, then a manufacturer's line-weight variation doesn't make any difference. If your fly rod will only give optimal performance with a specific line weight, then the line-weight variation might be significant." The Writer smiled. The Editor and the Caster both squirmed in their chairs.

"Well, I don't really believe that," the Caster said after a long silence.

"You don't really believe what?" The Writer showed no mercy.

"The part about rods handling different line weights equally well," the Caster answered. In the Writer's recollection, the conversation then continued along more reasonable lines to a very unreasonable hour, at which time we again parted friends.

Discussions about the design and action of fly rods have consumed and confused fisherman for more than a century. One might suppose some standards to have been reached in all this time, but that's not the case. For one thing, even modern manufacturers have refrained from joining forces to produce a set of definitions that would be helpful to consumers. Most makers will in fact say that such definitions are unobtainable, although I'm not sure that's true. For another, certain aspects of rod design and use are subjective, depending on how a rod "feels" to an individual user, which may be somewhat different than how it "feels" to another. Fly-rod action is thus like a tar baby; even the best of experts can become hopelessly entangled while trying to explain it.

We'll try in this chapter to extract some meaning from what's usually a black, gooey mess of conflicting terms and ideas. First, though, I want to offer a very basic idea that's become my personal yardstick over the years for measuring fly-fishing gear. The late A. J. McClane was best known through his long tenure as fishing editor of *Field & Stream* magazine, where he showed an uncanny ability to express reams of complex argument in a simple sentence or two. In 1965 after writing several thousand words on the characteristics of various fly rods, Al, who died in 1991, added this:

> The important thing in putting together an outfit is not to look for a line that will sail across the wide Missouri or a rod that will toss a lead sinker over the post office, but a modest set of tools designed to baffle a trout lying in plain sight.[1]

Any discussion of fly rods is inevitably linked to fly casting. Only in being cast does a fly rod seemingly come to life, bending and unbending in characteristic ways that reflect the rod's design and construction. The motions of an experienced caster seem almost effortless to any observer who sees a long, smooth loop of line unroll gracefully and drop gently to the water. It looks easy, but it's not. An accomplished fly caster is the result of years and years of practice, study, and muscle training. However, a beginner can be taught quickly to make casts that are adequate for the immediate satisfaction of catching a few trout, just as I can pick up a golf club or tennis racquet and immediately hit a ball even though I play neither sport. Many people limit their lives in such sports to just that sort of immediacy, which is fine to the extent that they're satisfied with it. Many others, however, want to know more, and in our case that includes a study of fly rods.

A fly rod is a flexible lever. That's a simple definition that may help you to conceptualize what a fly rod is and how it works, but a sharp-eyed reader will realize that we're in trouble even as we begin. In casting, the entire rod from the butt to the tip is being moved as it bends and unbends through the casting stroke. The rod thus has a number of dynamic properties that extend far beyond the idea of a basic lever. But for the moment, at least, let's stick with the simple definition: A fly rod is a flexible lever that's used to unroll a long weight—the fly line—through the air in a controlled manner.[2]

Intrinsic to this concept is what happens to the fly rod when it's used in casting. The object, of course, is to extend the fly line, leader, and fly in a more or less straight path from the fisherman to a distant fish. The fly rod, by virtue of its length, multiplies the motion of the caster's hand and arm. There are many examples in other sports of the same principle. The end of a baseball bat, a golf club, or a tennis racquet is traveling much faster than the hands that swing it. Nor is the idea a new one. Prehistoric man used the same technique to increase his spear-throwing efficiency with a primitive device called an adlatyl. This early gadget was made of bone or wood and was a foot or two long, with a socket at one end to support the spear butt. It effectively increased the length of the spear-throwing arm, enabling spears to be thrown with higher velocity and thus more killing power. While it's a long way from the hunters of woolly mammoths to the users of modern fly rods, some of the principles used are the same.

The motion of the caster's hand—and, consequently, the rod—takes place in two ways simultaneously. First, the hand and forearm are moved back forth in a more or less straight line. This helps to give an outward, straight-line impetus to the unrolling fly line while increasing the distance over which the rod tip and line are accelerated in casting. If, however, you hold a fly rod upright in your hand while moving your hand back and forth in a straight line, you'll immediately notice that the entire rod from butt to tip is traveling at the same speed as your hand. No mechanical advantage is obtained in this manner, and casting in this way is almost, if not completely, impossible. Speed and acceleration are obtained when the rod is rotated or moved through an arc. If you again hold your rod upright but at a slight angle to the rear, then rotate the rod forward to a slight angle in front, you'll see that while your hand has moved only a few inches, the end of the rod has moved several feet. Your hand and the tip of the rod have both moved through the same arc in the same time interval, but the tip of the rod has moved at a much greater speed.

At this point we have the tip of the rod moving through an arc or traveling in a circular path. This will likewise move the line in a circular path through the air, which we've already decided we don't want to happen. We want the line to go straight. In order for the rod tip and line to travel in a straight path, the rod has to bend in casting. This bending and unbending through the casting stroke is what translates the rotary motion of the caster's hand to the linear motion of the rod tip and line. This is part of what the caster feels as the rod is moved to propel the line. This is fly-rod action.

There's an old adage in fly casting by which beginners are advised to relax, to slow their casting-stroke timing, and "to let the rod do the work." Modern writers have correctly pointed out, however, that the rod does little if any work and that the impetus given the line in casting comes from the caster's physical effort as increased by the mechanical advantage offered by the rod. For example, Vince Marinaro in his wonderful 1976 book *In the Ring of the Rise* described an experiment by Robert Crompton, who had achieved a minor notoriety as a rodmaker in the years surrounding World War II:

> I have mentioned that old saw about "letting the rod do the work." The idea still prevails. The rod cannot make a cast any more than a baseball bat can hit a home run by itself. It is the caster's own muscle and energy that makes the cast. The rod, because of its small mass in cross section, cannot store up and release enough energy to make any kind of a cast. Robert Crompton once conducted a public experiment in which an ultrastiff rod was anchored upright in a vise, then the line was drawn backward to create maximum bend in the rod. On being released the line was dragged forward a short distance but could not get past the rod.

In a similar vein, Ed Mosser, a California tournament fly caster, and William Buchman, an engineer, once conducted an extensive analysis and found that approximately 83 percent of the energy in a cast was supplied directly by the caster's stroke and only 17 percent was supplied through stored energy in the springlike action of the unbending rod.[3] These results will vary slightly according to rod material and design, but the principle is immutable: Casters cast; rods don't.

I have often wondered, though, where the business about the rod doing the work came from in the first place. For all the effort that's been spent over the years at debunking this popular myth, I've never seen any attempt to explain how it originated. I did a little experimenting and found that at one time fly rods *did* do some of the work in casting in ways that might be surprising to a new generation of fly casters who have cut their casting teeth on modern graphite rods. I took one of my pet bamboo rods out on the river the other night; an 8½ footer rated for a light, four-weight line. In casting only about 10 feet of line plus an equivalent leader, it was immediately obvious that the weight of the short line—that weight which is nominally cast—was insignificant and was not in and of itself bending the rod during casting. The rod was bending of its own weight when moved back and forth in casting, and this bending happened to move the short line in a satisfactory manner. As I extended greater lengths of line in casting and applied greater loads to the bending rod, I began to feel the weight of the line in the casting cycle. It was still clear, however, that the moving mass of the rod itself was helping to propel the line through the air.[4] This, I believe, is the origin of "letting the rod do the work," although it was and still is quite true that the rod doesn't do anything by itself.

Because graphite as a rod material is so much lighter and stiffer than bamboo, the effect of its mass on the casting cycle is proportionately less, so much so as to be almost insignificant. You can duplicate the old effect, however, with a simple experiment. Wrap some fine lead wire around the tip of your graphite rod and also make a few turns about a foot below the tip. You are thus adding substantially to the rod's suspended weight—that rod weight forward of the grip—and the effect on the rod's casting action will be dramatic.

As a general case, the faster the line unrolls in the air, the more of it can be unrolled before it falls to the water. This means a longer cast, which is achieved through faster line speeds. Line speed is a common fly-casting phrase that's a little misleading because it doesn't mean the whole line is traveling faster through the air; it means the line is unrolling faster. Greater line speeds are in general obtained with stiffer fly rods. Because a rod is stiffer, it can be accelerated more quickly through the casting stroke. This makes the attached line go faster also, and thus more line is unrolled in the air. Some modern graphite rods are designed stiff specifically for high line speeds and distance work. Others are designed to be more flexible, enabling the airborne line to be unrolled more slowly and easily at close fishing distances. Still other designs are a compromise between the two, attempting to be sufficiently flexible for close work yet stiff enough for some distance when needed.

It will be clear to any fisherman of even moderate experience who takes the trouble to test-cast a variety of modern graphite fly rods that those rods do not all perform in the same way. They vary in their manner of bending, a characteristic of rod action that so far we've described as relative stiffness. There's more to it, of course, and as is so often the case in trout fishing the history of this development is the best explanation for its present form.

A couple of things had happened by the 1880s that affected fly-rod design enormously. Tapered fly lines of woven silk were widely available and offered a distinct weight over their long length that could be cast more easily than the earlier and less dense braids of horsehair, linen, or flax. Split-bamboo fly rods had also come into wide production by this time, their manufacture having been pioneered by Charles Murphy in Newark, New Jersey,[5] and subsequently by Hiram Leonard and his disciples in Maine and New York. Bamboo rods could be made stiffer in relation to their weight and length than any previous rods and thus provided the means for casting the new lines with greater efficiency and authority. Coincident with all of this was the growing popularity of dry-fly fishing, which then as now depended on the speed of the airborne line to dry the fly in the air.

F. M. Halford was the British doyen of the dry-fly method in the late nineteenth century, a man who we'll encounter at greater length in later chapters on the dry fly. For the moment, though, consider his surprisingly modern characterization of fly-rod action, as published in 1889:

> The action of a rod must be absolutely true and even in every direction from point to handle. There must be no weak place in it, and at the same time no part which is unduly stiff. It should return quickly. The meaning of this is, that when trying the rods, by imitating the action of casting and forcing the point forwards, thus bending the rod, the point should recover and spring rapidly back to a straight line, and when there it should not vibrate, but quickly regain its point of rest, and remain rigid. This simply means that the elasticity of the whole rod is both uniform and smart, the material of which it is built thoroughly good, and the tapering proportionately carried throughout its length. For dry-fly fishing it certainly should of the two be rather stiff than limber; but at the same time it is not recommended to use a thing like a barge pole, which cannot by any possibility cast lightly or with ease.[6]

Halford's description applies to modern fly rods in every respect. I point this out not only to illustrate some history, but also to make a point about Halford himself. In recent years Halford has become an angling cliché, representing a dogmatic and seemingly blind adherence to the dry-fly method. While some of this is true, it's a very narrow view of one of the greatest fly fishers at the turn of the century.

The late Lee Wulff became famous both before and after the Second World War for using ultralight fly tackle in trout and salmon fishing, urging his fellow anglers to use shorter and lighter fly rods in the interest of greater sport. Wulff was fond of poking holes in Halford's supposed dogma and in our many discussions often used Halford as an example of narrow-mindedness. Yet Halford also took to task the supposed angling masters of his time, men such as the widely published writer Francis Francis, who had said that single-handed trout rods should never be less than 10 feet long and that longer—to 13 feet—was better. Halford defied the conventional wisdom of his time in writing "with a short rod of 9 ft. 6 in., one who knows how to use it can put a fly in the teeth of anything short of a positive hurricane." Shades of Lee Wulff!

Halford, in his description of rod actions, added that "American rods . . . are too whippy . . . and seem generally to lack backbone." He thus began to make a distinction among rod actions that persisted for almost one hundred years and well into the 1970s; that of wet-fly as opposed to dry-fly action. In Halford's time virtually all American trout fishermen were using wet flies; the dry-fly method did not become generally popular here until after about 1910. To keep wet flies wet, meaning to avoid drying them out in casting, and to keep the multiple wet flies commonly used on a single leader from tangling in casting required rods that would flex deeply in use. These so-called wet-fly or soft-actioned rods normally produced a large and open line loop in casting, which unrolled slowly in the air to keep multiple-fly rigs wet and tangle free. This also required a certain kind of casting stroke—characterized by a full roll of the wrist at the end of the cast that places the rod parallel to the water's surface when finished—to keep the line loop wide open in casting and to ultimately place the cast straight on the river's currents. For anything other than wet-fly fishing with a multiple-fly rig, this casting method is relatively inefficient, especially with modern tackle. Interestingly, this came to be known as an eastern casting style because most (but by no means all) wet-fly trout fishing was being done in the eastern United States. Some contemporary fly fishermen still use this style, regardless of the rod they happen to be using, simply because this is the way they were taught by someone who learned it from someone else in a chain of instruction that extends back for almost a century. There are still a few modern graphite rods designed to support this style of casting, which they do well but at the expense of versatility.

As dry-fly fishing gained greater popularity here in the years after the First World War, the need for stiffer rods and the high-speed, narrow casting loops that could be produced in casting such rods became more and more apparent. Because a shorter rod can be moved faster than a long one and, to a point, at least, will help produce higher line speeds, fly rods became shorter, too. So by the 1950s, premium bamboo rods for dry-fly trout fishing

were for the most part between 7 and 8 feet long and stiffer than their often longer wet-fly counterparts. The development of higher line speeds was enabling some casters to cast much farther, a discovery that made line speed itself a goal of some rod designers and competitive fly casters.

Nowhere was this more true than on the West Coast, most especially California in the era between the two world wars. Here rod-makers and tournament casters began to work out designs in bamboo that would make possible the tight, fast loops so essential in casting for distance. Casting technique changed, also. It was gradually found that rapid acceleration of the rod in casting followed by an abrupt stop transmitted the greatest amount of casting energy into the unrolling line. This became known as a western casting style, characterized by an abrupt stop at the end of the forward casting stroke, usually with the rod finishing at some angle above the water and producing a tight, fast unrolling loop of line. Like the more open-loop eastern style, the western style has also persisted. Happily, and because they offer the greatest versatility in fishing, most—but not all—modern graphite rods are designed to be cast in this manner.

All of the fly-rod characteristics I've described were developed in bamboo rods during that material's golden age, which generally extended in this country from the 1870s until the 1960s and the increasingly widespread use of synthetic-fiber (fiberglass and graphite) fly rods. Bamboo rodmaking is by no means a lost art. There are presently between 100 and 150 commercial makers of such rods in this country, most of whom produce a very limited number of rods each year and many of whom make absolutely superb casting and fishing tools. But most fly fishermen most of the time are now using graphite fly rods, so that's where we'll place our descriptive effort.

The designs of most graphite rods are still holdovers from the best days of bamboo. This may sound odd because the materials are so different, but remember that a great deal of a rod's performance depends as much on its design as it does on the materials from which it's made. It's just as possible, for example, to build a stiff, fast-casting bamboo rod as it is to build a very flexible, soft-casting graphite rod. The introduction and wide use of fiberglass rods in the 1950s was quickly supplanted by graphite during the 1970s, and in both cases most of the major rod designers were those who had started their careers in bamboo.

Let's consider a couple of examples of what happened in the transition. There was one well-known eastern maker whose slow-actioned and very popular bamboo rods were characterized by relatively stiff, thick rod tips. This design accomplished a couple of things. The relatively thick tips broke less often than the thinner tips of other makers, so the company had fewer returns for repairs. Also the weight of the thicker rod tip kicked over hard as the rod unbent at the end of a casting stroke, and the momentum developed by that suspended rod-tip weight helped to propel the line. Here was a relatively slow-actioned rod that was perfectly suited to an eastern casting style. When the company, which still makes these bamboo rods, began to design and sell graphite rods, it quite naturally attempted to duplicate some earlier design successes. Thus their graphite rods were made with relatively stiff tips that forced the rod's bending action into the lower portions of the rod's length. Here again was a rod well suited to an eastern casting style, although the added effect of the heavy tip's kicking over was lost simply because

the comparative weight and resultant momentum of the graphite itself was so much less than that of bamboo. This particular company still makes graphite rods of this design, although they've since started making other designs in order to remain competitive as much of the country is tending toward what was at first a western casting style.

With a few notable exceptions, including the company I just described, every present-day American maker of graphite rods has at one time or another drawn upon the design influence of West Coast casters. What's evolved is what my old California friend Mel Krieger, widely known as a casting instructor and who counts present world champion Steve Rajeff among his former students, aptly calls a progressive action. There are various descriptions of progressive. Remembering that rod action describes the way in which a rod bends, a progressive-actioned rod bends

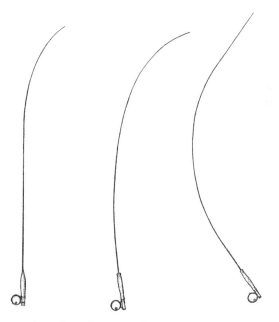

Modern fly-rod actions, left to right: tip action, progressive action, and butt action.

more in the tip than in the middle. The middle, in turn, bends more than the butt. Krieger applies the term "progressive" to the way in which the rod bends when cast with increasing lengths of line. On a short cast, the tip bends and allows the caster to feel even the weight of a short length of line. On a longer cast and under a greater load, the rod bends down into its middle. On still longer casts and under maximum loads, the rod bends well down into the butt section.

Most, but not all, graphite rods are now made with some form of progressive action. By this you may correctly infer that not all progressive actions are the same. This is in fact the case and would seem at first glance to make things awfully complicated. All you have to remember, however, is that this action can be designed in rods that are slow, medium, and fast.

As new forms of graphite fiber that were increasingly stiffer[7] became available over the past dozen years or so, many rod companies started making stiffer and stiffer—meaning faster-actioned—fly rods. In most cases, these were progressive-actioned rods in which the tip bent more than the middle, which bent more than the butt. While the relative proportions of the rod's bending sequence were maintained, overall stiffness was increased. This required faster casting strokes and produced higher line speeds, hence greater distance.

Over the last three or four years, most of the major rod companies have started to offer at least two types of progressive-actioned rods. There are those that are extremely stiff, require a fast casting stroke, and which will rocket a line to the end of almost any casting pool. While these allow plenty of distance in casting, this usually comes at the expense of delicacy for close work. The relatively fast casting stroke required by these rods is very demanding of a caster's timing because everything in the casting cycle is happening very quickly. This can make such rods difficult to cast well and is also tiring when multiplied over the hundreds of casts often made in a day astream. Partly in response to such complaints, many of the same rod companies now offer among their newer rods those that are either moderate-progressive or, in a few cases, slow-progressive in action. In such cases the advanced materials used in fast-progressive rods have been tamed into designs that are more flexible and softer, affording delicacy at normal fishing ranges of about 60 feet or less and being substantially less tiring to cast for hours on end. For the thoughtful trout fisherman who prefers moderation to pure muscle, such rods are an obvious choice.

The graphite fiber used in fishing rods came to us with the space age, having been first developed in England during the mid-1960s. Its use in American-made fly rods officially began with the introduction of a few graphite models at an American Fishing Tackle Manufacturer's Association trade show in 1973. Since that time a wide variety of graphite fibers has been developed by the aerospace industry, with varying characteristics of stiffness (modulus), tensile strength, and so forth that have and do play assorted roles in rod construction. Graphite fibers imbedded in a resin matrix, such as various epoxies much like the glue you can buy at a hardware store, are immensely strong; much stronger than steel or most other metals, for example, and substantially lighter. Such graphite-composite materials are primarily used as flat laminates in aerospace work, of which the wings on Stealth aircraft are one example. Interestingly, when defense and aerospace contractors need graphite-tubing technology, they often now turn to some fishing-rod manufacturers because much of the tubing technology has been refined in the course of making fishing rods. This same tubing technology has been applied by some rodmakers to such things as golf-club and ski-pole shafts, plus high-tech bicycle frames. Within this technology is the relatively simple key to the way in which graphite-rod actions are determined.

Raw graphite fibers are obtained by partially burning acrylic yarns at extremely high temperatures in special ovens, which leaves the fibers with a high percentage of carbon. There are a number of variables in this process that can be controlled, which allow graphite fibers of different characteristics to be manufactured. These hanks of yarn are then bounced up and down through a series of combs on a collimating machine that spreads the individual fibers more or less evenly in a single layer within a broad, thin ribbon of resin. The result is a flat, black material, about .005 inch thick, that looks a little like a rough linoleum floor covering. This called graphite pre-preg in the manufacturer's jargon. The graphite fibers themselves are about .0003 inch in diameter, and the evenness of their distribution within the matrix is critical. Any uneven fiber orientation will eventually show up as unevenness in a finished rod, a serious problem that has often led to an expensive and high rejection rate of material by premium fly-rod makers.

Rodmakers cut long, tapered patterns—called flags—from the flat pre-preg, and wrap these flags tightly around equally long, tapered steel mandrels. This assembly is then tightly wrapped with spirals of a tape that shrinks when heated, compressing the graphite-resin flag even more tightly against the underlying mandrel. The whole business is then heat cured in a large oven. This liquefies and then cures and solidifies the resin matrix. The steel mandrel is then withdrawn with the help of a very powerful hydraulic ram, and a rough rod blank is the result.

There are many variables in this process, almost all of which pertain in some way to rod action. Because the flag is tapered before being wrapped over the mandrel, there are usually more graphite fibers in those larger diameter sections that get the most wraps. This makes those sections stiffer. Correspondingly, fine-diameter tip sections typically get fewer wraps as their diameter decreases. These sections bend more easily. Thus the shape of the rodmaker's pattern or flag has a great deal to do with the action of a finished rod. Also, because the rodmaker is working from a consistent pattern, a particular rod can be made in large numbers with relative ease once the rod's manufacturing parameters have been determined.

Because the rod is a hollow, tapered tube, the relative stiffness of its various sections is also determined by its diameter. Other things being equal, a larger diameter tube is stiffer than one of smaller diameter. Thus fly rods have butts that are larger in diameter—hence stiffer—than their fine-diameter tips. The way in which diameter changes along the length of the rod also contributes to its action, of course, and rodmakers often design

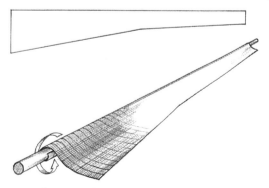

In making graphite rods, a tapered pattern is cut from a flat sheet of a graphite-fiber and resin matrix. The pattern is then rolled tightly around a steel mandrel and heat-cured. Rod action is partly determined by the shapes of both pattern and mandrel.

their mandrels with complex tapers to achieve a desired result. A hollow tube will tend to collapse across its diameter when bent with any force, and the forces of compression within a rod while casting or fighting a fish are enormous. Rodmakers are thus concerned with hoop strength, meaning the rod's ability to resist compression across its diameter. The resin matrix provides the basic resistance to this force, and different rodmakers invariably add a thin layer of reinforcing material—called scrim—that's at least partly oriented around the rod-blank's diameter in addition to the longitudinal graphite fibers in the resin matrix that help to govern the rod's action in the first place.

What we then have is a series of manufacturing steps that can be altered by a rodmaker seeking a particular sort of rod action: the selection of a graphite pre-preg according to the characteristics of its fibers, including stiffness and tensile strength, as well as the characteristics of the underlying resins; mandrel design, the complex tapers of which determine the rate of change of the rod's diameter over its length and hence its stiffness at any given point; and flag design, which determines the distribution and orientation of graphite fibers within the rod. All of these things can and do vary from maker to maker and from one rod model to another. If that's not enough to give you at least a minor headache, rodmakers also have another variable that makes all the difference. This is essentially the combination of their intuition and experience.

Some years ago I made a point of researching various theories on fly-rod actions and published a variety of articles on the topic by myself and others. For one of these, I asked Dave Engerbretson, the well-known western angling writer, to interview several rodmakers and casting authorities on that topic.[8] As expected, we found that most of the authorities disagreed with one another most of the

time. That's one reason why there are so many different kinds of fly rods. I think one of the most telling comments we got came from Jim Green, a well-known and highly skilled caster and rod designer. Green is one of those western caster/designers to whom I referred earlier as being seminal in the development of what's become the widely accepted progressive action in fly rods. As he told us about ten years ago:

> The thing a rod company has to sell is its own action. A rod designer can never please everybody, so he picks the one [rod action] that feels right to him. I can cast any rod, but I like one where I don't have to compensate for the design flaws. I pick it up, and it just seems to cast well. You can compensate for rod-design problems with the casting, but these aren't comfortable rods to cast. The idea that I try to build into a rod is that it always feels good regardless of the distance I'm casting.

For all the high-tech aspects of modern rod construction, it's still an empirical process. Green, who is less active professionally these days but still consulting, experimented with the design of a rod until it *felt* right. Because his rod actions were essentially based on his feel, they tended to be consistent from rod model to rod model unless he set out to deliberately create something different. This consistency of feel among various rod models within a particular brand is characteristic of most rod companies, and all such companies have found their advocates among anglers. But what feels right to one rodmaker doesn't necessarily feel right to another, which continues to lead to variations in rod actions among different makers. In the final analysis, *feel* is everything. This is why you should *never* buy a fly rod without actually casting it first.

The future of fly rods is changing, but slowly. There doesn't seem to be anything in anyone's crystal ball as dramatic as was the initial change from fiberglass to graphite twenty years ago. Largely because of the growth of various national fly-fishing media that's taken place during the same interval, the attention gained by new rod models is both immediate and widespread. The marketing of fly rods has thus become much like that of cars; many makers feel compelled to have at least a few new models to introduce with each new angling season. In recent years, the most apparent result has been more different fly rods than ever in the marketplace. Fly rods have consequently become more specialized in terms of both action and their intended use, which is all to the good in that fishermen have more rod choices than ever.

One long-term change you're likely to see is a switch from thermosetting resins in graphite rodmaking to thermoplastic materials. Thermosetting resins such as the epoxies presently used can be "worked" only once; after the material is heat cured, it can't be further manipulated. Thermoplastic materials, in contrast, can be reworked over and over again by simply reheating them. According to one company whose western rod shop I recently visited, this will not only add greater flexibility to the manufacturing process, but the different physical properties of some new thermoplastics may also become as important in rod-action design as the graphite fibers themselves. Specifically, such materials may give rebirth to solid as opposed to tubular rods, a concept that failed in the 1950s because the rods it produced were too heavy for their lengths.

Another change that's already started to happen is a general reduction in the diameter of graphite fly rods. This is enormously important, but little appreciated by most fishermen. When you move a fly rod rapidly through the air in casting, a good part of the effort on every cast goes to overcome air resistance and atmospheric drag on the rod. If you imagine a 9-foot rod having a ⅜-inch diameter butt as a long, thin, flat triangle, for example, the rod's surface area is about 20 square inches. The effort involved in waving something of this size through the air all day is perhaps now more obvious. The rod, of course, is a round tube and not a flat triangle, so the characteristics of air resistance and drag are somewhat different.

Fishermen as a rule don't understand this simply because they've never experienced anything other than the feel they have in casting their customary rod. A number of years ago I was able to cast and fish with a series of boron-fiber rods designed and built by Don Phillips of Connecticut. Boron fibers are similar to and slightly heavier than graphite and enjoyed a brief popularity among rodmakers in the early 1980s. Phillips pioneered their use starting in 1972, building solid (as opposed to tubular) boron fly rods of his own design in limited quantities for several years. Because Phillips' rods are solid, their diameters are extremely small—as much as 30 percent smaller at the rod butt, for example. Casting these rods was a revelation I found hard to believe. The ease with which these fine-diameter rods could be cast was amazing, primarily because air resistance was so much reduced. I really felt somewhat like a man on the moon, making giant leaps in an area of greatly reduced gravity.

While boron eventually fell out of favor as a rod material because the newer graphite fibers are just as stiff, and lighter and often less expensive, these same new graphites are allowing a gradual reduction in rod diameters. For one thing, because the graphite material is stiffer, less of it is needed to make a rod blank of equivalent stiffness. For another, the new graphites are also able to be used as scrim materials, which in conjunction with new and stronger resins allows for smaller tube diameters that are still strong enough to withstand the stresses of casting. Air resistance and drag are reduced as a result. This means that higher line speeds can be obtained with stiffer rods, and more importantly that even moderate- to slow-actioned rods can be cast more efficiently and with less effort.

1. See Merwin, ed. (1988).

2. There are three contemporary writers who have analyzed fly-rod action and performance at length: Ed Mosser, Don Phillips, and Ernest Schwiebert, all of whose works are cited in the Bibliography. Mosser's 1980 article on fly-casting dynamics is especially important, being one of the most lucid explanations I've encountered.

3. See Mosser and Buchman (1980).

4. This effect is obviously variable even among bamboo rods, according to their design. The rod I happened to be using has a relatively stiff, heavy tip that accentuated the effect I described. I have other bamboo rods with very fine, delicate tips that bend easily when casting a short line and behave in a very different manner.

5. Murphy was the first to successfully make and market split-bamboo rods in this country, although he certainly didn't invent them. That honor is often given Samuel Phillipe, a Pennsylvania gunsmith, who was apparently building such rods by the 1850s, even though much of this art's initial development had taken place earlier in England. It was Murphy, however, who gave the design its first commercial success in the 1860s. Murphy was eventually overshadowed by Hiram Leonard, who first copied Murphy's designs and then added his own genius to the art of rodmaking through the turn of the century.

6. See Halford (1889).

7. Graphite fiber stiffness is usually expressed in terms of modulus of elasticity, a number derived through a complex formula that expresses material stiffness in pounds per square inch. Modern rodmakers may thus refer to the graphite used in their rods as having a modulus (meaning modulus of elasticity) of 33 million (psi.) in the case of lower-modulus rods, or more than 50 million in the case of high-modulus rods. In the heat of competition, rod companies have beaten the modulus question to death in recent years: "My modulus is bigger than your modulus!" This sort of infantile advertising seems happily to be on the wane, and rodmakers are turning instead to better descriptions of their rod actions, which are much more helpful to potential users and customers.

8. See Engerbretson (1982).

10
Some Notes on Fly Lines

Peacock Alley in New York's Waldorf Astoria Hotel is a nice place for lunch, or so I thought at the time. The time was the early 1950s, and I was a young boy on his first solo trip, having taken the train in from Connecticut to visit a favorite aunt. She had long before escaped the family's rural routes, married a Greek artist, and was living what I knew in my own young mind to be the high life in New York. We had worked out the agenda several weeks before. Yes, she would meet my train at Grand Central. Yes, she would take me to lunch at the Waldorf, which I knew only as a kind of salad but desperately wanted to see. And yes, she would take me to Abercrombie & Fitch. The fishing-tackle department.

I don't remember much about lunch, except its hushed elegance and the hotel lobby seeming bigger and grander than life. Abercrombie & Fitch was another matter. This large Manhattan store, which finally folded in the late 1960s as I recall, was more than just a sporting-goods store; it was an institution. I had done enough reading by that time to believe that Abercrombie's was *it*; the skimpy tackle selections of our rural hardware stores would no longer suffice. My meager life savings were folded into a carefully buttoned-down wallet. I was ready.

This goggle-eyed kid dragged his poor aunt for hours through floors and floors of the world's best sporting goods. There were elephant's feet made into low ottomans that I got to try carefully after getting permission.

Real elevators with polite men who asked quietly where we wanted to go next. A gun room so awesomely elegant that I was frightened to go in and look beyond the door. Jack O'Connor, the great gun writer, whose columns I was reading in those years, undoubtedly shopped here, and I kept my eyes peeled for a face made familiar by magazine pictures. Finally we made it to fishing tackle.

I stood surrounded by a dream come true. There were rows and rows of shining fly reels from England in a long glass case. Bamboo rods shone like dull gold against the green felt of their rack behind the counter. Beautiful wooden cases with glass tops held thousands of flies, more than I had imagined could ever exist. If Ray Bergman, the wonderful writer whose 1938 book *Trout* I had by then read several times, happened to walk through, I wondered if I'd have the courage to say hello. Sure I would. I was a fisherman! This thought steadied me a little, and I started shopping.

I picked out one of the then-new fiberglass fly rods that fit my price range, a two-piece 7-footer that I still have and value for its A&F label. I found my first fly-fishing vest, one that had been designed not long before by Lee Wulff for manufacture under the Masland label. After checking all the prices on a rack of English fly boxes, I picked out a little Wheatley with a small lid on each internal compartment. I had a new Herter's HCH floating line at home that I knew would fit the rod, but I wanted one of the new sinking lines, too. When I set my things on a countertop, a gray-haired clerk came over to help.

"I'd like a double-tapered, sinking fly line, please. An HDH," I said as loudly as I could muster through a very dry throat.

"Well, sure. What size line does your rod normally—"

"It's rated for HCH, so I need a size smaller for sinking," I interrupted.

He reached under the counter, found the right line, and placed it with my things. "There you are, son. You know your stuff." He smiled.

I puffed up bigger than a boss rooster, paid my bill, and left with my aunt in tow. It was train time, so with hugs and kisses and admonitions she got me aboard. The long ride home after dark was an endless clatter of wheels on the New Haven, punctuated by the conductor's cries for Port Chester, Greenwich, Westport, and other towns on the way. Commuters in dark suits buried their heads in the evening papers while this small boy sat in the rear of a rail car, clicking the lids of a Wheatley fly box open and shut. Open and shut.

Old and New Fly-Line Sizes

CURRENT WEIGHT-FORWARD SIZE	OLD LETTER SIZE
WF3	IFG
WF4	HFG
WF5	HEG
WF6	HDG
WF7	HCF
WF8	GBF
WF9	GAF
WF10	GAAF
WF11	GAAAF
WF12	GAAAAF

Fly-line sizes at the time of the trip I just described were a mess. While fly rods were (and still are) being designed to cast a particular weight of line, the lines themselves were being sized and sold by their diameter instead of their weight. This made it extremely difficult to match a particular rod with the right line. That's why in the previous example I bought an HDH sinking line for a HCH-rated rod; the sinking line was heavier for its diameter, so an equivalent weight could only be realized by using a smaller size. The letter designations referred to line diameter. My HDH line was thus a double-tapered line with a .045 inch diameter (size D) midsection tapering to .025 inches (size H) at either end. I'll describe the vastly different modern system of fly-line sizes shortly, but first should point out that you'll encounter this archaic letter size system in all fly-fishing books written before the early 1960s. As a matter of historical interest and as an aid to understanding older books you might read, I've included a chart relating the old letter system to the modern numerical system.

The letter size system became a fly-line standard during the silk-line era, which generally extended from the 1870s through the 1950s. Because manufacturers were using the same material—braided silk—one maker's size D line weighed about the same as another maker's size D line, for example, even though the designation was based on diameter and not weight. After World War II, various synthetic materials such as nylon and vinyl came to be used in fly lines. These materials don't weigh the same as silk, of course, but the old system of sizing by diameter continued unchanged.

Myron Gregory of California was an active tournament caster from the mid-1940s until 1961, during which time he held a variety of casting titles. He was also an enthusiastic tackle-tinkerer and angling historian who was famous among his correspondents—of which I was one in later years—for his voluminous, single-spaced typewritten letters on a wide variety of fishing topics. Before he died in 1978, Myron's primary interests seemed to be lines and casting. He, more than anyone, was responsible for the 1960s change to a modern fly-line size system. I once worked with Myron in developing a magazine article about fly lines,[1] in which he described the possible origins of the letter size system:

> Exactly when, by whom, and why the letter system was established as a standard is still a well-hidden secret. I don't blame anyone for keeping the secret; whoever started the deal must have done so as a joke. While the letter-size standard came to refer to actual size, its major initial purpose was to establish a breaking-strength standard. As late as 1936, for example, B. F. Gladding advertised their "Saline" fly-casting "G" line as testing eighteen pounds. A possible clue . . . as to how the size and letter standard got its start may be found in an article by an Edward Chitty, published in 1839. He wrote that the thickness of the line should be about "the thickness of the 'D' string in the third octave in your sister's harp (to measure which, borrow her string gauge)."

In 1958, Gregory contacted some officers of the American Fishing Tackle Manufacturers' Association (AFTMA), asking if they'd establish a new fly-line standard based on line weight since the old dimensional standard had become meaningless. AFTMA quickly agreed and formed a committee, of which Gregory was not a formal member,[2] but on which he almost certainly exerted the greatest influence.

The end result was a numerical designation standard that defines fly lines by the weight in grains of their first 30 feet, regardless of diameter or type (such as floating or sinking). The 30-foot dimension is measured exclusive of any level front tip on a tapered line. This system was adopted by AFTMA in 1960, first appeared on fly-line labels in 1961, and has remained essentially unchanged ever since. It was—and is—finally possible for a fisherman to easily match fly rods and fly lines according to the labels on each. The lightest available line under this system is arbitrarily called a one-weight, the first 30 feet of which weighs a nominal 60 grains with a permissible (by AFTMA standards) range of 54 to 66 grains. Line weights progress through two, three, four, and so on up to a twelve-weight, the first 30 feet of which nominally weighs 380 grains with a 368- to 392-grain range.[3] Once again, I've provided a chart with these dimensions and also included the ounce equivalents for the respec-

Modern AFTMA Fly-Line Standards

DESIGNATED LINE SIZE	NOMINAL GRAIN (OUNCE*) WEIGHT OF FIRST 30 FEET	PERMISSIBLE RANGE (GRAINS)
1	60 (0.14)	54–66
2	80 (0.18)	74–86
3	100 (0.23)	94–106
4	120 (0.28)	114–126
5	140 (0.32)	134–146
6	160 (0.37)	152–168
7	185 (0.43)	177–193
8	210 (0.48)	202–218
9	240 (0.55)	230–250
10	280 (0.64)	270–290
11	330 (0.76)	318–342
12	380 (0.87)	368–392

* Ounce conversions based on one avoirdupois ounce equaling 437.5 grains.

tive grain weights, which will probably make the actual weights easier for most people to visualize.

Fly lines are also made in varying taper configurations and are designed to float, sink, or, in the case of special floating lines built with sinking tips, to do both. There's also a special, very-slow-sinking line that can be made to float if a silicone-based line dressing is applied. This is called an intermediate line. Under the AFTMA system, all lines are now labeled according to their taper configuration, their weight, and their behavior on or in the water. Most of these lines are about 90 feet long, more or less, depending on the model and maker. A level (no taper), five-weight, floating line is thus labeled L5F. A double-tapered, four-weight floater is a DT4F. A weight-forward taper, six-weight sinking line is a WF6S, while a floating version is a WF6F. The same line in an intermediate version is a WF6I. A floating version of the same line with a special sinking tip—commonly now called a sink-tip line—is a WF6F/S.

There are a couple of other designations you may encounter. One is for what's variously called a single-taper, shooting-taper, shooting-head line, or simply "head." These are used in distance casting and, just as important, for ease in quickly changing from one line to another. Shooting heads are usually about 30 feet long, tapered at the front like a normal line, and with a loop at the untapered rear end for attachment of a special, small-diameter running line. We'll talk more about shooting heads later in this chapter, but for the time being remember that their designation is ST—an eight-weight, sinking head is thus a ST8S. The second is the Triangle Taper, a novel line developed by Lee Wulff a few years ago in which the line tapers continuously from a fine tip up through an increasingly thick belly through its first 40 feet. A single such line is designed

to be used on rods of two different weight ratings. Thus a TT4/5F is a floating Triangle Taper line designed for four- and five-weight rods, being a four-weight in its first 30 feet and the equivalent of a five-weight over its first 40 feet. All of the foregoing should help you make some sense of the many line labels you'll see on the shelves of a well-stocked fly shop. It also all falls under what's commonly called the AFTMA System, although I hope someday the powers that be at AFTMA will rename the whole business the Gregory System, which would be a fitting tribute to the man who pushed the idea in the first place.

Before getting further into the various types of fly lines and how they're used, I want to backtrack a little for a look at how the lines are manufactured, followed by a look at how all fly lines perform in the air. Some knowledge of these areas has not only extended my own appreciation of modern lines, but also my ability to use them effectively; likewise it may be helpful to you.

Again according to Myron Gregory, the first plastic, polyvinylchloride (PVC), coated line was made in 1946 by the Rain-Beau Line Company, using a tapered core made of fiberglass filaments. Leon Chandler, who recently retired after fifty years with upstate New York's Cortland Line Company, has told me that Cortland was probably the first to really popularize synthetic lines with its 333-brand versions introduced in 1952. These lines, too, were made with a plastic coating, but over a hollow, tapered core of braided nylon to help make the line float. Although the design was popular, the hollow core eventually soaked up water, which made the line sink. At about the same time, Leon Martuch and Clare Harris, who had begun a small Michigan tackle company called Scientific Anglers (SA in streamside jargon) in 1946, were experimenting with plastic line coatings. Martuch's son once told me that his father was literally dunking hanks of line-core material in various plastics on the kitchen table and heat curing the results in the kitchen stove, trying to find a better fly line. Eventually Martuch and Harris developed a mechanism by which a braided, level core line was dragged through liquid plastic and then through a die with a variable opening. Changing the die's opening changed the resultant line diameter, allowing Martuch to make tapered lines and to control the line's weight at any point by changing the coating thickness. This basic process—a tapered coating over a level core—is the foundation of all modern fly lines and is still used today.

Martuch's early lines were technical marvels, but they didn't float very well, if at all. It was also Martuch who first solved this problem by applying microballoon technology to fly lines. By incorporating these tiny, hollow spheres into the liquid plastic coating, it was possible to vary the line's specific gravity. Martuch, who died in 1975, had quite literally invented the modern, floating fly line. He patented these developments in 1960 and 1962, and for the many years until the patents expired, other linemakers, including Cortland, made most of their fly lines (with their own proprietary changes) under license from Scientific Anglers. SA was bought in 1973 by 3M, which continues to develop and market lines under the SA name. These two companies—Cortland and SA—now produce the vast majority of the world's fly lines, both under their own labels and those of others.

Starting in the 1970s, an intense battle for market share developed between these two companies that has had and continues to have many distinct benefits for fly fishermen everywhere. In an effort to attract more customers, each company started developing and marketing ever-increasing numbers of specialized lines. There were suddenly lines specifically for saltwater fly fishing, for bass fly-fishing, slow-sinking lines for trout, fast-sinking lines for trout, stiffer lines for distance casting, lines with more sophisticated tapers and coatings—the list has become almost endless. Brad Jackson, who writes authoritatively about fly-fishing from his West Coast base, recently compiled a list of available sinking fly lines[4] in which I counted eight-five *different* lines, a number that would be even greater if multiplied by the available line weights!

The act of fly casting unrolls a fly line in the air. This much is self-evident to anyone who's learned to cast, but very few people are really aware of how and why this happens. I am very much in debt for my own understanding of this to Ed Mosser, a California caster and writer who some years ago was kind enough to send me some of his research materials on fly-casting mechanics.[5] By the end of this particular section, you should understand:

- Why fly lines are tapered at their end.
- What the taper does in casting and presenting the fly.
- Why different lines have different tapers, and how to choose among them.

That sounds like a tall order even as I write it, but it's really not all that complicated.

We'll begin with the start of a forward cast. This explanation is independent of fly-rod length or line size, so just assume we're using a rod and a normal floating fly line with some taper at its front end and with a normal leader and fly attached. I'm saying "we" in this example, by the way, because I'd like to keep you and myself both involved, although obviously only one of us is casting at a time.

At the start of the forward cast, the whole rod is tipped somewhat to our rear, and the fly line has just about straightened in the air behind us as the result of our backcast. The amount of line that's extended in the air is the only line available for the cast; we're not going to be releasing any additional slack. Now we move and tip the rod forward simultaneously and with moderate force. The line that was extended behind us accelerates forward with the rod, traveling in a straight path with the rod tip because the rod has bent during the casting stroke as described in the previous chapter. By the end of the casting stroke, the rod is tipped forward in front of us, and we stop the rod's forward motion as abruptly as possible.

The unrolling line loop is formed at this instant. The entire line was being accelerated forward during our forward rod motion. When we stopped the rod's forward motion, one part of the fly line—that part at the rod's tip—stopped also. The rest of the line still has considerable forward momentum and so it continues to move forward over the top of the rod in a long unrolling loop. The loop is shaped much like a long letter U turned on its side. Loops can be narrow or open, depending entirely on the caster's stroke and the position of the rod when stopped at the end of the forward cast. If the rod tip is stopped above the trajectory it followed during the forward cast, the line will collide with the rod or otherwise tangle. If the rod tip is stopped just a little below its own forward trajectory, the loop will be a narrow one. Finally, if the rod tip is allowed to travel well forward and down after the forward casting stroke—finishing well below its forward trajectory—the loop will be a wide and open one.

Except in certain circumstances that we'll cover soon, open loops are bad; narrow loops are good. Narrow loops are more aerodynamically efficient since they have less air resistance. They allow greater accuracy in placing the fly on the water. They also permit the most efficient transfer of energy through the unrolling fly line. Narrow loops are also high-speed loops; it's impossible to achieve maximum distance while casting with open loops.

Now we'll consider the loop itself in greater detail. We've stopped the action in mid-cast, so try to picture the unrolling loop of line as being stationary in front of you, the same U-shaped loop you've seen so often in casting. The straight line that makes up the bottom leg of the U is motionless, extending from the stationary rod tip to the bottom of the curve at the unrolling loop. The straight line that's the upper leg of the U is still moving forward. The line moves along the U's upper leg, travels around the U's curve, and then stops as it becomes the U's bottom leg. This is how the line unrolls, and so far things may seem fairly obvious.

At any given instant, that portion of the line traveling from the upper leg around the U's curved bottom—the loop—to the lower leg is subject to centrifugal force. This force puts tension on the lower leg of the U, but in this case the caster's rod tip isn't moving and the line that makes up the U's lower leg remains stationary. Centrifugal force within the loop pulls in the same way on the moving line that's the U's upper leg. In this case, there's little resistance at the end of the line—just the line, leader, and fly that are already traveling forward. Centrifugal force within the line loop pulls on the line, leader, and fly comprising the U's upper leg and makes them accelerate!

Not only is the free end of the line accelerating as the cast unrolls, but its rate of acceleration is increasing toward the end of the cast. Because the line moves through the loop with increasing speed, increasing amounts of centrifugal force are also created. That increasing force is being applied to less and less mass as the cast extends, because the upper leg of the loop is getting shorter. The net result is that the end of the line moves faster and faster as the whole line unrolls in the air, reaching its maximum energy and velocity at the instant the cast is fully extended. The pull or tug you sometimes feel at the end of a cast after the line straightens out is the final dissipation of all this energy. The acceleration and line-tip speed achieved in simple fly casting can be so great as to produce a sudden, loud *pop* or *crack* when false casting the line back and forth in the air. This noise is literally that of your leader and fly breaking the sound barrier, much like the cracking of a whip. If you do hear this sound while casting, slow your timing a little; such forces can easily pop the fly off the end of your leader.

The tension in the line along the lower leg of the U between the rod tip and the unrolling line loop is what enables a caster to "shoot" line. After the caster forms the unrolling line loop, slack line released by the left hand is pulled out through the rod guides by forces in the unrolling line, adding length to the cast. The amount of additional line that can be shot or added to the cast depends on the force with which the line is unrolling in the first place. Our example has now changed because the lower leg of the U between the loop and the rod tip is no longer stationary. There is still considerable tension on the U's lower leg, however; the drag of the shooting line as it runs through the rod guides is usually sufficient to maintain the shape of the casting loop in the air. On longer casts in which considerable line is shot, tension on the U's lower leg may be reduced to a point at which the remaining line at the top of the casting loop may tend to collapse rather than unroll smoothly. In this case, it's often necessary to check, or stop, the release of shooting line to make the line and leader turn over fully at the end of the cast. Ob-

viously, shooting lines of smaller diameters are most efficient and allow the greatest casting distance, which is why the rear portions of most standard, weight-forward lines are relatively thin.

We'll continue the same example while examining the effect of a taper on the forward end of the fly line. Our fly casting and fishing are done in a real world of windy conditions, with flies that are sometimes air resistant and difficult to cast. Our casting loops aren't

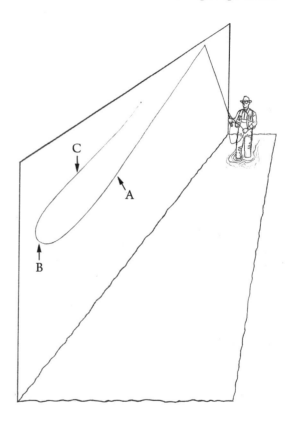

Mechanics of an airborne fly line: During a typical forward cast, the lower leg (A) of the U-shaped loop is stationary. As the unrolling line travels around the loop (B), it's subject to centrifugal force. This force causes the upper leg (C) of the loop to accellerate at an increasing rate—overcoming atmospheric drag—until the line is fully extended.

always perfect, either. In reaching for distance, for example, a poorly timed casting stroke may have given insufficient impetus to the unrolling line, the end of which may simply collapse in an awkward, tangled pile. Fly-line tapers help to solve these problems, at least most of the time. There are other times, especially when surrounded by rising fish, when I can make a tangle out of anything and have to sit for a minute to collect both my thoughts and my casting.

As a level line unrolls in the air, its energy—a product of its mass and velocity—is transferred from point to point within the line as the line travels or unrolls around the casting loop. A tapered line has less and less mass toward its tip because its cross-sectional area decreases with the taper. It is a basic premise of kinetics that as mass decreases, velocity will increase in order for the energy of the object—a moving fly line in this case—to be conserved. As the tapered portion of the fly line unrolls around the loop toward the end of the cast, the larger mass or diameter of the fly line in the rear is passing its energy to the smaller mass or diameter of the tapering fly line in front. (The same principles apply to fly-fishing leaders, as discussed in the following chapter.) Depending on the design of the taper—whether it's very short or very long, for example— the end of the fly line may be slowed down or even further speeded up. This effect is in *addition* to the acceleration effects already described for an unrolling line. The increase in speed produced by some tapers helps to offset the line's slowing down at cast's end because of air resistance and atmospheric drag on the line, leader, and the moving fly.

It may now seem apparent that different tapers in fly lines will have different effects. A very steep front taper in which diameter drops greatly in only a few feet will have a dramatic effect in helping the end of the cast to turn over or straighten with considerable force. Such tapers are useful in casting very large, air-resistant flies, such as bass bugs or saltwater flies, and are a feature of many lines designed for this sort of fishing. For most trout fishing that requires gentle delivery of a small fly, such lines are a disaster, often slapping the leader and fly on the water in spite of the caster's best efforts at delicacy. This problem has been compounded by newer, stiffer graphite rods that allow higher line speeds and correspondingly faster turnovers at the end of a cast. A number of the newer lines from major makers offset this characteristic with long, compound tapers at the foward end of the line specifically designed to dissipate the forces of casting and to deliver the fly gently. These tapers may range from 6 to 10 or even more feet long, while those on the rapidly tapered lines used for bass-bugging may be as short as 3 feet.

Stiffer fly lines seem to cast more easily than lines that are softer and more flexible and also seem to allow any given caster to cast farther. Increased stiffness is obtained by altering the fly line's coating, its core material, or both. Most major fly-line companies now offer both flexible and stiff lines, with the latter and most recent designs usually being touted as the lines to use for extra casting distance. Such lines also usually have a harder surface finish, which results in lowered friction against the rod guides in casting and increases the caster's ability to shoot greater amounts of line on any given cast. With the advent of modern, longer front tapers on the new stiffer lines, I've found no reason to go back to the older and softer finishes, even for normal fishing distances well under 60 feet. The softer finished lines will continue to have their adherents, I'm sure, simply because they have a more gentle feel and do work well at normal distances.

Exactly why stiffer lines cast more easily is something of a puzzle, for which I don't have a ready answer. In theory, a more supple line should cast more efficiently because the line itself bends more easily. This means that a casting loop will require less energy to be bent into shape in the first place, making more energy available for unrolling the line. On the other hand, the difference in relative stiffness between line models appears to be small enough to be almost insignificant in casting, thus allowing a slight trade-off for the many advantages of a stiffer line.[6] Stiffer lines probably cast better because they are more stable in the air and less susceptible to the rod vibrations from a typical, less-than-perfect casting stroke that can deform casting loops and add shock waves to the unrolling line, robbing the cast of energy in flight. Stiffer lines also allow the caster a better feel of the airborne line, simply because the entire structure of the casting loop is more rigid. Finally, stiffer lines are less prone to tangling because their stiffness makes loops of slack line lie in larger coils. As a general case, stiffer is better; at least until we reach the point at which stiffness creates difficulty in forming a casting loop, a point which none of the linemakers have yet approached.

Fly-line color is a widely argued question among fishermen, to which manufacturers have responded by continuing to offer floating lines in both dull colors and bright. I like bright lines. Fly lines that are white, hot yellow, orange, or some other highly visible color are more fun to cast because they're easiest to see in the air. I can thus watch my casting loops and easily see what happens when I mess up, or start experimenting with different casting strokes. Having also reached the age at which it becomes increasingly difficult for me to see a distant and small dry fly on the water, I have to increasingly rely on my judgment as to where the

fly is at any particular time. The high visibility of a bright line on the water helps in this regard, also. Some writers and fishermen maintain that the movement of a bright line in the air can spook trout in shallow, clear water. If a caster is so careless as to flash his airborne line over such fish in the first place, he deserves not to catch them. There's a leader of 9 feet or more between the line and the fly, and the only things that should be near the trout are the fly and the end of the leader. Given the right tactics, the color of a floating line is of little consequence to the fish and of considerable consequence to me, so I invariably wind up using lines that I can see the best.

Sinking lines are another matter. Most sinking lines are muted shades of gray, green, or brown to ostensibly blend in with the trout's underwater scenery. As we've noted in earlier chapters, the trout's vision is exceptional, so there's little doubt that the trout can see your sinking line no matter what color it is. It stands to reason, though, that muted colors will be less obvious underwater, and since those are the only sinking-line colors available, the question is moot.

Line manufacturers have yet to standardize their terms in labeling sinking lines, which can vary according to the rate at which they sink. One maker's slow-sinking line might be called a "Class I," for example, while another maker's similar line might simply be labeled "slow-sinking," neither of which offers much meaning to a fisherman wondering what line to use. Happily, in recent years most makers have also started to provide specific information on the sinking rates of particular lines, measured as inches per second (ips), which allows us to compare apples to apples when considering various alternatives both within and among the many brands available. Sink rates range from very slow, which is about 1.25 ips for an intermediate line, to very fast, which can be as much as 10 ips for some ultra-high-density shooting heads. Sink rates also vary according to line size within a particular type of sinking line, which is why such rates are usually specified as a range. Thus one maker's intermediate line has a sink rate of 1.25 to 1.75 ips within a size range of WF4I to WF10I. These rates are determined for sections of a particular line sinking in still water and not in a river's currents, which is another problem.

The object of a sinking line, of course, is to get a fly down in the vicinity of the trout and to keep the fly fishing properly at that depth for as long as possible. There are many different ways of accomplishing this—even with floating lines—that I'll be covering in later chapters, but for the moment there are a few other basic attributes of sinking lines worth noting. Until recent years, the thick portion, or belly, of all sinking lines sank faster than their thinner, less dense tips. This produces a sag in the underwater portion of the line that's most pronounced in high-density, fast-sinking lines. Because trout fishermen depend very much on feel to detect strikes when fishing deep, this sag sometimes translates into missed fish. In the past couple of years, some manufacturers have started increasing the density of their sinking-line tips in proportion to that of the rest of the line. This means a straighter connection between angler and fly and a much better feel in fishing.

When fished in moving water—and even when retrieved in still water—all sinking lines tend to plane upward. This means that water resistance against the line's diameter and length tends to push the line upward at the same time that the line's density is causing it to sink. The faster the current or the fisherman's retrieve, the greater the planing effect. This can force the fisherman into a choice or trade-off among different types of sinking lines. When fishing across stream or

downstream, as sinking lines are commonly used, a full-sinking line (one that sinks over its entire length) can be a good choice because the interaction of upward planing and downward sinking takes place on the line near the angler while the rest of the line and the fly remain at the desired depth. However, if you're standing in shallow water and fishing deeper water some distance off, which again is typical, a full-sinking line can become fouled on the nearby shallow bottom. This is a real nuisance that can ruin an otherwise fine day.

In that event, you can switch to a sink-tip line in which 5 to as much as 30 feet of the line's forward portion sinks at some designated rate and is backed by regular floating line that remains at or near the surface. This solves a number of problems, but primarily makes the underwater drift of the line's sunken portion more controllable by allowing the angler to manipulate the rearward floating line. The trade-off comes in the effect of planing, which is more pronounced on the floating portion of the line and most especially at the junction of the floating and sinking portions. There's a slight trade-off in casting, too. A full-sinking line casts like a rocket because it's smaller in diameter for its weight than a floating line and the effects of atmospheric drag are proportionately reduced. Sink-tip lines change dramatically in density between the floating and sinking portions, which produces an uncomfortable feeling in casting as the denser line tip flops over in the air. Such lines usually require a deliberate opening of the casting loop. Some makers have started to ameliorate this effect through a better blending and transition between the floating and sinking line coatings.

Pity the poor fisherman. On his home river where he fishes most often, he's doubtless become so familiar with water conditions that he knows he need only have a floating line and perhaps one of the many sink-tip varieties to drift a nymph or a streamer deep in one or two special runs. But when he goes on a trip, as more and more fly fishermen do these days, he needs to prepare for every contingency. This can mean a floating line, at least a couple of full-sinking lines of different densities, and five or six sink-tips in various configurations—all with the attendant reels or extra spools, backing, leaders, and so forth. All this, of course, is just to match one particular rod weight. If he takes more than one rod—say one light and one heavy—all of this paraphernalia is multiplied by the number of different rods. Lugging this stuff from airport to airport will eventually do wonders for your casting muscles, but there's an easier way.

Shooting heads. These short, single-tapered lines are a West Coast innovation dating from the 1930s and originally designed for distance casting. Their popularity has grown slowly, even in recent years, although the advantage they offer over carrying the requisite complement of full fly lines is enormous. Shooting heads are presently available within almost the full range of fly-line types, from high floating to ultra-fast sinking. Line manufacturers have yet to apply their new method of making sinking-line tips sink as fast as sinking-line bellies to shooting heads, but this is a logical extension of the new technology, so you'll probably see this in sinking shooting heads by the time this book is published or soon thereafter.

I'll use one of my own trips as an example to illustrate how I incorporate shooting heads into my own gear. You should be able to interpolate from this some answers to your own line needs. While packing for a couple of weeks' fishing in Montana and Wyoming, I know from previous trips that I'll be fishing with small flies for trout in shallow spring creeks and small ponds, and also that I'll be using both large and small flies on larger rivers like the Madison or Jefferson.

I'll take a light rod for the small fly/small water work; probably a four-weight, although your choice might be a little lighter or heavier. I'll also take a heavier rod for a little more muscle and distance on bigger water. In my case that'll be an eight-weight, but you might prefer a six or a seven.

For the light rod, I'll pack my regular reel loaded with the appropriate floating line. I'll use the floating line almost all of the time, even when fishing subsurface flies in the spring creeks and small ponds. Just in case, I'll throw in another reel for this rod, loaded with a sink-tip line for fishing more deeply. I've hauled this second reel back and forth from Vermont to the Rockies for almost twenty years without using it, but you never can tell.

For the heavy rod, I again take a reel loaded with a regular floating line. And again, this is what I'll use most of the time. By altering the leader, as described in the following chapter, the floating line works just as well for slapping a heavy Girdle Bug against the bank while fishing from a drift boat as it does for tossing a small caddis dry to the middle of a distant riffle. This is a compromise that no doubt costs me a few fish. The Girdle Bug might fish better with a short sink-tip, and the dry fly might fish better with a little lighter rod, but I long ago gave up the arduous hauling of enough tackle to optimize every contingency. To accommodate the many situations in which a sinking line is required, for the heavy rod I take one additional reel set up to take a variety of shooting heads of the same line weight but with different sink rates.

The 30-foot shooting heads roll up neatly into small coils secured with pipe cleaners. Each head fits into its own clear-plastic pocket in a wallet designed for this purpose. I've marked each pocket with a permanent marker as to the head's line weight and sink rate. These heads, by the way, happen to be made in different subdued colors according to their sink rate, so you might regard the labeling as superfluous. I can never remember which color sinks how fast, so I label them. On the reel itself, I sometimes use a special and readily available fine-diameter floating fly line that's sold specifically as running line and to which various shooting heads can be attached according to need. More often, though, I simply use a relatively soft monofilament line for running line. This is less expensive, but more importantly it allows me to fish more deeply with any given head because the fine-diameter monofilament minimizes the planing effect of water resistance. Monofilament also allows maximum casting distance by virtue of its fine diameter. Unfortunately it also tangles more easily and is more prone to damage by nicks and cuts than fly-line running line, so consider yourself forewarned.

Each of my five shooting heads, which range in sink rate from slow-sinking intermediate to an ultra-fast-sinking variety, has a loop at the rear for attaching the running line that remains mounted on the reel. The conventional practice is to have a loop at the end of the running line and to connect or change shooting heads by interlocking the loops. This is a real pain in the neck to do when you're up to your waist in fast water, or at any other time. Over the years I've come to attach shooting heads by simply knotting the running line to the loop at the end of the head, usually with a clinch or improved-clinch knot. When I want to change heads, all I have to do is snip the knot and tie on another one. This is not as strong as properly done interlocking loops, but has proved, for me at least, to be sufficiently strong for everything from landlocked salmon in Maine to British Columbia's giant steelhead. I would not use this method in tarpon fishing, for example, where maximum stress can be expected, but it's plenty for any trout you or I will ever encounter.

A good selection of shooting heads has re-

duced the number of reels in my luggage from more than a dozen down to four. I can change shooting heads in midstream quickly and without changing reels or restringing the rod, rapidly adapting to changes in water speed and depth as needed. The heads cast and fish well at moderate distances and allow me to reach out well over a hundred feet on those rare occasions when it's cast far, or catch nothing. Their primary drawback is a loss of line control on or in the water because the thin running line is difficult to manipulate once the cast is made. A floating line is still the trout fisherman's basic tool because of the control it affords in drifting any dry or subsurface fly. But for shotgunning a distant riffle with a nymph or streamer, shooting heads have no equal.

1. See Gregory (1978).

2. According to my old friend Leon Chandler, who was a member of this committee on behalf of Cortland Line Company, the other committee members in 1958 were Art Agnew (Sunset Line), Jack Dougherty (Gladding Corp.), Bob Crandall (Ashaway Line & Twine), and George Clement (Newton Line Company).

3. There are heavier lines that continue still higher on the same scale, but nine- or ten-weights are the heaviest you'll ever see used in almost any kind of trout fishing.

4. See Jackson (1992).

5. See Mosser and Buchman articles as cited in the Bibliography, most especially Mosser (1980), which deals with casting mechanics.

6. According to data I obtained from one line maker, their premium "soft" line is about 40 percent less stiff than their premium "hard" line, which they tout as a distance line. Both lines are still quite flexible; it's not as though the harder line feels like wire. Users of soft progressive-actioned rods who are dedicated to the use of small flies at distances under 50 feet may find the softer lines to be an advantage in casting because the line itself will consume less of the limited energy offered by a slower-actioned rod. It will, however, take a dedicated purist to tell the difference.

11
The Balanced Leader

A little tan mayfly was clinging tightly to the corner of my eyeglasses as a stiff downstream breeze tugged at its wings and tails. Other mayflies sailed downstream in the wind, furiously beating minute wings as they tacked for the sheltering hemlocks along the bank. I took off my glasses and held them against a nearby bush, gently nudging the little dun to safety. I was standing upright in the plunge pool under a low dam and was low enough to avoid spooking the dozen or so brown trout in the flat above, all of which were slashing avidly at the little flies being wind tossed across their pool. By virtue of my own concealment and the rising trout a short cast away, the whole setup looked like duck soup.

If you've fly fished for trout very long, you know your actions at this point are nearly automatic. You see a trout, and you put the fly there with no thought of the many complex steps in between. This is very much like what's been popularized as "inner" golf or tennis, in which the mechanics of a stroke are so automatic that you can "think" a ball onto a green or back to the baseline. Anyway, that's what I thought I did. The closest trout was about 25 feet upstream, so I false cast slightly to the side a couple of times to get the range and to avoid line-spooking the fish, and then dropped the fly about a foot upstream of the trout. If there had been no wind, the cast would have been perfect. As it was, the fly landed about 3 feet short. I punched the line out a little harder next time with a similar and now-frustrating

result. The trout kept rising, the wind blowing, and I pulled my line in to make some changes.

Like many fishermen these days, I was using a long, soft leader, the suppleness of which is ideal for fishing with small drys. Such leaders are now so universally recommended for dry-fly fishing that many people don't carry anything else. Now, however, the leader needed some obvious changes. I snipped off the fly and folded the knotless and tapered leader back against itself, trying to eyeball the differences in diameter between the fine tippet and the thicker midsection that would mark exactly where the leader tapered in diameter. A micrometer would have helped, but mine was in the same place that I seem to wind up keeping everything I need streamside—namely, in the car. I finally guessed, snipped, and then tied on 18 inches of 4X tippet that was both shorter and stiffer than the 3 feet of 6X with which I'd started. Once again I forced a couple of false casts into the wind, watching to make sure the leader was unrolling correctly in the air. This time the fly landed where it was supposed to, and the trout turned almost immediately to take the fly in a hard, splashing rise. I landed and released the fish at the lip of the dam, and proceeded to take several more from that position until the flies and the wind both quit at the same time.

Like most fishermen, I'd simply taken my leader for granted, assuming that what I used most of the time would work all the time and being surprised when it didn't work at all. This is an easy trap to fall into. Any self-respecting fishing-tackle store has a display board carrying a variety of knotless tapered leaders, clearly labeled by their respective makers as to their length, the diameter and strength of the tippet, and often the diameter of the butt, or thickest portion. It's easy, for example, to pick out a 12-foot, 5X leader with a .006-inch tippet for dry-fly fishing and to perhaps also get a spool of 6X, .005-inch monofilament for adding a finer tippet to the same leader in case you want to use even smaller flies. These leader sizes are commonly recommended by their makers for use with flies from size 16 down to 20, which happen to be in the same size range as the flies you've just bought for your evening's fishing. This kind of setup is the same as that often taught by introductory trout-fishing books and weekend fly-fishing schools, so, armed with confidence from this long chain of knowledge you head off to fish the evening rise. What you in fact have is an average leader that will help you to catch some of the trout some of the time under average conditions. As with fly patterns, a leader's help in catching a few fish takes most people into blaming the fish they *don't* catch on something else—a bad cast or an errant breeze or just plain fussy fish, to give a few common examples—instead of putting the blame on the leader itself, where it often belongs.

A fly-fishing leader makes the transition from the relatively heavy fly line to the essentially weightless fly and enables the fly to be presented in a natural manner. Almost all such leaders are tapered to enable this transition, and their points may be as fine as .003 inch, which is about the diameter of a human hair. The way in which a particular leader is tapered, and its length, stiffness, and diameters, all affect both your casting and the presentation of any particular fly; these variable characteristics have to be matched to the prevalent fishing conditions of the moment. The least important thing about

leaders is what many people see as most important: a fine-diameter, clear connection to the fly that's often considered nearly invisible to the trout. The acute vision of trout, however, has been amply demonstrated, and you can be sure that the trout can see even the finest of leader tippets. The importance of the leader is first and foremost a question of casting and fly presentation.

Understanding and being able to alter your leader to suit both your own casting and the variable conditions along the river will pay enormous dividends in the numbers of fish you catch. Very few people take the trouble to do this, but for anyone ready to go beyond trout-fishing basics, these are logical and important next steps. For example, in looking at different brands of a knotless, tapered 9-foot, 5X leader in a store—all labeled as to butt diameter, tippet size, and length— here's what you *don't* know from the labels: the relative stiffness of each maker's monofilament material; the way in which the leader is tapered; the relative lengths of the butt, tapered, and tippet portions; the actual diameters of the butt and tippet, which in practice may vary from the labeled dimensions; the relative elasticity, or stretch, of the leaders; the relative knot strengths offered by the different leaders, depending upon their materials—even the leaders' overall lengths can vary. In measuring a large variety of commercial leaders, all labeled as 9-footers, I found their lengths to range from 8 to slightly more than 10 feet!

All of these attributes bear in some way on leader performance. But don't get me wrong. It's perfectly fine to fish with off-the-shelf tapered leaders without any experimentation or modification. That's what most people do most of the time, and that's what I do if I'm in a hurry, which seems to be often. A little leader modification, however, can make your fishing a lot more satisfying, so to that end we'll look at both the history and theory of trout-fishing leaders.

The silkworm-gut leaders in wide use from about the 1880s to the 1950s are difficult to visualize in this age of synthetics. These weren't really gut, as being derived from the worm's stomach or intestine, but were made from the worm's silk glands. Each gland and its contents were hand stretched and drawn through a series of dies and then allowed to air dry as a stiff filament as much as 2 feet long. The drawing process gave rise to the "X" system of leader-diameter measurement; for example, a 4X gut strand was drawn through four successive dies to a reasonably consistent diameter of about .007 inch. Gut strands were relatively short and had to be knotted together to make a leader of reasonable length, with heavy strands at one end to mate with the stiffness and diameter of the fly-line point and fine strands at the other end to ensure a delicate delivery of the fly. Gut strands and leaders had to be water soaked before they were pliable enough for knotting and fishing, which meant keeping your leaders between damp pads in special boxes. They tended to rot with time, and their strength was generally unpredictable. In short, gut was a nuisance.

Nylon monofilaments were quickly adapted as fly-fishing leaders starting in 1939 with the work of the late Charles Ritz. Nylon could be had in a comparatively unlimited range of lengths, diameters, and strengths; it was relatively inexpensive and it wasn't subject to the organic rot and mildew that destroyed gut. It was Ritz who worked out the tapers in nylon that still govern most of our modern leader designs almost fifty years later. In the 1950s, Ritz described his fly-leader precepts in his wonderful book *A Fly Fisher's Life*:

> The butt of the leader should have a diameter equivalent to approximately 60 percent of that of the taper of the line. . . . The ends of tapered [silk] lines vary generally between .020 and .030 in.;

therefore the butt of the leader must be between about .014 and .018 in.

> The ideal is to have as long a forward taper as possible but which still remains controllable. It is desirable, moreover, to reduce to the minimum the loss of transmission of power, and in consequence to preserve the maximum of strength and rigidity over the greater part of the length of the leader. To achieve this, an ultra-rapid decrease [in diameter] near the point is necessary, and the total length must be divided approximately into:
> 60 percent of strength [butt section]. . .
> 20 percent of decrease [taper] . . .
> 20 percent of point [tippet]. . . .

Many experienced readers will doubtless recognize Ritz's 60/20/20 leader formula as being the same recommended by many modern angling books, notably those by the late and widely published Al McClane, who was also Ritz's close friend and occasional fishing companion. While Ritz's highly successful proportions have persisted, the caveats he offered at the same time are much less familiar, though equally valuable:

> The Rafale storm leader formula [the 60/20/20 style just described] for the leader is susceptible to slight modifications according to atmospheric conditions, types of line and dimensions of flies. In special cases, I content myself sometimes with shortening certain sections and, with experience, you can quickly get to know what must be done to achieve perfection.[1]

The best route to a quick education in leaders is to build some of your own, thereby gaining the experience with which to judge all leaders thereafter. Several monofilament makers and tackle companies offer kits for this purpose, consisting of numerous spools of monofilament in a variety of diameters and usually with a brief set of instructions supplied. I should note here that I'm referring to leaders made from solid monofilament; the newer braided leaders behave somewhat differently and have their own advantages and problems, which I'll discuss shortly. The complexity and variety of modern nylon monofilaments have increased dramatically since Ritz's time, and such changes have created some problems of their own. Most monofilaments now used for leaders are alloys of various types of nylon. Makers can thus alter various characteristics of the material, including relative stiffness for a given diameter, elasticity, tensile strength, knot strength, abrasion resistance, color, and resistance to the photochemical deterioration of nylon that's caused by ultraviolet light. Clearly, all monofilaments—and all leaders—are not the same.

One of the most important variables is stiffness. A leader butt that's too stiff consumes some of the cast's energy in bending and tends to open up the casting loop, which makes accurate casting difficult. The effect is especially pronounced with short casts—about 10 feet of line plus the leader, for example—when the extension of only a small amount of line requires a gentle casting stroke that lacks the force necessary to bend a stiff leader butt into a tight, accurate loop. A leader butt that's too soft or flexible may tend to collapse back on itself on longer casts, unable to overcome the drag and air resistance of the fly as the cast's energy diminishes toward its completion. To a certain extent, experienced fly casters compensate for this by varying the force of their casting stroke and the resultant velocity of the line according to what's needed to make the leader perform properly at any given distance. As we'll see in this and subsequent chapters, different leaders can be made to perform in different ways according to how they're cast; straight-line versus slack-line

casts are two examples. But one key to good leader design is this: Your leader must perform correctly with a cast of *average* force and length. Speeding up or slowing down your cast is something you'll be doing to get the most versatility out of your leader and should not be the primary basis for its design.

At present, no monofilament maker or distributor offers any kind of quantitative labeling as to material stiffness. There's simply no standard, although special testing machinery is available to measure stiffness directly—either in terms of the force needed to compress coils of a material or to compress the material itself. So although there could be a meaningful numerical system for stiffness, there isn't one because nobody's bothered. Without a numerical scale of LSU's (leader stiffness units, a term I just made up), you'll have to experiment. In order to have the method fresh in my own mind for this description, I did some experimenting the other day down on the river. Remember that the results I'll be describing apply very specifically to my own casting and tackle. Leader formulas are never ironclad, and you

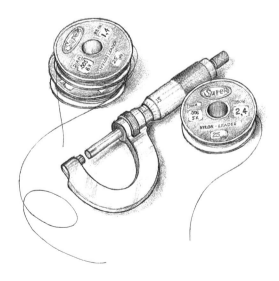

should be adapting them to suit your own tackle and casting style.

A micrometer is helpful. Although spools of leader material are usually labeled with their monofilament diameter, there can be considerable variation between the maker's indication and the actual diameter. For example, one of my tippet spools labeled as .005 (6X) mikes out at almost .007 inches. For that reason, I don't use it; the variation is too great. I use a different material that I've determined by actual measurement to be as labeled. You may get away without a micrometer by using leader-material spools all by the same maker, hoping that whatever errors there are in labeling are consistent. This will work as a general case, but your own measurements are inevitably the best route. I use a spring-driven Starrett No. 1010 thickness micrometer, which some machinists call a snap gauge, with an indicator dial that I can read to within .0002 inch, although anything that can be accurately read to within .001 inch is fine. Remember to use a consistently light pressure when reading diameters with any micrometer. If you're mashing the monofilament by screwing down the mike too tightly—a common beginner's mistake—you're obviously not getting an accurate reading.

Filling a fly-vest pocket with all the mono spools from my leader kit, I headed for the river and one of its many wing dams that I knew offered both a place to sit and a quiet backwater where I could experiment. The fly rod of the moment was an 8-foot four-weight built from one of the newer, stiffer graphites but designed with a slow-progressive action. It's a gentle rod that weighs in at a mere 2 ounces—a favorite of mine for small drys at less than 60 feet, which is the sort of fishing I do most of the time. By the time I got my waders on and rigged the rod *sans* leader, it was late morning, a time when a hatch of little blue-winged olives was due along the

riffles. I walked upstream, hoping for once not to see any flies at all. Fly hatches and rising fish invariably raise hell with my feeble resolve to tinker with tackle.

I sat on a wing dam next to a large backwater, dangling my feet over the edge as I spread out my leader spools on the rocks. I had scribbled a leader formula in a small notebook the night before, one that I'd adapted from Al McClane's 1953 book *The Practical Fly Fisherman* and had used successfully with a moderate-actioned, six-weight rod. Using a small tape measure, clippers, and a micrometer to check diameters when I forgot what strand I'd tied where, I assembled that 11-foot, 4X leader as follows: 40 inches .019 / 36 inches .017 / 7 inches .015 / 7 inches .013 / 7 inches .011 / 7 inches .009 / ending with a 30-inch tippet of .007 (4X). All the knots were blood knots, so named after a man named Blood (according to Ritz) and not for what you sweat in trying to tie them. I moistened the knots well with saliva before drawing them tight, lubricating the turns now in tightening to keep them from slipping and breaking later (see appendix on knots). I had already attached a short, permanent section of .019 monofilament to the end of my fly line, so I simply blood-knotted my new leader to that matching section. I stretched and tugged the leader hard between my hands, several feet at a time, to straighten it, removing the coiling effect created by the mono's "memory" of its many days wrapped around a small spool. The often-recommended process of massaging the leader with a piece of leather or rubber has the same effect, but for this you need to carry yet another gadget. Knotting a #16 Adams dry to the tippet, I was ready for testing.

At distances of more than 40 feet, meaning 30 feet or more of line plus the leader, the new leader worked fine. It fell reasonably straight on the water and delivered the fly gently in response to casts that I deliberately made with what was—for me, at least—average force. I could pop the fly on the water a little harder by pushing the cast, thus increasing line velocity and turnover speed. And I could put slack in the leader by deliberately underpowering the cast. These are all tests you can and should make with any dry-fly leader. So far, so good.

The fly in the ointment showed up in short casting. As I made casts that were successively shorter than 40 feet—all the way down to just casting the leader—the relatively stiff leader butt opened up the casting loop more and more. If I got a nice, tight but still gentle casting loop with about 8 feet of line, there wasn't enough force left over to adequately bend the leader butt into the same loop. This made the rest of the leader collapse in a wopse.[2] Rather than alter my casting, I changed the leader by building a more flexible butt section. This entailed clipping the .019 off the end of the fly line and nail-knotting a section of .017 to the line point to get a little more flexibility in the butt. Here's the formula for the final result, which again is specifically suited to a slow-to moderate-progressive-actioned four-weight rod and floating line when fishing flies of size 16 or less at the surface and at close to intermediate distances: 48 inches .017 / 24 inches .015 / 12 inches .013 / 7 inches .011 / 7 inches .009 / 7 inches .008 / followed by a 5X (.006) or a 6X (.005) tippet section ranging from 24 to 48 inches as required. I fish the same leader with 7X (.004) or 8X (.003) by adding a foot of 6X between the .008-inch section and the final, finer tippet.

The resultant leader is 10 to 12 feet long, depending on the tippet length, but its actually length is of much less consequence than its performance. Other than an arbitrary manufacturing standard, there's no reason why leaders shouldn't be 10.5- and 13.5-feet long, for example, rather than the now conventional 9- and 12-footers. In using this leader as weather and fishing conditions change, there are several easy options. If the wind kicks up, the tippet is made shorter and heavier and the casting stroke may become a little quicker, all of which will give better leader turnover in a breeze. Conversely, on a calm evening a long, soft tippet section—as long as 4 or even 5 feet—will allow me to throw lots of slack in the leader next to the fly when it lands and to thereby gain longer floats without dragging the fly. If a hatch of larger flies starts coming off the water and I have to start fishing bushy, air-resistant #12s, I can trim the leader butt and add about 3 feet of stiffer .019 material ahead of my normal .017. This combined with a heavier tippet, such as .008, and a more forceful casting stroke will allow the larger drys to be cast accurately and efficiently. All of these are changes that can be made streamside in just a minute or two, provided, of course, that you have the needed materials in your vest and that you've done enough experimentation on your own to know what changes to make.

The formulas I've given for custom leaders are partly dependent on the relative stiffness of the material from which they're made. Users of hard, stiff nylons such as those offered by Mason or Maxima will have to use slightly smaller butt diameters to get equivalent results, for example, while the ultra-limp nylons such as Plion from Cortland require a 20- to 30-percent increase in butt diameters for the same purpose. Some consistency in your own experimentation is obviously important, so start with a single brand of monofilament and stay with it until you learn to design your own leader tapers to perform as you wish. This is far more important than the particular brand of leader kit you choose in the first place.

There are a number of advantages to knotless, tapered leaders, the foremost of which is convenience. In recent years, stiffer fly rods have been used to cast stiffer fly lines with higher velocities to greater distances. All of this has led to a corresponding increase in the butt diameters and corresponding stiffness of most such factory leaders. These leaders typically now have butts ranging from .024 to .021, and with a couple of exceptions these leader butts are quite stiff. This stiffness helps beginners to avoid leader tangles in casting and to straighten their leader with the completion of a cast. Of necessity, manufacturers are selling tapered leaders designed to help the average fisherman catch the average trout. These leaders are generally adequate for the middle-weight line sizes (five through seven) that most people use most of the time, and certainly it's much easier to buy a bunch of tapered leaders off the rack than it is to tie up some of your own.

These knotless tapers are almost essential in certain weedy waters such as spring creeks and small ponds. Here the knots on custom leaders tend to pick up gobs of weed and algae when you're playing a fish, the water resistance of which can snap a fine tippet. Knotless leaders pick up weeds too, of course, but to a lesser extent, and when it happens they can usually be slid off the leader by manipulating the rod while you're playing a trout at the same time. Knotless leaders are also a big help if your casting isn't quite up to par, because the midair collisions of the fly, tippet, and leader butt on a bad cast are less apt to produce tangles.

Most knotless tapers these days follow the old 60/20/20 Ritz formula, which is still perfectly acceptable for most fishing on or near the surface. Many also have tippet sections as long as 3 feet or even more, which helps in slack line, dry-fly fishing. Contrary to what might seem to be a helpful assumption as you stare at a vast display of assorted knotless leaders, they aren't all the same. In trying various brands of a 9-foot, 5X knotless taper, for example, I found one with a .024 butt that was the same stiffness as another with a .018 butt. One leader was tapered in a 25/50/25 proportion, which is wonderful for slack-line, dry-fly work, while most others followed the more conventional Ritz tapers, which means they'll straighten more easily on the water. One or the other will suit your fishing style; both will not, at least not under similar circumstances. The only way to choose is to read the labels carefully and then, because such labels almost never specify a taper style or relative stiffness, experiment until you find one you like.

While knotless leaders have advanced considerably in the past twenty years in terms of taper sophistication and material strength, I still have a major complaint: Such leaders don't have the dimensional variation to adapt easily to a wide range of fly-line sizes. For example, one major maker offers eight different 9-foot knotless tapers ranging from 0X to 7X. Within that range, those leaders from 0X down to 5X all have .022-inch butts. The 6X version has a .020 butt, while the 7X version has a .019 butt. By reducing the butt diameters for those leaders with ultra-fine tippets, the maker has acknowledged the need for smaller, more flexible leader butts for use with the lightweight lines commonly used with small flies and light leaders. If, however, I want to use a 9-foot, 5X version on my three-weight line, I'm out of luck; the .022 butt is much too heavy. I have no choice but to take micrometer and clippers to chop up the knotless leader and rebuild it by tying in appropriate sections. What I think will happen over a period of time is the marketing of a broader range of knotless tapers designed and labeled for specific line weights. There will be 9-foot leaders all labeled "four-weight," for example, the butts of which will match that line size, and they'll be available in a broader range of useful tippet sizes. Until then, I'll keep building my own leaders, at least most of the time.

The new braided leaders that have become popular in recent years offer an interesting concept that's more successful in theory than in actual fishing. These leaders have a long, tapered butt section made of fine, braided nylon that's extremely supple. This section is followed by a section of conventional monofilament tippet material. The fly line to leader butt and the leader butt to tippet connections can sometimes be made by the interlocking loops that are incorporated by at least one manufacturer in these leader sections. This means no knowledge of leader knots is necessary, which for some people is part of the braided-leader's appeal. Once you've learned your leader knots, however, tying a good knot is just as fast or faster than fiddling around with locking and unlocking loops.

After experimenting with them for a full season, I found that braided leaders work extremely well under certain conditions; namely, fishing with small flies and fine tippets in calm weather. The extreme suppleness of the leader butt absorbs little casting energy in bending while transmitting that casting energy well to the tippet. In the wind, however, that same suppleness becomes a disadvantage because the wind deflects an unrolling braided leader to a much greater extent than it deflects a stiffer leader made of solid nylon. This problem is especially pronounced when fishing in a crossing wind, in which case the entire braided-leader butt tends to be blown sideways, and accurate casting becomes impossible.

There were a few other problems, as well. If you happen to get a wind knot—a simple overhand knot caused by casting faults—in your braided-leader butt, the knot can be al-

most impossible to untie. If your fly's hook point collides with the leader butt when you make a bad cast, it can bury itself barb-deep in the braid. I did this once, and it took almost half an hour of fiddling to extract the barbed hook from the fine, braided filaments. Because the braided-leader butt is made of a continuous braid, it can't be altered by tying in different sections to suit changing conditions. There are different taper configurations available in braided-leader butts, but the variety is limited. Finally, such braided leaders are more than twice as expensive as many conventional, knotless tapers, which in turn are substantially more expensive than those leaders you make yourself. While I'd happily pay almost any price for a leader that offered some sort of dramatic improvement, braided leaders do not as yet represent that sort of advance.

The most radical and recent change in leaders has been in terms of their relative strength. In 1953 Al McClane described a 5X (.006 inch) nylon tippet as having a rated breaking strength of 0.9 pounds, which meant any trout you hooked on 5X had to be played gingerly indeed. By the mid-1970s when he'd finished the most recent edition of his well-known angling encyclopedia, McClane noted 5X nylon as having a breaking strength of 2.5 pounds. Advances in nylon chemistry have now brought some .006-inch nylons to rated strengths in excess of 4 pounds, with comparable increases in other diameters as well. In recent years 8X (.003) tippets have become truly practical, with rated strengths in excess of a full pound.

Monofilament materials absorb water slightly and wet strength is somewhat reduced; strength is further reduced by almost any knot. Although less obvious, substantial improvements have been made here, also. At one time, for example, you could count on a simple wind knot in your tippet reducing your tippet's strength by at least half. In a leader tippet's typically small diameters and strength, this was critical and accounted for many lost fish. Modern nylon formulations have cut this strength loss down to about 30 percent or even less. This not only provides for stronger knots between leader sections and in attaching flies, but also allows a better safety margin for the wind knots you should have found and removed but didn't.

Nylon undergoes chemical deterioration with exposure to heat and ultraviolet light and so loses some of its strength with time. This effect is proportionately most pronounced in smaller diameters, so at the start of every new season I throw away all my tippet spools and buy fresh ones. In buying, I try to make sure the spools are from a recent batch and haven't been sitting for a couple of years on some dealer's sunlit shelf. Unfortunately, there seem to be no monofilament makers or distributors who date their spools, so it sometimes can be hard to tell if a spool's fresh or not. Monofilament and tippet spools with obviously faded labels are to be avoided. Most makers these days state they've added ultraviolet inhibitors to their nylon formulations to retard such deterioration, but I've always felt better safe than sorry. A few dollars for some new spools of nylon is cheap insurance.

Most of the time when fishing at or very

Two dry flies of different design tied on hooks of the same size. Air resistance in casting will be very different between the two, requiring modifications of both leader design and casting technique.

near the surface, I want my leader to float on the surface as well. There's a running argument among anglers extending back for decades as to whether or not the tippet should float or be submerged in dry-fly fishing. I can count on the fingers of one hand the number of times in the past twenty years I've had to submerge the tippet to get an otherwise recalcitrant trout to take a dry. I keep all or most of my leader floating with periodic applications of a paste-type fly dressing. In floating the leader, I'm sliding a dry fly off the water, not under it, every time I make another cast. I'm also inclined to work, or twitch, my dry flies often in fishing, which is almost impossible with a partly sunken leader.

On the other hand, it can be difficult to make a dry leader sink on command when you want it to do so, as in wet-fly fishing. There are various archaic remedies for this, ranging from rubbing the leader with streambank mud to treatment with a bar of hard soap. The object in either case is to get the light leader down through the water's surface-tension barrier. I carry a small, inexpensive bottle of Photo-Flo, which is a wetting agent used in photographic darkrooms to promote the even drying of films. It's commonly sold in any store that carries darkroom supplies. Putting a little of this fluid on all or part of the leader with a fingertip sinks that portion of the leader immediately. By the time it washes off, the leader has absorbed enough water to sink on its own. Be sure to rinse your fingertips afterward, since this wetting agent will sink your dry flies with equal facility.

That's not all there is to leaders, of course, as most of what we've discussed has dealt only with leaders used in fishing at or near the surface. Leaders for wet-fly and nymph fishing are covered in subsequent chapters on those methods. Perhaps the most important thing to remember at the moment is that your leader should suit your own needs and tackle, which may be quite different from those of the person who designed the leader you happen to be using. So experiment. Try different brands of knotless tapers. Tie your own. And learn about leaders.

1. See Ritz (1959).
2. Wopse is a word coined many years ago by the late Baird Hall, who wrote advertising copy for the Orvis Company in Manchester, Vermont. As I heard the story long ago, one of that company's more grammatically inclined secretaries turned to him with considerable concern.

"That's not a word," she said, expecting him to change it.

"Sure it is," Hall answered, smiling. "I just made it up!"

The word stayed, even as Hall passed on. A wopse is a tangled pile of leader.

12
An Angling Gadgeteer

ou're from the East, right?" the other fisherman asked after he had looked me over.

I stepped out of the water and joined him on a gravel bar as we watched a parade of drift boats loaded with fly fishermen on Montana's crowded Bighorn River.[1] "Well, yeah. As a matter of fact I am. But how did you know?" I asked in return.

"I dunno. You just sort of looked like it. I could tell." He smiled, wished me luck, and waded back out into the river.

I wondered about this and so took a head-to-toe inventory: brown wading boots, brown waders, dark green fishing vest with a couple of dark-green-painted spring gadgets on the front for my clippers and dry-fly goop, dark gray shirt, dark gray baseball cap with no corporate logo. I was generally covered in dull, muted colors, which I've always thought was important along any trout stream.

Then I looked at the other guy. He, I inferred, was from the West. His neoprene waders were a rich navy blue that partly covered a deep-purple synthetic-pile jacket, out from under which peeked the collar of a bright yellow shirt. His slate-blue fishing vest was bulging with overstuffed pockets, and there were three shiny pin-on reels on each side of his chest, each holding its appointed accessory that flapped and rattled as he walked. He had a new tan cowboy hat, of which I was a little envious, and his sunglasses dangled around his neck, held in place by a garish red band. This was the modern angler, fully equipped and looking like a big and bright tropical bird wearing sleigh bells.

Not wishing to engender yet another East-West fishing argument, I'll say immediately that I have many western angling friends who choose sensible fishing dress and know how to keep their accessory items to an equally sensible minimum. For decades the only choice of colors in waders and fly vests, for example, was tan or occasionally dark green. During the 1980s, a time when various national media "discovered" fly-fishing for trout and made the sport at least temporarily trendy, both manufacturers and fishermen discovered style. Suddenly there were vests and even waders in a range of colors, new kinds of fishing hats, special (and expensive) shirts for fishing in hot weather, and enough new accessory items to put the best-equipped fly vest at well over 30 pounds in weight. Most of these things sold very well for a time, at least, and some still do. But in seeing some of the new fishermen on the old riffles I'm reminded of a friend who told me he's recently taken up golf because he likes the clothes.

As you have probably gathered in progressing through this book, fly-fishing for trout is a richly traditional sport, which for many people—even newcomers—is a large part of its enjoyment. Happily, I've been told by several marketing gurus from the nether reaches of Madison Avenue that the 1990s mark a return to more traditional values somehow overlooked in the frenetic 1980s. Aside from the aesthetics of fly-fishing tradition, this sort of approach has a practical value in that more attention may be given to function rather than style. Traditions become such because they are functional; there's a *reason* for using an item of equipment or wearing a particular garment when fishing. We'll explore here some of those items and the reasons behind them, but be forewarned that my own approach tends to be Spartan. Although fishermen are notoriously gadget-happy folk, I'm delighted if I can find a way to avoid hauling yet another gadget around in my already-too-heavy fly vest. One thing you can't afford to be without, though, is a reel, which is a good place to start.

Reels store line, serve to balance the rod, should be aesthetically designed and thus pleasing in use, and are used in playing fish, which is the most important consideration.[2] While a reel of low quality can serve the storage and balancing functions, playing fish puts a premium on the reel's operating smoothness, and this usually comes only at a relatively high price. During the 1980s there was extraordinary growth in both the number of small companies making reels and in the variety of fly reels available. First-quality reels can be made with a few basic machine tools, which has allowed more and more new entries to that business as various makers found many anglers willing to pay a premium for the best in new equipment. This rush to market has produced a number of reels that are overdesigned, loaded with features of little practical value to most trout fishermen. While useful in salt water, where strong, long-running fish are encountered, for example, an internal drag system that will "stop a train," in the enthusiastic words used by one company to describe its reel models, is of little use to

most trout fishermen. In general, simpler is better, although this doesn't necessarily mean less expensive.

Different fly reels are available with a variety of drag systems, arrangements that mechanically restrain the reel spool's rotation and hence a fish pulling line from the reel. Many are based on the compression of special drag washers in the reel, while others are the caliper type, acting much like the disc brakes on a car. The best system for light (meaning normal) trout fishing is also the oldest: a simple click. Such arrangements are quite simple and almost foolproof. There's a small, toothed gear on the back of the reel spool, which—as it turns—engages a triangular metal pawl on the inside of the reel. The pawl is held under tension by a small, flat spring so that every time a gear tooth turns past the pawl, a little click is heard and

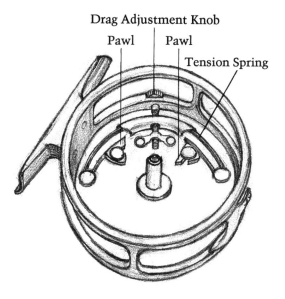

This classic, double-click-pawl drag system offers both light weight and a wide adjustment range, both necessary attributes of better trout reels. Each pawl in this case may be engaged or disengaged by simply rotating or flipping the pawl on its post as required.

some resistance is felt. The best click-and-pawl systems offer double pawls set against spring tension that's adjustable by a small screw knob somewhere on the reel. One or both pawls can be set to engage by taking the spool off and changing the pawls' position on their supporting posts, according to the range of tension desired. The points of the pawls are machined to an asymmetrical taper, which allows for greater resistance when line is going out than when you're reeling line back in, even though the pawls click in both directions.

These systems allow the greatest range of adjustment at *light* settings, much more so than other drag types. This adjustment over a light range is critical. Because leader tippets of 5X and lighter have evolved to greater strengths in recent years, more and more fishermen are using them with smaller flies over larger trout. Such fish almost invariably have to be allowed to run when first hooked on light tackle, and a smooth, lightly adjustable drag is essential for staying connected. The drag, by the way, should be set just tightly enough so the reel spool doesn't overrun and tangle when you give the line a sharp jerk. Additional drag is best supplied when needed by restraining the line between your fingers and the rod grip, or by gently applying fingertip pressure to the revolving reel spool. Heavier drag settings will only result in lost fish, something that most people learn the hard way. When you're not using the reel, back the drag adjustment all the way off to minimize the tension on the spring system during storage.

The question of balance is likewise simple although the answer is not especially precise. A heavy tarpon reel would obviously feel awkward on a light trout rod, but such reels aren't used in trout fishing anyway. Modern trout reels seem to weigh from a little less than 3 ounces to as much as 6 ounces. These reels will provide a balance point somewhere at or near the rod grip when loaded with line and attached to an assembled rod. You'll be using your entire arm if you're casting correctly and pivoting your wrist relatively little, so the question of balance is more a matter of comfort and proportion than a matter of casting dynamics.

Reel size is more important. Most fly-reel spools are relatively narrow, usually being about an inch wide, more or less. This is helpful because as increasing amounts of line are cranked onto the spool, its effective diameter increases and line can be cranked in more rapidly. Most trout fly reels are single-action, meaning one spool revolution for each turn of the handle. This means that a small diameter, wide spool—such as found on only a few fly reels—is an abomination because it takes so long to wind up your line. Given a normally narrow width, the primary consideration is spool diameter, which may range from as little as 2 inches to as much as 3.75 inches on larger trout reels. Light-weight reels with spool diameters of less than 2.75 inches are often recommended for use with light rods taking line weights of four or less, but such small reels pose problems in use. Fly lines kept on such small reels retain that small diameter in memory when pulled free for casting, and the numerous small line coils have to be removed by hand-stretching the line before you start fishing. Retrieve rates are proportionately slower than with larger reels, and both fighting fish and reeling in slack line are correspondingly more difficult. Finally, backing capacity is limited by small reel size unless you use ultrafine-diameter Dacron backing line—say 12-pound test—that offers the corollary drawback of increased tangles because of its small diameter. For all of those reasons I've come to use reels with a spool diameter of at least 3 inches on even my lightest rods with line weights down to one through four. Premium reels of this size are now light enough to balance well with lighter rods, especially if built with a weight-saving, click-pawl system instead of a more cumbersome and complex drag.

The majority of newer fly-reel designs incorporate a so-called palming rim, which is a wide, exposed flange on the outside circumference of the spool that allows increased drag to be applied by pressure from one's fingers or palm. In its modern form, this design was developed by the late Lee Wulff and was used by Farlow's, a Scottish maker, on that company's Lee Wulff Ultimate reels, which were sold during late 1960s. The design didn't become popular until American reelmaker Stanley Bogdan adapted the idea to his prototypes for the Orvis CFO reels in the early 1970s. For the past twenty years, the CFOs have been the finest production trout reels to carry an American label (they are manufactured in England), and their features—including the palming rim—have been widely copied by other makers.

Most trout fly reels are one of three basic types. There are reels without a palming rim, in which case the spool revolves within a light cage frame. This includes many of the better traditional models, some of which I still use. Other styles retain the cage frame and have added an outside flange to the reel spool. This has been the most common design approach in palming-rim reels. A few others are of an open-frame design, in which case a pair of posts extend from the back frame of the reel across the spool's width and their ends are hidden within the outside flange of the spool itself. In all cases, the reel spool is entirely supported by the central spindle, on which it revolves. The reel's frame, be it closed-cage or open, serves to help contain the line and to protect the reel from damage. Open-frame designs are generally the lightest in relation to their overall size, allow the easiest spool changes, and are

the most susceptible to physical damage if you fall or drop the reel on a rock.

I like open-frame designs because of their light weight and often use them for that reason. I should add, however, that in twenty years of using palming-rim designs I have yet to palm or finger the rim, even when playing trout in excess of 10 pounds. I started to palm a reel rim once after a big British Columbia rainbow hammered a drifting wet fly and headed downstream at an absurdly high speed. As I reached to palm the reel's rim with my left hand, the rapidly revolving reel handle caught my left thumb with a hard, loud whack that I can still feel. I screamed, lost the fish, and spent an hour afterward trying to decide if my thumb was broken. It wasn't, but might well have been. With any fly reel, regardless of design, I can apply and instantaneously release additional drag either by pressing the line against the rod grip with my fingers or by pressing my fingertips against the side of the revolving reel spool inside the frame and well away from the handle. I've also learned to let a big fish blow off its first head of steam before trying to apply other than minimal pressure.

Almost all fly reels are easily convertible from left- to right-hand winding. Many people still use their right hands to crank the reel, which means (for a right-handed caster) switching the rod from your right to your left hand after hooking a fish. This is archaic. Lee Wulff convinced me years ago to set up all my reels for left-handed winding, and I would urge you to do likewise (if you're right-handed). A little left-handed cranking practice will quickly alleviate any discomfort you feel in making the switch.

Extra spools are commonly available for almost all fly reels, the idea being that you can change lines by switching inexpensive spools and save the cost of an additional reel. This is both economical and a pain in the neck. Switching spools in a reel is easy while sitting at the kitchen table, but can be a nightmarish juggling act while standing in the middle of a river and trying not to drop a spool into the flowing oblivion around your knees. Instead of a spare spool, I carry an entire and fully rigged spare reel—in a zippered case to keep dirt out—that allows me to change lines with a minimum of fuss. While not inexpensive, it's substantially easier. This also provides the obvious advantage of having a complete spare reel in case I fall and land on my other one, bending it to the point of begin inoperable. I haven't done this yet, but that's attributable more to dumb luck than to my own somewhat dubious dexterity.

You'll need some backing line on your reels behind the fly line, and here again I have a suggestion that's counter to more traditional recommendations. Use 30-pound-test Dacron backing for everything, even on your light-line reels. This line is slightly larger in diameter than the more commonly suggested 20-pound test and correspondingly reduces the amount of backing you'll fit on a reel, but its larger diameter results in far fewer tangles both on and off the spool. The 12-pound-test braided Dacron recommended by some tackle companies for light-line setups on small reels is even worse because its turns on the reel tend to pinch into one another under even moderate pressure. This produces a stuttering kind of on-and-off tension when a fish runs, which in turn tends to pop fine leaders. Since most reelmakers specify how much 20-pound backing will fit on a particular reel with a full fly line of a certain size, you can reduce the recommended backing yardage by about 20 percent to get an equivalent yardage for 30-pound-test Dacron. All Dacron backing lines are available on small spools of stated line length, usually 50 or 100 yards, or in bulk spools holding a thousand yards or more. The bulk spools are much less expensive in terms of cost per yard and are a good bet if you're going to be spooling a number of reels. Never use monofilament nylon as a backing line; when rewound under tension—as in playing a fish—the nylon stretches, and the effect of this elasticity multiplied by hundreds of coils on a reel can deform the strongest of reel spools. Dacron has comparatively little stretch.

Filling the reel is easy in any case, but is easiest if the reel is mounted on the butt of a fly rod. Here's the procedure I and others use, which allows for a maximum amount of backing line. First I either make my longest cast with the line and rod of choice or just decide how long that cast will be, say, 80 feet. Then cut off the few feet remaining at the *rear* end of the fly line to allow for increased backing capacity. Wind the fly line on the reel first, and then wind backing on top of the line until the reel spool is filled to within ⅛ inch of its edge. This determines the capacity for your particular reel setup more exactly than any reelmaker's recommendation will allow. Then remove the backing and fly lines by winding them (separately) either onto spare reels or on a line-winding device sold for this purpose. Now the backing is wound on your empty reel, cranking with your left hand while using the fingers of your right hand to apply a slight tension to the line while moving it back and forth across the spool's width to apply the backing evenly. Having the reel on a rod butt and running the backing through the first guide above the reel makes this much easier than just holding the reel in your hands. Having spooled your predetermined amount of backing, the fly line is then attached and spooled in similar fashion on top to exactly fill the reel. The various knots used in this process are all illustrated in an appendix starting on page 298.

The foregoing process isn't simple, and you may at first be happier in just following the recommendations and stated line capacities that came in the directions sheet for your reel. Or you can just sort of guess at the whole business. Having gone through this process several hundred times over the years, I have to say that the first method I described is the best one, although it's the most time-consuming. It's also the only one to use if you're using a bulk spool of backing, in which case you can't tell if you're using 100 yards or 125, for example. A reel that's too full or too empty won't work as well as it should, and I have always regretted those times when I've hurried and filled my reel with guesses. Sooner or later I wind up doing it over again and doing it right. You should also be careful to avoid line twist, by the way, which if you don't will produce tangles every time you go fishing. Make sure the reel spool and the spool of incoming line are turning in the same direction when you're spooling your reel and *never* allow the incoming backing or fly line to come spiraling off and over its own spool from the side.

Just about all of my 3-inch light-line reels hold close to a hundred yards of 30-pound-test backing plus the slightly shortened fly line. This is more than adequate for the longest-running trout I would expect to encounter anywhere in the country when using line weights of five or less. With heavier lines ranging up to the eight- and nine-weights, which are the heaviest I use for any trout fishing, reel sizes and backing capacities are correspondingly greater. Dacron backing is now available in various brightly dyed colors in addition to the more traditional white, green, or tan. The idea is that making the backing more visible will allow you to better see what's happening in fighting a long-running fish, an idea that offers considerable benefit in saltwater fly fishing and relatively little benefit to most trout fishermen, who haven't seen their backing since it first went on the reel a dozen years ago.

Most people seem to assemble their gear with more thought about how they'll appear to other fishermen than about how they'll appear to the trout. In considering a variety of accessory items, though, let's consider the fish first. Distant objects in the trout's surroundings above the surface appear to the trout as a fuzzy band around the edge of Snel's Circle, the trout's circular window through which it views things above the water. Thus along most trout streams a fisherman is trying—whether he realizes it or not—to blend in unobtrusively with a fuzzy band of green streamside vegetation. We've already established that the waiting trout is alert to any movement, which is usually taken by the fish as the first sign of danger. Obviously, a fisherman moving around in a bright, white shirt against that dark green background is going to be more visible than a fisherman wearing a shirt of dark green or some other muted color. By the same token, the flashing of sunlight reflecting from a pair of bright metal clippers hanging from the angler's vest is also an abnormal and alarming event in the trout's compressed view of the stream bank.

Becoming as invisible as possible is an important part of modern trout fishing that will pay off in more and larger fish landed regardless of where you happen to fish. There are in every trout stream a few trout—those fresh from the hatchery truck or those trout in no-kill areas that have become educated and totally disdainful of fishermen—that will remain comfortably in plain sight of a wading angler no matter how he or she dresses or acts. Many people thus conclude that what they wear or do makes little difference because the trout are obviously not paying attention anyway. What these people haven't seen are the fish that disappeared under rocks and stumps at their first approach. On a few occasions, I have gotten such people to sit quietly with me behind a streamside bush for at least an hour while I enjoyed their incredulity as the larger trout gradually came out from cover to resume their feeding positions along a shallow flat. You will catch more fish by being thoughtful about what you wear; be conscious of the need to blend with your background.

The light tan that's by far the most popular color for fishing vests, shirt, and some rainwear is a poor choice that offers too much contrast between a fisherman and his background. Dark or medium green, offered by some makers of all the foregoing, is much better. In this case color value is probably more important than hue. In other words, it probably doesn't make much difference if your fly vest or shirt is dull green or dull purple, as long as it's some sort of dull color. The same holds true for hats. This means you can have your style, if not your color, and still catch your fish—at least within reason.

Flashing metal accessories are the other common sin. My favorite trout reels are a dull, gunmetal gray, which is both pleasingly elegant and also functional in being nonreflective. A bright, shiny reel that's pleasing to you is also shiny—and distinctly displeasing—to the trout. Like other fly fishers, I usually carry a few items pinned to the front of my vest for convenience. If I have a choice among brands, I pick those items that have a dull finish, most often green or black. If there is no choice, I hit the item with a little matte green spray enamel, which is periodically renewed as it wears off. I have yet to use camouflage cream on my face and hands when trout fishing, but I have seriously considered it. Some fishermen—even experienced fishermen—may dismiss all this as sounding like a toy commando getting ready for another raid. So much the better. As we fade into invisibility, we'll catch fish that the skeptics haven't been able to touch.

The last general criterion I use for clothing or accessory items is trying to decide whether or not I really need a particular gadget. In looking over a major fly-fishing mail-order catalog the other day, I counted twenty-one distinct items that I could pin on the front of my fly vest. All of these are indispensable, according to their makers, who would have me looking like a Christmas tree in full regalia. Of course, there's an even greater variety of things available to carry within my fly-vest pockets. This has produced kind of a contest among vest manufacturers; I think the current leader makes a version with more than thirty separate pockets. I dragged my old, dark green vest out of the station wagon last night—the vest I fish with four or five times a week—and counted the number of pockets I actually use. Seven. Including lunch.

In fairness, I'm fishing somewhere within the same 30 miles of river several times each week, when not traveling somewhere else, and have fished this area for more than twenty years. I know exactly what I'll need at any given time and just about all of the angling contingencies I might have to meet. This allows me to carry much less gear on a daily basis than I carry on a trip to distant waters. Here's a quick review of the various accessory items I use both locally and on distant trout-fishing trips.

Fly vest. Traditional versions are light tan and either all-cotton or a cotton/polyester blend with pockets on pockets *ad infinitum*. Colors darker than light tan are both preferable and less common. Some of the newer high-tech fabrics that became popular for fishing garments in the 1980s are lighter in weight and quicker to dry than cotton, but haven't yet been widely used in fly vests. They probably will be, and you might look for them. Larger pockets on the vest front— those designed for fly boxes—are usually oriented horizontally. A few designs offer vertical pockets, which I prefer because that design keeps the vest's bulk away from my elbows when I'm casting. It also seems that vertical pockets allow me more positive placement and fewer dropped boxes when I'm shuffling them around in midstream. Vests are either full (waist) length or a so-called shorty style that should come down to about your last rib. I usually wind up wading more deeply than I planned, so I stick with the shorter styles. Zippers on the pocket closures are a nuisance; Velcro works well and is much easier. As a general case, it's better to assemble everything you're going to carry in a vest before getting the vest itself and then to decide on a vest according to how you're going to use it. Make sure your fly boxes fit in the pockets. Remember that your vest should fit over a relatively heavy jacket, which is how you'll be wearing it some of the time. And make sure the vest's neck area is designed in such a way that the vest's weight—which can be substantial—hangs on your shoulders and not your neck. This last consideration is often a primary difference between expensive and inexpensive vests, the latter of which are well known for their ability to create sore necks during a long day on the river. Vests are typically unisex in style and cut, although there are now a few models designed especially for women. As with most things, quality construction is a must and should be self-evident.

Pin-on reels. These little round gadgets have a pin on the back for attaching to your vest and hold about 18 inches or so of line or fine-wire cable with a clip at the end for holding a small accessory item. They are spring loaded so the accessory item is automatically retrieved back up to the reel after being pulled down and used. If you're not happy with the clip on the end of your particular brand, replace it with a large, saltwater ball-bearing snap swivel, preferably a black one. While these little reels are handy for clippers or fly dope or anything else you use often, remember that all the things you hang on the front of your vest will eventually tangle in the bushes, with your line, your leader, or with themselves. Further, the greater the number of little hangy things, the greater the number of tangles. I use two of these, one for clippers and the other for a small container of paste-type fly floatant. Both are pinned fairly high on the vest near my left shoulder, which gets them as far away as possible from all the slack line I use in my right-handed casting. Many of these little reels come as shiny-metal versions, usually with someone's logo on the front. I paint them green, which not only cuts their glare but also covers the logo so I'm not an unwilling commercial for some tackle company. You'll have to decide how many of these things you need dangling off your vest, but remember that unless each one serves a function, holding an item that you need repeatedly and often during the day, the item is probably better off tucked safely in a vest pocket where it won't tangle.

But all fishermen wear these little reels, right? Sure. How about a dozen? Wrong!

Clippers. For decades fishermen have been using little fingernail clippers—the kind with the fold-out lever that presses the cutting edges together—to cut line and trim knots. These still work and cost less than a dollar in most chain stores. I think it was the well-known fly-casting instructor Lefty Kreh who first suggested some years ago in a magazine article that line tangles with hanging clippers could be reduced by taking off the protruding lever and using the clippers by simply squeezing them between your fingers. This led to a new generation of flush-cutting nippers without levers, which are a big improvement. Instead of having concave cutting edges, as fingernail clippers do, these have a straight edge that lets you trim more exactly. Most also feature a short needle at the other end for clearing obstructed hook eyes—invaluable. The needle on the version I now use is retractable, so I don't jab myself by accident, and happens to be long enough for use in tying a nail knot (see appendix on knots). Unfortunately, this model is only available in a bright metal finish, a problem solved with still more green paint.

Scissors. It's sometimes helpful to be able to drastically alter a particular fly with scissors. The other night, for example, I trimmed the hackle off the top and bottom of a big Cream Variant dry when I needed a cream spent-wing, which worked like a charm. The need doesn't come up too often, however, so you might keep your small, folding scissors in a small vest pocket. I use the smallest Swiss Army-type knife, of which there are several makers, which has a good pair of small scissors, plus tweezers, toothpick (also good for nail knots), knife blade, and a nail file, the end of which I've ground to shape for use as a small screwdriver. This lives in my trousers pocket whether I'm fishing or not, so I'm not counting it on my accessory list. You do need scissors of some kind that work for fly surgery better than line clippers.

Fly floatant. There are many varieties of this, all designed to waterproof your drys: small bottles of liquid in which the fly can be immersed and which you can easily spill; aerosol or pump-type sprays that coat your fly and your fingers at the same time; and various paste types, which are the most versatile. Paste dressings allow you to coat only part of the fly if desired, something that's often helpful when fishing low-floating emerger patterns, for example. Such dressings can also be worked onto all or a portion of your leader, making some or all of it float

as desired. During the 1970s someone discovered that Albolene hand cream, sold in large tubs in many chain drugstores, was a terrific fly floatant. This is a viscous paste that melts at fingertip temperatures, allowing it to be easily applied to a fly or leader. The cream was bought in bulk, melted and poured into proprietary containers by several companies for sale to fly fishermen at a very substantial profit. For many years its identity was a closely held secret, but now has become common knowledge. You can still buy it under various labels at fishing-tackle stores or get a lifetime supply for a few dollars at a drugstore. It handles poorly in cold weather, however, and you're probably better off starting with one of the many proprietary paste-type dressings sold by fly shops. These are now usually of more advanced formulations that handle well in the cold and come in a container that attaches easily to a pin-on reel.

Fly boxes. I have a long-standing and sentimental attachment to the English aluminum boxes by Wheatley, especially those dry-fly boxes with the individual lids on each inner compartment. Such boxes are about as traditional as you can get these days, but aren't without their problems. The spring latches on the inner lids are difficult to adjust so the lids stay closed when the top cover is opened, while still allowing the inner lids to be opened as needed. I have one such old box that I have to remember to open very carefully because I know three or four of the inner lids are likely to pop at the same time. More modern boxes are plastic and come in a rainbow of sizes, colors, and inner-compartment designs. I try to buy the largest box that will fit in its corresponding vest pocket. As a strength test, I put the box in a chair and sit on it gently, all 200 pounds of me. All my boxes have passed this test, except the Wheatleys, which are too valuable to test in this fashion and might not pass anyway. This perhaps sounds silly, but you won't think so when you pull an untested box from under a pile of duffle to find it broken and your flies spread over the back of your car.

There are five basic boxes in my vest, none of which are the widely used, closed-cell-foam variety. The foam liners in these boxes will rust a wet hook very quickly because the dense foam traps moisture around the hook point when you store a still-damp fly. The answer, if you like the new foam-lined boxes, is to carry a small, open-compartment drying box to hold the flies you remove from your leader during the day. After all these flies are allowed to dry thoroughly, they can be restored to their respective foam boxes. Those lovely looking and traditional sheep-skin-lined leather streamer books are to be avoided for the same rusty reason. All flies, regardless of type, will keep their shape best and dry best if stored loosely.

Some people organize their flies by color or size; I keep mine in order mostly by what the flies are designed to imitate. The object of whatever method you choose for vest storage should be to keep the flies from becoming damaged and to save time in searching through your vest. All my caddis imitations—dry, wet, emergers—are in one or more compartmented boxes in the left side of my vest. All my mayfly imitations are similarly kept on the right. Standing at the river's edge, I can watch what the trout are doing and then reach left or right as needed. My plastic boxes are for the most part clear, which further speeds the search for the right pattern once I get the right box. Dry-fly boxes, of course, should be deep enough to avoid mashing the flies, which usually means at least an inch deep for larger patterns. I have a third, smaller box for terrestrial patterns—ants, beetles, and the like. A fourth box is for flies I happen to use less often, such as stonefly drys and nymphs. The fifth box has long, narrow compartments

that loosely store my streamers and buck-tails. That's my everyday collection. On a trout fishing trip, where I need to carry a greater number of different fly patterns into the unknown, the number of boxes doubles with the general categories remaining the same.

Tippet dispenser. I have a long love-and-hate relationship with these things, which are so wonderful in principle and usually so woeful in practice. The concept is a small plastic container holding four or more tippet spools, which keeps them untangled and allows a length of a particular size tippet to be easily pulled out and cut, ready to attach to your leader. I have tried one or another new kind of these things every couple of years for what seems like forever, but have yet to find one that didn't tangle or fall apart. At the moment I carry my tippet spools loose in a vest pocket, which entails a little rummaging to find the right one. A wide rubber band around each spool keeps it from unwinding at random. Some vest makers have installed tippet-spool pockets on their vests, but this also can be a problem since the spool diameters vary widely according to brand. Because not all tippet spools will fit *securely* into all tippet-spool pockets, you'll have to check. By my own experience, the odds are the brand of tippet you like won't fit well into the special pockets on your favorite vest. So welcome to my dilemma.

Sharpening stone. The perennial advice from most sage angling writers has been to carry a small sharpening stone to use on your fly hooks before fishing them. Sharp hooks hook more fish, and even the smallest of flies can use a little touching up after hitting a rock or catching a fish or two. This is all good and true advice that I think has been included in almost every angling book since Walton because it sounds so good. I dutifully carried a small stone for years, but threw it away about ten years ago and haven't bothered to carry one since. I simply never used it. Hook sharpeners are critical with the larger hooks used in warm-water and salt-water fishing and also for really large trout, but much less so with small trout flies. Suit yourself.

Thermometer. All trout have distinct ranges of preferred water temperatures, and a thermometer can be helpful in locating streambed springs or other areas of cool-water flow where trout may congregate in summer. On my local river I found these places long ago and so don't bother to carry a thermometer anymore. I do carry one if I'm traveling, but have always felt I could live without it and am usually able to find warm-weather fish simply by looking around for feeder creeks and springs.

Light. Clip-on lights with flexible necks have become almost part of the uniform among trout fishermen. These allow the tying on of flies in poor light with both hands free. The price is tangling your casting line on the neck portion that sticks out of your vest front from its inner pocket. The ideal solution—if you can do it—is to use no light at all. Your eyes have slowly become acclimated to the growing darkness surrounding the late-evening rise of trout, but when you turn on your light to change flies you "lose your eyes"—meaning your night vision is subsequently diminished and will stay diminished for at least thirty minutes after you turn the light off again. I use a vest pocket to carry a small flashlight that I can hold in my teeth while tying on a fly. This avoids the tangling problems of gooseneck lights, and I can direct the beam by simply turning my head, while the gooseneck versions have to be continually adjusted by hand. First, though, I try to tie the fly on without the light, a task made easier even in near-darkness because I wear magnifying lenses.

Eyewear. Having reached the age at which I need granny glasses for tying on small flies, I keep a pair strung around my neck all the time. I used a small drill to make a hole in each of the earpieces and then added a loop of 30-pound-test backing line to hold them around my neck. Most chain drugstores carry a wide variety of these glasses at a very low price; you can try different magnifications to find the one that suits you best. Polarized sunglasses are essential for cutting surface glare and helping to spot fish. As with most things, you usually get what you pay for; inexpensive versions are often heavy and more easily scratched. I fasten these around my neck in the same way. Yes, they tangle with my other glasses, but I haven't found a better solution. Some new versions of high-end polarized glasses that I haven't yet tried do offer bifocal prescription grinding, so maybe there's hope. Polarized glasses are usually available with neutral gray or yellow- or brown-tinted lenses, the latter of which are supposed to make trout more visible by increasing visual contrast. I depend heavily on all my senses when fishing and dislike the color distortion produced by high-contrast lenses. Neutral gray is my color of choice.

Forceps. These are now widely available in tackle shops and are small pliers with locking handles that hold the slim jaws together, which means they can just be clipped to your vest. I clip mine to an inside-pocket flap where they won't tangle. Also called hemostats, they are very useful for removing small flies from deeply hooked trout, bending down hook barbs, squeezing lead split shot, and can even perform as an emergency fly-tying vise. These all used to be brightly finished, but black versions are now available.

Lead. It's occasionally desirable to attach a very small sinker of some kind to your leader to hasten its sinking rate when fishing wet flies or nymphs. Various kinds of small split shot are widely used, although I'm a current fan of the moldable, soft-lead putty sold for this purpose. This works especially well around the knots in my own custom-tied leaders.

Safety pin. I keep a couple of large safety pins pinned to the inside of my vest. They're useful for all kinds of things from tying nail knots to temporary fixes for broken wader suspenders or torn vests. I could also make a line guide or two from one of them in an emergency, fastening it to the rod with tape.

Tape. The silver-gray duct tape sold in most hardware stores is sufficiently waterproof to be useful in all sorts of ways. Pull about a foot from the roll, cut it off, and then roll it up into a little wad for carrying in your vest, which is a trick I learned from Lee Wulff. You can peel off small pieces from the wad as needed. If your waders have a smooth surface on either the inner or outer side (specifically, Seal-Dri's or Flyweights), duct tape makes a terrific, instantaneous patch for any cuts or leaks. This won't work on fabric-lined or coated waders, in which case you should also be carrying a small kit of the maker's recommended patching material.

Sunblock. This is easy to overlook until you get some stern skin-cancer warnings from your dermatologist or physician. Even a brimmed hat protects only against overhead sunlight and not the considerable sun reflected to your face from the water. The backs of your hands are another trouble spot, since they're continually exposed while fishing. Use it.

Insect repellent. Carry a small bottle with a high concentration of the active ingredient known as DEET. This substance will irritate your eyes and is very harmful to fly lines and other synthetics, so be careful. I carry mine further sealed in a locking, polyethylene bag as insurance against leaks. The bath oil called Avon Skin-So-Soft happens to be an effective albeit sweet-smelling insect repellent that's especially useful for small children or those with sensitive skin.

Net. A landing net will help you to land larger trout faster and more securely, thereby helping you to release them in better condition if that's your object (as it is mine). Many veterans disdain nets as a cumbersome affectation, and it is true that you really don't need one for smaller trout. Ideally, both the net frame and bag should be dark in color to avoid further scaring a fish while you're trying to get it calmed down and sliding gently into the net. Avoid nets with light-colored bags, frames of light-colored wood, and most of all those with shiny aluminum frames. I attach my net to a ring at the upper rear of my vest with an oversize spring-loaded reel, often sold as a key retriever. There are many horror stories about such attachments, such as when the net catches in the bushes, extends to the end of its spring-loaded tether, and comes shooting forward to hit you in the head. The tension on the particular reel I use is low enough to prevent such accidents and just strong enough to retain the net at rest. There are many other gadgets sold for attaching net to vest, and you may well discover something you like better.

Rainwear. I have a light, wading-length and hooded rainjacket that lives neatly folded in the large rear pocket of my fly vest. After having gotten soaked quite a few times because I left it at home or in the car, I now dry it off and replace it religiously after each use. Wading length means only slightly longer than my short vest and not waist or hip length, in which case the jacket would be dragging in the water. Since my waders come up under my armpits, I'm well covered.

Rainjackets of the newer breathable fabrics are the most pleasant to wear and also the most expensive. Your rainjacket will help to cut windchill even if it's not raining, an attribute I've found especially helpful when fishing the Rockies, Alaska, and British Columbia. Check fit carefully for freedom of arm movement in fly casting and remember the jacket should fit over *both* a warm underjacket and a bulky fly vest. As usual, dark green or other dull colors are the best choices.

Hat. There are all kinds of fishing hats, and their selection is often a case of intensely personal style. As a practical matter, that which is on the top of your head is the highest above the water and is the most visible to trout, so again dark colors are generally better. Other than that, you can go classically Tyrolean or Irish tweed or radically cowboy. Your personal geography might reverse the adjectives in this case. I will add that the *bona fide* cowboys with whom I've fished in the Rockies wear baseball-style caps when the wind kicks up, and leave their Stetsons in the car. Such caps are the least likely to be windblown off your head and into the river. A brimmed hat does protect both your face and neck from the overhead sun, which is especially important for those persons susceptible to skin cancers. Any visor or brim

cuts overhead glare so you can see better while you're fishing.

During one of my early Montana trips quite a few years ago, I screwed up my quaint eastern courage and bought a real Stetson. Stitched into the lining was a color illustration of a cowpoke using a similar hat to water his horse, the romance of which almost brought me to tears even though I dislike horses. The hat survived a week of rather self-conscious fishing, after which I realized the only way to get the thing back to Vermont without crushing it was to wear it. Blue blazer, gray slacks, The Hat, and I made it through the Denver airport without too many glances. There are lots of those hats in Denver. A few hours later I was striding smartly through Chicago's O'Hare, en route to another connecting flight, when I passed two elderly cleaning women taking their coffee break on a nearby bench.

"My, my!" one woman said in a loud stage whisper. "A synthetic J.R.!"

My fragile balloon burst, and I joined in their laughter while getting very red faced. The Hat, I'm relieved to say, has since become rain soaked, mud stained, many times mashed and reshaped, and is bedecked with a bunch of old flies. It's now a perfect image of nondescript, fly-fishing respectability.

1. The last time I published something derogatory about the Bighorn, George Kelly—one of that river's better guides and fishermen—sent me a strong letter of complaint for knocking his favorite spot. The trout fishing on this river is extraordinary, as a result of which it's also very crowded with fishermen and drift boats. If you've thought about going, by all means go. Fish early and late to avoid the crowds. At ease, George!

2. Modern fly-reel designs date from the nineteenth century, although I'm not providing their history here. You'll find an exceptional account of that history in Jim Brown's *A Treasury of Reels* (1990), which also provides an excellent bibliography on the same topic.

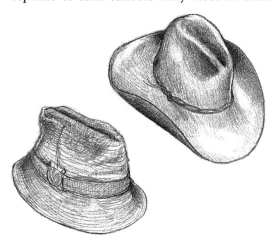

13
On Waders and Wading

Twenty or thirty years ago, I spent considerable time figuring out how I could wade far enough and deeply enough to reach the inevitably attractive far side of any given river. These days I'm apt to spend even more time figuring out how I'm going to get back. Wading is like that. Done correctly, it's the most important skill involved in catching more and larger trout. Done incorrectly or with little forethought, the consequences can range from spooked fish to a mild dunking. As an extreme case, improper wading can kill you.

The remote potential of a fatality has nothing to do with the waders themselves, however. There's a persistent mythology about waders that needs to be dispelled immediately; namely, that the waders can cause you to drown. If you take a deep spill, the water filling your waders will drag you down, according to one still-prevalent thought, while another holds that air trapped in your waders will force your head under the surface and drown you that way instead. Neither of these happens to be true, but unfortunately such beliefs are still common. Many writers have tried to correct these old-wader's tales over the years; foremost among them was the late Lee Wulff, who in the 1940s jumped off a bridge with his waders on just to see what would happen.

In the fall of 1989, I had just finished working with Wulff on a collection of his old magazine pieces that I had edited into a book, among which was the bridge-jumping story.[1]

He, Joan Wulff, and I were spending a day driving along the lower Battenkill in upstate New York, looking at Wulff's old haunts in the area where he had lived, fished, and written between 1940 and 1960. I pulled up and stopped at the old iron bridge over the Spring Hole, a deep and well-known pool in Shushan.

"Was this the bridge?" I asked him.

"Yes," he said, as we got out to look. "The downstream side. It was cold." He shivered with the memory of an October swim, and I looked off the bridge, wondering if I'd dare to make that plunge while wearing a pair of bootfooted chest waders. Almost forty years before, Wulff had written about standing on the bridge's edge, ready to jump:

> By going in with a vertical dive I felt I was making the conditions as hazardous as they could possibly be. The maximum amount of air would be trapped in my waders. My fly-fishing vest was on over my woollen shirt, although I had emptied from the pockets everything that would be damaged by water. I figured I was neither better nor worse off than I would be if I fell in while fishing. The water was swift enough to make swimming difficult and plenty deep enough to drown in.

Wulff then wrote about jumping headfirst from the bridge, surfacing, and swimming ashore easily, the air in his wader legs providing a little buoyancy and actually making swimming easier. He went on to explain what many people forget about waders and other objects in the water:

> Just for fun I did let my waders fill with water later and swam along with no difficulty because, ever since Archimedes made his naked dash through Syracuse shouting "Eureka!" every schoolboy has known that objects under water weigh only the difference between their weight and the weight of the water they displace. Submerged and filled with water my waders weighed a lot less than six pounds and no matter how much water I let into them, that water had no weight beneath the surface and hence could not handicap my swimming.

As he so often did, Wulff had graphically proven his point, one that's just as applicable to a more modern audience. Waders themselves won't hurt you, but your own carelessness might.

Some years ago, Montana outfitter Phil Wright and I were part of a small group fishing British Columbia's brawling Dean River at a time of fairly high water. We'd been looking longingly at the opposite side of a downstream pool while being intimidated by the deep and rough upstream riffle we'd have to cross to get to the far bank. A big trout rolled in the pool below, and that settled it. The water was cold, but not so cold as to be immobilizing, and I finally decided that as a worst case I'd be able to swim to shore in the pool's calm waters if I dumped while crossing the fast water above. The felt soles of my wading boots held well on the clean gravel bottom as I started out, holding a slim wading staff that Wright had assured me was stiff enough not to vibrate in the fast water. By the time I reached midriffle, standing sideways to minimize the flowing-water force on my body, the current's pressure wave had risen to my upstream hip and the wading staff was vibrating out of control.

The rocks under my feet started rolling. I started dancing on tiptoe, taking long hops, letting the current carry me downstream as the hops propelled me diagonally to the far shore. I made it, and later I made it back in the same precarious fashion. The point is that I had decided ahead of time what I could do if things went wrong. Had the riffle been above a rough canyon instead of a big, calm pool, I never would have tried it.

I've been able to wade large and rough waters from California to Maine and beyond for almost forty years with no more than a rare dunking and a few bruises, mostly by following some commonsense wading rules. These have been repeated often over the years but are worth your attention, so I'll restate them briefly.

Decide how you're going to get out of trouble before you get into it. If the answer isn't apparent before you wade a tough-looking spot, don't wade there.

If you're not a good swimmer, reduce your risks proportionately. On the occasions when I'm guiding fishermen, my first question is whether or not they can swim and how well. This often governs where we go fishing. The number of nonswimmers who blithely don waders and head for deep rapids is remarkably and regrettably high. A floatation vest is sometimes a good idea, even though it might feel awkward while you're fishing.

Use equipment appropriate for the river you're fishing. For trout fishermen this usually means waders with felt or woven-polypropylene soles; rubber-footed waders or sneakers are a greased disaster on trout-stream stones. Some rivers are notorious for their slippery rocks, such as the smooth ledges of Oregon's North Umpqua or the algae-covered boulders of Connecticut's Housatonic. In such cases, metal cleats or carbide-spiked wading sandals can mean the difference between fishing dry and fishing wet or worse. If a wading staff seems appropriate, by all means use one. They're common devices, and nobody's going to call you a sissy.

Keep your body sideways in the current; you need to minimize the surface area of your body that's exposed to the pushing water.

Shuffle your feet in small steps. Feel the bottom as you go, and go around—not over—large rocks if you can. You often won't be able to see exactly what you're stepping on or in underwater, so feel your way gingerly. All of my spills have come when I've neglected this, committing my balance to a long step and suddenly finding I had no stable place to put my foot. Sometimes I've escaped with a hop, skip, and jump; sometimes I haven't.

Use diagonals. The current is going to be pushing you downstream while you're trying to head straight across. Start somewhere *upstream* of your destination and then work your way down and across, using rather than fighting the current. Macho waders may ignore this at the expense of very tired legs.

Don't drink and wade. Nobody's going to give you a ticket for falling in after a three-martini lunch, but at best you'll look stupid, and you could be badly hurt. You need all your faculties, judgment, and then some to wade really difficult water. In such cases the noon wine at streamside is better followed by a nap than fishing.

Don't panic if you do tumble. If it's relatively shallow water, of course, you'll just get up again. If the water's deep and fast, ride it out and make your way to the closest shore. If the situation warrants, let go of your rod and shuck your vest. Better them than you. Try to ride through rapids feetfirst to fend off rocks. Protect your head. You might as well relax a little and figure you'll make it, because at the moment you haven't got a choice.

Be especially careful when fishing tailwaters below dams where a sudden release of water can leave you swimming in an area that was ankle deep a few minutes before. Power-generation releases sometimes take place according to a schedule you can determine before you go fishing but are often unpredictable. Before you venture too far across a broad shallow riffle, decide how you're going to get back when it's a waist-deep torrent, which might mean hiking a mile downstream to the next highway bridge instead of wading back by the same route you took earlier. Usually you'll have at least a few minutes to move when you notice the water rising, but be sure to keep an ear tuned for any change in the river's sound and an eye on the water level against your waders.

There's a graceful unrolling of airborne line before the fly settles to the river's currents, a small spot of color barely visible as it floats for a few feet through the riverbank's green reflections. Another step downstream and another cast. And yet another. All in a rhythm sometimes interrupted by a trout's slap and tug at the fly. You might cover a mile of river this way before lunch and yet another mile in the afternoon, catching a few trout and having an utterly blissful day. It's a daydreaming kind of fishing, rich with the feeling of flowing water around your legs and sunlight warming your back. Much of American trout fishing was like this in the days when you could, indeed, have a couple of river miles all to yourself. There is fishing like this on remote waters or even on popular rivers in their slow seasons, but such fishing is now rare.

More often in these days of crowded waters, your fishing is going to be constrained to a single spot; one pool perhaps, or even just part of a pool if that pool is a large, long one. A long tradition of angling courtesy—too often neglected these days—prevents you from wading into a pool or riffle already occupied by another angler, so you have to find your own spot and fish it without being able to range hundreds of yards up and down the river. In covering a long reach of water, you might stay with a favorite fly, a preferred casting distance, and your accustomed style of wading. Among the hundreds of trout in this long river distance will be a few willing to accept your standard approach, so your results are in general satisfactory. Being limited to a relatively short stream area, however, creates a whole new set of problems to which standard approaches offer few if any answers.

Foremost among these is wading. Sloppy wading scares trout. If you happen to frighten the trout in a particular pool, it used to be that you could simply go down or up to the next pool and try again. These days those pools are apt to be occupied by other fishermen, so that option is gone. Even worse, if you and another fisherman are sharing a long, flat pool, one angler's wading mistakes can ruin the fishing for both of you. The basic rule is to wade slowly and carefully. The relative necessity of this caution is proportional to current speed; in slow, flat water you have to be very careful indeed.

People often wonder how slow is "slowly enough" when wading flat, slow-flowing water. The answer's deceptively simple: Wade slowly enough so that you don't make any ripples in the water itself. This is usually the critical difference between catching a few small trout or catching several large ones. It's also difficult and requires enormous patience. I've kept track a few times recently and found it takes me about an hour to move 50 quiet feet through a knee-deep Battenkill flat, one slow step at a time and fishing occasionally as I go. There are times, too, when even this is too fast. Often when working the still tail of a long pool where I know several good trout will rise at dusk, I ease slowly into position and then stand still. For a little while I'll see nothing. After twenty minutes or so I may see a small rise against the bankside bushes, but I still remain motionless. After an hour there will likely be a dozen trout rising as close to me as 10 feet—large, wild browns that ignore me now if I don't move—all within easy reach of a gentle sidearm cast. I can usually catch several of them without having to move my feet, resting the water for a few minutes after landing each one until the others resume rising.

This doubtless sounds like a lot of trouble and effort, which it is. But for years I've watched other people fish the same pools with the normal cast-and-step routine that produces no more than a small brook trout or two. "I don't know how you can stand doing that," Ted Bayer complained to me one evening as we sat along the riverbank, waiting for dark and a hatch of flies. "I've watched you stand still for half an hour, then make one cast and catch a fish. I can't do it. I've got to cast or do something." To which I replied that I was doing something, too: watching.

Having parked near the river, most fishermen go through the same routine of assembling their tackle at the car—rigging the rod, fixing the leader, selecting and tying on a fly.

I might join my rod sections and attach the reel at this point, but take my rod down to the river before stringing it up. Usually I then wade slowly into position in the chosen pool, stand still, and watch for feeding fish. While I'm watching and standing still, I thread the line through the guides, reaching the upper end of the rod with my left hand by holding the rod in the middle with my right. (I'm standing in a pool and can't set the end of the rod on the ground to do this job.) This is safe enough in spite of the reel's weight at rod's end as long as you don't try to suspend that weight by holding the rod above its first ferrule, the middle in the case of two-piece rods. It should be obvious that doing this in the river instead of at the car allows you more time to watch the river itself before fishing and also allows time for the pool to calm down after whatever little disturbance you made on entry.

All this takes a few minutes, during which I may have seen and noted the positions of one or two rising trout that I might not have seen if I'd simply arrived with fully rigged tackle and started fishing immediately. If I wait and stand still longer, I'll see even more. There's a small dimple some 50 feet away where the current runs gently along the bushes. The water is only about a foot deep there, but it's shaded and quiet, the kind of spot that offers a trout both drifting aquatic

Ripples caused by sloppy wading scare trout.

insects and the occasional ant or beetle that drops from the leaves. The bushes are reflected on the surface as a green, wavy band through which I can't see the fish. There's another dimple in that reflection, just the merest disturbance in the calm surface. While I'm wondering how big the fish is, I bend a little and put my eyeglasses on to better scan the surface. Little ants drift around my legs, helpless in the surface tension, part of an afternoon mating swarm that's fallen on the river. I keep watching the distant shadows while adding a fine 7X tippet and knotting on a small flying-ant pattern. This time there's no dimple, but I can see the water's surface hump and retract almost imperceptibly as the fish moves slightly. It's bigger than I thought. By this time more than half an hour has passed. I've yet to fish, but I've learned a great deal about the feeding spot of this particular trout, a spot that will remain in use by this trout or another day after day, season after season, at this water level, and until the erosion of a spring flood changes the game. Such knowledge is priceless. There's a sudden splash behind me, and I turn my head to look.

"Hi! You gettin' any? Sure is slow today! Been fishing this river for three years and never saw it slower. Almost not worth goin' out."

The fisherman sloshed over for a visit about the water, weather, and lack of trout as the ripples from his wading spread over the length of the pool. I don't really remember what he talked about, but he talked a lot, and my occasional grunts were enough to keep him going. As I half listened, I watched the dark area near the bushes. There was no big wake from a spooked fish. There was no dimple. There was nothing at all and no indication that there ever had been. I turned to leave, suggesting to the other man that there might be a fish or two in this pool if he was careful.

"Well, that's nice of you, and thanks," he

said. "Course I wouldn't have bothered you if you'd been fishin', but it didn't look like you were doing much either."

"Nope. Not much," I said, leaving the water. "Not much at all."

Pocket water is a different game. From the tumbling waters of California's Mc-Cloud to the rough rocks of New York's Ausable, the question of stealth becomes almost secondary to simply keeping your balance while trying to get close enough to a likely spot in the turbulent flow. The high gradients of such streams mean much of the stream bottom is composed of large rocks that have been tumbled every which way in times of flooding. There are relatively few stable spots in which to plant your booted feet. Wading such rivers—or even just walking their rocky banks—can be exhausting.

One of the few places where I consistently use a wading staff is in the rough-water sections of New York's West Branch Ausable below the town of Wilmington. The rocks here have been likened to greased cannonballs, and the late Ray Bergman gave the stretch considerable fame in his 1938 *Trout* by noting that it's the kind of water one likes best before reaching the age of forty. I've passed that milestone, but still love the water for its rough wildness and large brown trout. The fish here at times seem almost everywhere—in front of the rocks, behind the rocks, along the edges of rocks, and most especially in the deep, slick chutes between the rocks, where the right fly at the right time can disappear in a shattering, explosive rise. I wade this water slowly, as much for self-preservation as for stealth, although stealth is a happy consequence. Deciding first where and how I want to present a particular fly, I then pick the position in the river's flow that will give me the best shot, working my way carefully through the rocks to that point. Having fished one spot, I pick another and so on, going slowly through the river and covering perhaps 200 or 300 yards in a full day's fishing.

Felt soles are adequate here—barely. I don't use cleats or spikes in this fast water, even though they'd be helpful, because of the noise they make against the underwater rocks. I likewise try to place my wading staff gently with each new step to avoid underwater clatter. The turbulent river has established an underwater background that's both loud and relatively constant, to which the fish are doubtless accustomed. Even with that roaring background, the metallic *clink* of a cleat or staff against a rock will be very evident. Years ago I saw violinist Isaac Stern have the misfortune of breaking a string in the middle of a New York Philharmonic concert, the little *plink!* of which seemed disconcertingly loud against the much broader sound of the orchestra. Stern brilliantly transposed his part upward and played flawlessly minus one string, but trout fishermen don't often get such second chances with wary fish.

You can pick your way through pocket water up- or downstream by using the pockets themselves as a kind of stairs. Wading from one pocket to another keeps you in the sheltering eddies behind the rocks so your exposure to the really fast water between pockets may be limited to only a few scary feet. Trout are holding in those pockets, of course, so make sure you fish a pocket before wading through it. The greatest danger here lies in getting your foot trapped rigidly between two rocks and then falling, possibly breaking a bone in the process or even worse. Make sure that your rear foot is safely anchored on the bottom before your other foot goes exploring. Remember, too, that even large rocks can be left precariously balanced by high water and might tip or roll under your foot. Test your weight with every step before committing yourself.

The payoff in such streams is that what's difficult for you is also difficult for other fishermen, many of whom give such water a wide berth. The fish see fewer fishermen, are often larger, and are usually found in greater numbers than in easily waded sections of the same river. If you're the kind of fisherman who likes to cover the water while moving quickly from place to place, fishing heavy pocket water can be physically brutal. But if you're willing to slow down a little and to carefully work your spots over a short section of stream, your wading skills can help you reach both more and larger trout.

Waders have changed a great deal since a French explorer described Amazonian Indians wearing latex-rubber boots back in 1736. By the 1820s, Britisher Charles Macintosh had figured out how to coat fabrics with the new rubber material, subsequently giving his name (with a *k* added) to a new kind of rainwear. Charles Goodyear of Massachusetts developed his rubber-stabilizing vulcanization process a few years later, and references to chest-high, stockingfoot waders were appearing in angling periodicals by the 1880s, although their development was probably about thirty years earlier. Chest waders with an integral boot foot apparently didn't come into use until the 1920s, after their development by Hodgman Rubber in upstate New York.

Today there's an enormous variety in brands, types, and styles of waders, but that variety is a very recent development. Fifteen years ago, waders were the trout fisherman's biggest headache. Brand variety was limited. Proper fit was difficult to find. Even new waders tended to leak, either immediately or after limited use. The now-popular neoprene waders were then just somebody's vague idea. By 1979, for example, there were only two brands of neoprene waders in limited

distribution; now there are more than twenty. If you used stockingfoot waders in the past, your wading shoes were either of soft canvas that allowed your feet to get banged up on the rocks, or of hard leather that dried to the consistency of steel after being used.

While the variety of waders has increased in recent years, the basic choices remain the same: bootfoot or stockingfoot styles in a choice of materials. Bootfooted chest waders—those waders with an integral, molded boot—are easy and fast to put on and remove again. Stockingfoot waders entail putting on (or removing) the waders plus wading socks plus wading shoes. As a general case, stockingfoot waders will better conform to your body, lowering your water resistance in fast currents, and their lace-up boots offer much better foot support and protection than the molded feet of bootfoot varieties. Most stockingfoots and their related gear also roll up into a smaller package than bootfoots, an important consideration if you're traveling. The price of these advantages is the inconvenience of stockingfoots, which will be aggravating if you're getting in and out of your waders very often during the day. In general, the older you are, the less likely you are to tangle with difficult water, and the more likely you are to prefer bootfoots for their ease in use.

Most stockingfoot waders are available in neoprene of various thicknesses, polyurethane-coated nylon, or plain brown rubber. The neoprene and rubber versions stretch when you move; other versions don't. Bootfoot waders are available in both traditional and modern coated fabrics and more recently in neoprene as well. Neoprene is the same waterproof material used in divers' wet suits; a kind of dense rubber foam that can be made waterproof at its seams (unlike wet suits) and has great insulating qualities. It's the material of choice for cold-water wading. Because the stretchy neoprene hugs your body and is also a good insulator, these waders can be horribly uncomfortable in hot weather. With that single qualification, neoprene waders are terrific. They are generally available in a wide range of sizes as well as shorts, talls, stouts, and special designs for women, so fit shouldn't be a problem. Their slimness and stretch are a big help to the actively wading angler. I have quite literally lived in these waders for a week at a time, when stranded by bad flying weather in the Canadian bush, and was perfectly comfortable through days and nights of heavy rain and wind. Tears or punctures in neoprene can be fixed easily, although you'll have to wait a few hours for the special cement to cure. If the waders do leak, however, you'll remain warm even in cold water thanks to their insulating properties.

During summer hot weather I usually switch to either the nylon or rubber stockingfoots; the neoprenes are just too hot, especially if there's any kind of a hike to the river. Both the nylon and rubber versions are very light and roll up into a compact package. Unlike neoprenes, they have no insulating value and are uncomfortable in water temperatures below the high 60s (Fahrenheit) if you haven't added some kind of warm undergarment. The nylon versions are prone to puncture by sharp objects, as when you ram your leg into an old barbed-wire fence, and most especially so by blackberry or rose bushes. These thorns catch in the fabric and then puncture the material with many small holes as you bull your way through the brush, so be careful to go around such bushes instead. The brown rubber versions can also puncture, of course, but are more prone to slices such as you might get from the sharp edge of a roadside guardrail. With the exception of multiple thorn punctures, both kinds of waders are very easily patched on the spot, either with duct tape or the manufacturer's

proprietary patching material, usually supplied with the waders. Both kinds are comfortable and loose fitting. I use both, but prefer the rubber versions because they stretch when I do.

Wading shoes have likewise progressed in recent years, and the greatest advance has been in the use of synthetic leathers. These thick, plastic materials look, feel, and are stitched like leather into ankle-high wading boots. Unlike leather, however, the material doesn't become stiff after it dries, so the boots are consistently easy to put on. Such boots are reinforced to offer superb protection against rock bruises and offer exceptional foot support that allows confident wading. Unlike some loose-fitting bootfoot types, a lace-up wading shoe shouldn't pull off your foot when you're pulling your leg out of knee-deep muck in some slow backwater. There are still several varieties of lighter canvas wading shoes available, which are sometimes less expensive but lack the foot protection of the heavier synthetic leather versions. Speed laces on your wading shoes will save you lots of time. These are the little D-rings riveted to some brands of shoes for lacing, through which the laces will pull tighter faster than through more conventional eyelets.

With your wading shoes you'll need some kind of sock for use between the shoe and the wader's stockingfoot to prevent abrasion of the wader foot inside the shoe. If a manufacturer says this isn't necessary with his particular wader, don't believe it. Heavy wool socks are okay, but I use a special neoprene sock made for this purpose. The neoprene sock doesn't absorb water, dries faster after use, slides easily on and off, and offers an additional soft cushion between my foot and the wading shoe. My neoprene socks also have a built-in gravel guard, a supplementary cuff that folds down over the top of the wading shoe. Ostensibly these keep small pieces of gravel and sand out of the shoe, but they aren't tight enough to be fully effective. If they were tight enough, they'd be difficult to put on. They do offer a handy place in which to tuck my boot laces after tying them, which keeps the laces from catching on rocks and other obstacles while wading. Several varieties of gravel guards are sold separately, if you're so inclined.

All of your waders should have felt soles for trout fishing because rubber-cleated soles are too slippery. Most such soles, by the way, used to be real felt but are now woven polypropylene, white, and about half an inch thick. It would be nice if the soles were dyed dark green or brown to match both the boots and the river bottom, but I've yet to see anything other than bright white. Integral metal studs are an option with some felt soles that I don't use because of their underwater noise. If I must have better traction, I'll use a pair of metal-cleated or spiked wading sandals over my felt-soled shoes or boots, knowing, however, that their noise may bother spooky fish.

I don't use a wading belt, although many people do. A belt around the outside of your waders at your waist might make some waders feel more comfortable. It will also reduce the amount of water you take in if and when you spill. I don't believe a belt is a safety consideration because it will neither hinder nor help your swimming ability in an emergency, so for that reason I don't bother. You will, however, need a pair of suspenders to hold up your chest waders; these are commonly sold in the same places that sell waders. Some wader models come with integral

shoulder straps so you won't have to bother with separate suspenders.

It's critical that your waders fit, which is not as obvious as it sounds. For example, if yours are short in the inseam and you start to take a normal step up a steep bank, the short inseam will restrict you suddenly and you may wind up flat on your face. When trying on new waders, the old rule says you should be able to put your foot comfortably up on a chair seat without having the waders bind in any way. Absent a chair, try standing on one foot and pulling your knee up toward your chest to make sure you've got plenty of free movement.

Although hip-length wading boots are popular, it's been several years since I've used a pair. I've found them comfortable, easy to wear, and invariably too short. Even when fishing a small creek averaging only a few inches deep, I always find a deeper hole or two that I have to cross or wade down through to avoid a jungle of alder bushes. The hip boots that worked fine all day suddenly become totally inadequate, and I'm left both wet and wishing for waders. I used to use hip boots for fishing stretches of meadow streams from the bank, and they were fine for kneeling in wet grass or crossing little boggy places. Now I use my knee-high rubber gardening boots for the same purpose, which is even easier, although the knees of my old trousers are now grass stained.

1. See Merwin (1989).
2. For an excellent review of wader history, see Calabi (1979).

14
Fly-Casting Magic

The old Delaware and Hudson railbed parallels the river for several miles, offering a path to distant pools that's much easier than pushing through the riverbank's alder jungles. It was a September afternoon rich with goldenrod yellow and the deep purple of old blackberry canes along the tracks. After an early frost or two, such Indian summer days bring hatches of little olive mayflies along the riffles, and sometimes swarms of small black or red flying ants that fall on quiet runs where the trout rise to them in gentle swirls while ignoring the mayflies completely. The railbed gravel crunched underfoot, and the noise startled a grouse into a rocketing flush from the nearby bushes. The bird sailed into a sumac thicket, its trajectory marked by the raised arm and swing of Bruce Bowlen, my companion, as he followed the bird's path with an imaginary shotgun.

We finally stopped at a rusty railroad bridge over a long, deep pool, waiting there to watch for flies and rising trout. Bowlen is an expert wing shot and also one of the smoothest casters I've met. He had spent almost fifteen years as a professional instructor of both fly-casting and wing-shooting skills, so I asked a question about which I'd often wondered: "So which is easier to teach—fly casting or wing shooting?"

"Shooting. There's just no question," he answered. "When a student swings and shoots at a moving clay target, the clay either breaks or it doesn't. It's a hit or a miss with

no in-between. If it's a miss, we can help correct problems with gun mounting or some other fault until the shooter starts to score regularly. Fly casting is more subtle. The student might make what you or I would call a bad cast, but the line still goes out on the water in some fashion, which makes the mistakes less evident. The difference between a good cast and a bad one just isn't as clear cut as a hit or a miss in shooting; it makes teaching fly casting that much more difficult.

"That advice, by the way, will cost you a sandwich." He grinned and held out his hand. There was strawberry jam, still tasting fresh from the berries' June picking, between thick slices of homemade bread wrapped in my small pack. We ate quietly and watched the river. In the late afternoon, a few trout showed with gentle rises along the bank, where we fished for them with a slowness that seemed to match the day. I recall little about the fishing, but the fly-casting thoughts have remained in mind. Foremost among such thoughts is a simple one that escapes most novices who have either read or otherwise gotten some basic instruction: There's more than one way to cast a fly line.

Over the years I've been able to work and to fish with many of the country's preeminent fly-casting instructors—people like Bruce Bowlen, Lefty Kreh, Mel Krieger, Lou Tabory, and Joan Salvato Wulff; each of them both teaches and casts differently from the others. It's obvious that there's no single correct method. But to anyone who has occasionally managed to wrap a cast around his neck instead of reaching the water, it should be just as obvious that there are more wrong ways than right ones. I won't presume to teach you fly casting here, because the written word isn't the best instructor. If you haven't already, you should start by going to one of the many two- or three-day fly-fishing schools offered by topflight instructors around the country, most of which emphasize casting skills. The second-best alternative to personal instruction is one of the several excellent videotapes currently available that cover basic casting skills; those produced separately by Kreh, Krieger, Doug Swisher, or Joan Wulff are especially worthwhile. What we can do here, however, is to look at some ways of handling your casts along a trout stream. These may be a little different from the conventional casting you were taught, but at various times you'll find one or another of them helpful.

As you become acquainted with various old and new trout-fishing books, you'll start running into names for all sorts of specialty fly casts. There are unique casts for throwing curves, throwing slack, throwing through holes in foliage, throwing with the wind, throwing against the wind, and on and on, with names like Positive Curve, Negative Curve, Galway Cast, Steeple Cast, Belgian Wind Cast, Tuck Cast, Reach Cast, Pile Cast, Puddle Cast, Ess Cast, and so forth. This can be confusing, and since some of the casts can be combined the confusion worsens; a Left Reach Pile Cast preceded by a Belgian Backcast Drop works well in a breeze with small dry flies when the current's flowing from your left to your right, but only if you can figure out what it all means. I am going to buck tradition a little by deliberately avoiding most of these names, suggesting instead that you use your understanding of fly-casting theory to simply adapt your casting as the trout and circumstances warrant.

Most beginners are taught to cast in such a way that their line and leader straighten as perfectly as possible on the water. This concept of straight-line casting is so ingrained that it's used by leader manufacturers to tout their products for their supposedly superior ability to straighten well at the cast's conclusion. These sorts of casts are the easiest to learn and require very little subtlety in practice. Unfortunately—though there are times when a straight-line cast is useful, most notably in streamer-fly fishing—such casts are usually self-defeating when it comes to catching trout. It is characteristic of most rivers and streams to have currents of different velocities—fast in the middle and slow near the bank is a common and simple example—that will tug and pull your drifting fly line and leader with varying degrees of force. Placing your line straight on such currents almost invariably creates drag, an unnatural and uncontrolled movement of the fly in or on the water that at the very least means refusals by trout, if it doesn't scare them outright. The problems of uncontrolled drag are central to fly fishing for trout, and many of these problems can be solved by adjustments in your casting.

Of course, adjusting your casting implies that you can control it in the first place. With basic casting practice, you should be able to cast narrow or open loops at will. In the real world of trout streams, where multiple current speeds, tree branches, high banks, and other obstacles create a far different casting environment from that of your lawn, you should also be able to cast overhead or sidearm (parallel to the water) with equal facility, plus backhanded as required. In all of these cases, you'll be creating an unrolling loop of line in the air, which loop you can modify as conditions warrant.

The speed with which the line unrolls during casting can be easily altered to change the way in which the line, leader, and fly land on the water. Being able to make these changes in casting depends on your understanding the dynamics of an unrolling fly line, which is partly why those dynamics were considered at such length in Chapter 10. Remember that on the forward cast, the rod is accelerated forward and then stopped. This gives a forward momentum to the fly line, which unrolls in the shape of a U tipped on its side. The bottom leg of the U is the line that forms between the rod tip and the bottom of the loop. For purposes of this discussion, no slack line is being released, and the bottom leg of the U is stationary while the top leg of the U is continuing to unroll as it travels around the loop.

The unrolling of the line loop is first dependent on the force of the cast; the harder you cast, the faster the loop unrolls, other things such as loop shape being equal. Second, the speed of the unrolling line is also dependent on the tension between the rod tip and the bottom of the loop. If you push the rod tip forward as the loop is unrolling in the air in front of you, that tension is decreased; the loop slows down and turns over with less force. Conversely, if you tug the rod tip gently backward as the loop is unrolling, the tension on the loop's lower leg is increased; the loop speeds up and turns over with greater force.[1]

This has numerous applications in fishing, all of which relate to your control of loop speed. For example, it's sometimes desirable to have certain flies land on the water with a good, hard *splat!* When fishing from a drift boat and casting big streamers or Girdle Bugs into the bank, this noise can sometimes help to get the trout's attention in a hurry. This is accomplished by a conventional overhead cast with the addition of a slight rearward pull on the rod when the cast is almost completed, speeding up the loop and turning the leader and fly over with more than normal force. The same technique is sometimes helpful when fishing large grasshopper or

stonefly dry-fly imitations, whether from a boat or by wading, because the large, natural insects are heavy and tend to hit the water hard. I should also point out that at times this sort of hard delivery scares rather than attracts the fish, and its continued use during a fishing day should be a matter of experimentation. There are some other specialized techniques that are derived from this little trick that are considered in later chapters on fishing with various fly types, but the point is that you can—and sometimes should— alter the turnover speed of your fly-line loop in mid-cast.

The same principle of loop-speed changes is what allows a proficient trout fisherman to quite literally cast around corners. In this case your casting is done sidearm rather than overhead, which means the unrolling line loop is on its side and parallel to the water's surface. The object is to have the end of your line and the leader land in a curve to the right or to the left as needed. If you deliberately throw a slightly open and underpowered loop, it won't unroll completely before it hits the water and will thus be curved to the right. This is sometimes called a negative curve, which implies reduced loop speed. If you throw a harder loop and perhaps pull the rod back slightly as the horizontal loop unrolls, the loop will be speeded up. The momentum of the unrolling loop will not only straighten the line but will also continue to carry the line point, leader, and fly around in a curve to the left, which is sometimes called a positive curve. This is exactly the same technique we used to splat a streamer hard on the surface, but in this case the momentum is used horizontally instead of vertically and a left-hand curve is the result.

Although the principles of curve casting are simple, it's very tricky in practice. A properly supple dry-fly leader with a long, flexible tippet is fairly easy to throw as a right-hand curve because such a cast is deliberately underpowered in the first place.

The same leader makes a left-hand curve almost impossible, because the supple leader and tippet are too long and soft to transmit the energy that makes a left-hand curve possible. If you expect to be consistently throwing left-hand curves—working upstream to rising trout along a series of fallen trees on the left bank of a river, for example—you'll have to modify your leader. A steep taper of relatively stiff monofilament coupled with a tippet shorter and perhaps a little heavier than what you normally use will enable left-hand curves to be thrown most consistently and accurately.

Curve casting offers obvious advantages in dealing with problems of drag, obstructions such as low-hanging branches, and fussy fish. Currents of conflicting speeds usually have to at least partly straighten the curve before dragging the fly, so curves often provide longer drag-free drifts. An accurate curve thrown when casting upstream to a particular trout means that trout sees the fly before it sees the leader or line curved to the

A left- or positive-curve cast.

right or left of the fish, which can be important in the case of skittish trout. Finally, left-hand curves can be thrown around obstructions, allowing fly presentations that are otherwise a physical impossibility. Consistent curve casting also requires substantial practice. You'll learn fastest if you practice with the same rod, line, leader design, and fly size on each fishing outing so that all your effort in practicing is devoted to method without introducing any variables in tackle. Changing from a small to a large dry fly, for example, means the air resistance of your fly has also changed. This in turn requires slight alterations of the horizontal-casting stroke—a little more force, in this case—changes you shouldn't have to worry about before learning the basic method.

Changes in loop speed can also be applied in other useful ways that are especially important in avoiding drag when fishing with either dry or sunken flies. The object in the following instances is to provide varying amounts of slack in the fine leader tippet near the fly. Because it will take the intervening currents a little while to pull this slack from the leader, the fly will usually be drifting without drag in the interim. This can be accomplished in a variety of ways, all of which are also dependent on a relatively long (about 3 feet or more) and fine leader tippet. For example, if your forward cast is underpowered and aimed slightly upward, it will collapse downward before fully extending the leader and fly. When done correctly, the fly will land adjacent to—but not in the middle of—several small, flat coils of slack leader tippet. This cast is especially useful when standing in very fast water and casting upstream into currents of much lesser speed. Fishing upstream into the slow currents behind a boulder, or casting from a riffle upstream into the slow water at the tail of a pool are two examples in which the rapid currents near the caster will otherwise drag the upstream fly immediately over the slower, upstream currents. This sort of cast is difficult to perform accurately—and impossible in much of a breeze—but can help you in taking some trout you'd otherwise miss from some difficult spots.

The method I often use—most of the time, in fact—is both simpler and more accurate. Again using a supple leader with a long tippet, I make a tight-looped forward cast with at least moderate force and stop the rod abruptly at about 45 degrees above the water. Depending on the effect desired, I may sometimes pull the rod back slightly to speed up the loop even further. A steeply tapered heavy leader would turn over hard in this case, as in the previous example of splatting a streamer fly on the surface. But my flexible leader and tippet simply straighten and then recoil slightly as the energy of the cast is dissipated. The tippet, being the most flexible, reflects the recoil the most, landing in a series of slack waves near the fly. This cast is easy to do with relatively little practice as long as you've learned basic loop control in casting. The velocity implicit in a tight, narrow loop is essential; a slowly moving, open loop won't provide as much of the essential recoil effect and in addition is much less accurate. Because this method depends on an abrupt stop of the rod at the end of the forward stroke, it's sometimes called a Check Cast, the name coming from an archaic British term meaning to stop.

This particular method is not new and has been "rediscovered" by various angling writers for at least a century. F. M. Halford described essentially the same technique in his 1889 book *Dry-Fly Fishing*, although Halford's application of the technique was limited by the stiffness of his silkworm-gut leaders. Vince Marinaro described similar sorts of casts in both his 1951 *Modern Dry-Fly Code* and also in his 1976 *In the Ring of the Rise*, both of which are must reading for

serious students of drag problems. The greatest strength of this method—other than that of at least temporarily avoiding drag in many situations—is its adaptability. With practice, you'll quickly start to get a feeling for just how much force—or lack thereof—is required to produce a certain amount of recoil and slack in the tippet. The same basic cast can be made to good effect at any angle—up, down, or across—and over currents of widely varying speeds. One happy consequence of this cast is that the rod tip is stopped and held fairly high above the water, rather than being low to the surface as in conventional, straight-line casting. This gives rise to another series of casting possibilities, which—in conjunction with the foregoing methods—are a key to catching difficult trout.

On a July evening some years ago I stood in an alder swamp, swatting mosquitos and trying to figure out how to catch the brook trout I could see rising in the slow creek channel a few bushes away. The ground was so mucky there was no place to comfortably crawl up to the bank to avoid spooking them. Wading the slow current was out of the question for the same reason. I walked slowly up to a bankside bush that rose to eye level and concealed me from the trout. The bush was barely low enough to permit a cast over its top, and there was a gap in the bushes on my immediate right—all of which gave me an idea.

It was a short cast of only 30 feet or so, which I made by reaching my rod hand slightly above the leaves. As the line unrolled in the air, I canted the rod to my right down through the gap in the bushes. By the time the leader and fly had landed above the trout, my rod tip was down near the water, giving me a straight connection between rod tip and fly. The trout obligingly rose, was hooked, and I slid it out of the water quickly between the bushes to avoid scaring the other fish nearby. I managed to take two other small brookies in similar fashion before the mosquitos and darkness drove me back to the car, thinking as I left about having invented the "Alder Cast" while smiling at the idea of adding yet another unnecessary name to an already long list of special methods.

This was the first time that I realized there are lots of things you can do with your rod and line *after* the forward cast is committed in speed and direction but before it lands on the water. If you've aimed your cast above instead of at the water, and if you've stopped your rod fairly high at the end of your forward stroke—at about 45 degrees above the surface, for example—you'll have from as little as two to as many as five or more seconds to make some additional manipulation of the cast before any portion of the line or leader lands on the water. Among other things, this time allows you to make what Doug Swisher and Carl Richards popularized as a "Reach Cast" in their 1975 *Fly Fishing Strategy,* which is certainly among the best of all modern books on trout-stream tactics. I'll consider reach casting in detail as part of a series of examples on just how that critical few seconds can be used to overcome problems of drag.

Let's assume you're standing in the fairly rapid currents of midriver and are trying to catch a trout that's rising in much slower water directly across stream and next to the bank some 50 feet distant. Your object is to place your small dry fly 2 or 3 feet upstream of the trout and to have that fly drift straight down to the trout without dragging. You know already that a straight-line cast won't do the job; the intervening currents will pull on the fly line, dragging the fly immediately and perhaps scaring the fish, causing it to stop feeding entirely. Some slack line or line manipulation will obviously be required to avoid drag. This can be accomplished in various ways, some of them more productive than others.

One commonly suggested method calls for wiggling the rod tip back and forth while the forward cast is unrolling in the air toward its target. This produces a series of ess-curves in the fly line and leader when they land on the water between you and the fish (the so-called Ess, Wiggle, or Serpentine Cast). If you make your slight rod-tip wiggles immediately as the line loop begins unrolling, those wiggles will be transmitted down the full length of the cast to fall as esses near the fly. If you wait until just before the line hits the water before making those wiggles, the line waves won't have time to travel down the full length of line and so will fall as esses in the water nearer to your position. Thus the intensity and timing of your wiggles control the extent and placement of slack-line esses on the water. In theory, the faster currents between you and the fish will have to remove those slack-line esses before the fly is dragged from its slow-water drift near the trout.

In practice, however, this is a terrible method. I think it's more widely recommended than actually used just because it initially seems like such a good idea. Unfortunately, the entire fly line on the water's currents comes under tension even though it's lying in ess curves. As the currents pull and push on the line, the line itself is pulled *through* the curves, which are not simply straightened by the current. The fly is often first dragged upstream and then down and then up as the line travels quickly through the curves, looking much like a python that's late for supper. One might suppose this cast to work better in a downstream direction, but even this is only partly true. When thrown downstream, the wiggles you created in hope of avoiding drag do straighten, but in the course of so doing still whip the leader and fly back and forth across the current, defeating your whole purpose. It's almost anticlimactic to point out that this cast is difficult to make accurately.

The aerial mend is a better option for avoiding drag in across-stream or across-and-downstream casting, although not without its compromises. Conventional mending is done after the cast has reached the water. Some additional slack line is then flipped with the rod tip in a curve up- or downstream to alter the speed of a drifting fly. An upstream curve is usually added to slow a drifting fly by reducing the amount of fly line being pulled on by the intervening currents, while a downstream curve most often increases drift speed by increasing the amount of line being pulled by the current. Even on casts of moderate length, it's difficult for most casters to place a line mend anywhere except in the line closest to their position after the line is on the water. A similar effect can be achieved simply by mending unrolling line before it hits the water. As the overhead forward cast is unrolling, simply move the rod tip a foot or two sharply to the right (or left, as required) and then back again. This creates a single horizontal curve that travels along the unrolling line until the line hits the water. The timing of your movement relative to the casts' unrolling in the air thus governs placement of the mend in the line when it lands. Once again, practice makes perfect, and eventually you should be able to use this method to place a mend anywhere from near your feet out to 60 feet and beyond.

While the foregoing methods all have their uses at times, reach casting as popularized by Swisher and Richards is usually far superior to any other option when fishing across stream or across and downstream with any fly that needs to be drifted drag free or otherwise controlled at or near the surface. Despite the method's effectiveness and simplicity, it's seen relatively seldom on most trout streams, and I often encounter people who have never heard of reach casting. It's a method anyone with a little ex-

perience can learn in a few minutes and almost immediately start catching more trout than would otherwise be possible. For purposes of the following example, we'll again be standing in the faster water of mid-river while casting a small dry to a trout that's rising in the slow, bankside currents across and very slightly downstream of our position.

Make your overhead, forward cast in conventional fashion while stopping the rod fairly high, aiming for a spot about 2 feet upstream of the rising trout. While the line is unrolling in the air, reach to the right—that is, upstream—with your rod and casting arm, allowing the line to fall to the water from that position. The line is thus placed on the water angling downstream toward the trout. Your movement to the right may have pulled the fly off target, landing it several feet short. Use a little more line in making the next cast, and you'll quickly get a feeling for just how much line is required to accom-

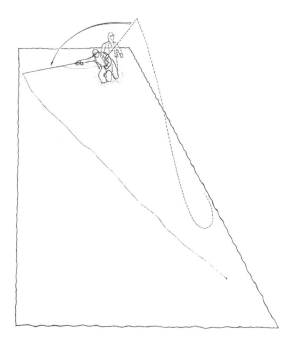

A reach cast.

modate both accurate fly placement and your upstream reach. If facing in the other direction—meaning the current will be flowing from left to right—a right-handed caster will reach to the left across the front of his body to accomplish the same effect.

From its downstream angle, starting above both you and the trout, the line will drift downstream in front of you and then below you as you follow it by moving your rod tip from right to left. The fly, meanwhile, will be drifting at a much slower pace in the gentle currents near the trout. Depending on the relative current speeds at your position and that of the trout, your rod tip and adjacent line may have traveled 16 feet fairly rapidly (assuming that's your reach from right to left as you follow the drifting line with an 8-foot rod) while the fly has had 3 or 4 feet of drag-free drift. Again, the principle is simple: Cast, then reach upstream with your rod while the cast is unrolling in the air. When the cast lands, follow it closely with your rod tip.

So far we've considered separately two basic principles of many specialty fly casts: controlling your loop shape and speed to get different results, and manipulating your line in the air before it hits the water. As you might well have guessed by now, some of these methods find their best results when combined with one another. Things may seem to become increasingly complicated as we go along, but that's just a matter of adding detailed descriptions of methods that are—with a little practice—both automatic and instantaneous when fishing a trout stream. Remember, too, that your understanding of the principles involved will eventually be far more important in your own on-stream experiments than trying to learn a series of specialty casts by rote. Ultimately, you'll find many ways to combine in actual fishing what you've learned in practice. For starters, though, I'll offer one example.

The low-hanging hemlock branches were reflected perfectly in the slow, curling eddy directly underneath, a mirror that was sometimes opened by the currents to give me a brief look through the surface before closing again as a translucent pattern of green shadows. Sometimes I could see the trout's upper jaw poking quietly through the reflections as the fish took a small insect. A few minutes later, a dorsal fin or tail tip would briefly show as the trout turned back down after another rise. There were no splashes and none of the spreading rings people associate with rising trout, just a subtle and shy brown trout busily and very quietly feeding.

I was standing as close as I dared without scaring the fish, about 40 feet distant and slightly upstream of the small eddy. After watching the trout for a while, I finally realized it was facing into the eddy's upstream currents, taking small insects drifting upstream along the bank. The main body of the river's currents was between us, traveling more quickly downstream in the opposite direction. I tied a small black-ant dry—my usual answer when a better one isn't apparent—to the end of a long 6X leader, dressed the fly, and made ready to cast.

I threw with a tight, fast loop, aiming to get the leader well back in the narrow space under the hemlock branches, and checked the cast abruptly in the air. Before the line hit the water, I reached leftward with the rod across my chest to place most of the line well upstream of the eddy. The fine leader tippet recoiled hard, and the little fly landed with several small coils of leader tippet close by. The drifting line was floating downstream in front of me, followed closely by my rod tip. The fly, meanwhile, was drifting slowly upstream toward the trout as the coils of tippet began straightening in the upstream eddy.

One second. Two seconds. Three seconds. By now I was reaching with the rod well to my right to follow the line's downstream movement, and the slack tippet that allowed an upstream drift in the eddy was almost gone. Four seconds. Got him! The little brown trout jumped once, splashing the overhead branches, and was quickly brought flipping against my waders, then released. I walked over and sat on a bankside log, surprised to find myself feeling drained and needing to sit.

Although the catching of that particular fish required the combination of many techniques described over the last few pages, I had not confronted the situation with a chart of possible casts. I just did it, not really figuring out exactly what it was that I'd done until afterward. Among the casting techniques we've discussed, this instance included a high-speed casting loop sufficiently narrow to pass between the overhanging branches and the water. The loop was fast enough to recoil the fine tippet when the cast was abruptly halted, providing slack tippet for the drifting fly. The rod was stopped high enough at the end of the cast to allow time for an upstream reach to the left, which prevented the faster, midstream currents from yanking the fly quickly away from the fish. Then, too, it was a lucky shot, one of the seemingly rare ones when everything falls together as one hopes.

Many trout-stream situations aren't as complex as the one I just described, nor are they always as demanding of technique. As you stand in midstream to watch quietly for fish, you may see a rise in the quiet water along a bankside log, another above a rock in midstream, and yet another directly upstream where the water slows on entering the pool. Each of these fish will require something a little different in your casting, adjustments you'll eventually make with little thought, but which are made nonetheless. You'll flow from one technique to another as simply as the river itself first curls around a rock and then glides along the bank, easily and with a harmony that makes everything somehow feel just right. That harmony is the magic of fly casting.

1. When releasing slack, or "shooting line," in casting, you may have noticed that too much slack causes the unrolling loop to collapse in making long casts. You have probably also discovered that checking or stopping the shooting line abruptly with your left hand restores the unrolling loop so the unrolling line can extend itself fully. In most cases, the friction of the shooting line being pulled through the rod guides is sufficient to maintain adequate tension on the U's lower leg. If, however, you try to release too much shooting line during a forward cast of insufficient power, the unrolling line loop will die before it completely unrolls simply because tension on the U's lower leg has been lost.

PART THREE

THE PUZZLE

15
Maple Leaves
and Mouse's Ears

Many trout fishermen still show a great reluctance to delve into aquatic entomology, perhaps because its apparent complexity seems intimidating or else simply not worth the effort. Many others seem to disdain it, being able to sometimes take trout with a handful of fly patterns that are generally representative of a variety of trout-stream insects, while showing a perverse pride in being able to do so without reference to "bug Latin." In either case, it's an odd attitude because aquatic entomology is the very foundation of fly fishing for trout, bringing to the sport something so simple as to be often overlooked: predictability.

Within a given reach of trout stream, hatches of different stream insects follow the same chronology year after year. Having fished the same river day in and day out for the past twenty years, I can tell you with reasonable certainty what flies will be on the water at a particular hour on any given day throughout the season. There's nothing unusual about this; any trout fishermen in any part of the country can tell you the same sort of thing if he's taken the trouble to learn his water well. Armed with this knowledge, a fisherman is then most likely to be using what proves to be the right fly pattern at the right time and place.

Variations in climate from one season to the next may alter the timing and duration of certain hatches, but not the order in which each occurs relative to another in a particular section of stream as long as the composition of the stream's insect community remains stable. Catastrophic events, such as severe flooding, bulldozers along the riverbank, or toxic-chemical spills in the river, may alter things considerably, of course, eradicating some kinds of insects and possibly allowing some new kinds to flourish. In that case, the hard-won lessons of which hatches occur at what times will have to be learned all over again. But in the main, hatches—and rising trout—are to a large degree predictable.

I may have learned over time that a large yellow mayfly hatches in certain areas of the stream on warm evenings in late June, and that in the same season this hatch occurs there will be hatches of little olive mayflies in late morning. This is aquatic entomology, like it or not. Even those who refer to their flies as "little brown ones and big gray ones" make use of this kind of knowledge, planning to be on the water when the "big gray ones" are prevalent and the trout are feeding heavily. Somehow, calling those big gray ones by their proper name—say, *Siphlonurus*, a large grayish-bodied mayfly genus common to the slow-water reaches of many trout streams—is held by some accounts to be unnecessary, affected, or both. It is neither, being just a name like Tom, Dick, or

Harry, and the name itself can convey considerable information.

Craig Mathews and John Juracek made this point especially well in their recent book *Fishing Yellowstone Hatches:*

> If an insect has a commonly accepted name we have used it. If it does not . . . we have used their real name, and yes, they're Latin. Many fishermen feel using Latin names is somehow akin to snobbery, but this isn't true. Since we have to call them something, and because it's just as easy to say *Hydropsyche* as it is to say "it was that caddis with tan wings and a brownish body in about a size #14 or #16," we have taken the Latin route when necessary.

This particular book is an exceptional example of a relatively new trout-fishing genre that you'll probably see a lot more of over the next ten or twenty years: regional hatch guides. If planning a trout-fishing trip to northern California, for example, sooner or later I'll be able to pick up a copy of something like *Northern California Hatches* that will tell me what important trout-stream insects hatch at what times on a river-by-river basis.

Such a book will have close-up color photographs of those insects as well as suggested fly patterns and fishing tactics. It will also treat mayflies, caddisflies, stoneflies, and midges in detail. And there will be similar and separate books for important areas such as Michigan and the upper Midwest, Colorado, Pennsylvania, New York, northern New England, and more. This sort of information already exists in any one of several books that treat trout-stream hatches on a national basis and indicate regional differences, but regional guides will be more helpful in detailing specific rivers as well as locally important hatches.

For that matter, I can telephone any one of many fly shops a few days before my trip and get an accurate account of just what hatches to expect on the rivers I'll be fishing. This sort of knowledge helps me—or anyone else—to determine a great many things ahead of time. If I'm planning to fish Idaho's Henrys Fork of the Snake in August, for example, and local guide Mike Lawson tells me by telephone to expect morning spinner falls of minute *Tricorythodes* mayflies, I know immediately that the fishing will require light lines and very fine, long leaders and so can pack my gear accordingly.

One reason for the reticence or resentment of many fishermen regarding entomology is probably the apparent assertion made by some popular writers that those who don't trouble to learn their angling Latin are somehow inept or otherwise second-rate trout anglers. "Every fly fisher *must* be able to identify the major groups of food organisms [italics mine]," according to one modern author, while another notes: "Both fly patterns that match the hatch and imitative techniques of fly manipulation are impossible without a thorough knowledge of fly-fishing entomology." Such statements are given as absolutes, are almost evangelical in tone, and are often resented by the thousands of trout fishermen who fish successfully—part of the time—with only an Adams dry or a Hare's Ear Nymph, for example. In recent years and particularly in fishing periodicals, there has been considerable backlash to this, a kind of reverse snobbery that extols fishing with "little gray ones" and that often substitutes flippancy for genuine knowledge.

Any understanding of aquatic entomology is not a prerequisite for successful trout fishing. You could embark on a coast-to-coast angling odyssey armed only with a box of small Hare's Ear Nymphs, for example, and catch at least a few trout at every stop en route. That such flies resemble the small nymphs of most trout streams is immaterial to many people. It's a fly, and it works; that's enough. But there will be other times during the same trip when you'll be surrounded by rising trout and utterly helpless as your little nymph is ignored. This particular hatch—which you can't identify—will be over after a while, and later in the day your little nymph may again be successful. The price of your ignorance—a price I've paid many times myself—is frustration, but it's only temporary. So while a detailed understanding of trout-stream insects isn't always necessary for catching trout, it will enable you to catch more of the trout more often. I'm not suggesting that learning some entomology is imperative, only that after a while you may want to explore it out of curiosity, occasional necessity, or more likely both.

A good place to start is with *Trout Stream Insects*, a book recently written by my Michigan friend and veteran tackle dealer Dick Pobst, which covers some major hatches of both eastern and western rivers, offers excellent color photographs of natural mayflies, caddis, and stoneflies, plus suggestions as to fly patterns—all in fewer than eighty pages. It's the best current short introduction to this topic of which I'm aware. The late Art Flick's venerable *Streamside Guide* offers similar information but is more limited in scope and of use primarily in the northeast. Those looking for more information will eventually turn to Ernie Schwiebert's *Nymphs*, Gary LaFontaine's *Caddisflies*, and Fred Arbona's book on mayflies, among other references, all of which offer wonderfully detailed information, but which will—perhaps—be more than some people wish to know. At the other extreme, you may eventually wind up tracking down articles about specific insects in scientific journals such as the *Annual Review of Entomology* or the *Journal of the North American Benthological Society*. My own interest in this area has led to the accumulation of a substantial li-

brary plus enough microscopes, nets, jars, and aquaria to equip a small laboratory, but this has been only because I enjoy it and not because I feel it's imperative in any way.

In recent years, fly-fishing knowledge has become increasingly specialized, and this is especially true of angling entomology. From about 1950 until the 1970s, there were a handful of general books on this topic, with Schwiebert's 1955 landmark *Matching the Hatch* being the most important. Now there are separate and quite large books on mayflies, caddisflies, and stoneflies, and more than one title in each case! Soon there will be popular books on just particular groups of mayfly species, and in current angling periodicals it's now common to see articles devoted to fishing the hatches of a single aquatic-insect genus or species. The trees to a certain extent are becoming more visible than the forest, and that's one reason I'll use the rest of this chapter and the next to consider certain aspects of trout-stream entomology in a general way. Another reason, of course, is that it's physically impossible to provide an adequate catalog of our trout-stream hatches within a chapter or two, which is why I've suggested a number of other references. Finally, the basic life cycles of aquatic-insect forms have been covered over and over again in numerous introductory angling books and are old hat to most fishermen, so let's try for something more interesting.

After several years of watching I finally noticed that the day on which my neighbor Sam started planting field corn for his dairy cattle always coincided with the start of the Hendrickson mayfly hatch on my favorite nearby trout stream. Eventually I asked him how he decided on what particular day to plant corn. He explained that the temperature of the soil 5 inches below the surface had to be at least 50 degrees at planting time, otherwise his seed corn would rot instead of germinate. Since his cornfields were subject to the same weather conditions as the nearby creek, it was then obvious that by the time Sam's fields had warmed enough for planting, the stream had also warmed to the point at which its spring insect hatches started to occur. Toward the end of every April thereafter, until I moved to another part of the state, I became a real pest, asking Sam each evening if he was going to plant corn on the next day. When he finally said yes, I could rig my fly rods and unveil a winter's worth of newly tied flies with all due confidence.

There is a delightful and very large folklore surrounding the relationship between the prevailing weather, seasonal changes in the countryside, insect hatches, and rising trout. In the Northeast, the old saw about spring fly hatches not happening until the new leaves on maple trees are the size of mouse's ears has been repeated for well over a century. Anadromous shad will be making their spring runs upstream in rivers farther south when shad bush there is in blossom, while farther north the white blossoms of this woodland shrub often mean the end of the Hendrickson hatch and the start of hatching "shadflies," which are a kind of caddis. One of my friends along the lower

Battenkill knows to plan on hatches of sulphur mayflies (*Ephemerella dorothea*) when the peonies in his front yard start to bloom in early June.

Although anglers have been slow to make the formal connection, this is all part of the science of phenology, which has been defined as "the study of periodic events in the animal and plant world as they are influenced by climate and weather."[1] Bird migrations are periodic—that is, recurrent—according to season year after year, as is the hibernation of various animals in colder climates. Assorted botanical events—the budding, flowering, and fruiting of particular plants—are also periodic season after season. Just like hatches of aquatic insects.

This goes far beyond the ancient linking of mouse's ears, maple leaves, and hatches of Hendrickson mayflies. As we consider phenology a bit further as a general case, keep in mind a developing parallel with aquatic-insect hatches. Most studies have dealt with plant phenology, starting with Carolus Linnaeus in eighteenth-century Sweden. Linnaeus set up a network of eighteen different geographic stations to record seasonal events in the lives of plants, establishing plant calendars that he related to climate and which he described in his 1751 *Philosophia botanica*. By 1938, A. D. Hopkins had proposed a fundamental bioclimatic law along the same general lines in a U.S. Agriculture Department publication:

> Other conditions being equal, the variation in the time occurrence of a given periodic event in life activity in temperate North America is at the general average rate of four days for each one degree of latitude, five degrees of longitude, and 400 feet of elevation, later northward, eastward, and upward in the spring and early summer, and the reverse in later summer and autumn.[2]

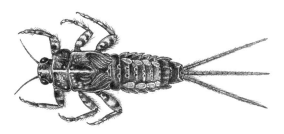

A Hendrickson (Ephemerella subvaria) mayfly nymph.

As things turn out, Hopkins' expressions of latitude and altitude are more significant than longitude in determining the relative timing of a botanical event such as the flowering of a particular plant species or other events such as the hatching time of a particular mayfly or caddis species. It's common knowledge, of course, that spring spreads slowly from south to north as the season progresses, and that higher altitudes have later springs than lower elevations. Hopkins' proposed law does generally conform to the old northeastern idea that spring advances northward at an approximate rate of 100 miles per week.

Various studies of plant phenology have produced the concept of *isophanes*, which was first proposed in the 1880s. These are lines drawn on a map that connect phenological events happening on the same date. For example, if a particular plant species bloomed on the same day in Baltimore, St. Louis, Topeka, and San Francisco, one line would connect all of those locations. Presumably, the same plant species would bloom later north of that line, and earlier to the south of it. These isophane maps resemble the form of so-called hardiness-zone maps common to seed and garden catalogs, which are probably more familiar and are usually based on minimum annual temperatures. Although more by accident than by design, these maps are also hatch maps, indicating roughly where in a particular region hatches of the same aquatic species will be occurring at the same time.

The growth and development rates—and consequent hatching dates—of aquatic nymphs and larvae are primarily governed by water temperature. Growth refers to an increase in size; development means maturation, such as the development of wing pads in a nymph that eventually become the wings of the flying adult. Both take place faster in warmer water than in cold, at least within the tolerance limits of the species.[3] Stream-water temperatures are in turn usually a partial reflection of their recent climatic history; being cooler during a cold, wet spring and warmer in a warm, dry spring, for example. Now consider this as it relates to the following description of plant phenology:

> Plants can be observed annually and dates recorded when growth characteristics occur such as opening of leaf-buds and flowers. These indicator plants may be considered as special, highly sensitive meteorological instruments that integrate weather factors, such as temperature, rainfall, humidity, wind, and sunshine, and show by their growth response the accumulative effect of these factors.[4]

The plants around my house bloom in the same sequence every year. Daffodils invariably come before apple blossoms, although the absolute calendar date of each, as well as the interval between them, will vary from year to year according to recent patterns of weather. The insects on my local trout river hatch in the same sequence every year. Hendricksons invariably come before sulphurs although the absolute calendar date of each, as well as the interval between them, will vary from year to year according to recent patterns of weather. Eureka!

Unfortunately, as anglers we have the "Eureka!" but not the gizmo. By that I mean that while someone could theoretically draw very accurate isophanes for aquatic-insect hatches over a map of the United States or that of a small region, it has yet to be done. The widespread data that would make such a map possible have never been collected, even though they exist as fragments in the memories and notes of trout fishermen nationwide. The hardiness-zone maps in seed catalogs do offer an approximation. As one example, for some years I compared notes with the late Lee Wulff as to the dates of certain hatches on the Vermont Battenkill near my home and on the Beaverkill near where Wulff lived, about 150 miles south. I was surprised to find that the dates of some important spring hatches were almost identical and found part of the answer in a seed-catalog map that had us both in the same zone in spite of the difference in latitude. The critical difference is in elevation. The Battenkill is farther north but at a lower altitude than the Beaverkill, a combination of circumstances that tends to produce an equivalent spring season in terms of the timing of hatches and rising trout.

Some knowledge of phenology can be extremely useful, even without a ready-made map of hatch isophanes for your particular area. Each time you go to your customary river, simply note by looking out the car window what plants happen to be in blossom (or similar botanical event) on that particular day. Note also what hatches occur on the same day along the river. After a couple of seasons of making these sorts of notes, a pattern will emerge that will enable you to accurately predict hatches without actually going to the river. Hendrickson mayflies and dog-toothed violets. *Brachycentrus* caddis as the shad bush fades. Peonies and hatches of evening sulphurs. Spinner falls of little *Tricorythodes* mayflies on calm mornings when cardinal flower shines red in summer meadows. Indian-summer blooms of fringed gentian and afternoon hatches of blue-winged olives.

Those things are part of my local pattern, while yours will vary with your geography. The principle is virtually universal. Just make sure that you use the same plants in the same location year after year as your indicators. I once made the mistake of waiting to fish our sulphur hatch until my own peonies had blossomed, instead of checking those down in the village that I'd watched the year before. Because my house is almost 500 feet higher in elevation, I missed the first five days of the hatch.

It was a lemonade evening, hot and muggy; the kind best spent in a big rocking chair on the porch of an old country hotel, with a pitcher of freshly squeezed lemons and water and sugar and ice close at hand. Thunderheads had filled the afternoon sky but were now passing to the northeast without rain, and the sky was clearing as the sun went down. The air was gradually becoming cooler, but not much, and I was grateful for the chill of the river around my feet as I sat on a rock and watched for rising trout.

A big yellow mayfly drifted on the surface past my legs, and I scooped it from the current. Large wings of pale-yellowish cream and a butter-yellow body marked with fine bands of brilliant orange. A Cream Variant—*Potamanthus distinctus*, if you prefer, which is a common northeastern mayfly—and one of many I hoped to see as darkness fell. If present in sufficient quantities, the flies are big enough to draw the attention of large trout, although it's a summertime hatch often ignored by many trout fishermen who still believe that both major hatches and rising trout have ceased by the start of summer.

I watched another yellow dun emerge at the surface, float briefly, and then go lumbering off through the still air as it headed for the shelter of the hemlocks. Its flight disappeared in a brown blur, and I was startled. There were almost a dozen cedar waxwings perched on as many hemlock branches overhanging the pool, and they were obviously waiting as I was, although not for trout. Another mayfly took to the air, and two of the birds went in long, swooping dives toward the same target. The mayflies were clumsy, slow fliers and easily taken by the birds, which made me wonder how enough of the insects could ever reach shelter along the banks and thereby survive long enough to reproduce.

There were more mayflies at the surface now, and even more in the air, which was also filled with darting birds. I heard a trout rise in the dark water near the far bank, the sound of a low, deep *chunk!* that one learns to associate with bigger fish. The fish fed once again as I watched, taking a dun from the surface with the same noisy authority. I had marked its location the second time, and dropped a big Cream Variant about 3 feet upstream of the fish. The fly drifted for only a few seconds before the trout took hard in a broad swirl, and birds, flies, and everything else disappeared from my mind as the trout made a long run upstream along the ledges. Eventually the fish came quietly to hand at the edge of the pool, hooked deeply and bleeding from its gills. It would never have survived if released, so I killed it quickly and placed it in the shallows before turning back to the pool.

It was almost dark, and the birds had disappeared. The mayflies were continuing to hatch in gradually diminishing quantities and were flying to the sheltering trees unmolested except for a couple of small bats that flew in crazily erratic circles over the water. The bright yellow insects were like points of light over the black water, and I could follow their flight easily until they disappeared among the dark green branches. It was obvious that in spite of all the predators attendant to their hatching that the mayflies had found their safety in numbers.

Mass emergences over a period of a few days to two weeks or rarely more are characteristic of most important trout-stream insects. These events are usually taken at face value by anglers—a hatch is a hatch, after all—but the ecological mechanisms at work in such cycles are extraordinarily complex.

For starters, aquatic insects are incredibly diverse. In previous chapters on stream ecology, we've already seen that certain mayflies, for example, will inhabit only areas of faster riffles, while other mayfly species occupy only areas of slower currents and backwaters. This sort of species separation based on habitat is often drawn much more finely in nature, and some of the best examples are found among certain filter-feeding caddisfly larvae.[5]

Many caddisfly species (but by no means all) common to trout streams are filter feeders, which means they construct fine, silken nets that filter minute bits of organic material from the current. After a net has accumulated some food, the larva eats the net and its contents and then builds another one.

As one progresses downstream from the headwater reaches of trout streams toward rivers of larger flow volume, the particle size of organic matter suspended in the current tends to decrease. As an extreme example, headwater areas may receive a large volume of falling leaves each autumn, which are shredded by certain nymphs and larvae specifically adapted to this sort of food, and the leaves are further broken up by the action of the current. The farther downstream one travels, the smaller the leaf particles become. In addition, other things such as diatoms, bits of algae, and drifting zooplankton all appear in increasing quantity in a downstream direction.

The number of different species of net-spinning caddisflies (meaning those in the family Hydropsychidae) generally increases likewise in a downstream direction. Net size likewise decreases, as does the general body size of those individual species making up the overall mix. Headwater species (e.g., *Arctopsyche*) spin relatively large nets in rapidly flowing water to make the most of an environment that's essentially poor in nutrients. Species more typical of a downstream environment (e.g., *Hydropsyche*) have adapted by spinning smaller nets in slower currents, a practice permitted by the increased amount of organic material carried by downstream currents. Such caddisflies are typically quite specific in terms of the current-speeds they inhabit, which means that even in the broad reach of a single riffle, certain areas will hold more individuals of one species than another.

The great diversity of specific habitats offered by North American waters—both flowing and still—is one reason for the equal if not even greater diversity of aquatic insects. There are, for example, some 600 distinct North American mayfly species found north of Mexico,[6] as well as approximately 1,200 species of caddisflies found either in the United States or Canada (or both).[7] Obviously not all of these are of importance to trout fishermen; some, for example, are warm-water species and don't occur in trout habitat. Still others are pond or lake forms not found in flowing waters. Most of those remaining don't occur simultaneously in any given trout stream but are distributed regionally and often only in certain areas of a given watershed. There is, however, often a greater variety of stream insects present in any stream than most fishermen suspect. As one example, John Juracek and Craig Mathews have cited a report of more than sixty mayfly species being found in Montana's Gallatin River, a well-known trout stream.[8] Part of this diversity is attributable to the diversity of habitats available in this particular stream, which might not be available in others, and many of these species are apparently found in such low numbers as to be unimportant to trout. Even so, it's a remarkably large number, especially when considered as only part of the aquatic community that also includes dozens of different species of caddisflies, stoneflies, midges, craneflies, and other aquatic insects in the same reaches of stream.

The coexistence of these many small creatures in the same limited area is a fascinating puzzle, some probable answers to which are even more intriguing. Let's start with a very simple analogy. There are two hungry rabbits in a garden, both looking at one short row of lettuce and one short row of carrots. If both rabbits attack the lettuce, there won't be enough lettuce to satisfy either. The same is true for the carrots. So the rabbits agree that one will eat only carrots and the other will eat only lettuce, thereby satisfying the needs of both animals. The rabbits have thus *partitioned* the garden's available resources between themselves. This is essentially the same concept of resource partitioning among organisms that we considered in a discussion of trout ecology in Chapter 4.

In real life, of course, things are much more complicated, so much so that I don't believe they've ever been fully documented although the concepts are firmly in place. Essentially, the many insect inhabitants of the streambed have over time partitioned the stream's available resources among themselves, not by decision, of course, but by evolving in increasingly specialized ways. Different but similar species may eat different foods or may eat the same foods but at different times, to give what's again an oversimplified example. The concept of different species coexisting in the same habitat by using that habitat in different ways at different times is at least part of the reason behind the fisherman's chronology of hatches. This brings us handily back to the idea of maple leaves and mayflies that began this discussion in the first place.

If all of the different mayfly nymphs present in a spring trout stream were to grow, mature, and hatch at the same time, their needs for food and living space would be far greater than the stream can supply. The familiar diversity of a trout stream's mayflies is often possible only if the stream's resources are partitioned among the different species over time. Consider two similar *Ephemerella* mayflies that coexist in many trout streams and use essentially the same habitat: Hendricksons (*E. subvaria*) and sulphurs (*E. dorothea*). Hendricksons hatch in early May, while sulphurs hatch typically four to six weeks later. During the winter, both are feeding and growing slowly. Hendricksons mature with the warming waters of early spring and then hatch, leaving the stream by the thousands. Their eggs are laid a few days later, and the newly born nymphs are almost microscopic as they disperse within the streambed gravel. Meanwhile, the related sulphur nymphs have several weeks of rapid growth and maturation before hatching, during which time they face absolutely no competition from their larger Hendrickson cousins with which they shared the stream during the winter.

Although there's certainly more to the whole process than just this one example, it is in large measure why we as trout fisher-men have our familiar chronologies of insect hatches that cycle through the seasons. Some of the other reasons are explored in the following chapter, where we'll look at some additional aspects of mayfly biology in particular. I hope meanwhile to have offered some simple tools with which you can learn over time to predict the dates of hatches along your favorite trout stream, and perhaps to have extended your appreciation of the insects themselves, regardless of what you choose to call them.

1. Hopp and Blair (1973) provide the definition and are also the most important source for the general aspects of this discussion.

2. See Hopkins (1938).

3. See the various papers by Sweeney and Vannote (as both joint and separate authors) for some excellent discussions of the relationship between nymphal development and water temperature.

4. From Hopp and Blair (1973).

5. See, especially, Alstad (1982).

6. See Edmunds, et al. (1976).

7. See Wiggins (1977).

8. See Juracek and Mathews (1992).

16
Some Notes on the Biology of Mayflies

There was suddenly a compelling need to lie.

The fishing on that particular morning had been extraordinary as mayflies blanketed the river, and the trout rose accordingly. It was an early-spring hatch that would not normally have appeared until late afternoon, but unseasonably hot weather had apparently brought the flies off several hours early. By lunchtime, both flies and fish had quit, and I headed for the car, for once quite sated with fishing.

As I stowed my gear, other cars began arriving, full of anglers who started rigging rods, donning waders, and getting ready for the anticipated afternoon hatch that I believed had already come and gone. One man walked over and asked the inevitable question as to how I had done.

"Not too bad," I answered, trying to match the twang made implicit by my Vermont license plates. I used a handkerchief to wipe any remaining moisture off my rod sections and began slipping them into their case as the man continued to stand behind me.

"So wha'd'ja get?" He wanted to know.

"Oh, I got a few," I answered. "Actually, it was a pretty good morning." He nodded and left, for which I was grateful. I hadn't wanted to say I'd come up empty, thereby seeming incompetent. And I certainly hadn't wanted to tell the truth. That it was one of the best fishing mornings of my life. That I'd taken eighteen brown trout in three frantic hours, including one that went almost 3 pounds. In that case, he would certainly have thought me a braggart and a liar. Politics as usual dictated the usual plausible answer: Yes, a few small fish, and none too large, thank you.

Besides, if I *had* told him the truth, I would also have had to tell him that the day's hatch had already come off the water, thereby ruining his afternoon before he even got started. So I left well enough alone, and left.

After lunch and a nap, I drove back slowly along the river just to see if my guess about there being no further hatch was correct. I parked next to a long pool that held a dozen fisherman, all standing waist-deep in the river and about 50 feet apart. It was 3:30 P.M., which is the textbook hour for this particular hatch on a sunny, late-April afternoon. I could see no flies on the water or in the air. Nor did I see any of the energetic casting that might indicate some trout activity was taking place. Most of the fishermen were just standing and quietly waiting.

There was considerable loud griping in the local tavern that night about how this rare 90-degree April day had made both mayflies and trout uncooperative. The trout, it seems, would rise by the book or not at all. I had started my dinner early and so left as the crowd was continuing to gather. There was just enough daylight left for a quick trip to the river before heading to the motel, so I drove back to the same pool I'd fished that morning. The air had cooled just enough as it grew dark to bring a shiver or two as I stepped over the guardrail and walked down to the water's edge. What I saw was beyond belief.

The water was covered with drifting mayflies. At least a dozen trout were rising steadily within an easy cast of where I stood. They must be spinners, I thought quickly, because it's cool enough for the recently hatched flies to have molted, mated, and returned to the river for egg laying. I snatched a fly from the water's surface and saw that its wings were still dull gray and partly opaque, not the clear, hyaline wings that characterize almost all mayfly spinners. It was a freshly emerged dun, one of hundreds and hundreds that were emerging as they had this morning—at an hour unheard of for this particular species whose supposed predictability had fostered a long tradition of afternoon angling.

I ran up the bank, hurriedly rigged a rod with the morning's successful dry fly, and ran back down, not bothering with waders or vest. After catching a pair of small browns and one much larger, I finally hooked a still bigger trout—one that I'm certain I would not have had to lie about—that finally sheared my leader tippet on an underwater rock. By then it was too dark to change flies or even to fish. I could still hear an occasional rise, and by looking very carefully could still see flies here and there on the water. Once again, I had had the river to myself, so no one saw me leave, shaking my head at the day's events and my own wonderful, dumb luck.

The river in this particular case was upstate New York's Beaverkill, and the flies were Hendrickson mayflies. But the example could just as easily have been any one of a number of other American trout streams, and the flies could just as easily have been a different species. On an average July day on an average western trout stream, for example, one can reasonably expect to see hatches of pale morning duns (*Ephemerella inermis* or *E. infrequens,* two slightly different species with the same common name and similar habits) at about eleven o'clock in the morning. These are an important and widespread western hatch about which the same sort of tradition is developing as to timing as pertains to afternoon-emerging Hendricksons in the East. But like Hendricksons, the PMDs (as pale morning duns are often called)—and *all* other mayfly species—don't always behave as they're supposed to.

If a particular species of mayfly hatches at three o'clock in the afternoon, like you, I greet them gratefully and fish for the trout that rise in response. But I also greet them with a little curiosity, wanting to know, for example, why they didn't hatch at eleven in the morning or six in the evening instead. And why they're hatching on this particular day instead of last week or next. Mayfly hatches are often too periodic to be construed as random events. If they're not random, there must be some reasons for their regularity.

Water temperature is apparently the overriding determinant governing both the timing and intensity of mayfly hatches. This seems almost self-evident and is already part of many well-established angling traditions. For example, we have been told by numerous angling authors over many years that spring mayfly hatches begin when stream temperatures reach the mid-50s (Fahrenheit) and remain there for several days in succession. As a corollary example, we have also been told that Hendrickson mayflies will hatch at about 3:30 P.M. on warm spring afternoons, which happens to be the hour at which water temperatures usually reach their daily peak at that particular season. This emergence schedule is very apt to be true on an average day on an average trout stream during an average spring season. Unfortunately, most trout fishermen seem to have taken these averages as absolutes, which they most certainly are not, and are confounded when things don't happen according to the fisherman's perceived schedule.

A similar problem exists with so-called hatch charts, which have been widely published since the 1970s for various regions or particular rivers to indicate what hatches typically appear at any given time during the spring, summer, and fall seasons. Once again, such information is (or should be) based on the average emergence dates of various insect species over a period of many years. The actual date on which such emergences begin can vary by as much as several weeks, depending on that region's recent climatic history as reflected in changing patterns of stream temperatures. Many fishermen still believe such charts to be ironclad, travel several hundred miles to fish a particular hatch on a certain date, and are sometimes dumbfounded to find that the flies either emerged during the previous week or probably won't appear until several days after it's time to go home. Accurately compiled hatch charts are immensely valuable, giving one an idea of what to expect at any particular time and place, but should never be given as gospel nor taken as such.

It should be evident by now that the influence of water temperature on hatch timing isn't as simple as it first appears, which is indeed the case. For example, the rate of change in water temperature over a period of several weeks is probably more important than the absolute water temperature on any given day. I have had superb dry-fly fishing to hatches of Hendrickson mayflies during

late spring storms that howled with snow and driving sleet, days on which only a fool would be on the river and during which no mayfly in its right mind would consider hatching. But mayflies, of course, don't have minds, while they do have thermal histories that determine their growth and development. In this particular case, several warm weeks had brought the nymphs to maturity, at which point they were hatching come hell or bad weather.

Trout-stream mayflies grow, mature, and hatch according to their accumulation of thermal units over time. I give this as fact although it hasn't been scientifically established for *all* mayflies, just a few species. A thermal unit is some undefined unit of temperature over time that's analogous to the degree-days you've probably heard mentioned in conjunction with either agricultural or home-heating weather forecasts. At a certain temperature—say 32 degrees, although the actual value may be somewhat higher—a nymph's metabolism and activity are low enough so that no growth or development is taking place. If exposed to a 10-degree increase over a ten-hour period, the nymph becomes more active, feeds to a greater extent, and some growth is enabled. By this example, in which I'm using hypothetical numbers, the nymph will have accumulated one hundred thermal units, which will have corresponded to a certain amount of growth.

Now let's say the stream cools off a little with bad weather in late spring. The nymph accumulates a lesser number of thermal units during this interval, which means it grows at a reduced rate. During the following two weeks, the weather turns unseasonably warm and the water warms likewise. Now the nymph is accumulating thermal units at a greatly accelerated rate, growth and maturation proceed rapidly, and at the end of two weeks the nymph emerges at the surface as a winged mayfly five days before its long-term average date for this particular river.

The number of thermal units required for the maturation and hatching of mayfly nymphs is apparently species specific. That's one of several reasons why different mayfly species hatch in temperate-zone trout streams at different times during the spring, summer, and fall.

Assume for the moment that we're occasionally fishing the emergences of a particular mayfly species over a period of about three weeks, which period encompasses the first and last actual hatching dates of this species for the season. Some experienced trout fishermen have noticed that the emerged duns seem to be larger at the beginning of this period than they are at the end. In actuality, the difference in body weight of individual mayflies sampled at the beginning and end of this period may be as much as 40 percent, which is substantial. As a practical matter, this means that all mayfly duns of a particular species are *not* all the same size, which is contrary to popular belief. In some cases, this range may encompass almost three hook sizes, the difference in which is sometimes enough to cause refusals by trout if the wrong size is used at the right time.

The reasons for this phenomenon are also temperature related, and help also to explain why some mayfly species may be more abundant than others in any particular river. Adult mayflies of a single species typically lay their eggs in a stream intermittently over a period of several days or even weeks. This means that the eggs hatch at different times, a difference that may be exaggerated by short-term changes in water temperature. During the rest of the season and over the winter, the nymphs are feeding and growing, but are not all the same size. This is first because some hatched later than others, and, second, because as individuals they are subject to slightly different conditions in the stream; some may encounter more food than others and thus grow more rapidly, for example.

In the spring as water temperatures increase, the nymph's growth, meaning an increase in size, becomes independent of its development, meaning maturation and the development of such things as wing buds and gonads that will be used as adults. By very rough analogy, the sexual maturation of people is essentially independent of their height and weight. As the nymphs' thermal-unit threshold is approached, they begin to hatch, with the larger ones usually coming first. Their species-specific trigger of accumulated thermal units causes all of the nymphs to hatch over a short term, even though their body sizes may be quite varied.

Female mayfly adults of smaller-than-average body size will in all likelihood develop fewer eggs than females of the same species that are larger. As a general case, this means the smaller flies will be less successful at perpetuating their species than larger ones. Different trout streams have radically different temperature profiles over time, which will vary within sections of the same stream and also from region to region. The available thermal units in a particular stream over time will likewise vary, which has a dramatic influence on the species mix of mayflies found in any particular body of water. One particular creek, for example, may usually offer water temperatures over time that are especially favorable to the development of larger-than-usual nymphs of a particular mayfly species, the adults of which will lay greater-than-normal numbers of eggs and continue the cycle. At the same time and place, temperature conditions will be less favorable to another species, producing smaller-than-normal nymphs at hatching time, fewer eggs produced, and lesser numbers of nymphs in the stream. If temperatures are cold or warm enough to prevent the completion of a particular species' life cycle entirely, then that species will be absent. Over time, a given reach of stream will approach a dynamic equilibrium in terms of the variety of species present and the numbers of individuals of each species. This is a concept developed by several aquatic entomologists over the past twenty years, which is sometimes called the Thermal Equilibrium Hypothesis.[1]

All of the foregoing is obviously influenced by other factors. For example, if the physical habitat required for a particular mayfly nymph is missing from a stream, that species won't occur there, regardless of the stream's thermal characteristics. Burrowing mayfly nymphs that require a soft substrate aren't found in bedrock creeks, for instance. Further, any missing links in a typical stream's food web—such as a lack of algal growth for any reason—will obviously constrain the numbers and kinds of its inhabitants, as will any unusual attributes of water chemistry such as the acidity caused by acid rain.

If everyone happens to be home, my driveway at the moment hold three vehicles; a dark-maroon station wagon, a light-gray station wagon, and a black pickup truck. I happened to look out the other evening and noticed a swarm of mayfly spinners flying up and down in the air near the cars. When I went out to check more closely, I was amazed to find that all the spinners were hovering closely over the hood and roof of the gray vehicle; there were none over the black truck or maroon station wagon. Because I had always supposed that such mating-mayfly activity takes place over water, I then assumed that the insects took the dull light reflecting from the car to be the same as that reflected by the riffles in a nearby stream.

This explanation would have been satis-

factory except for the fact that the other cars had attracted no mayflies while seeming—to me, at least—to offer equally attractive and stream-imitating reflections. This was—and is—confounding. I grabbed one of the little flies from the air and stood staring at it while it rested on my fingertip. The fly's minuscule brain would easily fit on the head of a pin with room left over for more angels than I could possibly count. Yet somehow this fly and several dozen relatives had made a deliberate and unanimous choice among three adjacent and similar reflective surfaces.

As trout fishermen our collective knowledge of mayfly spinners and their behavior is very superficial, which is surprising considering the great extent to which mayfly nymphs and duns have been studied by anglers. Here's a brief summary of what most anglers have taken as common knowledge about a mayfly's life cycle.

The mayfly nymph hatches into a winged adult, called a dun by fishermen and a subimago by entomologists. Technically, however, duns aren't adults because they aren't yet sexually mature. The dun flies off into the nearby bushes, where in a matter of

Mayfly spinners.

hours or a few days at most it molts, shedding its entire skin from wingtips to tails, and becomes what fishermen call a spinner, which is an imago to entomologists. The spinner has clear wings, while the dun's wings were merely translucent and most often tinged with gray although sometimes another color such as cream. The spinners return to the river in the evening, often to riffle areas, where they swarm in clouds a few feet above the surface. The individual flies show an erratic up-and-down flight pattern within the swarm, which is why they're called spinners.

Male and female spinners encounter each other in the swarm and mate, the pairs often seen flying while attached to one another in the process. The females then dip to the water to release their fertilized eggs. Both males and females eventually fall spent and *en masse* to the surface, where they die and drift flush in the surface tension with wings outstretched, becoming easy prey for avidly feeding trout.

This is all true as a generalized case, but almost all trout fishermen of my aquaintance have taken the common scenario as being true of all trout-stream mayflies, which simply isn't so.[2] Swarms of some mayfly species may take place a mile or even more away from the river, or may occur 100 feet or more in the air overhead. In either case, the spent adults may appear suddenly on the water, causing a rise of trout that catches anglers unprepared since the obvious clues of nearby and visible swarms have been absent. Still other species that are noted for their characteristic late-evening swarms may have been prevented from swarming by winds or bad weather during several consecutive evenings, and so will instead swarm, mate, and fall to the water in the calm of early morning. Again, the trout will feed eagerly, but often in the absence of fishermen who follow patterns more rigid than those of either mayflies or trout.

Under ideal conditions, closely related members of the same mayfly genus may show consistently and radically different behavior as spinners. Hendrickson mayflies (*Ephemerella subvaria*), for example, are well known for their late-evening swarms a few feet above riffles, while spinner falls of western Green Drakes (*E. grandis*) apparently occur in the early morning before daylight and so are of little importance to anglers.

Finally, while mayflies as a group are indeed ephemeral, meaning short-lived as adults, the term must be taken in a relative way. Adult mayflies do not feed, so their brief existence is oriented entirely toward reproducing their own kind. Some species characteristically hatch, molt, mate, and fall to the water within a few hours, of which the common *Tricorythodes* mayflies are a good example. Others may molt and then be able to wait in the bushes for several days or longer until weather conditions are most conducive to swarming. I have, for example, kept Hendrickson spinners alive in cages for as long as sixteen days, although I'm sure the adults were so weakened by the end of that time as to be incapable of swarming or mating.

Obviously, the behavior of mayfly spinners and its implications for trout fishing are enormously varied, far more so than accounted for in many angling books, which so far have provided only cursory treatment of this important stage in a mayfly's life cycle. Without getting too far into the idiosyncracies of individual species, which is a broad topic beyond the scope of this book, there are a few things you can note that will be helpful in predicting and fishing spinner falls along your favorite trout stream.

First, simply be aware of the kinds of mayflies that have been hatching during recent days. Sooner or later, there will be one or more spinner falls of the same flies that may produce excellent fishing. Even sparse or intermittent hatches of some mayflies can assume much greater importance as spinners, because while the duns may have been emerging sporadically over several days, the spinners will return as a very large group all at once.

The weather is obviously important. Most mayfly-spinner falls will occur when the air temperature is between 65 and 75 degrees, when there is no wind, and when the humidity is relatively low. Intervals of such weather can be determined well before heading to the river just by listening to weather forecasts and being aware of when the ideal conditions might occur. The first such period—morning or evening—after several stormy days is the best possible time, because while duns will likely have been hatching during that interval, the same flies will not have been able to swarm and thus will probably have accumulated in great numbers.

Because mayfly spinners drift flush with the water's surface, they are hard to see. So if you suspect that the trout are taking spent—meaning feeding on spinners—check the surface very carefully. Because trout have learned that spent mayflies aren't about to escape, the trout's riseforms are usually very gentle when feeding on spinners, and the riseforms are usually—but not always—a good clue. Other flush-floating insects such as flying ants will cause trout to rise in similar fashion, so don't base your fly selection on the riseforms alone.

Because the numerous books on angling entomology published during the past thirty years have covered many mayfly species in vast detail, there's a growing tendency among trout fishermen to believe we've learned all there is to learn about such flies. If nothing else through this chapter, perhaps you've come to appreciate just how much information is missing from the angler's files. I can, for example, suggest that a particular mayfly nymph will hatch at three in the afternoon on April 30 from a particular pool, and have a variety of well-founded reasons for that suggestion. But suppose it turns out to be a very windy day, and the emergence is less prolific than expected. Do some of the nymphs somehow know the wind is blowing and postpone their hatching for a day or two? Can these nymphs sense and react to changes in water density from changes in barometric pressure in turn caused by changing weather patterns? Are they sensitive to subtle changes in concentrations of dissolved gasses, such as a reduction in oxygen tension caused by a falling barometer?

I don't know. But it's become increasingly apparent that such answers and ideas as I've been able to obtain continue to produce an even greater number of questions, so there's little danger of removing the element of luck from our favorite sport.

1. See the various papers by Sweeney and Vannote (either as joint or separate authors), from which much of this discussion has been derived.

2. The most in-depth study I've obtained concerning the behavior of mayfly spinners is that published by the entomologist Eino Savolainen in 1978, which was based on his work with a variety of mayfly species in Finland. The genera covered in this study—*Ephemera, Siphlonurus, Heptagenia, Leptophlebia, Caenis,* and *Centroptilum*—are well represented in many American trout streams.

PART FOUR

THE GAME

17
Those Old-Fashioned Wet Flies

It was late summer and low water. The creek that had come thundering past our house in April was reduced to a quiet gurgle among the dry stones. My father and I stood watching a spot where the trickling flow swept weakly into a small pocket under a stump, from which it emerged to join the big river a few yards farther along.

"There's a trout there," he said. "Do you want to catch it?"

I was still quite young and had recently started fly-fishing, although by then I had also read a great deal of Bergman, McClane, and others, and thought myself something of an authority. I looked skeptically toward the stump, where I could see no trout. "How do you know there's a trout there?" I asked my father. "Can you see one?"

"No, I can't see one. I just know," he said quietly. "Watch." He tied a small Brown Hackle wet fly to his leader, a fly pattern almost as old as fly-fishing itself, and made a couple of false casts in the air toward the stump. Finally he allowed his line to fall across the bare rocks, settling the fly in the slight current at the edge of the stump. The fly sank quickly and drifted down in the shadows. As I watched, the line gave a perceptible twitch, Father raised his rod tip, and in due course a foot-long brown trout was slid splashing and flopping onto the rocks.

I was incredulous, so much so that the incident remains in my mind with exceptional clarity decades later. Three things came distinctly to my own life from that event, the first of which is that I have never since passed up a chance to drift a fly through the shadows of a stream-bank tree stump. Second, I subsequently paid much greater attention to whatever my father had to say about anything. And finally, I continued to fish traditional wet flies with considerable affection and enjoyment, not only for the rich fabric of memories they offer, but because they work.

There's an old, leather fly wallet in my own collection that tells much of the wet-fly story, which in turn may help to correct some modern and very prevalent misconceptions. Written clearly with a stylish hand inside the front leaf is the following notation: "John S. Beecher. New York. April 15, 1840." By that date, it's the oldest American fly wallet of documented age that I've seen in many years of looking. The only one I've examined that's known certainly to be older was hand dated in Edinburgh, Scotland, in the 1830s and is now in the collection of the American Museum of Fly Fishing. Fly wallets that can be documented from before the American Civil War are quite rare; together with rods, fly lines, and loose flies, they were used, worn out, and discarded, rather than being treasured and passed along like grandfather's musket or the family's silver teaspoons. For lack of any other reason, I attributed this wallet's survival to the fact that most of its contents fell from American angling fashion after about 1860, and therein lies the tale.

Beecher's wallet is divided into hand-sewn pages of parchment or heavily oiled paper (I'm not sure which), each side of a page being further divided as three hand-sewn pockets, each one open at its top. The whole affair is about 5 inches wide, 8 inches deep, and 2 inches thick, being covered by an elegant, tooled-leather wrap secured with a miniature belt and buckle. Each pocket holds half a dozen wet flies of the same size and pattern, coiled neatly together on their gut snells. These flies, of course, predate the invention of the eyed hook, which Henry Hall developed in England during the late 1870s. Absent any hook eyes or metal loop to which a leader could be tied, early flies were usually snelled on blind-eye hooks, which means a short length of silkworm gut or other line was tied directly to the hook shank before the fly itself was constructed. The other end of the short snell was usually fashioned onto a small loop, which was used in attaching the snelled fly to one's leader. The gut snells on Beecher's flies are rather fine and appear to be about 8 to 10 inches long; I haven't tried to uncoil them for fear of breaking them. The snells on later Victorian-era American wet flies were typically both heavier and shorter, often being about 6 inches long.

Many experienced anglers know that wet flies are the oldest artificial-fly form, having been traced at least as far back as the thirteenth century in western Europe. There is, however, the equally prevalent and incorrect assumption that all old wet flies were like the large and gaudy Victorian patterns popular in America from after the Civil War until well into the 1920s. More of these recent Victorian flies have survived in various collections than flies of any other historic vintage, so as artifacts they are encountered by the greatest number of people. These same flies are often colorfully bright and visually appealing to fishermen and nonfishermen alike and have colorful names, too—all attributes that have helped to make the image of such flies representative of *all* trout-fishing history rather than a minor part of it, which is closer to the truth. The white, red, green, and gold Royal Coachman wet, which was so christened in a late-nineteenth-century Vermont kitchen, is one example, as is Henry Wells' Parmachenee Belle, a red-and-white brook-trout fly that Wells named after his favorite lake in western Maine.

Beecher's wet flies are older than any of the gaudy classics by several decades. They are uniformly small, drab, and wonderfully imitative of aquatic-insect forms, fully the equal of the best modern efforts in that regard. There are even a few extended-body mayfly imitations in Beecher's collection, representing a technique of tying large insect imitations on small hooks that didn't become widely used until the 1970s but which Beecher's flies anticipate by more than a century. Small, imitative wet flies—as small as a modern size 20, or less than ¼ inch long—were in use by British anglers at least since the early 1700s and probably well before. Their construction depended mostly on one's ability to fashion miniature hooks from small sewing needles, a skill common to many adept anglers of that period and ex-

tending back to before the fifteenth century. Other fly-tying techniques were also sufficiently developed by that time to allow the construction of small wet flies that could be used effectively with the finest of horsehair leaders.

The ancient British tradition of small, drab wet flies was developed over centuries of fishing for often-selective brown trout, which was substantially more difficult than the brook-trout fishing that characterized much of nineteenth-century American trout fishing. The brook trout here were, for a time, both more plentiful and often less demanding of fly pattern, which is partly why the so-called fancy flies blossomed in popularity after the Civil War. Such flies succeeded in spite of themselves simply because our brook trout were easily caught. As our trout water became more heavily fished, as brook-trout populations declined, and as brown trout were introduced to American waters starting in 1883, the fishing became more difficult. With this the popularity of brightly complex wet flies began to fade, and such flies are now best seen as a brief aberration in a centuries-long time line of imitative wet flies and fishing.

When properly tied and fished, wet flies are subtle flies and have almost always been such. There's certainly nothing flashy about a "Dun Cut" wet fly with a "body of black wool, wings of blackest Drake Jay"[1] (probably a precursor of our modern Black Gnat), a pattern commonly attributed to Juliana Berners, a British prioress, sometime before the year 1450. Walton, Cotton, and others through the seventeenth and eighteenth centuries were fishing such flies in small sizes and often in deliberate—if somewhat crude—imitation of whatever insects the trout happened to be feeding on at particular time. Many of our modern fly patterns have their roots in this era, with still-popular wet flies such as the Cowdung, March Brown, Blue Dun, Alder, and Woolly Worm being essentially unchanged after several hundred years of use.

While many of the flies have remained the same, however, modern trout fishermen have simply forgotten—or never learned—how to use them. The subtleties of wet-fly fishing have been largely overshadowed by the relatively recent and high-tech glitz of graphite and the search for increasingly sophisticated fly patterns. For example, both now and centuries ago, the most common wet-fly method is to cast quartering downstream (meaning across the current in a downstream direction) and to then let the fly or flies play across the current. A more sophisticated method was described by W. C. Stewart, who plied his wet flies in the tumbling streams of the northern British Isles. Stewart used his 1857 book *The Practical Angler* to advocate fishing wet flies upstream without drag, a radical suggestion at a time when almost all of his cohorts worked their flies down. His arguments for this approach eventually evolved as the classic, upstream dry-fly method, which we'll consider in a later chapter. For the moment, though, Stewart's observations are more important as they pertain to wet-fly fishing:

> The last advantage of fishing up[stream] is, that by it the angler can much better adapt the motions of his flies to those of the natural insect. And here it may be mentioned as a rule, that the nearer the motions of the artificial flies resemble those of the natural ones under similar circumstances, the greater will be the prospects for success. Whatever trout take the artificial fly for, it is obvious they are much more likely to be deceived by a natural than by an unnatural motion [meaning drag].

Stewart was as particular about his wet-fly patterns as he was about tactics, and the following criteria he offered are tremendously important even now:

> The great point, then, in fly dressing, is to make the artificial fly resemble the natural insect in shape, and the greater characteristic of all river insects is extreme lightness and neatness of form. Our great objection to the flies in common use is, that they are much too bushy; so much so, that there are few flies to be got in the tackle shops which we could use with any degree of confidence in clear water. Every possible advantage is in favour of a lightly-dressed fly; it is more like a natural insect; it falls lighter on the water . . . and there being less material about it, the artificial nature of that material is not so easily detected; and also, as the hook is not so much covered with feathers, there is a much better chance of hooking a trout when it rises. We wish to impress very strongly upon the reader the *necessity of avoiding bulky flies* [italics are Stewart's *and* my own].

Even now, many flies—most especially wet flies—as found in most tackle shops are overdressed; that is, made with an excess of materials or, in Stewart's words, "too bushy."

Like others both before and after his time, Stewart emphasized the use of soft, flexible materials in wet-fly design; hackles, for example, so soft "that when a . . . [wet fly] is made of one of them, the least motion [in the water] will agitate and impart a singularly lifelike appearance to it." For the most part, Stewart found such hackles among the wing feathers of small land birds such as starlings and plover, as well as neck hackles from grouse, which are still commonly used. The widespread efforts in this country during the past twenty years at breeding rooster hackles of superior length and stiffness for dry flies have produced as corollaries large numbers of hen necks featuring long, fine, but still very soft hackle feathers in a wide range of sizes and in both solid and mottled colors. While stiff rooster hackle is too immobile in the water for most wet-fly applications, many modern hen necks are superb for this purpose and are widely available in fly shops. In that respect, at least, wet-fly anglers have never had things so good.

Stewart called his wingless flies "spiders" because that's how they appeared to him, although they don't imitate spiders *per se*. (The word "spider" in modern angling refers to certain dry flies with oversize hackle that don't imitate spiders either.) Modern anglers frequently call them simply soft-hackled flies, which is a name offered most often in recent years by Sylvester Nemes of Montana, who has written two recent books specifically on those types of flies. Stewart eventually settled on three such patterns—Black Spider, Red [Brown] Spider, and Dun Spider—which I've included in the fly-pattern section of this book because they offer the best of all trout-fishing worlds: a generous dose of tradition and a high degree of modern effectiveness.

Surveying older books on wet-fly fishing shows frequent reference to another important term often overlooked in modern wet-fly fishing—entry. This refers to the way in which a wet fly enters or penetrates the water's surface and how the fly performs in the currrent. A wet fly with slim wings tied to lie close to its body and made with just a turn or two of very soft hackle will penetrate the surface with relative ease and will swim smoothly without creating a wake when pulled against or across the current. That's good entry. A bulkier fly, or one with its wings cocked higher above the body, may not sink as quickly and may be more unstable in flowing water, tending to flip-flop in the current or to plane back upward to the surface.

That's poor entry. As is so often the case with all flies, a wet fly's design and construction can thus have as much to do with its relative success as its pattern or choice of materials.

Wet flies were—and sometimes still are—fished in tandem. Two or three to sometimes as many as ten or more flies were fished on a single leader, spaced along its length by dropper loops. The entire assembly was known as a "cast," and one might fish a two-fly cast, a three-fly cast, and so on. It was possible by this means to present the trout with a variety of offerings at once; a Leadwinged Coachman as the point fly, say, with a Montreal on the drop (middle), and a Gray Hackle on the dib (uppermost fly). "Dib" refers to a technique known as "dibbling" that's unique to multiple-fly casts and

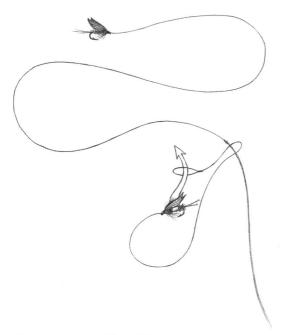

One easy method for adding a second or dropper fly involves simply looping a snelled fly around the leader above the tippet knot.

still very effective. When fishing multiple wets on a relatively short line, raising your rod high will cause the uppermost fly to dance, or "dibble," along the surface of the water while the flies (or fly) farther down the leader remain submerged. The sunken flies (or fly) put enough tension on the leader to allow control of the dibbling fly, making it behave much like an active caddisfly. This erratic movement can drive trout nuts, provoking hard, slashing strikes. In the absence of a hatch, or trout feeding on a particular type of insect, I often try a pair of wets in riffles or boulder-strewn pocket water, using my long reach with a 9-foot rod to swim the flies around the rocks and then raising my rod slowly to dibble the uppermost fly through the likely holding water.

Rigging a wet-fly dropper is a little more complex now than it was in the days when gut leaders came with dropper loops and snelled wet flies could be attached or removed by interlocking their loops with those of the leader. The most commonly recommended method is a 2- to 3-foot-long tippet section—5X, for example—attached by a blood knot to the next-heavier section above, which in this case will likely be 3X nylon. The tag, or free, end of the heavier section isn't trimmed close after tying the knot but is left about 6 inches long for attachment of the dropper fly with a turle or other knot. This heavier section protrudes from the blood knot at right angles to the leader, which helps to keep the dropper fly from tangling while being cast or fished. If the point and dropper flies aren't of the same size, the larger or heavier of the two should always be used as the point fly so its greater weight and momentum in casting will be at the end of your leader to reduce the likelihood of tangles.

I still snell my dropper flies in much the old style, rather than tying blood-knot droppers, although I'm sometimes ridiculed by a companion for so doing. Usually the laughter dies down, however, when the reason becomes apparent. I use a turle knot to tie a short section of monofilament—usually 4X to 1X, with the heavier calibers being for larger, heavier flies—to the fly. At the other end of the short section I tie a perfection loop or a double surgeon's loop (see the appendix on knots), making the whole assembly about 4 inches long. This gets attached to the main leader above the tippet knot simply by passing the fly around the leader and through the loop on its own snell. When pulled tight, the resultant loop is tight to the main leader and is kept from sliding downward by the tippet knot just below it. The fly is now held more stiffly at right angles to the leader by the doubled snell than it is in the case of single filament from a blood-knot dropper. It's also easier and faster to add or remove a dropper by this method instead of retying a whole new tippet with another blood knot. The only drawback to this technique is the pressure it creates by pushing against your tippet knot when a fish is hooked on the dropper. If your tippet knot is poorly tied, this method will cause it to fail sooner than it might ordinarily. If your tippet knot is correctly tied and consequently of full strength, you should have no difficulty.

Perhaps the most important modern attribute of classic wet-fly fishing is that so few other fishermen follow that route. Even on popular, hard-fished streams, an entire generation of trout these days might never have encountered a pair of small, March Brown wets swimming slowly across their riffle, which of course enhances the likelihood of their success. I once had a banner afternoon on a tumbling stretch of Montana's Madison with a pair of small Partridge-and-Green wet flies during a caddis hatch, often taking fish when I was able to dibble the dropper around the rocks. Another fisherman watched from the bank and, when

I finally waded ashore, asked what I'd been using. I showed him one of the small wets and explained why I thought it looked like an emerging caddis. He smiled indulgently at the two wet flies on my leader and said something about old-timers. If I'd said trout were taking on the dibble, he would have thought me crazy.

By far the most common wet-fly method still involves casting at a downstream angle across the river, letting the cast swing in the current until it hangs directly downstream, and then retrieving the cast slowly upstream for some distance before casting again. This is typically done with a floating fly line, which means the cast is fishing no more than an inch or two below the surface. This is easy to do and is therefore often suggested as a beginner's method, although a sinking-tip or even a full-sinking line may be required for deeper or faster currents. It's a good way for a novice to catch a few trout in faster water, but usually several things go wrong, often at the same time: the fly used is too large; it swings too fast in the current; and many trout seem to swirl and bump the fly without being hooked.

Remember that in the absence of a specific, imitative need for a large fly, your wet flies should be small. This means size 14 or 16 for general use; smaller if need be. This is just a matter of matching the odds. There's a much greater number and variety of small insects than larger ones in all trout streams. Assuming that you're just fishing the water and not trying to match a particular insect, your drab wet flies will be generally imitative of a greater number of things to which the trout are accustomed if the flies themselves are small. If fishing a two-fly cast, I usually use a pair of 16s to start and typically of the same pattern.

Fly speed, meaning the speed at which the

fly swings in the current, is very important and usually easy to control. Note that if you cast straight across stream, the current will catch your line immediately and drag its curving belly very quickly across the flow. The movement is typically too fast to interest any trout in the fly. If you cast straight downstream, there's no line belly for the current to catch, and the line doesn't swing at all. It should be immediately obvious that the speed of your swinging fly depends in part on the angle at which you cast across the river, so adjust the angle accordingly.

Once the cast is made, you may have to mend line by flipping slack up- or downstream to slow the fly or speed it up as required. Once you've learned to anticipate the current's effect in a given situation, you can make such line mends in the air before the unrolling fly line lands on the water as described in Chapter 14. In any case, once the cast has landed and is swinging in the current, be sure to follow the drifting fly with the rod tip. If you hold the rod still, the size of the dragging line belly increases during the fly's drift, and the fly speeds up. If you follow the drift with the rod, you can either slow the drift or maintain a constant speed.

Trout often seem to splash and miss swinging wet flies; at other times you may just feel a little bump while seeing a swirl where you imagine the fly to be. Anglers often attribute these short strikes to the trout's reluctance to take the swinging fly with any enthusiasm, but it's usually not the trout's fault. Excessive fly speed often causes misses, but there are other causes, too. Trout are specifically adapted to capturing items drifting to them in the current, which means an emerging nymph or a drowned mayfly adult will often quite literally be carried by the current into the trout's mouth as the trout moves to intercept its food. Further, when the trout does open its mouth to grab something in the current, its gill covers also

flare, which creates an underwater vacuum within the mouth that pulls in both water and the object of the fish's attack. Your wet fly is swinging on a leader made taut by the current, and while the fly's movement may have attracted the fish, that same fly's suspension in the current doesn't conform to the trout's feeding habit. The fly hasn't drifted with the fish on the strike nor has it been sucked in the fish's open mouth, which means the trout either missed the fly entirely or the hook simply scrapes the end of the fish's jaw rather than being taken fully. In the latter case, you'll feel a little bump and then nothing as the trout returns to its feeding station, probably frightened to the point of being uncatchable for an hour or two.

There are several solutions to this common problem, which can be used separately or in combination. The most important is mending line and following your drift with the rod tip to avoid excessive fly speed. While following your drift with the rod, keep the rod tip at a slight angle above the water rather than pointed directly down at the fly. This provides a little curve of slack near the rod that can be sufficient to allow the trout to turn with the fly on the strike. When drifting flies across and down, you'll be holding your fly line pinched firmly between your right index finger and the rod grip so when a trout does strike you can respond immediately just by raising your rod tip. When fishing downstream, trying to set the hook too quickly often just pulls the fly from the trout's mouth. You can avoid this by keeping a few inches of slack between your right-index-finger grip and the reel. When a trout hits your swinging fly, raise the rod and release your index-finger grip at the same time, releasing the slack. Sometimes, at least, the release of a little slack on the strike will mean the difference between a bump and a trout.

Finally, you can boost your odds a little

with downstream wet flies by considering the hook design on which the flies themselves are tied. Most wet flies and other types are tied on hooks with a round, sometimes called "perfect," or sproat bend in which the hook point winds up being fairly far forward and under the fly's body. I try to find and use Limerick-style hooks in tying wet flies, a hook style that places a bit more of the hook-bend's metal to the rear of the fly itself. Having more of the hook's weight farther to the rear of the fly seems to provide more stability in moving water, thus a better wet-fly swim. Limerick-style wet-fly hooks also seem to offer a slightly higher hooking percentage when fishing down and across, probably because this style's hook point is a little more to the rear of the fly than is found with more conventional, round-bend styles. Your chances of finding commercial wets tied on Limerick-bend hooks are almost nil, at least in this country. The hooks themselves, however, are still being made in England (by Partridge of Redditch) and are imported into this country, so you can either make such flies yourself or have them made by any competent flytier.

A dead screech owl lay half buried in the roadside bank of snow, looking so much like another reddish brown lump of mud that I almost missed it while walking past. I picked it up and felt the large primary feathers of its wings, which were both strong and soft in texture, a softness that helped the owl cruise silently over the nighttime meadows. I decided quickly that such feathers would make terrific wet-fly wings, recalling at the same time that possession of the protected owl—alive or dead—was a violation of fish and wildlife laws. So I left the owl as I found it, minus a couple of feathers that I took home and transformed into several small wet flies.

Several months later, Rich Norman and I stood knee-deep in the long, flat water above Wilmington on New York's West Branch Ausable, separated from one another by about 200 yards of slow-moving river. I tied one of the little wets to a long 6X tippet and rubbed the fly with some mud scooped up from between my feet. I cast about 50 feet across the broad flat, and then just waited. The line drifted slowly on the surface for a few seconds and then gave a quick twitch. I pulled, and a small rainbow pulled back, jumping once or twice and making a commotion that was all the more gratifying because my upstream partner—an excellent fisherman—hadn't caught anything yet.

"So whaddit take?" Norman hollered down as I released the fish.

"A Screech Owl," I yelled back. He resumed fishing, and I cast again also. This time the line drifted longer over the slow currents, eventually assuming a broad ess-shape before I again felt a little twitch and again connected with a little rainbow.

"What's a Screech Owl?" Norman hollered again as I released the second trout.

"A wet fly," I yelled back, and resumed casting. After a long, quiet drift, the line lay in a series of broad squiggles between me and the sunken fly and I again felt a little bump and connected with a third trout. As I released the fish, I turned and saw that Norman had come downstream to stand behind me, watching from the bank.

"How did you know you had a fish?" he asked. "I was watching your line and didn't see anything. I don't see how you could even feel anything with all that slack line in the water." I thought about that for a minute or two and finally said I'd just felt the fish take. I gave him a couple of little wets, and he disappeared back through the bushes and upstream.

The fishing of the moment had nothing to do with the magic of Screech Owl wet flies—

there are other feathers just as soft and effective and perfectly legal, which owl feathers are not—and everything to do with a kind of sixth sense that comes with wet-fly experience. It's often more productive to fish your wet fly dead-drift either across or upstream. Since you can't see the sunken fly, and because the fly is drifting (hopefully) without drag, it can be very difficult to tell when you have a strike. Some people, of course, are better at this than others, and the ability of those anglers to detect strikes often seems extrasensory or magical. There's no magic involved, however, just practice, experience, and—most of all—a substantial amount of concentration.

While many people seem able to master the techniques of slack-line casting at various angles relative to the current, most of which were described in Chapter 14, fishing a sunken fly with such casts seems even more difficult. You'll be most often helped by fishing a relatively short line and—more than anything else—concentrating. If you're watching the birds or the sky or talking to another angler, you'll miss more fish than you hook. If there's nothing in your mind but the drift of the fly and nothing in your eyes but the river, you'll catch them. Fishing wet flies in this manner is very much like fishing with dry flies you can't see, which only means that you should be able to visualize the fly's location and its behavior even though you can't see the fly itself. This is tense fishing indeed, and I'm often quite tired after an hour or two spent bent and concentrating on an unseen, drifting fly.

Many anglers use some sort of strike indicator in such fishing these days—some sort of small, visible bobber attached to the leader. Although I'll discuss these gadgets at length in a subsequent chapter on nymph fishing, almost all such arrangements are clumsy both in casting and fishing. Generations of wet-fly men have been drifting their casts without such modern aids, and I guess I'm crusty enough to suggest you learn your wet-fly skills without those sorts of crutches. You'll be a more effective angler for having made the effort.

Fall River in northern California is one of the world's great spring creeks, meandering slowly from its source at Thousand Springs through a gentle valley past Fall River Mills and on to the Sacramento system. It holds a strong population of wild rainbows, some often quite large, and its slow, clear flow makes for demanding dry-fly fishing, which is how most people fish here. Access is limited by a wide assortment of private riverbank holdings, and much of the river is fished from little aluminum prams with small electric motors that allow easy travel up and down the broad currents.

I had anchored at twilight slightly upstream of a small tributary, the currents of which extended for several yards into the much larger and more slowly flowing river. As I watched, one trout rose, and then another as a hatch of small caddisflies brought trout to the surface. I was fishing as a guest of the late Tim Bedford of Oakland, who had recently retired from an engineering career with Kaiser Corporation and who was perhaps best known for the superlative bamboo rods he made in very limited numbers. As I headed to the river, Bedford had given me several small wet flies tied with simple bodies of dark green herl fronted with a turn or two of softly mottled partridge hackle. When I made some comment about old-style flies, Bedford had smiled. "Try 'em," he told me. "They love 'em!"

It was almost dark when I finally knotted one of Bedford's flies to a fine tippet, and I knew there was time for only one fish. I chose what appeared to be the largest riseform, some 30 feet away, and softly dropped the little fly about 3 feet above it. The fly sank a little. I twitched it slightly, then let it dead-drift. I twitched it again, then let it drift. I saw the end of the yellow fly line dart forward and gently raised the rod tip. There was at first a dead, heavy weight that seemed to turn slowly in the water, but which then rapidly accelerated into the black currents of the main river, pulling line from the reel in a long, chattering whisper.

The fish stopped, then slowly swam back toward the creek mouth as I recovered line on the reel. There was another, shorter run, and then another. In a few minutes the trout wallowed on its side at the edge of the boat, and I scooped it up gratefully in the net Bedford had also provided. I slipped the little wet fly from the corner of its jaw, and watched the last colors of the evening light play across the fish's side. I leaned forward to hold the fish briefly in the current until it had the strength to swim from my hands into the dark water; a rainbow of at least 5 pounds that's still the largest stream-resident rainbow I've taken in the lower forty-eight. It was a big fish taken in country then new to me, one made all the more special for its having taken the oldest of trout flies.

1. See McClane (1953).

18
Streamers or Bust

Zonkers, Buggers, and Muddlers sound more like the noontime specials at a Cockney restaurant—side dishes, perhaps, for your bangers and mash—than the names of our most popular streamer flies, but such is the state of modern fly boxes. Streamers have become meat flies; slinky, wiggly things you throw with a heavy leader for big fish. These are the flies you might cast with some desperation after the trout have refused your delicate, no-hackle hors d'oeuvres, served ever so carefully with the finest of leaders. When all else fails, it's streamers or bust. Or so it seems these days.[1]

Of all the basic trout-fly types, streamers are the only ones that are uniquely American, having come to prominence here during the years between the two world wars. Streamer flies started as baitfish imitations in concept, long, slender flies that could be darted in the current to attract larger, fish-eating trout. Various people have been given credit for originating this style: Theodore Gordon, the late Catskill flytier, who was apparently making his large Bumblepuppy shortly before 1900; Alonzo Bacon, who was making trout flies with long, streaming hackles—such as the Rooster's Regret—in Maine at about the same time; Herbert Welch, fabled originator of the still-famous Black Ghost streamer and also from Maine, who claimed to have invented this style in the early 1900s; and finally William Scripture, who was making similar flies in western New York at about the same time, but

used long hair from a deer's tail instead of feathers for the wing, giving rise to the name "bucktail" for what was (and is) essentially the same sort of fly. Since many of the larger wet flies used for trout at the turn of the century were undoubtedly taken as small minnows (rather than insects), the origins of streamer flies are more a matter of degree and intent than outright invention and will probably remain forever obscure.

Streamer flies probably reached their peak as an art form with the work of Carrie G. Stevens, who first tied her celebrated Gray Ghost pattern in the little western Maine community of Upper Dam in 1924. Stevens' work echoed the colors of the then-popular fancy wet flies for brook trout, but her flies were and are unusual for their long, slim proportions. Many of her streamer patterns are superbly imitative of smelt, which are still a principal forage fish for trout and landlocked salmon in Maine's Rangeley Lakes region, where she originally worked. While the Gray Ghost is one of a handful of older streamer patterns that remain popular, most modern versions of the same fly are rather stubby looking and have little resemblance to the slim grace of the originals. I've included an original Stevens dressing in this book's color plates so you'll be able to judge the difference.

Surprisingly, and throughout the streamer fly's brief history, attempts at precise imitation of particular baitfishes have not been commercially durable, and today's most popular streamers manage to look like everything and nothing at the same time. Imitative flies have existed and do still exist, of course. The late Lew Oatman of Shushan, New York, developed a series of elegant streamer patterns during the 1950s to imitate many of the baitfishes found in the lower Battenkill, near his home. Then there were Sam Slaymaker's Little Trout patterns, bucktails imitating juvenile trout by species. More recently, Dave Whitlock, the talented Arkansas flytier, developed what he called a "match-the-minnow" series of streamers, and Ernest Schwiebert included a collection of specifically imitative marabou streamers in his 1978 book *Trout*. While all of these patterns have gotten national publicity by one means or another and at various times, none has persisted in the majority of modern fly boxes, where Buggers and Zonkers are usually the flies of choice.

I regret that a great deal, because many of those imitative patterns are both elegant and effective, while Buggers and Zonkers merely

Three popular streamer styles, top to bottom: Muddler, Zonker, and Woolly Bugger.

catch fish some of the time and are about as elegant as they sound. Many imitative patterns are difficult to tie well—a well-tied, feather-wing streamer is more difficult to make than most dry flies, which may surprise some people who don't tie their own—and that difficulty has limited their general availability and resultant popularity. This accounts in part for the popularity of such simple streamers as the Woolly Bugger, of which I can tie three or four in the same time it takes me to carefully tie one of Oatman's Golden Darters, for example. While both will take trout at times, the Woolly Bugger is more profitable for commercial tiers and thus more widely distributed. It's also easier to fish well, which is another part of the story.

Of all the trout fisherman's options, streamer flies are the most difficult. Drys,[2] wets, and nymphs are all sometimes taken by trout without being manipulated in or on the water after the cast is made. The success of streamer flies usually depends on their lifelike motion, and the best streamer fishermen are wizards at bringing life to the feathers with twitches, line mends, and abrupt stops all in the course of a single cast. This is not easily done, which is probably why streamers lag far behind all other trout flies in commercial sales nationwide. But streamers are usually the best general fly choice for tempting larger-than-normal trout in most rivers. Obviously, your streamer fishing will be most productive if you fish such flies thoughtfully and deliberately rather than as a last resort when nothing else is working.

Like other flies, streamers have the basic attributes of pattern, color, action, design, and size, all of which will affect your results at any given time and place. Pattern is simply the recipe list of materials used in the fly's construction. The fly pattern may be imitative, such as the late Art Flick's Black-Nosed Dace bucktail, or generalistic, such as a White Marabou streamer or Black Woolly Bugger. Questions of imitation are both logical and simple and usually a matter of imitating the baitfishes prevalent in a particular river at a particular time. If, for example, brook trout in a northern river are feeding heavily on an early spring run of smelt, a smelt-imitating streamer is an obvious choice. Certain hackle feathers offer obvious ideas; a light-and-dark-barred grizzly-hackle wing suggests the parr marks of young trout and also the barring of certain minnows and sculpins, while the dark center stripe of a so-called badger hackle appears much like that of the common dace of many trout streams. While imitation can be especially important if trout are feeding on a concentration of baitfish, it's usually less important than color, size, and action for reasons that will be apparent as we go along.

Color affects the extent to which your fly is visible to the trout. While the colors of imitative streamers are dictated by the object of your deception, many of the most popular streamers aren't directly imitative, and so color is more a matter of choice. The most effective single colors for all trout streamers are white, yellow, or black. In general, the distance at which trout are able to see your fly depends on the underwater contrast between that fly and its background. Since black usually offers the greatest such contrast, especially in murky water, it's the underwater color most visible to trout and is an obvious choice. An all-black streamer is like almost nothing in nature, but the wide success of some patterns in this color is at least partly attributable to their high visibility. Yellow is probably most effective in clear but tea-colored water, and white is usually a good bet in clear water of neutral color. Different trout species seem to respond to color in different ways, with black being the best choice for rainbows and cutthroats, yellow for cutthroats and brookies, and white for browns. This doesn't mean, of course, that you won't catch a brown trout on a Black Marabou or a Yellow Muddler, but is generally reflective of average catches over many years of trout fishing. If you're not bothering with deliberately imitative flies, the basic color choices help to make pattern selection simple.

Action is equally important. Some streamer-fly materials are softer and move more easily in the water than others. Soft marabou fibers and the flexible fur on a strip of rabbit hide both wiggle well in the water—more so than stiff bucktail fibers, for example—and are widely used for that reason. A streamer fly's action is ultimately dependent on the angler's manipulation of the fly in the current, but the built-in wiggle of soft materials makes certain flies seem even more alive and thus more effective. The marabou-based Woolly Buggers and rabbit-fur-based Zonkers, in a set of basic colors, derive their effectiveness from their action, offering enough wiggle to sometimes pull trout for even the most inept of anglers, which is largely the basis for their wide popularity.

Design refers to the way in which a streamer is constructed, as opposed to the list of materials specific to a particular pattern. Conventional streamers are based on a long feather or hair wing fixed to the front of a long-shanked hook. If your casting is other than perfectly smooth, the long wing sometimes becomes tangled under the hook, and the cast is wasted because the fly then won't fish properly. The Matuka-style streamers that became popular in the 1970s are one design solution to this problem, in which the wing is bound to the hook shank by a tinsel or wire ribbing, which prevents the wing from tangling in the hook. Woolly Buggers solve the same problem differently by having the marabou wing tied at the rear of the hook where it won't tangle, while the forward hackle is short enough to be also tangle free. Zonkers have their rabbit-strip wing tied in at both the rear and front of the hook, which in yet another manner solves the tangling problem.

The question of size may not be as obvious as it appears. At different times and places, huge, size 3/0 streamers 5 or 6 inches long and miniature streamers about an inch long tied on little size 12 hooks will be appropriate. Most trout fishermen carry a few streamers in size 6 or 8 and let things go at that, which is a mistake. I'm partial to fairly big streamers tied on #2 or #4 hooks, believing in the old adage about how big fish like a mouthful. As a general case, larger trout will respond to larger streamers very well at normal or higher water levels. In summertime low water, however, such a large fly hits a quiet pool like a big rock, and at those times I often go to the other extreme, using ultrasmall streamers that are 1 to 2 inches long and tied sparsely. In addition to questions of stealth, such little streamers are most representative of both small, young-of-the-year trout and juvenile minnows that larger trout are accustomed to seeing and feeding on during the summer. One study of predation by brown trout in Michigan's Au Sable river, as described in Chapter 5, noted that large, predatory browns ate almost five times as many small trout less than one year old than they did trout a few inches longer and between ages one and two years,[3] all of which reinforces the arguments for small streamers in summer.

The trout's underwater world is a place of changing light and shadow and often considerable noise if the water's moving quickly in pocket water or a riffle. Within that world are sticks, twigs, bits of leaves, and other debris tumbling in the current, random bits of motion that when considered together form a pattern to which the trout has become accustomed and learned to ignore. Suddenly something in the current some distance away moves quickly in a way that's different from the natural motion of objects in the current. The trout, being acutely sensitized to movement in its surroundings, first catches the movement peripherally and in milliseconds is immediately focused on the moving object.

As the trout watches, the thing comes closer, being carried down by the current while apparently struggling to swim across the stream at the same time. The thing looks superficially like others the trout has seen, little minnows that the fish has caught and eaten. The trout's aggressive behavior was reinforced by the pleasant sensation of amino acids from the minnow's flesh interacting with hundreds of taste cells in the trout's crushing jaws. The little streamer fly starts to dart past the trout in the current. The trout has learned from capturing other minnows that speed is everything and attacks with an astonishing flurry of spray at the surface.

While we don't have to interrupt this scene for a commerical break, writers do have the luxury of instant replays, a luxury that doesn't pertain in ordinary fishing. With that in mind, let's take this trout's-eye view example and replay it a couple of times to examine some alternatives that will also give some insight into basic streamer tactics. In each case, we'll start with the trout having suddenly perceived something new and different in its underwater environment. It's important to realize that this perception usually happens with incredible swiftness and focuses the trout immediately on whatever it is that's different from the ongoing background of the stream. By analogy, it's much like a person's sitting and half listening to some muted Muzak in an office, a sound that's unconsciously tuned out and against which the drop of a coin on the floor sounds like a clap of thunder, even though it's not really all that loud.

As a first case, the trout is again holding in the current, scanning the flow both for food and possible danger. The following takes place in the span of about two seconds: A few feet upstream something splats on the water, creating air bubbles and bright patterns of light on the mirrored undersurface of the river. The thing again superficially resembles a minnow and immediately starts to skip across the surface above the trout, making small splashes as it moves away from the fish much as a real minnow skitters along the surface when pursued. The thing is getting away. The trout's attention is captured and it attacks all in the same moment, its primitive brain having processed an enormous amount of information in microseconds, a process based on predatory behavior the fish has learned and instantly recalls. In this case, the behavior of your streamer fly fits within the trout's experience, which in turn enables the trout to react.

As a second case, the trout is scanning the current as before. It sees and focuses on something moving in the current, which may or may not have been preceded by a splat or splash. The thing doesn't look like any minnow within the trout's memory nor does it act like one. The trout watches, its instinctive and aggressive response to the object's movement held in check by the unfamiliar. That thing pulses in the current, long fibers of black marabou waving like the fingers of a magician. It is obviously alive and of a size that means it could be edible. The trout, still uncertain, doesn't move, and the fly passes downstream out of view and untouched.

Here comes another one. The fisherman has merely cast again to the same spot, although of course the trout doesn't know this is what's going on. The thing again drifts toward the trout while moving across the current, fluttering and wiggling in the flow. The trout turns and follows the fly for a few feet, watching its movement, and then darts back to its feeding station in the current,

leaving a boil on the surface behind the swimming fly. The fisherman flinches, smiles, and tries again.

Another black wiggly thing comes drifting down toward the trout, obviously alive and acting like food although resembling nothing on the trout's familiar menu. The trout is agitated; instinct fights with uncertainty, and for all its wonderful sensory capabilities the trout has no logical process with which to evaluate and decide. The thing wiggles near the trout. The trout reacts, attacks, and then turns back in the current. The fisherman feels a hard pull and sets the hook, smiling this time more broadly and feeling the fish's weight. Having finally taken a trout on a Black Woolly Bugger, let's rewind our angling tape again to try a couple of other common scenarios.

Again we have a trout occupying a particular spot in the flow, let's say in the deep water along the outside curve of a river. This time we'll fish a big White Marabou streamer, one we like to use not only because it sometimes moves big fish but also because we can see it well while making it swim a few inches below the surface. The trout rests in the shadows, which provide a secure hiding spot and also enhance the fish's ability to see out into the dimly sunlit pool. An upstream splat captures the fish's attention; muscles tense and body fins flares slightly, it's ready to attack or to run, depending on whether the splat was caused by a falling grasshopper or an otter. It was neither. As the fish watches, a big, slinky white thing comes undulating through its upward field of view. As before, the trout's inclination to attack something alive and moving is checked by its lack of experience with this new food. As the fish watches, several of these things slither overhead in the course of several minutes. Finally the building instinct to attack overcomes all else, and the trout rushes toward the surface and the fly. At the last split second, the trout sees the streamer, not as a fake, which is a decision trout are incapable of making, but as resembling no food in its several years of experience. The trout closes its mouth and returns to the shadows, the momentum of its rush having meanwhile taken it splashing through the surface and over the fly. At the moment the big brown trout rolled over his fly, our fisherman yanked the rod, only to have the loose line come flying back to land in coils at his feet. With shaking fingers, he changes flies, exchanging the big White Marabou for a slightly smaller Badger Matuka, which looks very much like the dace common to this particular river.

The trout, meanwhile, is in its old position, but still very agitated. Its muscles are still tensed with the energy of its attack, just as they had been after it had gone slashing through a school of shiners at dawn without managing to catch one. Something moves again in the current above and upstream of the trout, and the trout focuses. It's a large dace, a cripple that flutters weakly in the current with short, slow darts. It seems to fit the dace pattern registered long ago in the trout's brain, and the trout's attack is both immediate and violent. The fly disappears in a broad, strong swirl, and our fisherman shouts with excitement. The trout senses something wrong immediately and bores hard and deep into some sheltering rocks, pulling line quickly from our fisherman's reel. A leader knot catches in a root crack near the trout's head, and the trout shakes its head violently, snapping the leader and giving slack-line heartbreak to our fisherman, who knows he's just lost one of the biggest browns he's ever seen. The trout, meanwhile, turns to rub its jaw against an underwater root, dislodging the fly, which drifts slowly away in the bottom rocks. In this case, the trout was hooked with a ''bait-and-switch'' tactic common to experienced streamer-fly artists, through which a trout is

first located and excited with a nonimitative but very active streamer and subsequently hooked with a more imitative pattern.

Finally, we'll pay another visit to the same big brown trout for a look at a few of many possible reasons why trout *don't* take a streamer at a particular time. In this case, it's the same kind of warm June evening, but exactly one year later. Our fisherman is back, hoping by some twist of fate to catch the fish by duplicating the circumstances, but armed with a heavier leader. Again, the big White Marabou flutters and teases about our trout, which eventually turns suddenly under the fly. The fisherman sees a broad yellow flash and a heart-stopping boil on the surface near the stump. He stops to change flies, oblivious now to both the fading light and swarming mosquitoes, while the trout turns over and over again in his mind. Again he chooses a Badger Matuka, and again our trout holds, still agitated, in the deep water of the bend. The fisherman casts, mends line upstream, and starts to flutter his fly weakly through the shadowed water.

There's movement again in the dim water upstream of the trout, which watches, motionless and alert. The moving form appears as a dace, and the trout lifts a foot above the bottom and then stops, waiting for the dace to come closer. Something is missing.

Black-nosed dace, a small trout-stream fish commonly fed upon by larger trout.

There's no dace sound. By neural process and long habit, the trout has filtered out those sounds created by the stream and the trout's own movement and should be able to sense clearly those low-frequency sounds of 5 to 50 cycles per second that are *uniquely* characteristic of swimming dace of this particular size. This dace doesn't match perfectly the dace pattern in the trout's memory, and the trout remembers its trauma with other dace that weren't a perfect match. The trout settles to the bottom, relaxes slightly, and remains motionless, ignoring the fly that our fisherman casts repeatedly and with growing frustration over the pool.

There are other things wrong, too. There has been no dace smell, and the trout knows the characteristic odor of dace very well through long experience. It's a smell measured underwater in parts per billion, and one to which the trout is acutely sensitive. The electricity is wrong, also, which the trout also senses. As the dace drifted closer, its weak electromagnetic field—one unique to dace—should have intersected the similar but slightly different field unique to the trout, producing a minute pattern of electrical interference that the trout has learned to be characteristic of its encounters with real dace. At some future time, an ingenious fly-tier will concoct a marriage of metals within a fly to produce a miniature galvanic cell that duplicates this natural effect, but that time is far distant. For all of these reasons and quite possibly more, the trout doesn't move. Our fisherman leaves, frustrated. Our trout, having reached seven years and slightly more than 8 pounds weight, spawns for the last time that November and then slowly dies. The carcass washes to the tail shallows of the pool, providing a Thanksgiving Day feast for an adolescent raccoon. The trout's skull is scraped clean by caddis larvae during the winter and is finally pulverized by the shifting stones of an April flood.[4]

Muddler Minnows are a special case, being the most versatile and effective member of the currently popular streamer trio that also includes Buggers and Zonkers. The basic design of a bulky, deerhair head and collar fronting a slim mottled wing was worked out by Don Gapen of Minnesota during the 1930s for brook trout in the Nipigon region of Ontario. Al McClane praised the fly in a 1949 issue of *Field & Stream* and, together with the widely published Joe Brooks, had much to do with the Muddler's subsequent popularity. The fly is most commonly described as a sculpin imitation. Sculpins are small fish specifically adapted for life on the bottom of trout streams—unlike most other trout-stream fish, they have no internal air bladder, for example—and are often a favored food of large trout. While Muddlers are certainly effective when darted along the bottom to mimic a sculpin's behavior, the fly is usually not fished in this manner and is widely known as being effective at all depths, including at or near the surface where sculpins are never found.

Unlike Buggers or Zonkers, conventional Muddlers are made of rather stiff materials and don't find their great trout appeal through a built-in wiggle. The conventional Muddler's muted and mottled color scheme is generally suggestive of a wide variety of baitfishes and, in smaller sizes, at least an equal number of other trout foods such as grasshoppers and large dragonfly nymphs. More important when considered as a streamer fly, the Muddler makes noise. The fly's deerhair head and rather stiff collar push water when darted through the current, producing underwater vibrations that are undoubtedly sensed by trout. No other streamer fly of my acquaintance produces this effect, at least not to the same extent, which together with its color scheme is the basis for the Muddler's success.

The Muddler style has since been adapted to a wide variety of streamers ranging from variously colored Marabou Muddlers, which are the most popular in the Rockies and west but that also work well on eastern rivers; to deliberate sculpin imitations, such as the Spuddler and Whitlock Sculpin, designed to be fished deep; to very small conventional Muddlers tied on wet-fly hooks, the so-called Mini-Muddlers popularized by veteran fly-tier Fran Betters on New York's tumbling Ausable. All of these versions have their times and places, but the conventional Muddler is still the most versatile.

There are a few considerations that can make your conventional Muddlers more effective. Most commercial versions are sadly overdressed, and Muddlers are most effective when the winging materials are either trimmed down or originally tied to give a very slim profile. The deerhair collar should be short, flared, and relatively stiff to best make its contribution of low-frequency sounds underwater. Head shape is another problem. Many versions have round, barrel-shaped heads that are effective in pushing water, but which also have the sometimes annoying tendency to keep the fly waking on the surface. It can take considerable soaking before the deerhair head absorbs enough water to sink well, and while a surface-waking fly is sometimes effective, I more often find it a nuisance. Some versions designed for deep fishing have tapered, chisel-shaped heads that are most imitative of sculpins and also cause the fly to plane downward in the current. My own conventional Muddlers are tied with tapered heads for the same reason of downward planing, which with otherwise conventional dressing gets the streamer a few inches below the surface where both I and many trout most prefer the fly to be.

Muddlers can be tied weighted with turns of fine lead wire under their gold-tinsel bodies, which gets the fly down and can be important in flies designed to scour the bottom.

As a rule, however, I don't like weighted streamers. They're awkward in casting because of the added weight, and I believe the added weight also deadens the fly's action in the current.

"It's not a fly! It's a lure!" When he said the word "lure," Vince Marinaro drew the word out in a long, low sneer that placed streamer flies somewhere below worms in angling's social register. Some years before Vince died in 1986, we were sitting on one of the benches behind Charlie Fox's house along the banks of Pennsylvania's Letort. I knew Vince casually. We had fished together a few times both on his Letort and on my own Vermont Battenkill, and I'd also published some of his work. I'd just had the temerity to suggest that a large streamer might work better for the Letort's big browns than our endless fussing with the little dry flies Vince loved so much. I admired both Marinaro and his work a great deal, but Vince didn't like temerity and could be downright crusty, getting red faced and very emphatic while chewing harder on the ragged butt of an ever-present Dutch Masters cigar. After a while he calmed down and explained at great length that real trout flies imitated natural insects. Streamers don't imitate insects and were thus lures in Marinaro's admittedly Anglophilic view.

That distinction is still held much more widely among British anglers than in this country, where a fly is a fly is fly, meaning anything from a crude leech pattern to a delicate Blue-Winged Olive imitation. But a consideration of streamer flies as lures is important in fishing them in that luring or goading a trout into striking a streamer is different from the outright deceit implicit in fishing with imitative dry flies, for example. Experienced bass anglers long ago learned that while plug color and size are important—as with streamer flies for trout—the way in which a plug is retrieved through the water is an art unto itself, one that makes all the difference in actually catching fish, and something that seems to have escaped many otherwise competent trout fishermen.

In its most rudimentary form, streamer-fly fishing is down-and-across casting with a sunken fly that then swings in the current, its movement punctuated by a rhythmic raising and lowering of the rod tip that pulses the feathers. Another step and another cast; over and over again in a method that plays the odds over a long reach of water that sooner or later one of many available trout will slash at the fly. It's a traditional and still-effective method that works with the full range of fly-line types, from floating to sinking, according to the depth and speed of the current. There doesn't have to be more to streamer fishing than this, but there can be.

The full range of specialized fly-casting techniques, as described in Chapter 14 and including mending line, aerial mends, throwing curves or slack, and deliberately throwing a very straight line, can be applied to streamer fishing with exceptional results. In general, your effectiveness will only be limited by your own willingness—or lack of it—to experiment. Throwing a left curve will get your fly behind a downstream stump, for example, to a pocket of water that might otherwise be unreachable. You can use a combination of mends and slack line to keep your streamer fishing straight across the river's currents and broadside to the fish rather than coming tailfirst to the trout as in the case of a downstream swing. This was a favorite tactic of the late Joe Brooks, who called it the broadside drift and described its use for large western trout, although it works well everywhere at times. You can throw a perfectly straight, flat cast toward the bank, finishing with your rod low as the fly lands, which allows an immediate fast retrieve to convince the trout that a minnow has splashed and is trying to escape in the same instant. Or fish your streamers upstream, stripping line rapidly back with the flow to keep your feathers alive in the current. Much of this is not easily done, but I didn't say it was easy. Only that it works.

1. While many recent angling books cover streamer-fly fishing in a peripheral way, there are very few works devoted solely to this topic. The most recent of these is my own *Streamer-Fly Fishing* (1991), which elaborates on many of the points covered in this chapter.

2. The plural reference to dry flies is drys, not dries. In an angling context, this evolved during the early years of *Fly Fisherman* magazine, when publisher Don Zahner and I worked at developing a style sheet to provide some continuity in the magazine's text. The precedent we used in this particular case came about during Prohibition, when persons on opposite sides of that political question were known as "wets" or "drys."

3. See Alexander (1979).

4. Some of this will sound like science fiction, even to the experienced fishermen, but it's all quite plausible and based on well-documented research concerning the senses of trout and other fishes. The ability of trout and many other fish to use an electromagnetic sense in feeding has been neither proved nor disproved. Sharks do have this ability, and their electromagnetic senses are extraordinary. Paul Johnson, the veteran and widely respected researcher at Berkley and Company, has hypothesized the use of a similiar sense by largemouth bass and has suggested that bass lures might someday incorporate the electrical fields characteristic of certain baitfishes. See Johnson (1984).

19
Nymphs

I couldn't decide which sound was more appealing, the sharp sizzle of morning bacon or the muted rushing of Montana's Big Hole River that I could hear through the open windows of Phil Wright's bankside house. Wright and I had quickly become friends through our mutual involvement with *Fly Fisherman* magazine during the 1970s, and I had just as quickly accepted his invitation for a few days' fishing at his Montana home, from which he ran a well-known outfitting and guiding business before retiring several years ago. I was watching the river and contemplating my maiden voyage to the West when Wright poked me in the back, handing me some coffee as I turned.

"The first thing we're going to do," he said, smiling, "is to get rid of your quaint."

"What do you mean?" I was puzzled. "My quaint what?"

"Your Eastern quaint. Your quaint little flies. Your quaint little rod. Not to mention your quaint little casting. This is the West, Buck-O!" Wright knew full well that I'd first learned to fly fish while growing up in the Northeast, with all the tactics and tackle that implied. "Quaint" was also a favorite word of his, usually derogatory, which probably came from having spent time in earlier years with his wife, Joan, in and around Concord, Massachusetts—about as quaint as you can get—and later in the Aspen, Colorado, area—sort of *nouveau* quaint—before settling in Montana, where he escaped quaintness altogether.

Wright twisted the knife still harder, enjoying my polite discomfort immensely. "For openers," he said, "you'll be fishing with one of these." He pulled a fly from his shirt pocket and dropped it in my outstretched hand. I distinctly remember its being one of the most godawful looking flies I'd ever seen.

"Phil! What is this thing?" It was a large, chenille-bodied fly with several pairs of white rubber legs and palmered over Woolly Worm style with long, brown hackle. The thing was obviously lead weighted under its body and was tied on a big, black wet-fly hook, the kind that was originally designed for Atlantic-salmon flies.

"A Yuk Bug! Quaint, huh?" Wright smiled broadly and then explained that a Yuk Bug was really a kind of ersatz nymph that worked especially well in the rough-and-tumble waters of the Big Hole when the early summer flood of snowmelt was starting to drop. I was skeptical, but kept the fly in my pocket through breakfast and also through the mandatory casting practice on Wright's little pond, which he used to make sure his guests were basically competent before setting out in a drift boat for the day's fishing. My casting, at least, passed muster, but I still regarded the fly in my pocket as a problem.

Later, while drifting in Wright's Mac-Kenzie boat with himself at the oars, I politely—if dubiously—followed his instructions about slapping the bug hard on the water a few inches from the bank and pulling the fly back with short strips of the fly line. The weighted fly sank quickly out of sight in the fast water, but I made a point of watching it a few times when it neared the boat, marveling at the way its rubber legs and hackle wiggled and waved in the water. After a while I developed a regular cadence of plop-strip-strip on repeated casts, which was finally interrupted by a violent yank on the other end of the line. A foot-long rainbow jumped once and then came flipping to the boat, the Yuk Bug stuck in its jaw and looking like a garish mustache. At that point, I became a believer, plopping and stripping more attentively during the day and catching an embarrassing number of fish. It was yet another kind of nymph fishing, and my quaint was cured, at least temporarily.

Many years later I've decided the reasons for the wide effectiveness of the Yuk Bug, Girdle Bug, Bitch Creek, and similar big, rubber-hackled nymphs are twofold. First, they have considerable inherent action, derived mostly from their soft-rubber legs, which pulls trout with the same wiggly appeal common to Woolly Bugger and Zonker streamer flies, the materials of which likewise move easily in the current. When confronted with a wiggly anything of edible size, the instinctive response of many trout is simply to attack the fly in a feeding reflex. A fly's imitative qualities, in this case, are usually less important than its wiggle, which lures or goads the trout into striking.

But the big western rubber-legged flies are more than just wiggle. In a very general way, they resemble in size and color the huge salmonfly nymphs of the *Pteronarcys* (stonefly) genus common to many fast-flowing western rivers such as the Big Hole and Madison. Such nymphs are 2 inches or more long at maturity—about the same size as a big Yuk or Girdle bug—and are available to the trout all year because most of these nymphs spend three years in the river before emerging as adults. By late June or early July in most such rivers the mature nymphs are crawling over the bottom in a migration toward the riverbank, where they clamber out and emerge as adults in the riverside willows. At such times enormous numbers of these big nymphs are available to trout, and big, dark, rubber-legged nymphs can be devastatingly effective.

There are similar large stonefly nymphs in many eastern rivers, too, although usually in much lesser numbers, and big, black Girdle Bugs work well in places like Connecticut's Housatonic and in New Hampshire's big Androscoggin. Most anglers work the Housatonic's lovely no-kill water above Cornwall Bridge with small drys or nymphs and long, fine leaders, for example, but the rare individual there who starts slinging a big rubber-legged nymph when nothing else is happening may find himself—as I once did—too busy unhooking trout to notice the frowns of his more genteel angling neighbors.

Imitation and fly behavior are the keystones of modern trout tactics. A dry fly drifting naturally without drag depends on its imitative qualities for success. That a rapidly moving streamer fly will often pull trout is often based more on the fly's movement than its pattern. Successful nymph fishing is typically a simultaneous mix of both attributes, using a deliberately imitative fly and making it behave in a natural manner, which is often difficult because the fly is underwater where you can't see it. Further, because different kinds of natural nymphs behave in radically different ways underwater, some knowledge of this behavior is obviously helpful in fishing any particular nymph pattern. There can be so many ifs, ands, and wherefores involved in nymph fishing that it seems as if the method might have been invented by an attorney.

Which it was. George Edward MacKenzie Skues was a British solicitor practicing near the Strand in London during the early part of this century. He was also a lifelong trout fisherman, plying his art mainly on the Abotts Barton water of the Itchen, a placid chalk stream near Winchester where Skues fished—often alone—for fifty-six years. Within his lifetime (1858–1949), Skues became justly famous as the father of modern nymph fishing, a man who used quiet, determined logic to tumble the dry-fly temple built so rigidly by F. M. Halford and his followers along the same rivers just a few years before. Skues' legacy is clearly evident in many of our nymph patterns and tactics even now, which makes him worth a closer look.

As the story generally goes, Skues at first fished the slow-moving chalk-stream water with an upstream dry fly in the fashion cemented in the minds of anglers by Halford with his 1889 book *Dry-Fly Fishing*. After trying a number of different drys over a difficult fish, Skues tried yet another one, a dry fly that happened to be so poorly made that it quickly sank. The trout took the sub-

G. E. M. Skues.

merged fly immediately, shattering Halford's dogma within Skues' well-ordered mind. Dry flies were supposed to be more effective than sunken flies, but obviously this hadn't been the case of the moment. Clearly, Halford was at least partly wrong. Skues began some successful experiments with upstream wet flies, and eventually described his results in such British publications as *The Field* and *The Fishing Gazette*.

Conrad Voss Bark, formerly a fishing correspondent for *The Times* of London, has been closer to the British angling scene for many more years than I, and so I include his brief description of what happened next, which Voss Bark wrote in 1976 by way of introduction to a reprinting of Skues' work:

> We, of a later, perhaps more permissive, more tolerant generation, can barely comprehend the fury that broke over Skues' head. The code of the dry fly on chalkstreams was paramount. The dry fly, and the dry fly only, had to be fished at all times and without exception. Nothing else could be allowed or tolerated. When Skues said that the dry fly, admirable enough when the trout were taking duns or spinners on the surface, was inadequate to deal with trout feeding on nymphs ascending through the water, and that therefore the traditional and older method of the upstream wet fly might legitimately be used to deal with them, the anger of the purists knew no bounds. In the atmosphere of the times it was not only heresy but rank bad manners—like cocking a snook at the archbishop—and the archbishop was Halford, by then idolized, and growing more rigid in his age.[1]

Skues' early work, which he described in his 1910 book *Minor Tactics of the Chalk Stream*, dealt primarily with fishing upstream wet flies to individual rising trout. Then, and in his own words:

I had supposed for a long time that the wet fly was taken on these occasions for a nymph in the very act of hatching. But after a while the presence in the mouths of some of my captures [trout] of nymphs with no show of wing led me to experiment with short-hackled patterns dressed to imitate nymphs. . . . In the succeeding eleven years I had made other attempts to represent nymphs—but I was hampered by the need to carry out hateful and messy autopsies to ascertain on what my trout were feeding, until towards the end of that period I was struck with the idea of using a marrow scoop to extract the contents of the trout's stomach in a single operation. The method proved completely successful, and time after time I was amazed to see what a huge proportion of these contents were nymphs—and how few were the winged flies.

Skues goes on to describe washing the stomach contents and putting them into a white plate so he could see them clearly. The plate was kept at his fly-tying bench, where:

I was able to dress (and compare in the water by the side of the natural insects) representations of the nymphs I had extracted, resembling them in size, contour, proportions and color. I did not need to use these patterns when the trout were feeding on the surface, for then the dry fly was at once easier and more effective—but on those many occasions when the trout have been devoting their attention to the nymph and neglecting the floating fly I have found the appropriate pattern of nymph great medicine, however bright the weather and however smooth the water.[2]

Skues' second book, *The Way of a Trout with a Fly*, was first published in 1921, and contains a series of nymph dressings that are modern in every respect. Millions of anglers see nymphs of almost identical style in modern catalogs and shops every year, albeit with little if any thought of Skues.

Halford, meanwhile, had simply declared that nymphs were impossible to adequately imitate for the sake of fooling trout. After examining the forms and movements of some live mayfly nymphs in a jar of water, Halford had written (in 1889):

How is it to be expected that a timid, shy fish like a trout . . . should mistake that motionless, supine compound of dubbing, silk, quill, and hackle drifting helplessly and lifelessly like a log down the stream, for the active, ever-moving larva sparkling in the sunshine.

Skues over a period of years proved Halford wrong, although certain circumstances have combined to give Halford a poor modern reputation he doesn't totally deserve. Even though Halford went out of his way in writing his 1889 *Dry Fly Fishing* to avoid deprecating wet-fly fishing,[3] his disciples and acolytes were less cautious and elevated dry flies to the rigid code they eventually became. In later life, Halford assumed a similar stance, perhaps because he believed his own press clippings, that the band of anglers surrounding him must be right simply because they were so worshipful.

Shortly before Halford's death in 1908, and after a number of Skues' articles had appeared, the Skues-Halford affair produced a brief confrontation between the two at the venerable Fly Fishers' Club of London. Halford, egged on by a small group of supporters, stood severely before Skues and said, "You cannot fish the Itchen in the manner you describe."

"But I've done it," Skues replied.[4] It was point, match, and set in a simple sentence. It's important to realize that Skues was fishing deliberately imitative nymphs upstream to trout rising or otherwise visibly feeding near the surface, and that the rules of certain British angling clubs were subsequently modified to allow nymph in addition to dry-fly fishing, but only the upstream nymph and only when cast to feeding fish. Although this was a remarkable change from the rigid dry-fly rules of a few years previous, it's still a far cry from modern methods in this country, where nymphs are fished in all directions relative to the current and often fished when no trout are visibly feeding. Skues would have found some of these tactics ill-mannered, to say nothing of how he would have regarded a modern, wiggly Girdle Bug. Skues' legacy in this country comes not from his challenging a structured dry-fly code, which change had little effect in America where the fishing was less structured anyway, but in his methodical and studied approach to fishing with nymphs, which almost seventy-five years later is still the best route to successful nymph fishing.

Trout display most of the same behavioral patterns when feeding underwater and removed from the angler's view as they do when taking floating flies at the surface. Degrees of selectivity, the trout's individual food preferences, and behavioral patterns that may also be unique to individual fish aren't changed by the mere fact of feeding in midwater or near the bottom. While many trout fishermen readily acknowledge the frequent selectivity of surface-feeding trout because the trout's refusal of a particular dry fly is easy to see, relatively few appreciate that the same sorts of things happen at all levels of the stream. This understanding is intrinsic to successful nymph fishing.

Before examining how trout selectivity pertains to nymph fishing, we need a few definitions, because "nymph" itself has become a hazy word. *Nymph* can be strictly construed, referring only to the aquatic, im-

mature forms of mayflies, which was Skues' definition. Immature stoneflies, dragonflies, and damselflies are also properly called nymphs in a biological sense, which means all have an incomplete metamorphosis, hatching directly as adults from fully grown nymphs without passing through the sort of pupal stage used by a caterpillar in changing to a butterfly, for example. In modern angling terms, caddis, cranefly, midge, and other aquatic larvae that undergo complete metamorphosis—meaning they do have a pupal stage—are usually also called nymphs, which is technically incorrect but survives in usage. The same term is often extended to other trout-stream life forms, such as freshwater shrimp and aquatic sowbugs, that complete their life cycles underwater but are nymphlike in size. The angling term "emergers" refers to those immature forms that are in the immediate process of changing to an adult form, such as a caddis pupa swimming to the surface or a mayfly trying to drag itself from its nymphal shuck in the surface tension. The distinction between nymphs and emergers is important because the fishing methods employed are often quite different; emergers are discussed at length in Chapter 22.

Because most trout-stream insects hatch *en masse* over a period of a few days to a couple of weeks and at different times of the year according to species, the availability of certain nymphs to trout varies dramatically with the season. While a specifically imitative Hendrickson mayfly nymph may work especially well in late April before the adult emergences of early May, for example, it's a poor choice for June fishing, when there are no mature Hendrickson nymphs in the river. Basic stream habitat is another major consideration governing just what kinds of nymphs are found where, which was explored at length in chapters 15 and 16. To give just one example, the large western *Pteronarcys* stonefly nymphs that are so popular with fish and fishermen may be abundant in the tumbling, rocky reaches of a western river above a reservoir. In the widely famous tailwater fishery below the dam, however, the biota has changed considerably, with stoneflies being absent almost entirely and certain caddis, *Baetis* mayflies, and midges predominating. This sort of knowledge should obviously have considerable effect on your choice of nymph patterns.

Because trout encounter differing quantities of different nymphs at different times and places in all trout streams, the trout often become selective, just as they do when more obviously taking one kind of mayfly in preference to another visibly at the surface. For example, trout that have become accustomed to seeing and feeding on vigorously active *Potamanthus* mayfly nymphs over several consecutive June evenings will likely hammer an imitative, large cream nymph after the first twitch or two, but just as likely will have ignored the little olive nymph that you tried first. As with other styles of trout flies, you can select and fish your nymphs based on the common attributes of color, size, shape, design, and behavior. Although I'll consider these one at a time, remember that trout see all of them simultaneously and that in general no single characteristic is favored to the exclusion of another. They are *all* important.

Shape means simply that your nymph should have the same overall physical form as a corresponding natural. There's as much difference in shape between a corpulent dragonfly nymph and a slim, swimming nymph of the *Ephemera* mayfly genus as between a horse and a hippopotamus, even though both might be of the same overall length. This is especially important because under certain conditions trout will first see your nymph as a silhouette and may initially identify or reject it based on shape and size.

Size is almost obvious. I say "almost" because, while your nymph should match the naturals in size, most immature aquatic forms are growing during the several months or more they spend in the stream, so the question of size becomes more variable than might first appear. In general, most nymph patterns are tied to resemble naturals of a size close to maturity, which should be taken as a maximum.

Color is a complex question. There's little question that trout can differentiate between nymphs of similar color value but of different hue, medium olive and medium brown, for example, which would appear to be identical if photographed side by side with black-and-white film. The color tones of natural nymphs are also not the solid blocks of color they appear to be at first glance. I have photographed many natural nymphs in special aquaria and enlarged their images several hundred times by projection. Examining the projected images often shows small areas of red, green, brown, and yellow, for example, on the surface of a nymph that seems superficially brownish olive and nothing else. I don't know to what extent trout are able to discern this, nor do I know what Darwinian advantage the minute color patterns offer the insect itself. It has been well demonstrated, though, that many successful nymph patterns are based on colors achieved by blending differently colored dubbing furs rather than relying on a single color.

Translucency or the lack of it is also part of the color question. Almost all nymphs are translucent to varying degrees, which is part of what can make an imitation seem to be lifelike. Examining your artificials when they're wet will show you not only the color change of the fly's materials in water—usually a darkening—but when side- or backlighted will also reveal the extent of the fly's translucency. A translucent effect can be imparted to many nymphs by roughing up their dubbed-fur bodies so the fine fibers of fur soften the fly's image when viewed in back- or sidelighting. This is often why scruffy-looking nymphs work better than neatly tied ones and is also partly why a well-chewed version that's taken several fish usually works better than the same nymph fresh from the box. For that reason, I often use a little toothbrush to gently tease dubbing fibers along a nymph's body after tying the fly.

Design is another basic question that's amost limitless and best shown by example. A nymph can be tied weighted with lead fuse wire under its body or not, depending on how quickly you want it to sink. Light-wire versus heavy-wire hooks of the same size offer a similar option. Frank Sawyer, the near-legendary British nymphing expert, originally tied his famous Pheasant Tail nymph without legs (hackle) because the little naturals he observed folded their legs against their body when swimming, which seemed to make legs superfluous on an imitation. I deliberately spread the fine tail fibers of smaller mayfly nymphs when tying them, which mimics the tails of many naturals at rest or slowly sinking. Others clump their tails in tying nymphs, feeling—perhaps rightly—that it makes no difference. Although many mayfly nymphs have prominently waving gills along each side of their thorax, many common imitations don't emulate this characteristic. Ernest Schwiebert has published many nymph patterns incorporating fine ostrich-fiber gills ribbed with gold wire along the thorax, which I've tried extensively and found to be both wonderfully effective in fishing and horribly time-consuming in tying. As I said, design questions in nymph imitations are almost endless and to a large degree are independent of specific patterns, but perhaps I've cited enough examples to fuel some thoughts of your own.

Your fly's behavior is critical and is derived largely from your knowledge of specific nymph species, your casting plan, and your rod and line manipulations after the cast is made. It would take a very substantial book to adequately review all the possible combinations implicit in the previous sentence. By far the best modern work covering that topic is Schwiebert's *Nymphs*, in which Ernie spends considerable time relating nymphing tactics to specific insect groups, based on their behavior. The importance of that concept is enormous, which makes *Nymphs* must reading for would-be nymph fishermen. For the moment, though, I'll use just one example from my own experience to illustrate what I mean.

The big mahogany duns that hatch along upstate New York's Ausable River in September are an odd mayfly hatch for many anglers because these *Isonychia* mayflies usually (and *not* invariably) crawl above the water on streamside boulders before emerging from their nymphal cases rather than emerging in the stream itself in typical mayfly fashion. On windy days the big duns are sometimes blown back into the river, and at such times dry flies like Art Flick's Dun Variant can produce spectacular results. Usually, though, nymph imitations are more important than drys.

These nymphs are rather round bodied, almost cylindrical, a dark purplish brown with a prominent white dorsal stripe, and three short tails that combine to be rather like a broad paddle at the rear of the natural. They are fast-water nymphs, holding themselves partly erect in the current and using the fine hairs on their forelegs as a filter with which

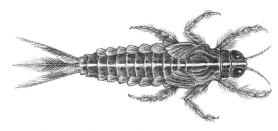

Isonychia mayfly nymph.

they gather drifting organic matter from the flow. Most important, they are excellent swimmers thanks to their muscular body shape and tail structure, being able to dart in the current with the rapidity of little fish. As the nymphs migrate to boulders in and along the stream for hatching, they are available in unusual numbers to trout. The secret in this case is a lightly weighted imitation fished in short darts across the current and through the quieter pockets behind and around big rocks that extend above the surface. Dead-drifting or simply swinging your nymph in the current won't do nearly as well; the fly must have a darting motion and preferably in a logical direction, which means not straight upstream in fast water.

The river's brown trout often respond viciously and with no hesitation to this technique, which fits well within the frame of their immediate experience with natural nymphs. Of necessity, it's short-line fishing in fast pocket water, where fly control is essential. And although I usually use the lightest practical tippets in most nymphing situations, in this case I try to err on the heavy side, using 3X with these #12 nymphs simply because the trout hit the rapidly moving fly so hard.

There are almost as many ways to fish nymphs as there are different nymphs themselves, from basic approaches like the down-and-across wet-fly swing to more sophisticated examples involving across-stream slack-line casts or casting small nymphs upstream to rising trout as Skues once did. I won't take the space here to try to describe them all; many are amply covered in works by Brooks, Schwiebert, Swisher and Richards, Whitlock, and others. One deserves mention simply because its name has changed. The so-called outrigger technique has often been attributed to Chuck Fother-gill, who apparently developed it during the 1970s as a means of dead-drifting nymphs deep in the faster waters of mountain rivers near Aspen, Colorado. Using a floating line, a long leader with enough small lead shot or strips spaced near its end to put the fly near the bottom, and a small nymph, the cast is made up and across stream a short distance. As the fly sinks and drifts past the angler, the rod is held very high, so high that the line and leader are almost perpendicular to the water, but without putting any tension on the leader or fly. The weighted leader and fly drift deeply—which is where the trout are in fast, broken water—and without drag. During the ensuing years this same method has come to be used often with slightly weighted nymphs combined with long, fine leader tippets and without any additional weight on the leader itself. In either case it's a very effective way of dead-drifting an artificial deep without having to resort to a sinking line. These days the same tactic is commonly called high-sticking, which I've described not only so you can try the technique but so you'll know what your guide's talking about when he or she tells you to "go high-stick a little Hare's Ear through that riffle."

Another technique also deserves mention, partly because it's been the most controversial method in all of fly-fishing during recent years: the use of strike indicators. When fishing with a floating line and casting a nymph upstream, it's often very difficult to tell when a trout has taken the sunken fly when you can see neither the fish nor your nymph. Sometimes the line and leader will pause slightly or dart forward, indicating a strike, but even this takes both concentration and practice to detect. As a shortcut in this method, some sort of strike indicator—literally, a floating bobber of some kind attached to the leader well above the nymph—has long been suggested by various writers.

Ray Bergman and others in the 1940s and 1950s suggested a dry-fly dropper above a drifting nymph, the movement of which would indicate a trout's having taken the unseen fly below. The concept languished until the 1970s when Dave Whitlock started publicizing the use of a small section of fluorescent fly line slipped over the leader butt for use as a strike indicator, correctly noting that the little section of bright line would be easy to see and follow in the current. Now there are little brightly colored foam balls sold for this purpose, as well as adhesive-backed bits of brightly colored foam that can be folded over one's leader at the desired point. There are even commercially available nymphing leaders that provide the whole setup as a unit, ready for the addition of a fly. At its best, this arrangement allows even skilled anglers to detect hits on nymphs they'd otherwise miss. At its worst, the same setup allows a drift-boat guide to rig strike indicators and nymphs for neophyte anglers who then plop them over the side and sit waiting for something to yank the indicator underwater, which of course takes no skill whatsoever. Meanwhile, the letters columns of assorted fly-fishing magazines have been boiling over with commentary as to the ethics of the whole business, which to some at least seems little removed from baitfishing.

I will beg the question by pointing out that after numerous experiments with various rigs of this type I've gone back to dry-fly droppers. First, I never expect to catch anything with a plastic ball, bright-yarn tag, or piece of stick-on foam. I sometimes catch fish with the larger drys I use as strike indicators. Second, almost all of the newer commercial indicators designed to be added to one's leader are abominations to cast; dry-fly droppers are easier to cast. Third, it's easier to add, remove, or change a dry-fly dropper than it is to perform the same operation with most commercial indicators.

Dry-fly droppers also fish better at greater distances. I often use a #12, or #10 Royal Wulff dry as a highly visible indicator, trailed by about 2 or 3 feet of 6X tippet and a #16 slightly weighted Hare's Ear nymph or similar pattern. I can cast this rig 30 or 40 easy feet upstream in a little run and am able to follow the high-floating dry exactly as it drifts back trailing the unseen nymph. At those distances, I simply can't see a flush-floating foam indicator no matter how brightly colored it might be. The same technique works with across-stream slack-line casts, as well. Even at distances of 40 or 50 feet, which is well beyond that considered practical among the red-plastic set, any dragging of the little Wulff or other dry dropper is quickly evident and can usually be corrected with a line mend, which means the trailing nymph will also then be drifting correctly. Just as evident, of course, is the instant when the dry dropper hesitates or is yanked underwater by a trout's take of the nymph.

My suggestions about dry-fly droppers are deliberately given from a practical rather than an ethical view. I do have one observation, though, for neophyte fly fishermen whose guide wants them to spend the day drifting an indicator-and-nymph rig over the side of a slowly moving boat. If you choose that route, at the end of the day you may very well have caught a large number of fish. You will also have learned absolutely nothing about fly-fishing for trout.

1. From Voss Bark's Introduction to the 1976 edition of Skues (1932, 1976).

2. From Skues (1932, 1976).

3. For example: "In treating the advantages of dry-fly over wet-fly fishing, I am most desirous of avoiding any expression which should tend to depreciate in any way the skill exhibited by the experienced and intelligent followers of the wet fly." Halford (1889).

4. This particular version of that famous conversation is adapted from Schwiebert (1979).

20
The Upstream Dry Fly

The young man had spent the evening sorting several dozen dry flies into assorted boxes, stowing them carefully into the pockets of his fishing waistcoat for the next day's fishing. Meanwhile, his bride of two days had tearfully collapsed in a nearby chair, woefully facing yet another day alone while her new husband fished the trout stream near their rented Adirondack cottage.

"You love fly-fishing for trout more than you love me!" she sobbed, seeing her dreams of connubial bliss disappearing in a jumble of waders and fly rods.

The young man rushed to her side, desperately trying to think of a way to console this new light of his life. He put his arm gently around her trembling shoulders, smiled reassuringly, and said with perfect logic: "That's not true, dearest. I love you more than wet-fly fishing."

By the 1930s, the period from which that oft-repeated anecdote dates, American dry-fly fishing had in some respects become a parody of itself. The popular conception that true gentlemen anglers fished only dry flies upstream was firmly ensconced not only in many fishermen's minds, but also in the public mind, where the image was lampooned by the likes of John Taintor Foote, whose 1924 novel *The Wedding Gift* poked not-so-gentle fun at the fishing foibles of his angling peers. Such humor often played on the supposed—and now outdated—role of wives as stubborn innocents acting as foils to their angling-doctrinaire husbands. Cartoonist

H. T. Webster, whose wry wit brightened the pages of the *New York Tribune* during the same era, often featured fly fishermen in his cartoons, one typical example of which showed a demure wife enduring a swarm of blackflies about her head while wistfully watching her smiling husband flogging a trout stream some distance away. Webster called the scene "Life's Darkest Moment," one of a series he drew under that title, and humorist Ed Zern included the cartoon in his 1945 book *To Hell with Fishing*. Zern also added the following note:

> Personally, I don't get the point of this cartoon. As far as I can see, it's an ideal honeymoon, and I don't know what Mr. Webster could be driving at. I spent my honeymoon fishing for smallmouth bass. I had to. Trout season had ended.

Things have changed. For one thing, while still statistically a male-dominated sport, there are probably more women fly-fishing now than at any other time since the 1890s. What hasn't changed is the popular and incorrect perception among trout fishermen that dry flies are best fished against the current and that such fishing is somehow more challenging and thus better than any other means of fly-fishing for trout.

As a general case, dry-fly fishing is the *easiest* of all options simply because you can see what you're doing. Streamers, wets, and nymphs are all usually invisible below the surface, yet all need to be carefully controlled in the current, which can take considerable skill. Dry flies are visible on the surface and are thus more easily controlled; at worst, your mistakes, such as a dragging fly, are immediately evident. Then too, a trout's taking a dry is also very apparent, even in the case of quiet rises, all of which is usually more obvious than a quiet take of a sunken nymph that you can't see. While dry-fly fishing probably gained its formidable reputation and social status because it's more demanding of skill than simply swinging a wet fly in the downstream currents, sunken-fly fishing at its best is far more subtle than fishing dry.

The basic tenets of the upstream dry-fly method were described by W. C. Stewart, a British wet-fly artist, whose 1857 book *The Practical Angler* suggested the then-radical technique of fishing wet flies upstream for a variety of still-valid reasons: The flies drifted back in the current without drag and were thus more representative of natural insects. The trout, being blind to the rear, could be approached more closely from below. An angler fishing upstream scared fewer trout and to a lesser degree than an angler working downstream and directly into the trout's upstream view. The immutable logic of Stewart's wet-fly method was eventually incorporated into the dry-fly tactics widely described by Halford and others in late-nineteenth-century England, who also strongly equated social standing with technique. Gentlemen thus fished upstream and dry.

By the time American dry-fly fishing began to be widely practiced in the years after World War I, the attitude as well as the technique had been imported. While numerous changes were made in adapting the technique to American waters, which are more diverse and have a greater variety of insect hatches than the British chalk streams, many of the sport's most widely published American practitioners, such as George La Branche and the insufferably opinionated Edward Hewitt, were as adept in the realms of New York society as they were on its trout streams. Even though they and others experimented widely with methods other than upstream dry flies, their obvious elegance and skill continued to give a special and still-persistent aura to the upstream method.

There were, of course, and still are some practical considerations that make fishing drys upstream appropriate. In 1913, Samuel Camp included the following note in his *Fishing with Floating Flies*, which was—and still is—generally indicative of the prevalent thinking of dry-fly fishermen:

> The dry fly man . . . has no option in the matter; regardless of all other factors for upstream fishing, the practical fact remains that the floating fly cannot be fished downstream for when thus cast it is drowned almost at once.

In 1953, the great Al McClane used part of his book *The Practical Fly Fisherman* to discuss various ways of fishing drys downstream to good effect, but still concluded that

> you cannot reasonably expect to get your best dry fly fishing by fishing downstream every day . . . casting upstream is certainly most effective.

Both time and changes in tackle and technique have proved Camp, McClane, and others at least partly wrong. Fishing dry in a downstream direction is often more effective than fishing up, typically allowing better control of the fly with less effort than is required when wading against the current. (The reasons and tactics for downstream drys are explored at length in the following chapter.) There are times, however, when fishing upstream drys is still the most productive route, and we'll examine some reasons for that after taking a look at just what dry flies are.

Dry flies are imitations of winged, adult insect forms that have spent part of their life cycle as nymphs or larvae in the stream and have emerged or returned as adults at or near the water's surface.[1] These adult imitations are specifically designed to float and to be fished on the surface. A separate class of dry flies called terrestrials is specifically imitative of land-based insects, such as ants and grasshoppers, and is treated in another chapter. So-called emergers are specifically imitative of insects in the brief transitional, or emerging, stage between nymphal or pupal forms and adults and are also treated separately in their own chapter. The actual differences in these fly patterns sometimes depend on nothing more than the angler's intent in fishing with them; some dry patterns imitative of mayflies could also be considered as emergers, for example. The distinctions are thus somewhat artificial, but angling tactics when using these groups may also differ, which is why they're not being considered as a unit even though all are fished at or near the surface.

Dry flies are often specifically imitative patterns, frequently having been designed to represent a particular species of mayfly or caddis or other insect and sometimes just the male or female of that species if the two differ in size or color. A conventional Hendrickson dry fly, for example, is commonly cited as imitating an adult female *Ephemerella subvaria* mayfly, while a Red Quill dry imitates the slightly smaller and more reddish male of the same species. As with other kinds of flies, some dry flies are more generalistic while still being imitative. The Adams dry is the best-known example of this sort, and its dull gray body and mixed hackle colors are generally representative of many varieties of mayflies and caddis. There are so-called attractor drys, too, such as the Royal Wulff or Humpy, that by virtue of their bright colors or unusual design seem to im-

itate little in nature, but even these flies have an imitative basis. The Royal Wulff is tied in conventional mayfly style, its bright red floss body darkens to an insectlike shade when wet, and the fly probably derives its wide popularity from its white wings, which make it easy for fishermen to see the fly on the water. Many modern dry flies such as the Gray Wulff that are now seen as general purpose as opposed to specifically imitative show an imitative basis in their histories. Lee Wulff once told me, for example, that he first tied his now famous and widely used Gray Wulff during the winter of 1929–30 as a deliberate imitation of the large *Isonychia* mayflies that hatch along New York's Ausable River in the fall.

Until the late 1950s, matching dry flies to the natural hatch of the moment was usually an empirical process often governed by tradition that simply noted, for example, that #12 Light Cahill drys worked well on the Beaverkill in mid-June. Modern anglers who have decided ahead of time where they're going to fish can usually check some published reference as to the hatches often prevalent at the time of their trip and obtain drys specifically imitative of those hatches ahead of time. This is obviously less haphazard and consequently more productive. It also represents a growing trend toward dry-fly sophistication that finds its American roots in Ernest Schwiebert's 1955 *Matching the Hatch* and in the 1971 book *Selective Trout*, by Doug Swisher and Carl Richards. While both these books remain important, my favorite modern references are more recent: Fred Arbona's 1984 *Mayflies, the Angler, and the Trout* for mayflies, and, for caddis, Gary LaFontaine's 1981 *Caddisflies*.

There are many dry-fly anglers who stubbornly refuse any dash of science in their sport, preferring to fish instead with what amounts to little gray ones and big brown ones, for example, generally matching their flies to what happens to be on or around the water at any particular time. There are still others, including some very expert dry-fly anglers, who use only a couple of dry patterns—say, an Adams and a Chuck Caddis—in various sizes, arguing that further imitation isn't necessary. I think of one man in particular who follows the latter route, which is made all the more convincing because he's very adept at catching large numbers of trout, and who Lee Wulff and I hashed over one day some years ago when the trout weren't rising and we had nothing better to do. At the time, Wulff made the perceptive observation that while the man did catch considerable trout with his deliberately limited fly patterns, the same man wasn't learning anything except how to fish those same flies over and over again.

Many of these arguments derive from a precept that I placed at the start of this book; namely, that almost any fly will fool some of the trout some of the time. If that particular fly happens to be fished with uncommon skill, then the numbers of fooled trout correspondingly increase. But I have spent too many years not catching trout for lack of the right fly in too many places around the country to avoid placing a premium on imitation. Assume for the moment that we have a group of trout in a pool, all feeding on one kind of adult mayfly at the surface. A dry-fly imitation that's close to the naturals will probably get a response from some—but not all—of the trout. This is the sort of dry-fly trout fishing that most people have experienced.

A more specific and successful imitation, if fished correctly, will draw a strike from every feeding fish without exception. That, quite simply, is how you know you have the right pattern on at any particular time. There have been some rare nights of large hatches on the nearby and notoriously difficult Battenkill when by some fluke I've had exactly the right fly. The river's normally skeptical browns have hit the fly hard and immediately without their characteristic long inspections and refusals. On each of those few evenings I've managed to take more large browns in a few hours than in the whole preceding month, which I'm certain was a matter of exactly the right fly at the right time. Duplicating such performances has almost always proved difficult, although not always impossible. At the very least, such events provide a yardstick against which to measure subsequent efforts.

As your dry fly floated gently and without drag over a trout in the slow, clear water at the tail of a pool, you may have been close enough to have seen the fish move slowly upward under the fly, drift back with it slightly, and then return to its position without rising. On making a second cast, you may have seen the trout move again, but not as far, and again return to its lie without striking. On the next and subsequent casts, the trout didn't move at all. Fortunately, this is a common scenario. I use the word "fortunately," not because I begrudge you the trout, but because the incident offers so much food for angling thought.

In the first instance, the trout rejected your dry fly from an inspection distance of a few inches. In the second, from a distance of a foot. Finally, the fish was able to reject the same fly at a distance of about 2 feet or however deeply the trout was holding in the stream initially. By some mechanism that's still not completely understood, the trout has quickly learned that the series of identical flies passing overhead are not worthy of a response. Fishermen often attribute such events to pure luck, but luck has nothing to do with it.

As you may recall from previous chapters, all trout exhibit selectivity in feeding that's present to different degrees at different times and under different circumstances. A trout that's been feeding heavily on little olive mayflies during each of the past four afternoons will be most likely to rise to a little olive dry on the fifth afternoon, assuming a continuation of the same hatch, because the trout's feeding behavior has become temporarily patterned by the abundance of a particular insect. The same thing happens in shorter intervals, such as during a hatch when a trout feeds on the abundance of one kind of insect to the exclusion of all other kinds. The trout, in this case, has formed what's called a *searching image*[2] in its brain that comes from repeated, short-term exposure to—and acceptance of—a series of identical natural flies. Some insects floating on the surface toward the trout match this image and are likely to be eaten; others—including your dry fly, perhaps—don't match and are ignored.

The searching image can be likened to one missing piece in the center of a large jigsaw puzzle.[3] The various colors and complex shape of the missing piece are unique to its space. All those parameters must be matched by a single piece for completion of the puzzle. The trout's brain makes that kind

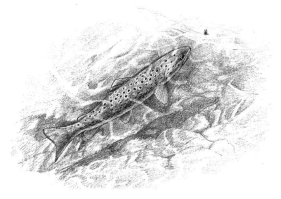

Will he or won't he? The trout's decision-making process may be even more complex than previously imagined.

of match with each insect it accepts, very much like a digital computer searches for bits of data that match certain established criteria—both with blazing speed and conspicuously lacking any human power of reason. The primitive brain of a trout, however, does all this with a speed—still unmeasured—that makes our most sophisticated computers look like child's toys. Interestingly, the trout's brain probably uses a parallel-processing method—seeing and attempting to match the fly's various characteristics simultaneously rather than one at a time, which is similar to a design premise behind most modern supercomputers.

These sorts of examples are at the current frontier of both the behavioral sciences and of trout fishing, and some may resent my having compared the working of the brain of their idyllically favorite fish with the techno-wizardry of Seymour Cray or IBM. This sort of thinking, however, gives even greater credence to a technique the late Vince Marinaro called "The Game of Nods," which can be vastly instructive to all trout fishermen who trouble to follow its simple rules.

A short while ago, we used as an example a trout that rose to inspect our dry fly and refused it. On subsequent and repeated casts, the trout didn't move at all. Let's say we now change flies from a tan to a light-gray dry of similar size. After a cast or two, it's evident the trout isn't moving to this one, either. No progress, except that the gray version has been eliminated and that, in itself, is progress of a sort. Let's put a tan fly back on, one size smaller, and trim the hackle from the bottom so more of the fly's body is in contact with the surface. Again the trout rises to within a few inches of the fly and turns back down in refusal. The trout has just told us we're doing something right, but not exactly right; the trout has not told us—"nodded," in terms of Marinaro's game—exactly *what* it was we did partly right. The next time we cast, we give the fly the barest of twitches— no more than half an inch—when it's a foot upstream of the trout. The trout rises smoothly and takes the fly unerringly. Having taken the trouble to learn from one trout what was acceptable, we then use the same trimmed down little dry with subtle twitches to take another half-dozen fish from the same pool. The Game of Nods depends on being able to work for some time over a visible fish without disturbing it, changing flies and noting the fish's reaction to each, which is often possible with careful casting and little movement. It is a time-consuming, nerve-wracking, exacting business that can be immensely rewarding in terms of trout.

Modern dry flies fall within a series of categories that are all useful at times, although not always at the same time. These groupings are determined by fly *design* and not pattern; each design can offer a slightly different representation of the same insect to the trout.

Conventional drys are what most people think of when considering dry flies, represented by a style that evolved in New York's Catskill Mountain region generally between 1900 and 1950. These are, for the most part, mayfly imitations with a few hackle or hair fibers for the tail; a slim, tapered body of floss, spun fur, or quill; hackle wound radially at the front of the hook, extending at right angles to the hook shank; and often with paired wings of wood duck, quill fibers, hackle tips, or clumped hair, also at the front of the hook. The overall effect should be one of sparseness, giving lightness and life to the fly on the water, an effect typically diminished by an excess of materials in tying—a common fault. This category also includes variants and spiders tied with longer hackles

than normal for a given hook size and usually without wings. The latter flies work especially well for fishing the water in the absence of a hatch, landing lightly and floating high on calmer waters and often getting rises from larger, otherwise reluctant fish. Spiders and variants have fallen from general use in recent years, perhaps because they're not easy to tie, but their effectiveness remains undiminished.

Modern, thorax-style drys place the hackle and wings about a third of the hook shank's length back from the eye or front of the hook. This is a better approximation of the position of the wings and legs of natural mayflies and thus offers a more realistic silhouette to the trout. The tail fibers are often splayed into a Y-shape, which gives greater stability on the water and a greater likelihood of the fly's landing upright. As originally described by Vince Marinaro in his 1951 classic *A Modern Dry-Fly Code*, the thorax style has hackle wound around and through the paired wings in crisscross fashion, which splays the hackle widely and causes the fly to ride very high on the water. This is both effective and difficult to do, and most commercial versions of this style simply feature a single, upright clumped wing with conventionally wound hackle. I routinely trim the hackle on the bottom of such commercial flies, which don't follow the original thorax design anyway, so the fly floats flush on the surface tension. This makes such commmercial ties float upright more consistently and, I believe, also makes them more effective.

Parachute drys date back at least to the 1930s, but didn't become widely popular until after being described in Swisher and Richards' 1971 *Selective Trout*. Most parachutes utilize a single, clumped wing— rarely paired and divided wings, which are also very effective in this style, but harder to tie—again placed a third of the distance back from the hook eye. Hackle is wound horizontally around the base of the wing, extending in a circular fan shape around the top of the fly above the body. The effect of the horizontal hackle is quite literally like a parachute, landing the fly gently and almost invariably right side up on the surface. Of all the commonly available commercial dry-fly styles, parachutes are probably the most imitative of newly emerged mayflies at the water's surface. Their flush-floating design means they won't float as long or as high in rough water as more conventional styles will, however. Parachute ties are especially effective as small mayfly imitations in hook sizes 20 and smaller because the tying style doesn't obscure the hook point and gap with hackle or other materials. Many commercial parachute patterns are made with a white-hair, upright wing—regardless of their imitative purpose—to enhance the fly's visibility. Such wings are quite realistic when viewed against the sky from below, but are starkly white when seen from below against shadows or dark bankside foliage, which is a glaring imitative error. Wings of imitative gray or another appropriate color will work better in such cases, although at the expense of your being able to see the fly easily.

No-hackle drys enjoyed a flurry of popularity after being described in Swisher and Richards' *Selective Trout* in the early 1970s, although their once wide use seems to have dwindled, and this style is absent from most mail-order catalogs and fly shops these days. This style of mayfly imitation is still superbly effective in smaller sizes for hyperselective trout, and I suspect, again, that its diminished availability is mostly because the flies are difficult to tie correctly and thus not high among the priorities of most commercial fly-tying houses. No-hackle drys feature tails splayed in a Y-shape for stability and duck-quill wings tied to extend upright from the sides of the body about a third of

the hook shank's length back from the hook eye. Bodies are made of finely dubbed fur or synthetic fiber of appropriate colors.

The comparadun style of mayfly imitation was so named by Al Caucci and Bob Nastasi, who introduced it in their 1974 book *Hatches*. The name is unfortunate, sounding like someone's idea of slick marketing, but the design is ingenious and is largely derived from the earlier Haystack style established by Fran Betters to imitate the mayfly hatches along New York's Ausable. Comparaduns also have splayed, hackle-fiber tails for stability, and finely tapered bodies of dubbed fur or synthetic fiber. The key design element is the wing—again located about a third of the way back on the hook—which is composed of deerhair fibers tied upright and splayed through a 180-degree arc from one side of the fly to the other. When splayed in this fashion, the fibers serve to imitate the wings and legs of the naturals simultaneously and hold the fly upright on the water. This low-floating design is easy to tie and is widely available in a full range of sizes and colors. It has consistently outfished more conventional drys for me over many years and is often the first style I reach for when I encounter trout feeding on adult mayflies.

Spent-wing drys are mayfly patterns representing the so-called spinner stage, adult mayflies that have returned to the stream for mating and egg laying and that subsequently float dying on the surface, wings outstretched; their lives at this point quite literally spent. The design is relatively simple, with the only major variations coming in choices of winging materials. A relatively long tail is comprised of a few slightly splayed hackle fibers; bodies are often made of dubbed fur or closely wrapped quill; the wings are tied horizontally, often about a third of the way back on the hook shank, and configured much like the wings of an airplane. I usually use wings of pale gray (*not* bright white, as is commonly done) polypropylene yarn, which is a common solution. Most commercial versions are grossly overdressed; remember when tying or buying that a very few yarn fibers as a wing go a long way. Other solutions include wings of hackle fibers or hen-hackle tips; the former may be worth a try if a trout refuses your more durable poly-winged pattern.

Another major dry-fly category includes all down-winged flies, meaning those adults that have their wings parallel to their body rather than upright as in the case of adult mayflies. This includes adult caddisflies, stoneflies, and midges, of which caddisflies are the most important to both trout and fishermen most of the time. For the moment, I'll consider just caddisflies.

Caddis drys are either of a high-floating design, which is most imitative of both newly emerged adults that remain very briefly on the water and of egg-laying adults that hop and skip actively along the water's surface, or of a flush, low-floating design, which is usually most representative of spent adults. While many anglers now carry

Modern dry fly styles, clockwise from top: conventional, comparadun, parachute, no-hackle, and thorax.

a selection of high-floating caddis drys, relatively few carry and use flush-floating patterns, which can be enormously effective at times.

High-floating caddis drys are characterized by no tail (caddis don't have tails); a slim dubbed or floss body that's sometimes palmered with short, stiff hackle; a down wing of hair fibers or slips of duck quill tied in at the front of the hook; and usually some additional hackle wound radially in front of the wing. All of these attributes contribute to a high-floating fly that can easily be twitched or worked gently on the surface in imitation of the natural's behavior. Al Troth's Elkhair Caddis is the basic and most widely used style in this category, which also includes such flies as Eric Leiser's Chuck Caddis (made with woodchuck hair) and the venerable Henryville Special.

Flush-floating caddisfly drys are used to a much lesser extent. This isn't because they don't work—they work wonderfully at times—but because they've been given much less attention in the angling press. The basic design elements of a slim body and down wing are retained in this case, but the wing itself is more often cut from a feather of appropriate color or made of hen-hackle tips to be more imitative (than clumped hair) of the natural's wings. Hackle is placed only at the front of the fly and is used more sparingly than in high-floating versions. Some versions use parachute-style hackle—while retaining a down wing—to good effect.

Flush-floating caddis conclude this list of basic dry-fly types, although I realize I've omitted a great many other styles that some anglers will also see as basic. I've tried to concentrate on those that are most widely available commercially; certainly there are others that at times will work just as well or even better. Too long a list will start to seem like work, and I promised earlier in this chapter that we'd cast a fly or two upstream.

Another little olive mayfly disappeared in a brief dimple, and I could see the trout clearly as it scanned the surface for more. It was a good fish for this little spring creek, a brown of 18 inches or so. The fish was holding in the slow current directly underneath a barbed-wire fence. The lowest strand was about 2 feet above the surface, and from where I was kneeling in the grass some 30 feet downstream I counted three small drys dangling from broken tippet sections along the wire. I cursed the wire. I also cursed Dave Corcoran and Greg Lilly, who had kindly—or so I thought at the time—given me directions here from their nearby Bozeman, Montana, fly shop.

A downstream approach would have been been duck soup, feeding a little dry from upstream on a slack line down with the current and under the wire. The fence was a good one, there were some range cattle on the other side with which I had no inclination to go waltzing, and crossing the fence to get above the fish might have meant an irate rancher. So that choice was out. What the hell.

I tied on a little No-Hackle Olive and worked out some line in the air, quietly and deliberately casting a couple of feet below the trout to get the range and rhythm for the next cast. As the fly drifted back, I pulled another 4 feet of line from the reel, roll-cast the drifting line into the air, made a single backcast, and then tried to shoot a tight, fast loop under the fence and slightly to one side of the fish. The cast checked abruptly a few inches above the water, and the fly bounced back a few inches on a slack leader tippet about a foot above the trout. I watched through a seeming eternity as the trout tilted slowly upward, took the fly and started to turn gently downward. My response was immediate and unfortunately enthusiastic; snapping the leader with a sloppy, heavy-handed strike. It was a victory of sorts, since

I had, after all, gotten the trout to come to the fly and had managed to avoid the fence. I still feel like an idiot, though, every time I recall that particular fish—which is often.

Upstream dry-fly fishing is sometimes a matter of necessity, as in the previous instance in which there was no other choice. At other times, such as when wading and fishing larger rivers, usually in a down-and-across manner, I might spot a trout rising upstream of my position. There's usually little point in getting out of the river and walking around and above the trout for the sake of getting a downstream throw. It's usually more important to fish upstream to the trout immediately, before the fish stops surface feeding entirely.

Sometimes, fishing upstream is simply a better choice. Pocket water is one example, in which case pockets of quiet water behind boulders serve as upstream stairs for the wading angler, who can move slowly from one pocket up to another while remaining for the most part removed from the more difficult, faster water between the rocks. Such pockets are usually triangular in shape, with the broad base of the triangle (and the slowest water) being immediately behind the rock, from which the pocket of slower water tapers to a sharp point farther downstream. Many trout—and often the largest—will hold at the downstream apex of a pocket, in that narrow area of slow water several feet downstream of the boulder that interrupts the faster flow. This sweet spot is easy to fish by casting a dry upstream on a relatively short line, checking the cast in the air to provide a foot or so of slack tippet near the fly.

In this case, and most often in others involving upstream angling, the line, leader, and fly are drifting back to the fisherman, who has to gather the accumulating slack by stripping line with the rod tip low, maintaining contact with the fly and ready for a strike. As the fly drifts still closer, I often start to raise the rod tip to slowly pick up the gathering slack line. This puts me in position for a roll-cast pickup, which literally lifts line, leader, and fly off the water by making a forward roll cast in the air before starting the normal false-casting sequence. If a trout hits as the rod is partly raised, I make a roll-casting stroke immediately, counting on the force of the rolling line being sufficient to set the hook.

It's possible to get extremely close to rising trout—even large, normally shy fish—from directly downstream and even in slow, clear water. Close in this case means a dozen feet or even less if you don't scare the fish by sloppy wading, although I usually choose a more comfortable (for me) casting range of 25 to 35 feet when approaching fish from below. In this case, the river's currents between you and the trout straight upstream are often of constant speed, minimizing drag problems. You can use a cast curving to the left or right (as appropriate) to place the fly a couple of feet upstream of the fish so the trout sees the fly before the leader. Or you can simply cast straight upstream, placing the fly a few inches to one side or the other of the fish's head. Slapping the water with the line or leader butt in the immediate vicinity of the rising trout is the greatest sin common to this method and will scare the trout immediately. Remember when fishing in this manner that because the fly is placed close to the fish, it may be taken almost immediately. You must be ready for a strike as soon as the fly lands on the water; there's no time for fiddling around.

If a particular trout stream offers enough room, and if I don't have a specific reason for fishing upstream, I most often fish dry in an across-and-downstream direction. Working or twitching a dry fly on the surface, which I do often, is more difficult when fishing upstream because an upstream slack line is harder to control. Fly tackle, tactics, and patterns have all evolved to a point at which downstream dry flies are perfectly plausible, which wasn't the case during much of this century, when the upstream dry fly ws *the* method of choice. Casting your feathers against the current is still a worthy method if you have a particular reason for so doing. Just keep in mind that it's not the only way.

1. Technically, the newly emerged mayfly dun, which many dry flies imitate, isn't "adult," or sexually mature, until it molts for a final time in the air or elsewhere along the stream after emerging, but I've considered it as adult for purposes of this definition.

2. See the various papers by Neil Ringler cited in the Bibliography.

3. In the narrow construction of behavioral scientists, *searching image* connotes an image formed of a particular food in the mind of a predator that literally blinds the predator to other food forms. As an alternative, some have suggested "predator preference" as the basis for some selective feeding behavior, in which case the predator sees all available food forms and makes choices among them. In either case, however, the predator has to see and have some mental image of its prey. A grasshopper floating downstream amid a flotilla of blue-winged olive mayflies is certainly not invisible to the trout, which will—rarely—divert from its mayfly meal to eat the grasshopper. I thus use the term "searching image" in a broader sense to mean simply the way in which a trout visually perceives a particular food form. See the various papers by Ringler, especially Ringler (1975).

21
Dry Flies Downstream

Angling mythology is usually a matter of convenience. It's much easier to say, for example, that Theodore Gordon invented American dry-fly fishing[1] at the turn of the century—a claim Gordon himself never made—than it is to explore the dry fly's real roots. The optical phenomena associated with Snel's Circle—that window in the water's mirrored surface through which trout view dry flies from below—have been much described as they pertain to trout fishing, but are usually dismissed as pertaining only to flat, smooth water and thus of limited value. Even our dry flies are subject to the convenience of myth, which holds that drys designed to be highly imitative of natural insects aren't necessary in the fast, broken water of most trout streams.

None of these myths happen to be true. They are widely held not because they make some aspect of trout fishing more effective but because they make it easier. It seems almost to be a case of angling ignorance becoming trout-fishing bliss, even though the consequence of such thinking is the catching of fewer trout than would otherwise be possible.

This is perhaps most true with dry-fly fishing, which a century of tradition holds is an upstream method. That tradition is still remarkably pervasive, with many anglers even now believing that fishing drys downstream is a poor tactical choice if not physically impossible. Of all our modern tactics

for trout, downstream drys are the newest, an approach being used by more and more anglers with each passing season. As you struggle to wade upstream against the current with tangles of fly line drifting back down around your legs, a simple suggestion will make your life easier and will also sometimes bring more trout to net. Turn around.

In referring to downstream dry-fly fishing, I specifically mean those casts made at various angles to the main current, ranging from directly across stream—perpendicular to the current—to directly downstream and parallel to the flow. If you have a choice, some intermediate angle is usually best. I found in checking my own habits that I try, if possible, to wade to a position that allows a cast at an angle of 20 to 30 degrees—measured from an imaginary line perpendicular to the current—down and across to cover a rising fish.

Although I never give it too much thought while actually fishing, the extent of the downstream angle is fairly critical. Casting straight across the current means the likelihood is greatest that your line will fall across currents of varying speeds, which generates the most potential problems with drag. Casting straight downstream with a slack line usually means the fly line will be in a single current lane, so drag problems may be minimized as long as you can feed additional slack into the straight-downstream drift. But this creates problems in hooking fish, since you'll most often be pulling the fly toward the front of the fish's mouth on the strike. The straight-downstream approach also means the line, leader, and fly will be suspended in the current over the fish when the drift is concluded, and the fish may become frightened when you slide the line over its head and off the water for your next cast.

Within this set of downstream problems, fishing at some angle across the current is a compromise. A downstream angle will help somewhat in reducing the drag problems intrinsic to across-stream casting and also help to avoid the hooking problems and spooked fish common to a straight-downstream approach. The advantages of this method are enormous and include the following:

- It's physically easier than working against the current. Not only do you avoid the effort of wading constantly upstream, you don't have to wrestle with the constantly accumulating slack line characteristic of upstream dry-fly work.
- Your dry fly will cover more water more effectively. Longer drag-free floats are often possible with this method because slack line can be slowly added to the drift, something that's impossible with upstream fishing.
- Your hooking percentage will improve. Careless accumulation of slack in upstream fishing accounts for many missed fish simply because you then can't respond fast enough to a stike. Down-and-across dry-fly fishing means you can most easily control the tension—or lack thereof—on the line between you and the fly, which allows a precisely timed response when the trout eventually rises.
- You'll pop fewer tippets. Again because of the precise control allowed by this method, the timing and force of your hook setting can be very deliberate. This in turn

means you'll be breaking off fewer fish, especially when fishing with ultrafine leaders and drys smaller than size 20.

- The fly can be worked or twitched. Trout that have refused a dead-drifting dry can often be induced to rise if the fly is twitched briefly on the surface and then allowed to resume its drag-free drift. This is easily done with a down-and-across approach and is more difficult to accomplish by any other means.
- Multiple drifts are possible on a single cast. After your initial down-and-across cast has finally started to drag, you can use your rod to slide the line, leader, and fly upstream without lifting them from the water. Then lower your rod to create slack, which allows another drag-free downstream drift to cover either more water or another fish.

For all of these reasons and more, I find myself now fishing this way most of the time, after first starting to experiment with down-and-across drys almost twenty years ago. If the river or stream is large enough to allow this method—meaning about 40 feet wide, or more—it's a good way to fish blind (meaning not to a specific, rising fish) and dry, wading slowly with the current and casting down and across to drift your dry fly over likely spots along the bank. But it's a good method for crowded waters, too, in which case the presence of other anglers up- and downstream may mean you're constrained to perhaps only 100 feet or so of a pool or run. As usual, the best way to explain the technique is to try it out in a trout stream, so let's run through a typical down-and-across situation.

This time we'll fish Montana's Madison, specifically the section near the highway bridge for the road to Cliff and Wade lakes and a few miles downstream from the popular stretch near the Slide Inn. Remember that although I'm using a specific river section for interest's sake in this example, the techniques I'm describing can be applied to almost any river. The Madison here is wide, rough, and fairly fast, with most of the fish concentrated near shore, either associated with current-breaking boulders or with the bank itself. In previous years here, I've sometimes raised big trout, especially rainbows, from the fast water at midriver, but eventually learned that carefully fishing the banks and pocket water along the edge was more productive of trout.

It's a perfect day for dry-fly trout fishing, overcast with an off-and-on gentle drizzle and no wind. The sky reflects as a flat gray on quieter river pockets that I can see from the car while putting on my gear, and I smile with the realization this will make both natural flies and rising fish easier to see than would be the case in bright sun and wind-ruffled water. I carry my unassembled rod sections downstream along the bank, planning as usual to use the rigging-up time as time to also watch the river for clues as to what to use and how to use it.

Finally I come to a good-looking, long pocket of slowly flowing water behind a huge rock that's about 15 feet from shore. The pocket is about 8 feet wide, extends some 30 feet downstream, and looks as though it should hold fish, so I stop to put my rod together and to watch. There are some small mayflies visible in the quiet water behind the rock and a couple more fluttering past in the air. My baseball-style cap makes an adequate net that I use to snare an airborne mayfly for a closer look. Small, about a size 20. Medium-olive body. Gray, upright wings. Two tails. It appears to be one of several *Baetis* species, although that probably won't make too much difference as long as I've got the general idea of what's on the water.

I sit down on a rock at the edge of the river that gives me a good view of the downstream

pocket and proceed to string the rod, stretching the leader hard between my hands to straighten it and to test its knots. A new tippet is mandatory, my old one having been stretched and abraded in catching some cutthroat over on the Yellowstone yesterday afternoon. I tie in a new section of 6X about 3 feet long, gauging its length against my outstretched arm. It's long enough to recoil adequately when cast, adding slack near the drifting fly, and of sufficiently fine diameter that it won't overpower the fly on the water. Finally I tie on a #20 Olive Parachute dry of a size and color to mimic the natural I caught, keeping the clinch knot very loose and well lubricated with saliva until finally drawing the knot tight. Keeping the knot loose and lubricated until the last moment of tightening helps to keep the tippet from curling like a Christmas ribbon when it's pulled around the narrow radius of the hook eye in the knotting process. A little paste-type dressing is daubed on the fly, and I use the residual dressing on my fingertips to wipe and dress the leader as well. I want all the leader to float because I expect to be twitching the fly occasionally, and a sunken leader will pull the fly underwater in that event. Okay, trout; I'm ready.

The hatch is sporadic, as they often are on gray days such as this one. As I watch, mayflies appear on the pocket's surface in twos and threes, floating briefly before taking off and flying into the nearby bushes. Finally there's a rise. Not much of a rise, just a little wrinkle in the water down near the end of the pocket. As I watch, the fish comes again, and I can see the tip of its tail wave briefly above the surface as the trout turns quietly back down. I pointedly watch a small dun as it drifts near the trout's position. Sure enough. This time I see part of the trout's upper jaw gently break the surface as the fly disappears.

In this case, I could either walk around on the bank to get below the fish and thereby cast upstream, or simply get a little closer and fish down. I elect to fish down and so wade very quietly for a few feet downstream along the bank, stopping and standing still when the fish is about 40 feet across and downstream of my position. There's about 15 feet of faster water between me and the quieter stretch that holds the trout, which I'll have to account for in trying to avoid drag. I check and find the bushes behind me are fairly low, so there's plenty of room for a conventional, overhead cast. I extend line in the air, aiming my false casts well away from the fish to avoid spooking it. Changing direction slightly, I aim the final forward cast about 3 feet upstream of where I believe the fish to be, stopping the rod abruptly at about 45 degrees above the surface to straighten and then recoil the tippet and fly before they land. Simultaneously, I reach with the rod to the left across the front of my body to place the line farther upstream in the faster current nearby.

At this point, I've completed a typical down-and-across-stream dry-fly cast. The fly and some adjacent slack leader tippet are drifting slowly and without drag down toward the trout; the fly line in the faster currents nearby is moving more rapidly downsteam and is being followed with my rod tip; and the rod is *still* being held as high as it was at the completion of the cast. This last point is vital and usually overlooked.

I've described in previous chapters the necessity of following the drifting line with your rod tip in this case, which helps to prevent a growing belly of line dragging in the current. If the whole casting process is concluded with your rod tip high above the water, you can further minimize drag by slowly lowering your rod as you follow the drifting line. There are thus two distinct rod motions conducted at the same time. One is a horizontal, downstream movement as you use the rod to follow the drifting line. The second is a gradual, downward movement of

the rod toward the surface of the water, which feeds line into the drift in a precisely controlled fashion. This allows a longer drag-free float than is possible if the rod is lowered at cast's conclusion as is most often done. It also means that I can stop lowering the rod at any time, twitch the fly briefly, and then continue lowering the rod so the drift continues without subsequent drag. Finally, if a trout comes to the fly, my slow rod lowering means I'm in direct contact with the line, leader, and fly, ready to set the hook deliberately and gently. If drag problems are circumvented by the more common method of using line mends or other means of placing slack line on the water, contact with the fly is not nearly as direct and both deliberate hook setting and fly twitches are correspondingly more difficult, if not impossible. Once again, keep the rod tip high above the water, lowering it gradually and deliberately as you follow the drifting line. This is the single most important factor in successful down-and-across-stream fishing with dry flies.

My little olive dry drifted in the company of a natural a few inches away, which the trout took in a quiet swirl as my fly floated past unheeded. I let the cast continue to drift below the trout as the current swung my line well away from the fish's position. Finally, I judged the line to be far enough away from the trout that I could safely pick it up with the rod for another cast without scaring the fish. I cast as before, slowly swinging and lowering my rod to follow the drift. This time as the fly approached the fish, I stopped lowering the rod. I could see the fly coming to the end of its slack-tippet tether and at that point gave it the merest of twitches—moving it perhaps half an inch—and then began lowering the rod slowly again to drift the fly drag free. The fly floated another few inches downstream, and by this time the rod was extended to my right as I followed the more rapidly drifting line. The trout came quietly, taking the fly in a small dimple, and

I pulled the rod gently to the side, setting the little hook firmly in the corner of the fish's jaw.

There was a boil on the surface as the trout turned and headed swiftly downstream toward a little island, pulling line from the reel as I stumbled in pursuit along the shoreline rocks. Fortunately, the fish ran downstream on my side of the island and settled in a still backwater where the battle was concluded. Measuring 22 inches by my pocket tape, it was the largest brown of the afternoon; my largest, in fact, from that particular river, but its release by no means marked the end of the day. The gray drizzle and little olive flies continued until amost dark, and trout continued to show among the rocks and along the bank for several hours. Sometimes I'd wade out into the fast water to be better able to drift small drys down and across to rising fish near the bank. And sometimes there were pockets like the first one that were best fished down from near the bank itself, although none seemed to offer fish as large as the first one had. By the time I quit, the rain was seeping around my rainjacket collar and into my shirt. It had become cold, and I alternated between shivers and smiles while hiking back to the car. The smiles were the best part. There could be few things worse, I decided, than fishing in the rain and not catching anything.

Drag is the dry-fly angler's greatest demon, yet a slight and natural movement of the fly can be very helpful in raising difficult trout. The difference between natural and unnatural movement can be hard to discern but is vital in drawing strikes from trout when using drys in either slow or fast water.

Sometimes drag is self-evident. Line swinging in the current pulls on the leader and fly, making the fly skim across the surface contrary to the flow and with an obvious wake. This becomes quickly evident to anyone with just a little trout-fishing experience, and many people have learned the basic techiques, such as line mending, that are necessary for drag-free drifts. Drag, however, is not always so apparent.

If you watch a group of mayflies (or any other small objects) floating in the current near one another yet each separated by a few inches, you may notice that their positions relative to one another seem to change slightly; one seems to speed up and gain on the others, while a moment later one seems to slow down as the distance between it and the others momentarily increases. The naturally drifting flies are floating in the same primary current but are obviously not always drifting at the same speed. This at first glance seems to defy logic, but there's a good reason for this phenomenon that you can see for yourself if you study the current closely. The flow of all rivers and streams is turbulent and irregular, almost never laminar and of consistent, even speed. There are little whorls at the surface resulting from the current's moving over rocks or logs at the bottom, tossings and turnings and upwellings of water that travel to the surface where their energy dissipates and their momentary interruptions of the surface flow eddy and disappear. All the various currents are self-similar, taking place in the same way and otherwise resembling the larger scale flow of the river itself. But they happen at different scales or to different degrees and at times that are—to fishermen—unpredictable. Those inclined to mathematics will recognize this description as being the self-similar geometry of fractals. The nonlinear aspects of turbulent water and its fractal geometries are a new science that's beyond a mere trout-fishing book, although sometime in the future that won't be the case. The bottom line is that those fractal currents—the little whorls, boils, and eddies in the otherwise smooth flow—will drag your fly in a subtle manner sometimes undetected by you but not undetected by a trout.

In recent years, this has come to be known as *microdrag*, which is a term—having mentioned it—that I'll omit henceforth, preferring to rely more on fly-fishing theory than on its already overgrown vocabulary. A fly is either dragging or it isn't, and anything in between is only a matter of degree. At distances beyond 20 or 30 feet, such subtle drag effects can be impossible to see, although they're detected readily by trout at the fish's inspection distance, typically a few inches. There is one way you can tell if this is happening that I don't recall having seen described before. Instead of watching your distant fly to see if it's dragging, watch the position of your fly relative to other floating objects nearby. If your dry fly is floating near a natural insect, a bubble, small stick, leaf, or anything else on the surface, watch them both. When the dry fly attached to your leader appears to move slightly away from or toward the nearby, naturally drifting object, the fly is probably dragging even though you can see no wake and the fly's movement is not otherwise apparent. If this movement of the dry fly relative to the other object stops, you're doing fine. If it persists, let the fly swing well away from the trout's position and try another cast. Slack leader tippet near the fly is usually the best solution to this problem, but doesn't always work because the little fractal currents at the surface are—

for our purposes, at least—random, intermittent, and unpredictable.

Deliberate movement of the fly is another matter. Many anglers have caught onto this idea since Len Wright published his landmark 1972 book *Fishing the Dry Fly as a Living Insect*, which dealt mostly with fishing caddis drys in seductive twitches—what Wright called the "sudden inch"—on the surface. What still seems to escape many fishermen, however, is just how that movement should be conducted and just how much is enough. Carefully—and not very much—are the essential answers.

A trout scanning the surface for food sees many odd bits of flotsam in the surface tension; bits of bark and leaves, small buds fallen from trees, all sorts of things of a size and superficial resemblance to natural foods that the trout nevertheless rejects outright, making no movement or other response. Things floating on the surface—including natural insects and dry flies—create indentations in the surface tension. When viewed from below, such indentations are minute prisms, bits of flashing light that show up markedly on the mirrored undersurface of the stream. During a hatch of mayflies or caddis or a fall of mayfly spinners, large numbers of identical insects make identical patterns in the surface tension, light patterns that by their repetition probably help the trout to cue on the naturals well before they become totally visible to the fish in the more limited and closer range of Snel's Circle (the trout's window through the otherwise mirrored undersurface of the water).

Within this realm of sunshine and shadow, where much of the ceiling is a mirror of the bottom pockmarked with the bright indentations of floating objects, the most conspicuous attribute of any floating object is movement (or lack of same). As we've discussed several times already in this book, trout are acutely sensitized to movement in their surroundings. The movement of a floating object is even more apparent to the trout than is the movement of an object below the surface, because surface movement adds another dimension: light. A naturally drifting mayfly or caddis at first offers the trout only its characteristic light pattern at the surface. If the same insect flutters or moves slightly, its light pattern moves even more distinctly. To humans, the difference is the same as that between the headlights of numerous parked cars and the giant flashes of neon signs in Times Square. Our attention, like that of the trout, is riveted by that which is different from everything else.

The insect's movement has focused the trout on that insect's particular light pattern and position well before the insect has drifted close enough to be totally visible. The trout might respond immediately, swimming close enough to the insect to examine and eat it, or, more often, will wait, still focused, for the the insect to drift within full view. If the insect—now our artificial dry fly—goes dragging away across the surface in a manner that from below looks like the fiery trail of a skyrocket, the trout will likely ignore it. The fish may associate that "insect" behavior with the trauma of a prior catch-and-release experience, or the fish may simply find such behavior beyond the realm of its experience and ignore the dragging fly because the fish has no basis for a response. Other fish will find the insect's odd behavior threatening and will stop feeding entirely.

Having looked above and below the surface, it should be obvious that the most common approach to fly movement involves no more than a gentle, short twitch when the fly is a foot or two upstream of the fish, followed by a drag-free drift and, hopefully, a take. In the absence of a strong wind, most insects don't flutter wildly across the surface for 1 or 2 feet before stopping, but many do move an inch or two before pausing to drift quietly once again. The technique, by the way, is not a new one, although many fish-

ermen regard it as such. It has appeared for many years off and on in British angling works as the "induced rise" or "induced take," meaning the fly is deliberately moved to coax an otherwise reluctant trout.

Some dry-fly designs lend themselves more easily to twitching than others, and your use of this technique is governed by a combination of fly design and current speed in addition to the way in which the trout happen to be responding on a particular day. Flush-floating designs—such as parachutes, no-hackles, comparaduns, and spent spinners—can only be twitched cautiously and gently in relatively slow-moving, quiet water. The same movement imparted on a fast-flowing, rough surface will most often drown the fly quickly. Conversely, high-floating, traditional drys with stiff, radial hackle—as well as heavily hackled caddis patterns such as the Elkhair Caddis—can be twitched to good effect on broken water as well as on the flat, smooth sections of slower runs and pools.

The differentiation of dry-fly designs based on water types is a newly popular concept, but also one subject to a great deal of myth. It's commonly held that trout rising in fast, broken water are less selective than those rising in the flat, calm waters of a pool. The popular reasoning is that trout can't see drys as well when feeding in broken water and that the various optical phenomena associated with Snel's Circle (see Chapter 8) only apply to trout taking insects from a flat surface, again as is found in slowly flowing pools. Such common beliefs are wrong, and the only reason trout might seem less selective in fast, broken water is because they simply have less time to scrutinize the fly.

I was sitting on a big rock in midstream some years ago, which happened to be in the middle of a rough section of upstate New York's West Branch Ausable. Having taken a good twenty minutes to struggle my way a dozen feet through the rapids and to the rock, I wasn't anxious to wade farther and so sat there for a couple of hours, fishing the adjacent pockets occasionally and watching both trout and intermittent hatches of mayflies and caddis. If you don't already know, this particular river has a worldwide reputation for both rough-and-tumble water and for brown trout. Much of the stream is of a steep gradient, which means much of the trout fishing is done in fast, broken rapids.

Various trout would rise occasionally in the nearby currents as I watched, and after a while the precise locations of their rises began to show a pattern. Within the standing waves and white water in front of me were numerous small slicks, smooth-surfaced glides that in many cases were only about a foot long and a few inches wide, though sometimes larger. At distances of more than a dozen feet, these little slicks were almost invisible in the surrounding turbulence. It was within these slicks that the rises *invariably* occurred. The trout were not slapping at caddis or taking the little olive duns as the flies bobbed among the standing waves of the rapids, but almost every time one of the flies drifted along one of the small slicks—bang!

The observation hit me like Newton's apple. While I claim no comparison with the late physicist, it was immediately obvious that the reasons for the trouts' feeding pattern were twofold: a fly on the slick was drifting—however briefly—in a predictable manner and was thus easier for the trout to target for an accurate rise than a fly in the adjacent rough water; and the smooth surface of the slick made the fly easier for the trout to see. I tried a little Royal Wulff dry, which is a common recommendation for broken-water trout, and did catch a couple of small browns. But from my close vantage point I could also see the underwater flashes and the surface boils that marked numerous

refusals in the fast water. Next I tried a small, No-Hackle Olive that was a close match for the little mayflies that were occasionally popping off the surface among the rocks. With very short casts, often no more than the leader, I specifically targeted the little slicks where the trout were rising. Over the next hour, trout after trout came to the little fly in quick, flashing rises and with no refusals that I was able to detect. I didn't actually catch very many, being too excited and usually pulling the fly away from the fish in an overeager response to their rapid rises. But then—as now—the emerging concept was far more important than any fish that might have come to hand.

The various trout-feeding phenomena associated with Snel's Circle—which essentially means that trout can see dry flies on the surface very well at close range—do pertain in fast-water dry-fly work, contrary to the wisdom of the concept's many critics, who have frequently claimed it pertains only to selected, slow-water situations. The reason is that smooth-surfaced glides both distort Snel's Circle relatively little and are

Even in generally fast, choppy water, trout will usually surface feed in small, slick areas found adjacent to areas with a rougher surface.

usually present even in broken water. An analogous and better-known situation occurs in many trout lakes and ponds, where on quiet days, given a calm surface, the rises of trout to emerging midges and other insects are often widespread. If a breeze ruffles the surface, the trout often stop surface feeding, even though the insects are still present. This halt in feeding activity is undoubtedly because the ruffled surface makes the insects less visible to the trout. And so it is that the slick-surfaced glides in an otherwise choppy riffle or rapid are the preferred areas of surface-feeding trout.

As a practical matter, this simply means you shouldn't leave your low-floating, imitative patterns in the car when you head for a riffle. While your no-hackles and comparaduns won't float as well or as long as heavily hackled drys in rough water, they will amost invariably produce more fish. Granted, because the duration of the trout's inspection is shorter in fast water, you may be able to get by with less imitative patterns or designs. This is what most people do, which I think is terrific. But by following them down the riffle with more imitative, low-floating drys, we'll catch a few trout the others haven't been able to tempt.

Fishing drys down-and-across stream has proven so effective and so often much easier than any other route, that I fish this way almost all the time as long as where I'm fishing offers sufficient room for the kind of overhead or sidearm casting this method requires. Obviously, down-and-across stream doesn't pertain to small, brush-crowded waters, for example, where an upstream dry fly is usually the best tactic. On any particular river, I might fish a high-floating caddis down and across even in the absence of a hatch, making a series of casts to the bank as I walk slowly with the current, alternately twitching the fly and letting it

drift drag free. At other times, and especially on crowded waters, I may be fishing little drys down and across over several fish without moving my feet for an hour or even longer. In this case, a refused fly swings gently away from the trout without scaring them, so there's plenty of time for all the fly changes and pondering that go along with difficult fish.

The basic method should sound familiar by the time you've progressed this far, because I've already suggested similar strategies separately for wet flies, nymphs, and streamers. If a trout refuses my drag-free or twitched down-and-across dry, I can try tempting the fish *from my same position* with a wet fly or streamer, or with a nymph twitched and then dead-drifted in front of the trout's nose. Perhaps at this point down-and-across-stream fishing with a carefully controlled fly is starting to sound like the Holy Grail of modern physics, a Grand Theory of Everything that accounts for the taste of pickles and the origins of the universe all at once. It is. Less presumptive and less important, certainly, but still an increasingly apparent fact of trout-fishing life.

1. Gordon was an American angler and flytier who lived alone in a small Catskills cabin in upstate New York at the turn of the century. He wrote widely—and with insight and wit—in a variety of periodicals, describing his experiments with both flies and tactics for trout. In 1890, F. M. Halford sent Gordon a series of British dry-fly patterns, which Gordon worked at adapting to American waters. Gordon has often been described as the father of American dry-fly fishing, but was not so described in his lifetime, nor did he claim the honor. Dry-fly fishing in America preceded Gordon by at least fifty years and probably longer, although it didn't become widely practiced here until the 1920s, well after Gordon's death in 1915. Gordon's many contributions were important, but invention of the dry-fly method was not among them. See, most especially, McDonald (1947).

22
Emergers

So far I'd been on the receiving end of a trout's no-hitter—no strikes; no swirls; no bumps. I had spent several hours over the past two evenings gently casting dozens of different fly patterns over trout that were rising sporadically in the slow-moving currents of a late-summer pool. The lack of any results at all seemed remarkable, and I was quickly becoming obsessive about the whole business. There was no discernable hatch to match, yet individual trout were making gentle swirls in the smooth surface at intervals of five minutes or so. Such fish can often be taken on small terrestrials in summer or sometimes on spent-wing imitations of minuscule mayflies, but neither my little ants nor my miniature spinner patterns had drawn a rise.

Ordinarily, the best solution to this problem involves wading out into the current lanes that have held feeding trout and using a small net to seine the flowing surface. You'll thus catch some samples of whatever the trout have been eating and will be able to select an appropriate imitation. The price of this knowledge is frightening the trout in the immediate vicinity by walking into their feeding areas, but the information gained should also produce fish in other parts of the stream on the same day as well as for the next day or two, perhaps, under similar conditions of time and place. It's a small sacrifice, which I'd tried on the second evening to no avail, wading out, scaring the fish, scanning the surface, and seeing absolutely nothing.

I spent much of the next day hammering out a contraption I thought would provide an answer. For anchors, I filled a couple of coffee cans with concrete mix, sinking an eyebolt in each for attaching ropes. A piece of window screening made up the net that I nailed to long dowels for support. Then I whittled a couple of large, tapered floats from an old, foam lobster pot that I'd picked up long before during a surf-casting trip and fastened the floats to the upper dowel. Perfect. This contraption could be held perpendicular to the current by its two anchors, where it would do all my insect-collecting work unattended as I fished. After fishing, I would only have to check my anchored screen to see what, if any, insects had been emerging and had perhaps escaped my notice. It was a brilliant ploy.

I got a few strange looks from anglers walking to other parts of the river as I lugged all this stuff to the pool where I'd spent the past few evenings in frustration. Let them wonder, I thought. Soon they'll see my rod bowed in triumph and hear the splashing of a hooked trout. I carefully set out my net in the tail of a pool where the trout had been rising last night. After a few adjustments to the anchors and ropes, the net was held firmly across a couple of feet of current, the floats supporting its top so that everything from the surface to a depth of about 18 inches would be filtered and held by the screen. I waded about a hundred feet upstream to the middle of the pool and then stood still for the half hour or so it would take for the pool to calm down and for the trout to begin rising.

Rise they did. Eventually trout began to show intermittently with the same gentle swirls of previous nights. Once again there was no visible hatch, nor could I see anything drifting at the surface around my waders. I cast, drifted, twitched, and floated everything I could think of over the fish, but again to no avail. It was almost dark when I finally said to hell with it and waded down to check my net. I played the beam of my little flashlight over the dripping screen, looking for anything wiggling among the bits of leaves and sticks captured from the current. The impossible became quickly obvious. Other than some minor debris, the net was empty.

This was so discouraging that I quit fishing entirely during those August evenings, concentrating instead on the morning spinner falls of *Tricorythodes* mayflies and on the afternoon hatches of olive *Baetis* flies that came in September. It was a full year later that I discovered the answer, one that may already be apparent to a few experienced fishermen from my description: microcaddis, a term now generally used by anglers to describe numerous caddisfly species less than ¼ inch long. That answer came not from my anchored drift net—which later did work well during other hatches of larger insects—but from a brook trout that finally took a small ant on one such evening of sporadic, quiet rises. I used a small plastic, syringelike device to pump the fish's stomach, and squirted the results into my palm after letting the fish go. A half-dozen, miniature caddis pupae floated in my hand. They were small enough to have been washed around the sides of my net, rather than lodging against the screen, but obviously large enough to attract the trout's attention as the little pupae drifted and wiggled just under the surface.

These days miniature solf-hackled wet flies are the commonly prescribed but still seldom-used answer for that problem of imitation, and the little Partridge-and-Olive wets I tied later that night on #24 hooks seemed to match the naturals in size and color. Such little flies don't sink readily, and I tied a short length of fine lead wire along each hook shank before dubbing the body and adding hackle. I found in trying that wrapping the hook shank with lead wire as I do with some larger flies was too bulky for the little hooks, but the small, straight section of lead wire was sufficient to keep the fly underwater and not waking at the surface when twitched.

I'd like to say the trout fell all over themselves in taking my little wets, but they didn't. I did catch some, though, which was a big improvement. I fished the little wet fly on a long, fine 8X tippet in the low and clear water, using slack-line casts down and across the slow current to the fish. If everything fell just right and I was able to briefly twitch and then dead-drift the little wet near the trout, I sometimes saw the floating leader dart on the surface when a trout took the fly. Mimicking both the appearance and the behavior of the little pupae was essential. If those imitative attributes were not both supplied by me, the trout simply didn't respond. As with other kinds of flies, the appearance and behavior of emergers are both critical.

E*mergers* has come to mean artificial flies that represent the appearance of aquatic insects during the brief interval of the insects' transition from nymphal (mayflies and stoneflies) or pupal (caddisflies and midges) stages to the winged, above-water stage. Emergers thus include a range of artificial flies, from those fished totally wet, such as imitations of mayfly nymphs or caddis pupae ascending to the surface, to those fished "damp," meaning low-floating on or in the surface tension, such as an imitation representing a mayfly or caddis partly emerged from its nymphal or pupal shuck.

The word "emerger" is relatively new,

having come into general usage among trout fishermen during the 1970s, but the concept is not. Although no modern fisherman has, to my knowledge, actually seen any fifteenth-century trout flies, most of the dozen fly patterns described in a circa 1450 British treatise are relatively simple and could easily have been taken as emerging insects by brown trout of similar vintage. It will likely never be known whether this was a matter of imitative accident or an angler's intent that was never made completely clear. In a 1932 collection of his own work, published as *The Chalk-Stream Angler*, G. E. M. Skues mentioned a diary that was kept by a Reverend Durnford as a record of fishing along England's Test between 1809 and 1819. Skues noted Durnford as having said the throats of trout were stuffed with "nymphae of the gnats ascending through the water before they take wing." Skues himself, who is widely known as the father of modern nymph fishing for his work in this field before his death in 1949, used emergers—although not by that name—as a stepping-stone to his theories of nymph design and fishing. His early work, as it appears in his 1910 *Minor Tactics of the Chalk Stream*, involved fishing wet flies upstream to feeding trout in much the same manner as modern emerger patterns are sometimes fished. We now seem to have come full circle in that after a preoccupation with dry flies and subsequently with nymphs through much of

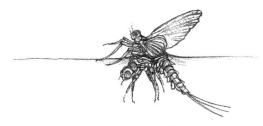

Mayfly emerging from its nymphal shuck, and the basis for many so-called "emerger" fly patterns.

this century, emergers are again the hot topic in trout fishing.

Interestingly, emerger patterns are much less standardized than other sorts of flies in terms of their design, and relatively few specific emerger patterns have gained national acceptance. This may be because our fascination with this style is relatively recent. Then too, the popularity of emerger flies coincided with the rapid growth in national fly-fishing media during the 1970s, which meant—and continues to mean—that the many diverse ideas concerning emerger-pattern styles get national exposure almost immediately. The pattern-selection process among anglers has thus remained unsettled, so there's as yet no series of emerger flies with the widespread popularity of the late Lee Wulff's series of dry flies, for example.

Many old wet-fly patterns were—and still are—doubtless taken by trout as emerging insects. Some mayfly species, for example, shed their nymphal shucks underwater, traveling to the surface with their wings partly unfurled and looking very much like a conventional winged wet fly. Other wet flies—notably the old soft-hackled styles—look very much like emerging caddis pupae. To that extent, very little has changed. What has changed in recent years is the intent and methodology of anglers designing and fishing emerger patterns, both of which are becoming more deliberate and less an accident of tradition. Most notably, the design and fishing of such patterns is being increasingly based on new understandings of the appearance and behavior of specific insect types.

Emerger patterns haven't yet evolved into distinct categories, but there seem to be four distinct types based on the depth at which they're designed to be fished. Ascending types represent nymphs, pupae, or emerged adults traveling upward from the stream bottom to the surface. These can include many conventional mayfly-nymph patterns, various caddis- and midge-pupa imitations, and partly winged imitations of certain *Ephemerella*, *Epeorus*, and other mayflies that have emerged underwater.

Floating types represent the various immature forms that accumulate immediately under the surface before breaking through the surface tension. Many kinds of caddis and midge pupae as well as some mayfly nymphs sometimes drift for extended periods, quite literally bumping their heads on the undersurface of the water before being able to break through the surface-tension barrier. Pupal and nymph imitations dressed on light-wire hooks and fished near the surface fall within this group, as do so-called floating nymphs. These last are nymph- or midge-pupae patterns dressed with enlarged wingcases, now often made from buoyant materials such as a fine, closed-cell foam.

A third group, which I call emerging patterns, includes those flies representing an insect that's partly broken through the surface tension and has begun to crawl from its pupal or nymphal shuck. Included within this group are many so-called suspender patterns that extend in some way both above and below the surface. Picture, if you will, a small dry fly tied with a dubbed-fur body, no tails, and short, stiff hackle wound radially at the head. When the fur becomes wet, the body hangs below the surface since there are no tails for support. The hackle at the head, meanwhile, supports the fly in the surface tension and keeps it from sinking. When viewed from below, the overall effect is much like a small caddis or midge just starting to scramble out of the water. The fly I've just described is often called a Vermont Caddis, which I believe first evolved during the early 1970s from George Schlotter's fly-tying bench at Shushan on New York's lower Battenkill. More important than the name, however, is the above-and-below concept, which is not unique to this particular fly and is very

effective in imitating a variety of emerging mayflies, caddis, and midges.

In the same category of emerging-type patterns are various caddis and mayfly imitations tied with full or reduced wings, with reduced or no hackle, and featuring some representation of the empty nymphal or pupal shuck still attached to the rear of the fly. Although these patterns are designed to float low in the water, more of the fly's parts remain above the surface than extending below it, which is exactly the reverse of suspender-style emergers. Essentially these are reduced-form dry flies, with the trailing shuck substituted for the tails. This style hasn't been tagged with a name that I've heard widely used; I just call them shuck flies, which is an inelegant reference to their most obvious feature. Various patterns suggested by Swisher and Richards use a tightly drawn, reversed hackle for the shuck, while others—notably the so-called Sparkle Dun series described in recent books by Craig Mathews and John Juracek—depend on a few yarn fibers to accomplish the same purpose.

Closely related to the previous category are the so-called stillborn- or crippled-insect imitations, meaning those representing emerging insects that have become trapped by their own shucks during emergence or trapped by dirt and dust on the surface film. These might be identical to the shuck style I just described, or might simply be a dry fly tied in somewhat deformed style—a No-Hackle dry deliberately tied to lie on its side is one example. The object in this case is to present something slightly different to a trout that's choosing among hundreds of identical adult insects at the surface, something sufficiently different to attract attention but not so different as to cause a trout's refusal.

All this may sound incredibly arcane, even to anglers of some experience who are disinclined to be that fussy as to fly pattern. There are many times, however, when trout *are* that fussy, and one's attention to emerger patterns is becoming an increasingly well-known approach to catching more of the fish more of the time. During any given insect hatch, including those of both caddis and mayflies, trout will most often show a tendency to concentrate their feeding on emergers. This is especially important because, as a rule, the larger the trout, the greater the likelihood that it will be feeding on emergers *only*, rather than on a random selection of nymphs or pupae, emergers, and adults—all of which will often be at or near the surface at the same time. This usually holds true, by the way, for all four major trout species and is just as true in California waters as in Maine, plus all those waters in between.

There are a variety of reasons for this preference, most of which probably apply simultaneously and all of which are intrinsic to the nature of trout as described in earlier chapters. At the early stages of a hatch, as nymphs or pupae start migrating to the surface in increasing numbers, trout encounter increasing numbers of identical food forms behaving in more or less the same manner. The fish then abandon what may have been their random feeding on items drifting in the current and concentrate exclusively on this newly abundant food, a concentration that takes place most readily if the trout have already had a day or two's experience with the same hatch. As the hatch progresses over time, increasing numbers of insects usually accumulate near the surface, where the surface tension provides a partial barrier to their emergence. Emergers are thus what a trout encounters in the greatest numbers and are usually the basis for the searching image formed through experience in the trout's brain, an image the trout uses in selecting prey items that usually must match that image or be rejected.

A trout's propensity to continue its selective feeding on a single prey type has been shown in various laboratory tests to depend on the frequency of its encounters with that prey.[1] In other words, and by the previous example, the trout will continue its selective feeding on emergers as long as those emergers are drifting by the trout in sufficient numbers to hold its interest. The actual number of encounters per unit time required for this response seems to be highly variable and depends partly on the idiosyncracies of individual trout, variations in behavior that may be shown by individual fish and are based on the sum of their prior experiences as individuals in the stream. In general, a drifting-emerger concentration that provides a trout with three or four encounters per minute is enough to maintain selective feeding, although I've seen such selectivity maintained by only one exposure every four or five minutes in cases when no alternative prey—such as nymphs or adults of the same or a different insect—has been readily available. Trout can and sometimes do, in other words, become highly selective to emergers of a particular type even if the hatch is sparse or intermittent.

In the middle of a mayfly hatch, when the water is becoming covered with floating emerged adults, an angler's logic might have the trout feeding on the adults in greater numbers. A few trout will usually do this, which further leads the poor fisherman into flailing the water with dry flies and catching relatively little. Most of the trout, however—and almost invariably all of the larger ones—will continue feeding on emergers until that stage of the hatch has largely disappeared, only then switching to the floating adults that remain and only if the trout is still hungry and hasn't been frightened. Again the reason is simple: The trout, having locked onto emergers first, has no reason to switch to adults until the supply of emergers diminishes toward the end of the hatch.

There are other reasons, also. One relates to the gospel of efficiency that governs trout behavior in the stream environment, which means in part that successful trout will learn over time to capture the greatest number of calories (as food) with the least effort. Insects are terrifically nutritious. The larval forms of most mayflies, caddis, midges, and other trout-stream insects average around 4,000 to 5,000 calories per gram of dry weight,[2] which is substantially greater than the most elaborate, diet-blowing dessert known to man. Emerging insects are at their nutritive peak; once mayflies, caddis, and midges start emerging, they stop feeding. Instead of storing energy through growth, they are expending it. The caloric value of an emerging nymph is slightly higher than that of the corresponding adult mayfly, which makes the emerger of slightly greater value to the fish. This may be one reason—but by no means the only one—for the appeal of emergers.

Emerging insects may also be selected by trout on the simple basis of opportunity. They are often easier for the trout to catch than certain adults—most notably, many caddisflies—that leave the water's surface very quickly. Larger fish, especially, often feed on emerging caddis and usually avoid making the slashing, slapping surface rises that are usually characteristic of smaller trout chasing the quick-flying adult caddis. It may also be true that larger fish feel less vulnerable to predators in feeding an inch or two below the surface rather than from the surface itself, although I don't believe this to be very significant. A final factor that's most important in hard-fished areas is that trout gain experience with artificial fly patterns over time. Since emergers are still fished less frequently than more standard drys during a hatch, most trout will have experienced the artificial emergers less often and will often be more easily duped by those sorts of flies.

Deciding whether or not to use an emerger pattern—and if so, which one—is a matter of observation and experience. By ex-perience I don't necessarily mean all the knowledge accumulated over many years of trout fishing, but rather some knowledge of what's been happening along the stream over the past couple of days. If, for example, you've seen small, tan caddis hatching during the previous two afternoons but have had indifferent results with your caddis drys, then the third afternoon is the logical time to try an appropriate emerging pupa or surface-emerger imitation—fly styles that you might well have tried in the first place. This is only common sense with emergers added to the traditional equation. The other necessity—observation—is a little more difficult.

Given rising trout and a hatch of insects—and assuming you've decided to use an emerger pattern—there are three things you need to observe before selecting a fly: Are the feeding trout actually breaking the surface with all or part of their upper jaw? Are their apparent rises leisurely, or are they hard, sometimes splashing swirls? Are the trout in fact taking the type of insect that seems most prevalent on the water, or are they taking something else you haven't noticed? Finding the correct answers to these questions *before* actually beginning to fish has enabled people to catch more and larger trout than anything else since trout discovered worms.

If the trout's snout can be seen breaking the surface consistently as the fish rises, that fish is usually taking something that's at least floating flush—if not higher—in the surface tension. During a hatch, this typically calls for either suspender- or shuck-style emergers to imitate a particular mayfly, caddis, or midge, depending on what adult naturals you happen to be seeing at the same time. If all you see are swirls at the surface or an occasional dorsal or tail fin breaking the water as the trout turns—meaning you don't see the trout's head at all—the fish is taking a little deeper. In this case you'll most likely want an appropriate mayfly nymph imitation tied on a light-wire hook, or a caddis or midge pupa imitation that will fish a little deeper.

The speed and character of the trout's rise also provides some clues. In general, leisurely rises mean the fish's targets are moving slowly or not at all. Among possible emergers, this is most common to smaller mayflies, midges, and—sometimes—caddis. At other times, the rises or swirls near the surface are more vigorous, indicating targets that are either large, fast-swimming, or both. Again, among emergers this sort of response is most common to rapidly swimming caddis pupae. Trout also respond this way often to certain larger mayflies that have emerged underwater and are swimming to the surface with their wings partly unfurled, the best-known examples of which are Hendricksons (*Ephemerella subvaria*) and certain *Epeorus* flies such as the Quill Gordon (*E. Pleuralis*) in the East and the so-called Pink Lady (*E. albertae*) in the West.[3] Agressive subsurface swirls are also characteristic of the trout's response to large swimming mayfly nymphs—such as Brown Drakes (*Ephemera simulans*)—at the times of their emergences.

While the trout's behavior should give you some idea of the sort of emerger that's re

quired and how to fish it, those by themselves aren't enough of an indication. If there's only one kind of adult insect visible on or near the water and most of the trout are feeding with the same sort of underwater swirl, then you're probably home free; the choice of emerger pattern should be fairly obvious. But it's easy to get fooled.

It's also easy to be overconfident. Hatches of small, olive-bodied mayflies are common on almost all American trout streams during the early fall, as are swarms of small flying ants. Both are apt to be a late-afternoon event. The olives drift upright on the current and are easy to see. The ants are tiny, float flush in the surface, and are hard to see from any distance. Trout respond to drifting olive emergers and to the ants in much the same way, with gentle swirls at the surface. I am embarrassed in counting the many times I've confidently fished olive emergers on afternoons when olive duns covered the river, only to eventually discover the fish were on the ants all the time. Masking-hatch situations, when more than one insect form is present and trout are feeding on the less-obvious form, are very common. Those cases in which the less-obvious insect is floating flush, whether ants or other small terrestrials, mayfly spinners, or spent caddis, are especially troublesome because the insects are very hard to see without *careful* examination of the surface from a close distance. After forty years of trout fishing, I am still sometimes suckered by this, being so enamored of and confident in my emergers that I occasionally forget to look for anything else.

A splashy or violent riseform often—but not always—means the trout are taking emerging caddisflies.

There are three basic methods of fishing emerger patterns: with a drag-free dead-drift; a dead-drift with periodic twitches; or a swimming retrieve with a speed and direction to generally match that of the emerging naturals. Each method is appropriate only in certain circumstances that are for the most part determined by the kind of insect hatching at the moment, its typical behavior, and the depth at which trout are feeding on the hatch.

Most of the time I fish emerger patterns to rising fish by using a variety of slack-line casts in a down-and-across-stream direction. This approach is by far the most versatile because it allows a dead-drift, an intermittent twitching, or an active-swimming presentation to be made from the same position. It only works well, however, with imitations that are fished at or near the surface. Fishing down and across stream, even with slack-line casts, usually doesn't allow the fly to sink very far. If the fly needs to be deeply sunken, as in making a swimming retrieve from the bottom toward the surface, another casting direction is needed.

After cutting their way out of their cocoons amid the stream-bottom stones and gravel, almost all varieties of caddis pupae swim rapidly toward the surface, where they either emerge immediately or drift for some interval just under the surface-tension barrier. The rapid ascent often draws an aggressive response from trout, most especially in relatively fast water. Over the years a variety of specialized techniques have been developed to imitate the vertical movement of emerging caddis and other insects, of which the well-known Leisenring Lift[4] is one example.

The basic method, and one that's common to all such techniques, is simple. First, the fly must be sunken to some depth. A weighted fly might be used, weight might be added to the leader, a sink-tip line might give enough depth, or these methods might be used in some combination, depending on the speed of the water and the depth desired. A relatively short cast is made at some angle ranging from directly across stream to straight upstream of the angler's position. As a rule, the greater the upstream angle, the deeper the fly will sink before drifting back past the angler's position. As the fly drifts back down, line is mended on the water and accumulating slack is gathered to keep the fly from being dragged upward.

As the sunken fly passes your position and continues to drift downstream, either put some tension on the drifting line, slowly raise your rod, or both. The object is to make the sunken fly swim toward the surface while *at the same time* being carried downstream by the current. Adding a twitch or two to this movement will imitate the naturals perfectly. The most common mistake in this approach is giving the rod no horizontal motion while it's being raised, which makes the fly rise upward and *against* the current in an unnatural fashion. Remember that ascending pupae and nymphs are being carried downstream while moving upward. You can best imitate this movement by moving your rod horizontally to follow the drift and raising your rod at the same time.

This vertical, swimming retrieve is an excellent method of imitating emerging caddis in fast, broken water. In this case strikes are apt to be violent, so a relatively heavy tippet is a must. In slower currents, trout are apt to be feeding in a more leisurely fashion and closer to the surface. Across-and-downstream casting will allow better drag control in slower water, where the fly can be allowed to sink as it drifts above the trout and then stuttered and twitched toward the surface as it approaches the fish. Giving too much movement to the fly is the common sin in this case, and your twitches should be interspersed with dead-drift intervals to not only imitate the naturals but also to give the trout a target that can be accurately attacked. Rises will usually be more deliberate in this case, which allows you to strike in more deliberate fashion and permits the use of finer tippets.

Fishing certain emerger imitations entails not only imparting the right behavior to the fly, but being sure it's taking place in the right part of the stream. For example. there are some June evenings along the gentle flats of Vermont's Battenkill when the midstream brookies are quietly sipping little Rusty Spinners. All seems perfectly normal until the silence is interrupted by a violent splash or swirl near the bank. Years ago, I attributed such events to a startled muskrat or mink; now I know they're caused by larger brown trout chasing nymphs in the stream margins, specifically, nymphs of the big Yellow Drake mayfly (*Ephemera varia*) that migrate in limited numbers to slow, bankside water before emerging. These flies emerge sporadically on June evenings, when the occasional large, pale yellow duns draw relatively few rises. The nymphs are another matter.

This particular nymph is an agile swimmer, which, together with its large size, accounts for the trout's violent attack. Some years ago I abandoned the midstream sippers and tried fishing the big nymphs along the bank at dark. This was difficult because on the brushy Battenkill it entails standing half buried in the alders, roll-casting the nymph toward midstream, letting the fly swing around and down into the shallows, and then twitching the fly rapidly straight back upstream through the quiet water near logs and rocks along the bank. If I managed all this without spooking the fish, which was relatively seldom, the trout's response was remarkable; hard, slashing strikes on a tight line that meant I missed more fish than I hooked. I finally gave it up as too much work but still fish the same nymph sometimes from midstream, casting toward the bank. This occasionally works, but not nearly as well, I believe, simply because the nymph is traveling from the bank to midriver, which, in the trout's view, is the wrong direction.

The late Charles Brooks, in his very useful 1976 book *Nymph Fishing for Larger Trout*, went quite properly to great lengths in relating his nymph and emerger patterns to specific insects. He was also extremely critical of the way in which such patterns were named and sold by most fishing mail-order catalogs:

> One of the catalogs I have lists over seventy nymph patterns; five were named after the dry fly the natural hatched into, four were named after their creators, some had names of untraceable origin, some had suggestive names, and the rest were more or less descriptive. This is a good example of the thorough muddle we are in with our nymph patterns at present.

Charlie's comment helps to make an important point, which is that by their very concept emerger patterns need to be related to the corresponding naturals. Your choice of fly pattern and size as well as your tactical choices are all based on that relationship. Seeing a listing for a #18 Olive Floating Nymph tells you a great deal. Emerger. Slack line. 6X. Down-and-across. Good for certain *Baetis* mayfly hatches. On the other hand, names such as Sloan's Emerging Caddis or Steve's Hunchback tell you almost nothing. The common trend is toward generalized emerger patterns in an attempt, I suppose, to make things simpler for more people. But when the trout get fussy, such generalizations can be more of a handicap than a help.

1. See, for example, the various papers by Ringler.

2. See Cummins and Wuycheck (1971).

3. Juracek and Mathews (1992) give an excellent description of this western *Epeorus* mayfly.

4. Named after the late James Leisenring, a Pennsylvania wet-fly fisherman whose 1941 book *The Art of Tying the Wet Fly* resurrected many of the soft-hackle fly concepts popular in Britain a century before. Leisenring's work was expanded by Vernon Hidy in the 1971 *The Art of Tying the Wet Fly and Fishing the Flymph*, which remains as one of the best books ever written on wet-fly and nymph fishing.

23
A Time for Terrestrials

Black clouds curled around Red Mountain and swept quickly up the valley. The big maples turned silver and gray as leaves by the thousands turned their pale undersides to the gathering wind. I got out of the river and walked up to the shelter of a covered bridge just as the rain starting clattering on its metal roof. There was a quick flurry of hail amid occasional spits of lightening and the echoes of thunder in the hills. Stream-bank alders bent and tossed deeply toward the water in the gusting wind, and small branches went skidding and twisting through the air, then splashing into the river. It was a furious few minutes, exhilarating to watch from my secure spot sheltered by the trusswork bridge. And then it was over.

The hot, humid August afternoon resumed as if never broken by the storm, whose passing was marked only by a few small branches and leaves floating into the current. The black macadam of the Cambridge-Arlington road steamed in returning sunlight, quickly becoming as dry and hot as it had been before the rain. Although it had rained hard, the storm had passed quickly enough not to raise or muddy the river, so I walked back down to the quiet, alder-shaded run where I'd seen several trout rising earlier in the day.

The river was quiet and cool, its summer temperatures kept quite low by numerous springs along the banks and bottom and the shade trees along its margins. There were little blips and bubbles against the far-bank

darkness where water dripped from the alders, and several times I started to cast until the dripping water repeated itself and I realized I'd been fooled. Finally, there was the merest wrinkling of the smooth surface amid some green, drifting leaves. Then another. Soon I could see the quiet riseforms of half a dozen trout feeding almost imperceptiby at the surface. I smiled and rummaged in my vest for a little box of terrestrial patterns, happily counting my trout before they were caught.

Terrestrials—meaning land-based insects such as ants, beetles, grasshoppers, and crickets—are an important part of a trout's diet in most trout rivers throughout the world. Terrestrial patterns and related tactics for fishing them have evolved very slowly over several hundred years, but took a giant step with the work of Vince Marinaro and Charlie Fox in the spring-creek country around Carlisle, Pennsylvania, starting in the 1940s. Marinaro described his experiments in his 1950 landmark book *A Modern Dry Fly Code*, which remains even now one of the most important trout-fishing books of this century. Subsequent, separate books by Fox, Ernie Schwiebert, Marinaro, and others helped to make fishing with such flies an accepted, worldwide practice, although their lessons are still too often ignored by many trout fishermen.

Because of their work and the subsequent experience such information has allowed, the rising trout I confronted were a puzzle with an obvious answer. The wind and rain had likely disloged numerous small ants, beetles, and other land insects from the trees and bushes, tossing them to the water's surface where they drifted helplessly in the slow current. There were no apparent hatches of aquatic insects; I could see no little mayflies floating on the surface, nor any caddis or midges flying nearby. Terrestrials had to be the answer, and so armed with confidence I knotted a #22 Black-Fur Ant to a long, 7X tippet. I gave the fly the merest whisper of floatant, wanting it to float low in the surface tension, and wiped the leader with floatant, also, hoping to keep it on top as well. I dropped the fly and leader on the surface at my waders to let the oily film of excess floatant dissipate before casting to the fish. Finally done fussing, I cast.

It's fun being right, especially when trout give you so many chances to be wrong. Having thrown about 30 feet down and across the current with a slack-line cast, I watched the little fly disappear in a small dimple. I raised the whole rod gently to set the hook—carefully avoiding the kind of wrist-flexing, strong yank that breaks fine leaders—and was rewarded by the long, strong pull of a trout heading deep for the far shadows. It turned out to be a brook trout of 10 inches or so, and I cradled it gently next to my waders while using my small pliers to slip the little hook from its jaw. The trout flipped and was gone, and I turned to look for another.

There was laughter and splashing above the bridge, then some waves spreading over the pool. The trout stopped rising, and I turned upstream. Damn! Half a dozen people floated on inner tubes under the bridge. A seventh tube held a large Styrofoam cooler and was fastened with an old rope to the flotilla's rear. I reeled in my line and backed out of the pool as they drifted closer.

"How far is it to Shushan?" a young girl asked as she drifted by.

"About six miles," I sighed. "But the river's low. You'll have to walk some at the riffles." I recognized one of the teenagers at the end of the line and stayed to say hello.

"Somebody meeting you at the Shushan bridge, Ellie?" I asked.

"Yes. Dad'll be there with his truck. Or so he said when he dropped us off. There's lots more behind us. Sorry about the fishing." She shrugged.

"Have fun," I said. And left.

Terrestrials are often an afterthought among trout fishermen who find their glory in spring and early-summer days of mayfly and caddis hatches and scores of rising trout. Yet such hatches persist at most for a few hours each day and become less prevalent as the season progresses into summer and early fall. Terrestrials are the only insect group fed upon by trout that are generally available to the fish all day every day throughout most of the season. As such, they are enormously important.

These insects fall, drop, jump, hop, or are windblown from shore onto the water, where they drift and are eaten by trout. The numbers of terrestrial insects in or on the water, and consequently the numbers being eaten by trout, are dependent on the activity level of the insects themselves. In winter, when cold temperatures in the area of most streams mean that terrestrials are generally dormant, such insects typically comprise less than 1 percent of the trout's diet. Summer's warm temperatures mean there's lots of insect activity along the riverbanks, more of them are falling in the water, and more of them are eaten by trout, which at this time of year may find 60 percent or more of their total food consumption in the form of land insects.[1]

The trout's dependence on terrestrials in summer is based not only on the increased availability of those insects, but also on seasonal decreases in the available masses of aquatic nymphs and larvae. The multitudes of mayflies, caddis, and stoneflies on which trout fed heavily in April and May, for example, have largely hatched by the end of June or mid-July. They are replaced by small, juvenile aquatic forms of the same species that are less available to the trout because the juvenile insects are both minuscule and cryptic, hard to find as they hide in small fissures amid the stones. With a few exceptions, those species of mayflies and caddis that do hatch into the summer and early fall are smaller than those that emerge earlier in the season. While fed upon heavily by trout, their dietary importance is proportionately less.

The importance of terrestrials also varies on a diurnal basis, meaning within any given twenty-four-hour cycle along the stream. Grasshoppers are more active on warm afternoons than on chilly evenings or mornings, for example, which has obvious implications for your fishing. The last time I floated Montana's Madison River with Bob Jacklin as an able and entertaining guide, we had a terrific, warm afternoon of tossing little hopper patterns toward the bank. Trout came to the fly quietly on that day, tipping up and sipping the little hopper instead of making the slashing rises that are so often described in accounts of grasshopper fishing. As late-afternoon shadows stretched across the river, the action began to slow. Jacklin rested the oars, tipped back his battered Stetson, and announced it was time to change flies.

"Too cold," he said. "The sun's gone, and so are the hoppers. Try a little caddis." As usual, he was right. On both counts.

Ants are the most important. All 8,800 named species of ants are of the insect family Formicidae.[2] This name refers to the pungent formic acid that is characteristic of all ants. For some reason or reasons unknown, trout seem especially partial to ants. Some people have attributed this preference to the trout's purported liking for formic acid, but this has never been scientifically demonstrated. It has, however, given rise to a half-legendary yarn that's almost always mentioned whenever trout and ants are discussed.

As the story generally goes, the late Edward Hewitt had recognized the trout's inclination to an ant diet but was at a loss to explain it. Then, according to angling folklore, Hewitt deliberately ate some ants, tasted the strong formic acid, and gave that taste as a reason. This, however, is not the true story, which has been considerably exaggerated over time. In checking my old copy of Hewitt's 1929 book *Telling on the Trout*, I found the original anecdote, which is also an excellent description of what can happen when trout start feeding avidly on ants:

> One evening, on the Neversink, we noticed a great rise of trout in the large pool at the Big Bend. They were located where the current runs along the ledge. My son and I fished for about two hours without hooking a single one. We tried all patterns of flies with no results. There were large numbers of small black flies in the air, sometimes even clouds of them, as well as other insects, and even larger flies. Finally, one of these clouds came around my head, and as I opened my mouth to speak one or two them got in it, and to my surprise they tasted quite bitter. These were small flying ants, and were bitter with formic acid. . . . The fish were evidently taking these small flies on account of this taste, and would not touch anything larger until these insects had all disappeared. I took some No. 18 flies and cut down the wings to make them about

the size of the flying ants, and at once began to get fish. We took a dozen good-sized ones in a little while. Since then these conditions have been repeated a number of times, usually toward the end of May.[3]

Hewitt's many contributions to American trout fishing in the years before World War II were substantial and summarized in his 1948 book *A Trout and Salmon Fisherman for Seventy-Five Years*. He was also well known for being occasionally irascible, often opinionated, and somewhat eccentric. He was not, however, so eccentric as to deliberately chew on a fistful of ants just to get their flavor.

Trout encounter ants in a couple of ways, both of which are important and quite different from one another. First, ants of different sizes and colors exist along most trout-stream margins during the spring, summer, and fall. Individual ants enter the stream by various accidental means and are available at largely random times to drift-feeding trout. Second, mating swarms of winged flying ants may at times fall on trout streams in incredible numbers. Hundreds of thousands of small, *identical* insects may suddenly blanket the surface over a period of a few minutes, producing an hour or two of highly selective feeding by the trout. If you're caught without a flying-ant pattern of the right color and size at such times, you might as well sit on the bank to watch the trout rise. Fishermen commonly regard both cases—that is, random drift feeding on individual ants and heavy feeding on mating swarms—as being sporadic and impossible to predict and therefore difficult to fish. A little common sense, however, plus some new knowledge about ants can greatly stack the odds in your favor.

As we've seen, trout recognize and accept distinct food items based on prior experience with those items. This selective effect can be short term, as when trout come to recognize and feed heavily on a hatch of a particular mayfly or caddis that occurs abundantly over a period of several days or weeks. It can also be long term. After a larger trout eats a few crayfish, for example, it has learned that crayfish taste good, what they look like, how they behave, and how to catch them. For the rest of the trout's life it will encounter crayfish intermittently in the stream in quantities that are limited but still sufficient to reinforce the fish's feeding behavior in ongoing fashion.

So it is with ants. Starting with the days of their earliest surface feeding as juveniles, most trout encounter ants intermittently all their lives—day after day and season after season. These encounters typically occur more often with ants than with any other single food form, terrestrial or aquatic. The ants are present in limited numbers on days of heavy mayfly or caddis hatches, and the ants are present in the same numbers on days when there are no hatches. By analogy, ants for trout are a little like comfort foods for humans, a cup of warm milk that offers the reassurance of long familiarity. Adult trout, of course, do not have any emotional attachment to ants, but I believe their long familiarity with ants is the basis for the trout's well-known preference.

This seems more plausible to me than the common hypothesis that ascribes the trout's ant preference to the taste of the formic acid common to all ant species, which is an oversimplification. For one thing, ants contain other powerful chemicals called pheromones that are used in communicating with other ants. Even though these chemicals are present in minute quantities, such quantities fall within the trout's sensitivity range. So although there probably is some chemical basis for the ant's appeal, formic acid may or may not be the only one. Undoubtedly ants taste good to trout; otherwise, they wouldn't be eaten. The appeal of ants, however, is based on the trout's long-term experience, of which taste is only a part.

The appearance of ants in the stream drift is not as completely random as commonly supposed. Some days, times, and places will be better for fishing with ant patterns than others. This gets very tricky and is a real unexplored frontier in trout fishing. Here's why. The appearance of ants in the drift—and their availabilty to trout—depends on the ants' behavior and activity along the stream margins. Ants that are active along the bank appear in the drift with greater frequency than ants that are relatively inactive. So far, so good. But different species of ants show widely different activity levels under specific conditions of temperature, humidity, and other factors.[4] At any given time of day, some species—little red ants, for example—are more likely to apapear in the drift than others—say, little black ones. The trout, of course, can and do readily discern the difference. Some will feed on any old ant that drifts down the pike; other fish will accept only that which they are accustomed to seeing.

At this point, some readers will charge me with having taken the ant question to a ridiculous extreme, but I don't think so. The following may help to illustrate just how complex the picture can become. In 1975, one Michigan ant researcher counted eighty-seven *different* ant species in an area slightly greater than 2 square miles, which is much less than that encompassed by most trout streams.[5] When you realize that many of these species can be represented by hundreds or thousands of colonies in the same small area, each hosting an equivalent or even greater number of individual ants, the imitative problems for the trout fisherman may be more apparent.

But not impossible. Happily, almost all ants come in one of three basic colors: black,

medium brown, and cinnamon (a dull, reddish orange). A selection of basic ant patterns in these colors and sizes from #10 well down into the 20s will cover almost all of your bases. The exceptions are flying ants, which I'll cover shortly, and those cases in which multicolored ants—say, those with a dark head and a lighter rear portion—are prevalent. In the latter case—and usually after trout have refused your standard ant patterns—you'll have to carefully look along the stream bank to see exactly what's crawling around in the grass. While some surveys exist that detail what kinds of ants are found in particular trout-fishing areas, reviewing them is an enormous task and well beyond the scope of this book. That's why I and most others settle on a set of basic patterns and go exploring if and when the standard versions don't work, which is seldom.

As a general case, you can expect your best fishing with ants during hot days of high humidity. More ants will be more active at such times than at any other. The humidity is important because many kinds of ants (but not all kinds) start to become desiccated and slow down when the air is very dry. Hot, muggy afternoons are thus generally better than cool mornings or evenings.

Be alert, too, for opportunity. Storms and strong winds can mean greater than normal numbers of ants being blown into the water. Check the wind direction, and be sure you fish along the bank where wind is carrying ants into the water instead of the opposite bank where the wind is pushing ants *away* from the river. A tree newly fallen into the river may still be home to a colony of large carpenter ants, which may also be common to the tangles of brush and deadfalls that accumulate at bends in the river. A long expanse of bare gravel at river's edge will likely offer few ants to the stream drift, while a stretch of overhanging grasses along the bank may offer a great many.

Flying ants are another matter. In this case, ants appear not occasionally in the stream drift over several hours but almost instantaneously and in large quantities as flying swarms fall to the surface. Although other terrestrial insects sometimes offer intervals of abundance—the population peak of a multiyear cicada cycle, being one example—none are as consistently important as flying ants. Fishermen have paid much less attention to ants than to mayflies or caddis, for example, and several modern angling writers have puzzled in print about the unpredictability of ant swarms. When flying ants are on the water, trout will very often touch nothing else, which makes the question of predictability very important.

An ant colony, composed of thousands of ants, is often likened to a single, living organism. As that organism grows, becoming populated with increasing numbers of ants, it seeks to reproduce. Among the various methods used by different species for starting new colonies, one of the most common is a mating swarm. Bert Hölldobler and Edward Wilson, in their massive 1990 book *The Ants*, described various factors that trigger such mating swarms. The following passage offers several clues to trout fishermen:

> One of the commonest triggering stimuli is rain, especially in species that occupy dry habitats such as deserts, grasslands, and forest clearings. A typical species in this respect is *Lasius neoniger*, one of the most abundant ants in abandoned fields and other open enviroments in eastern North America. This small formicine emerges in immense swarms in late afternoon in the second half of August or the beginning of September. The flights almost always occur within 24 hours of moderate or heavy rainfall on warm, humid days with little wind. For an hour or so the air seems filled with

winged ants, rising from the ground like snowfall in reverse. After mating, the queens find themselves on moistened soil that is easier to excavate. They are also protected from desiccation due to overheating.

The example just given does not mean that a flight of ants will inevitably occur under the conditions described, only that it's more likely at such times than others.

Ants also undertake mating swarms at times of day that are unique to the species involved, a factor that is apparently both endogenous and circadian, which means based on an internal, twenty-four-hour biological clock. The nuptial flight of one kind of carpenter ant[6] almost always peaks between 3:30 and 3:45 P.M., for example. In my area of southern Vermont, this often takes place on warm afternoons in early May and coincides *exactly* in time with the Battenkill's famous hatch of Hendrickson mayflies. Winged carpenter ants are usually on the water during at least two or three days of the two-week interval occupied by the mayfly hatch, at which times most trout are ignoring the mayflies altogether and feeding heavily on the ants instead.

There are thus four things fishermen can note that will make the appearances of flying ants predictable instead of the random events they seem to be initially. First is the species of ant involved. Second is that species' diurnal activity cycle, which is unique to that species and determines the time of day during which flights are likely to take place. Third is the kind of day that triggers such flights. Fourth is the season or seasons in which flights of that species are prevalent. Unfortunately, things here are easier in theory than in fact because, while the nature of the puzzle has been made clear, some of its pieces are missing.

In a few cases, perhaps, one or more myrmecologists (ant scientists) may have cataloged those ant species prevalent in an area that happens also to encompass several trout streams. With some assiduous research and inquiries to a state entomology department, one might be able to find a technical paper something like "A Catalog of Ant Species of West-Central Michigan," which is a title I just made up. Once that information is obtained, you'll have to determine which of those species are apt to be found within a mile or two of the river in question, a determination that might be difficult to accomplish. Because ants utilize a wide variety of habitats that are often unique to a particular genus or species, not all of the listed species will be of interest. Assuming that a determination can be made, you'll then have to research the life histories of those species that seem pertinent, hoping to find information as to their activity levels and swarming behavior under varying conditions. At the moment and for the foreseeable future it's almost a certainty that at least some of the required information doesn't exist simply because the requisite scientific research hasn't been performed, even though its methodology is well established.

The alternative, which will work almost as well, involves the old empirical approach to trout-stream entomology; namely, discovering over time what flies work well on any particular day and season. If you do encounter trout feeding on flying ants that have fallen to the stream, make note of the following: the ants' size and color (e.g., black, hook-size 22); the month and date; the time of day; the ambient air temperature and, if possible, relative humidity; and the weather pattern over the prior two days. As we've seen, flying-ant swarms appear according to specific circumstances that vary with the kinds of ants involved. This means that your observations in a particular area of a particular stream should assume a pattern over

several seasons, and bingo! You'll eventually be able to predict with fair accuracy the appearance of specific flying ants, which means you'll have the right artificial fly ready at the right place and time.

Various ant imitations can be effectively fished dry or wet, but in either case a drag-free dead-drift is almost always essential. Ants trapped in the surface tension are drifting almost completely inert and are sitting ducks for trout, which usually take them in very gentle, sipping rises. Unlike some hatching mayflies and most caddis, which sometimes flutter on the surface and can be imitated by twitching your fly, any movement of your ant pattern should be done as a last resort and only after a difficult fish has spurned your best drag-free efforts.

Ants that appear randomly in the drift are almost always wingless workers, and their hourglass shape is easily imitated with a ball of material at either end of the hook shank with a turn or two of hackle in the middle. There are presently four basic styles of artificials. The first was apparently developed by the late Bob McCafferty in Pennsylvania during the 1940s, in which the body is made of lacquered, black-silk tying thread. This produces a glossy black body that's quite imitative, but difficult to keep floating, so I use this style for my wet patterns. Bodies of dubbed fur are easier to make in a wider variety of colors and also seem to float better and longer, so I use this method for all of my dry ants.

The other two styles involve synthetic materials and are newer. The so-called McMurray Ant depends on two minute, black-painted (or other color) cylinders of balsa wood glued on either end of a short monofilament section. This assembly is then tied to the hook shank and, with the addition of a little hackle, becomes an instant ant. This pattern is a puzzle to me. I've used it to good effect with large brown trout on New York's hard-fished Beaverkill, but the trout in Vermont's Battenkill have ignored it completely. The latter fish seem to prefer smaller, fur-bodied imitations. The fourth and last style involves bodies constructed of black (or other color) closed-cell foam. I have not experimented to any degree with foam ants, which seem perfectly plausible, simply because my older styles have continued to work well.

Flying-ant imitations can be likewise simple, but most such imitations I've seen ignore both the structure of flying ants and the way in which they almost invariably lie on the surface. The wings of such patterns—be they hackle tips or yarn fibers—are usually attached at the patterns' midsection along with the hackle. The wings of the naturals, however, are attached to the body behind the head and well forward of the natural's hourglass waist.

Spent ants lie on the stream's surface in a very characteristic way, at least according to my own observations. The ants are *all* lying on their sides with their bodies in a slight curl and with both wings extending to one side. Hundreds and hundreds of spent, winged ants will be seen floating in exactly the same manner; natural ants floating upright appear to be the exception. Lately, instead of tying my flying-ant imitations in conventional, upright style, I've been tying both wings on one side of the hook shank to duplicate the drifting naturals. I'm not ready as yet to say this makes a difference, but it's easily done and might be worth some experiments of your own.

Other terrestrial imitations are also important, of course, although ants are so important and so little explored by fishermen that I've given them most of this chapter. Beetles, inchworms, moths, leafhoppers, crickets, and other insects along the stream are all eaten by trout when such insects accidentally enter the drift. In the absence of the predominance of any particular terrestrial form, trout will likely be sipping just about anything that comes along. Working to such fish is then a matter of playing the odds as to what the fish is probably seeing most often. Usually, that means some sort of ant. The next most likely item is a beetle.

Beetle imitations progressed mightily during the 1940s and 1950s, when Marinaro, Fox, Schwiebert, and others discovered that such imitations could be tied flat. An opaque small feather or feathers tied flat on the hook shank with a little hackle underneath is an excellent imitation of small beetles. Marinaro's famous jassid pattern, which featured one or two feather "nails" from a jungle-cock neck tied flat on a small hook is the classic and still very effective example. Foam-bodied beetles have become popular in recent years. These are also easy to make and float especially well. But in the small sizes—meaning size 18 and smaller—that are often necesary for successful beetle patterns, the flat-feather-wing style is more easily constructed and more effective.

These days when I encounter gently sipping trout on warm afternoons, I first try a small ant if nothing else is indicated. If the ant doesn't work, I try a small beetle. One

A flying ant adrift on the water's surface.

or the other *almost* always works, which is just as true on Idaho's Henrys Fork as it is on Pennsylvania's popular yellow Breeches Creek. The exceptions can prove very difficult and may be due to a temporary abundance of a particular kind of inchworm falling from trees along the bank, for example. In such cases, you'll have to go exploring, autopsy a trout, ask the locals, or—most likely—all three.

1. See Lord (1946).

2. Much of the technical material in this section on ants is drawn from *The Ants* by Bert Hölldobler and Edward O. Wilson, a massive work both scientifically and—at about 6 pounds— physically that was published in 1990. Wilson is a Harvard professor best known for his Pulitzer-winning *On Human Nature*.

3. Hewitt (1926, 1930).

4. For example, one species of common carpenter ant has been shown to begin foraging activity at ambient temperatures greater than 36 degrees F. and to cease such activity at temperatures greater than 79 degrees. In contrast, some members of the ant genus *Lasius*, which includes some common woodland ants, don't even start foraging until ambient temperatures reach 84 degrees F. Obviously both types won't be equally available to trout under all conditions, all of the time.

5. See Hölldobler and Wilson (1990).

6. *Camponotus herculeanus*. See Hölldobler and Wilson (1990).

PART FIVE

SPECIAL SITUATIONS

24
High Water and Low

It was a bum day all around. Except for the kid.

The kid was terrific, mostly because he didn't say much while listening very carefully and waiting for his chance. He looked about fourteen, all arms and legs and big eyes. I had won the kid and his father in a kind of lottery, having offered a day's guided fishing as one of many items sold at a fishing club's benefit auction the previous spring. They had made the winning bid, so eventually we had arranged by telephone for a morning meeting at the river.

It was September, the time of year when equinoctial line storms roll through the mountains with cold rains and tatters of mist as recurrent cold fronts collide with the warm highs of Indian summer. The fishing can be terrific or awful, depending on the unpredictable weather. At the moment, it looked awful. It had rained all night, the river was a torrent, and the nearby high peaks were invisible behind low clouds and a cold, misting drizzle. As the man and his son assembled their gear from the back of their station wagon, I drank warm coffee from a Thermos, pulled my rain hood a little tighter and found myself hoping most of all that the man had a sense of humor.

He didn't. We tried bucktails, wets, and nymphs in one of the rain-swollen pools for an hour without a touch. I had explained that conditions were more difficult than usual, but he wasn't listening. He wanted fish and was catching none. The river was rotten. I

was a failure. He was a failure. Finally, I gave him a couple of large Black Ghost streamers and pointed to some runs downstream where he might move some fish along the willows. He grunted, took the flies with no word of thanks, and headed down along the riverbank. His son, meanwhile, had remained sitting on the rocks behind us, hunkered down under a red vinyl poncho and watching without a word.

I watched his father depart and then turned, smiling with relief. "C'mon, kid. It's your turn."

We walked back up past the cars, where I grabbed the Thermos and another box of flies, and then up the road to the top of a long, tumbling rapid. We sat together on a big rock near the water. I poured coffee; the boy shook his head when I handed him a cup. "Go ahead, son," I said. "It's cold out, and this'll help. Besides, you're big enough."

He took the cup with a wide grin, the first I'd seen that morning. I asked if he wanted to catch some trout, and he nodded. I explained how the river had risen by a couple of feet overnight and how the trout moved to the edges to escape the faster than normal flows at midriver. I rigged his leader with a pair of little Hare's Ear wets, and showed him how to flip his line into the current, let it swing around, and how to twitch the little flies back up through the quieter water next to the bank. "You don't have to cast," I said. "Just flip it out and then wiggle the flies slowly back behind the rocks. I'll walk partway down and watch while you pick your way along the edge. Don't try to fish the whole roaring river. Just pick one little spot at a time and fish that. Holler if you want help."

I left him with that advice and walked partway back to the cars where I could sit and watch. Looking downstream, I saw the small figure of the kid's father disappearing around a distant bend. When I looked back, the kid's rod was bent over, and he was hauling a foot-long brown trout into the air and onto the bank. He pinned the fish against a rock with a soggy sneaker and worked for a while at getting the hook free. Finally he stood up and used both hands to stuff the trout headfirst into the front pocket of his jeans. Then he started fishing again.

As he worked slowly down along the bank toward me, I saw his rod jerk upward a few times, so he was apparently getting strikes but not connecting. Eventually he was standing on a large boulder in front of where I sat, working his flies behind the rock and through the swirling pocket that stretched for 20 feet downstream along the bank. His rod came up again, this time attached to another small brown that splashed next to the fast water. As he worked the fish back upstream toward the rock, the dropper fly on his leader danced along the surface where it was taken in a splashing rise by a second brown.

"Awesome!" he yelled. "I've got two! Wha'do-I-do, wha'do-I-do . . ." His words all ran together, and he jumped to the bank as I scrambled down to help. Together we managed to corral the trout against the moss and sticks, and I showed him how to kill them mercifully with a stone. Ordinarily, I might have encouraged him to release the trout, but these fish seemed very important. I pulled a small plastic bag from my vest.

"Here. Use this," I said, laughing. "Those won't all fit in your pocket." He was em-

barrassed by that, but still smiling. I headed for the cars after asking him to follow along.

His father and I reached their station wagon at the same time. He looked cold and wet, and no, he hadn't caught anything, dammit! He opened the tailgate and began angrily throwing his gear inside. "You know," he started, "you've got a hell of a nerve getting us all the way up here . . ."

"Dad! Dad!" The boy walked up to the car, waving his bag of trout. "I got three! I got two on one cast!"

"Wonderful," the man said, but he obviously didn't mean it. The boy's smile disappeared. "Get your stuff in the car, and let's get going." I leaned against the back of their wagon and watched the boy go quickly around to the side door, put his wet gear and fish on the backseat floor, and get in the front seat, where he sat very still. I yanked my hand away from the tailgate just in time as the man slammed it shut. He brushed past me without a word, started his car, and fishtailed a little on the wet road as he accelerated out of sight. The kid was terrific, I thought again, but he sure had a long ride home.

Almost all of our common trout tactics and tackle are geared to fishing rivers and streams at their normal late-spring and early-summer levels. But, like the piece of bread that always lands butter side down, it will inevitably rain hard during some of your fishing trips, and you'll then face the choice of either fishing in high water or perhaps not fishing at all. Conversely, the weekend you've reserved for trout fishing in the mountains may ultimately prove to be at the end of the driest summer in twenty years. When the fields of August corn look as brown as the large dust clouds raised by your car along a gravel road, the fishing can appear equally dismal. In either case, you won't be having textbook trout fishing. Both high and low water present some unique problems in taking trout—problems that aren't usually insurmountable, just different.

There are several basic considerations in deciding whether or not to fish a flooding river or one that's higher than normal at any particular time. High water is a relative term, of course, and a river that's a few inches to a foot above its seasonal norm is usually more fishable than one that's in severe flood. Turbidity is another problem. If the rising waters become only slightly off-color, the fishing may actually improve, while if the river becomes a sea of mud, sand, and silt, the trout will have difficulty in seeing your flies. Temperature is a factor that may change with the water level, and the response of both trout and hatching insects will sometimes depend on the extent and direction of the temperature change. The rapidly changing weather patterns accompanying a storm, such as periods of high winds followed by calm air, will affect not only your fishing and casting but also the possibilities of insect activity and feeding trout. This means that a small portable radio tuned to the National Weather Service broadcasts can be a substantial help, telling you, for example, that winds are expected to drop by five in the afternoon. Finally, there's your own safety. You'll have to judge the rising waters carefully to decide just where you should wade and where you shouldn't

It's important to realize that all the streams in a given area aren't necessarily affected equally by heavy rains, so if a particular river floods you may have another option nearby. Trout ponds and lakes are the most obvious choice, often being little affected by rain. Most well-known trout rivers around the country also have trout ponds within their drainage systems that you can find most easily by asking at a gas station or tackle shop. Among flowing waters, spring creeks and other streams primarily dependent on subterranean groundwater flows are usually affected the least by heavy rain, perhaps rising only an inch or two and becoming slightly off-color from surface runoff in the immediate vicinity. Mountain streams and others with a steep gradient—including larger rivers with such streams as their headwaters—are the opposite extreme, in which case the surface runoff from a deluge will be rapid and usually occur over a wide area. Such rivers rise quickly and often become turbid because their wide drainage areas usually include areas of mining, construction, logging, or other erosive activity that allows silt to enter the stream.

Sometimes the flooding effects of heavy rains are mitigated naturally in certain stretches of a stream or river. This means that a little exploring can often save your fishing if your customary area becomes too high or too muddy to fish at all. For example, there are two primary branches of the Battenkill near my southern Vermont home that behave quite differently after a substantial rainfall. The East Branch is comprised of a series of steep mountain tributaries, which rise very rapidly and often become quite muddy, extending that influence into the main river itself. The West Branch meanders slowly through a series of swamps several

miles upstream of the main river. These slow meanders reduce the erosive force of the rising waters and settle some of the silt and mud from the flow. This means that the water discharging from the swamps is usually the clearest water available, even though a deluge may have increased its volume, which makes it a logical area to fish when high water turns the main river downstream the color of milky coffee. Even if you're fishing an unfamiliar area, the relatively flat headwater areas of swamps and beaver bogs should be evident on a topographic map and are probably worth a look if a day or two of rain has otherwise ruined your trip.

The reservoirs and dams associated with tailwater trout fisheries have a similar mitigating effect. A couple of years ago Bill Herrick and I enjoyed a spectacular day's fishing during the Hendrickson mayfly hatch on upstate New York's Beaverkill, after which our evening celebration over dinner in Roscoe was dimmed by the slashing of rain and wind at the restaurant windows. By the next morning the Beaverkill was in flood beyond fishing, its normally quiet pools turned muddy brown as stumps and trees floated down rapid chutes that had been yesterday's quiet riffles. The motel parking lot was full of disconsolate fishermen griping among themselves about the rain while others stowed their wet gear in station wagons and left for home a day early. We drove over the mountain to the East Branch Delaware, a tailwater fishery below a large dam, where that river was both clear and at its normal spring level because the effects of flooding were being absorbed by the upstream reservoir. Not only was the river perfectly fishable, but we had it all to ourselves on that rainy day, apparently because the Roscoe crowd had blithely and wrongly assumed that all rivers flood equally at the same time.

At other times, a river's rising water levels can mean that particular stream is the best possible choice. After water temperatures have made their seasonal rise to the mid-50s, which happens by late spring in most areas but still later in others with late-melting snowpacks, both trout and insect hatches become active. For the rest of the season, and well into fall, rising water has a unique effect on the trout, in general causing the fish—especially large ones—to feed aggressively for a short time. This is so predictable that a weather forecast including heavy rain is often enough to send me to the river on short notice, hoping to be there in time to catch the first rise of water.

For the trout, rising water levels in the stream mean a temporary abundance of food in the drift. Earthworms, ants, and other terrestrial fare get washed into the stream, and the increasing currents also dislodge greater numbers of aquatic insect larvae and nymphs. Both rain and the increasing turbulence add increased amounts of oxygen to the water and the runoff from a sudden summer storm may start to cool the entire river by a few degrees. I don't know whether trout, based on their experience, anticipate all of these events as the river first starts to rise or whether they merely react to such events as they happen. In any case, during the first hour or two of rising water the fishing can be extraordinary as the fish seem to lose all their previous caution. It is an especially good time for taking very large trout on streamer flies.

By the time rising water levels have peaked, the fishing has usually tapered off. The water may have finally become too discolored or too high to fish effectively, or trout may simply have become full and ceased to feed. As the water starts to drop and clear, however, there's often another apparent feeding spree that lasts from one to several hours until both the river and the fishing have returned to normal. A radical, short-term change in water level, as occurs with a heavy rain, disrupts the trout's social hierarchy within the stream. The feeding positions chosen and defended by individual trout during normal flows often are no longer available in the growing currents of a flood. It's been shown that a disruption of the trout's social order greatly increases the fishes' vulnerability to angling.[1] As the river starts to drop and clear, trout are often easier to catch than at times of normal flow, probably because their pecking order has not yet been reestablished.

Let's assume as a last resort that you have to fish either a flooding river or one that's at its high-water crest after a storm. The pools and riffles with which you've become familiar have turned into forbidding torrents that you couldn't fish even if you dared wade near them. In this case, many of the trout will have moved into slower water, and that's where you'll find them: in the slow currents on the inside edges of river bends instead of along the outside bend as usual; in backwaters and sloughs that hold only minnows and bullfrogs at normal levels; and—most important—along the edges behind rocks, along logs, and in under the bushes, all the sorts of places that offer quiet water and shelter from the current. These are all likely spots to fish a wet fly or nymph or streamer. Remember that, as a general rule, increasing turbidity means that black is the underwater color most visible to trout, which means, for example, that a Black Gnat wet fly or Black Woolly Bugger may be more effective than something like a March Brown wet that matches the brown color of the water.

High water doesn't necessarily prohibit dry-fly fishing, either. The hatching activity of most aquatic nymphs and larvae (or pupae, more precisely) is established according to species by an accumulation of degree-days as reflected by water temperature changes over some time period from spring into summer. If, for example, some *Baetis* mayflies are due to hatch on a particular afternoon around three o'clock, some will still attempt to hatch even if water levels have risen from normal over the previous few hours. As a result, you may see trout rising in quiet backwaters where the emerging flies accumulate despite a heavy rain, torrential currents nearby, or both. Most people are surprised—and thus unprepared—when this happens.

Then, too, the end of a storm often brings clearing, calm weather, the sort of weather that's ideal for a heavy fall of mayfly spinners. The mating mayflies, of course, have no idea of water level. They will swarm, mate, and then fall to the water as long as atmospheric conditions are suitable and whether the river's in flood or not. Once again, trout will take these flies as the floating insects accumulate in quiet water along the shore or elsewhere, even if the water is relatively turbid. I have more than once watched out the window as violent thunderstorms have blown off to the northeast, seeing at the same time a clear sunset in the southwest accompanied by a dropping wind. Once again, it's time to head for the river, where the calm evening may bring trout rising quietly at the edge of a flooded hayfield instead of in their customary—now torrential—riffles.

Low water is more difficult, mostly because it's more demanding of both observation and patience. The flows of many trout streams are at a seasonal low by late summer and early fall. Rapids have turned to quiet riffles, and the deep pools of May have become long, shallow flats. In some areas, the rocks and snags along the edges that sheltered springtime trout will now be bone dry. And in such cases the trout will often have become concentrated in the remaining, deeper pools for their own safety. Such trout can be relatively easy to catch, but first you have to find them.

Because low water usually coincides with hot weather, water temperatures at such times are critical for both fish and fishermen.

Some of the best-looking pools and deep pockets may be devoid of fish simply because the water is too warm. If a check with your stream thermometer shows the water has reached the 70s, and if the recent weather history and water levels mean that's been the case for several days or more, you should probably do what the trout have already done; namely, find some cooler water.

Sometimes this can be easy. As a general case, the farther you travel upstream, the cooler the water becomes since headwater reaches are almost invariably cooler than the main flow. The mountain stream starting near my home stays below 65 degrees Fahrenheit all summer, even in very low water, as it tumbles through shaded ravines before reaching the valley. The fishing here for small brook, brown, and rainbow trout is excellent, even on hot afternoons in late August, although most people who try it scare more fish than they catch from the stream's clear pools. By the time the same stream has flowed over a dozen miles of broad, open riffles in the downstream valley, it has absorbed considerable sunlight and has taken additional heat from the rocks along its shore. Its water temperature may have increased by 10 degrees in as many miles, and the fishing is terrible. Such trout as remain in the lower pools are lethargic, clearly stressed by the high water temperatures, and catching them offers little sport.

There are sometimes exceptions to this temperature regime that can be tricky. In recent years, numerous beaver have dammed many of the headwater tributaries of the Battenkill in southern Vermont, which has had the net effect of slowing the water and allowing it to absorb more sunlight—and thus heat—in any unit of time. The water is warmer than one might expect in these headwater reaches, sometimes reaching the low 70s in late August. In contrast, the water in the main river a few miles below the junc-

tion of most of its tributaries is almost invariably 5 or 6 degrees cooler thanks to the addition of cooler groundwater from several large springs in the bed of the main river itself. In this particular case, hot-weather fishing is inevitably better in the cooler reaches downstream rather than upstream.

The extent of your ability to search upstream for cooler water may be limited by posted land, or in the case of large river systems because it's simply too far to travel. In such cases you should be looking for areas of cool water within the river itself. I knew one man who took this question so seriously that he wore a thermocouple attached to one of his ankles when wading a trout stream. This temperature probe was connected by a small wire to a dial mechanism fastened to his waist that instantaneously showed variations in water temperature as he moved about in the river. Such devices are relatively small, common, easily obtained, and are probably the best means of learning over time those special stream areas offering trout a refuge in times of low, warm water. They also require more thought and effort than most people seem willing to expend.

Even without a thermometer, there are some cool-water clues for which you should be watching. The most obvious are tributary streams that offer water that's colder than the main river and thereby attract trout. You might encounter such streams by accident or by deliberately locating them on a topographic map when you plan your fishing day. Springs along the stream margins may also offer cool water and attract fish, but will be harder to spot. Often the stream-bank vegetation around a spring will be different from that prevalent along most of the river, and a patch of light green against an otherwise dull green or gray sage background along the bank often indicates an important trickle of cold water. Failing anything else, turbulent rapids and riffles will offer the most oxygen to fish in warm-water periods and can thus be productive, as can areas of stream that are more or less continually shaded by overhanging trees or brush.

The tendency of trout to seek cool-water refuges at certain times of summer low flow is proportional to the increasing temperatures of their customary river habitat. The warmer their river becomes, the greater the numbers of trout that will be seeking cooler water. Many popular trout streams around the country that depend on surface runoff for most of their flow volume can become very warm in summer, often reaching the high 70s and sometimes even the low 80s. In such extreme cases, large numbers of trout become concentrated near the mouths of cooler tributaries, which poses a serious question of angling ethics. Such trout are often sitting ducks, being relatively easy to catch in large numbers as long as they're not spooked in the process. Scaring the fish and forcing them to actively disperse into the warm water of the main river is stressful to the trout. Catching and releasing them puts an even greater strain on the trout's ability to survive. Under the general angling regulations that pertain in most states, it's perfectly legal to fish in such areas. You'll have to decide, however, on the extent to which this shooting of fish in a barrel fits your personal code of sportsmanship and fair play. Certainly, if the water in the main river is much over 70 degrees Fahrenheit, the survival of trout caught and released near a tributary mouth may be doubtful, in which case they are better left alone.

Given low, clear water that's sufficiently cool to allow trout to maintain their positions in the main river, there are a number of tactical problems that are a little different from those encountered at normal water levels. Most of these problems center around the need for even greater than normal stealth on the angler's part. Low-water fish can be easy to catch, but only if they aren't frightened.

As usual, the first step is to spend some time quietly watching the river where you plan to fish. In the absence of one of the sparse hatches of small mayflies, caddis, or midges common to late-season trout streams, the undisturbed trout will most likely be rising very intermittently to small terrestrials, meaning little ants, beetles, or other insects that have fallen into the stream from grasses and brush along the banks. Such fish are often more skittish than usual in low, clear water, and their riseforms are most often gentle and hard to spot. Very often you'll see the trout themselves spread out in shallow-flowing flats that are a foot deep or perhaps even less, rising occasionally and ready to spook at your first false move. This is probably the most consistently difficult situation in all of trout fishing, in which case I sometimes say to heck with it and search instead for an area of riffles or deeper water where the trout will be less easily frightened. But let's give it a try.

When fishing low, clear water, the first rule is to stay hidden from the fish. The second and equally important rule is not to wade at all if you can avoid it. Take the time to look over both the fish and their long pool from well downstream or while hiding behind some bushes or in the grass. Some fish, by virtue of their position in the stream, will be reached more easily than others. There may be a series of bushes behind which you can crawl to get within casting range while remaining on the bank. Or one of the several gravel bars exposed by the low water may offer a path you can take, slowly, crawling out toward the fish on your hands and knees. If you must wade, which will greatly diminish your chances, then wade as if walking on eggs. Slowly. Very slowly, and making no ripples whatsoever. In almost all shallow-water cases, you'll be approaching the fish from downstream to make an upstream or up-and-across-stream cast. Sometimes I'm able to wade with sufficient care to get within 30 feet or less of trout feeding in shallow water. At other times, a rock rolls underfoot, making me ripple the water while catching my balance and spooking the trout immediately.

Sentinel fish can be a problem. I use that term not to mean that certain trout are actually standing guard, but rather those fish that I didn't see and then spooked. If sufficiently frightened, the rapid upstream escape of such fish will in turn scare the trout you're sneaking up on, and all will be lost. Often when I'm moving very slowly and carefully, however, sentinel fish will likewise just move off slowly, feeling vaguely threatened by my presence but not panicked into full flight. This sort of response doesn't usually seem to bother other trout upstream.

The object of all this sneaking around is to get within a relatively short cast of the fish. It may be that you can throw 70 or 80 feet of line plus a 14-foot leader and a small fly without spooking shallow-water trout, but I can't. While I can cast that far, gentleness and accuracy are lost. In this case I'm looking for a cast of about 20 to no more than 40 feet that I can throw accurately and gently while kneeling or hiding behind a low bush. Given sufficient caution on your part, feeding trout in shallow water can often be approached from downstream even more closely, so by all means do so if it's possible.

Most often in this low-water game, no mistakes are allowed. Delicacy and accuracy are at a premium with your first shot at the trout. Leaders will most often be as long as you can handle in casting—as long as 14 feet or even more—and lines will be light, meaning a that four-weight or lighter is best. Once a fish is hooked after a long stalk and gentle cast, don't horse it.[2] Play the fish quietly and keep steering it gently toward shore; this kind of handling will often keep the hooked trout from splashing wildly at the surface and disrupting the pool. If you play your cards—and your fish—right, you may be able to take several trout in succession from the same stretch, sometimes even without having to move yourself.

All the usual cautions about wearing subdued clothing and moving carefully pertain most especially to low-water trout fishing. Your tackle should be on the light side, as I mentioned, not necessarily in the interest of greater sport but simply to minimize the impact of line and leader on the surface. The one equipment item I use that's a little unusual is a pair of gardener's knee pads that buckle over my waders. Many chest-wader models now have integral knee pads, which are adequate to protect the waders from abrasion but are insufficent padding for my knees when I'm crawling over gravel. The extra pads are a godsend when spending much of the afternoon in the prayful attitude required by low-water trout and are widely available through most gardening catalogs.

Low water means easily frightened trout and requires greater than normal caution on the angler's part.

"What an awful story!" Bill Herrick shook his head and frowned at the river as we sat together on the bank. I had just finished telling him about the man and boy I'd guided up north during a day of rain and high water. About the boy who had been so happy with three small trout, and about his father who had been so miserable about not catching any himself.

"But I guess I can understand it," he added. "I've known people who can get that serious about it, too. They just seem to lose all their perspective, but that doesn't seem like much fun."

The river where we sat was high from a late-spring rain, turning our productive pool of yesterday into what seemed like today's total loss. The water was still relatively clear, however, and the weather still warm, so there was hope. As we watched there was a splashing rise in among the submerged alder branches that were normally a foot above the surface. A little tan caddisfly flew out from the leaves and skated erratically through the downstream air. The trout had missed.

"Hey!" Herrick exclaimed, reaching for a box of flies. "Did you hear that? That was a big one! Which side do you want?"

"I'll cross over on the highway bridge," I said, laughing at his excitement. "How do you know it was a big one?"

"They're *all* big ones, Buster," he smiled. "Just ask that kid friend of yours instead of his grouchy old man!"

1. See, for example, Bachman (1984) or Vincent (1975). Both describe the impact of hatchery-trout introductions on wild populations, noting a short-term social-order disruption as one result. Both note the increased angling vulnerability of wild fish during this interval. My suggestion is that flooding has a somewhat similar disruptive effect, including that of a short-term increase in angling vulnerability, until near-normal flows resume and social hierarchies are reestablished along with the trout's customary feeding stations.

2. Old-timer's jargon. "To horse" means to play a fish with unnecessary roughness, potentially allowing the fish to break free, and with little finesse.

25
Merrily Down the Stream

There were icy October mornings on the Bighorn, with stars so clear and close as to seem easily touched before dawn. Our fingers froze to the raft's metal valves as we struggled to pump it up in the darkness, filling the back of Jim Ellett's truck with its strange and black ballooning shape. The river was black, too, at the landing, and my companions were only silhouettes, moving quietly, stowing tackle and gear for a day's fishing.

Sunrise brought a little warmth and the cackling of cock pheasants from hayfields along the river. The grasses and brush along the riverbanks were covered with rime, long feathers of frost that glittered in the growing sunlight. We didn't talk much. It was too early and too cold. The oarlocks creaked loudly as Ellett leaned his big arms and back into a stroke that sent us gliding downriver. I cast a big—very big—White Marabou Muddler toward a log along the bank and watched in fascination as the supple feathers waved and wiggled their way slowly downstream in the dark water.

There was a broad, yellow swirl, and then the authoritative pull of a large brown trout heading for deep water, taking line as it went. I released the fish—a trout of about 3 pounds—at the boat's edge, and then broke the silence. "That's *exactly* the way it's supposed to work!" I hooted.

"So do it again," Ellett said, adding a long, slow smile that meant he thought it might

not happen quite so fast next time. As usual, he was right. Other good fish came to our flies that day, but there were long intervals when lots of hard casting brought nothing at all. But there was always the river—a source of constant interest as we drifted for mile after gentle mile, wondering about what would be around the next bend and then the next.

There have been other rivers, too, and other fish; the big landlocked salmon that nailed a Supervisor streamer and vaulted over the bow on my canoe on Maine's big Penobscot; rainbows that eagerly took drifting nymphs in the green water of Arkansas' White River as we floated slowly in an old jonboat with lawn-chair seats; trout from Montana rivers and those of Idaho and California; and even larger trout taken while drifting rivers farther north such as Alaska's Naknek. Float fishing—that is, fly-fishing for trout from a moving boat—has become ever more popular in recent years. So much so these days that MacKenzie drift boats, the double-ended river dories common in the Rockies and Northwest, can be found on eastern waters such as the big Delaware in New York and on New Hampshire's Androscoggin, while canoes and jonboats—traditionally used in the Northeast and South, respectively—are now sometimes seen on the more placid trout rivers of the West. For most trout fishermen, accustomed to working a trout stream by wading, float fishing is a radically different game.

In most trout fishing as done by wading, the angler's fly, leader, and line nearest the trout move in the current while the line nearest the stationary angler remains more or less in one spot. Most of our many tactics for controlling a fly and averting drag are based on this actuality. If float fishing, however, when casting a fly from a moving boat, both ends of the line are moving—often at different speeds—and the tactical problems of casting and fishing assume an added dimension.

Being able to fish any given river of adequate size from a drifting boat can be a mixed blessing. Certainly a greater length of river is covered than can be fished in a day's wading, and float fishing means you'll be covering areas that wading anglers can't usually reach. Floating also may be the only way to fish a particular area, perhaps because posted land prohibits shoreline access or because some areas are just too much of a hike from the closest road. On the other hand, your drifting boat often passes quickly by the likely spots for trout along the bank, giving you one cast or perhaps two before a promising area is left behind. A wading angler can take his time, working such spots carefully and often more productively.

The kind of boat from which you'll be fishing is also a consideration. MacKenzie or drift boats are relatively stable, and allow casting and fishing while standing up except in very rough water. Large inflatable rafts, such as the Avons commonly used on western rivers, are sufficiently rigid so you can stand up gingerly, but you'll probably do most of your casting and fishing from a sitting position in rubber rafts as well as from canoes and narrow jonboats. You will in any case have to adapt your tackle, casting, and fishing technique to the special needs of float fishing.

This sort of fly-fishing also has an undeserved reputation as being muscular, requiring heavy tackle for flinging huge streamers and big weighted nymphs against the bank for hour after hour. I began to learn otherwise almost twenty years ago in watching Mary Renschtler float fishing Montana's Big Hole from a rubber raft with a pair of hired guides, one to run the oars and the other to attend to her tackle and fish. She was at the time an elderly widow, who years before with her husband had been involved in a now-famous Atlantic-salmon club on Canada's Moisie River, and who for a time made an annual trout-fishing pilgrimage to the area of Montana where we happened to meet. She was often fishing with small drys when I met her and used a matched pair of exquisite Leonard bamboo trout rods. Upon hooking a fish, she dutifully played it near the boat and then handed the rod to the guide, who netted and unhooked the fish after handing over her second rod so she could meanwhile continue fishing. She caught just as many trout as I did while flailing away with a heavy rod and big nymphs and did so with considerably more elegance. We visited in her Park Avenue apartment the following fall, catching many of the same trout over again in late-afternoon conversation, and her only complaint—made quite sternly, but with twinkling eyes—was that I'd put too much water in her whiskey while fixing drinks. I promised to do better.

Float fishing puts a premium on your ability to read water. As the boat drifts downstream, it's often slowed by a guide at the oars and kept a comfortable cast from the bank. Likely spots along the bank pass by one after another as the boat moves along. Some people try to cover as many of these as possible, giving each spot a cast, a few twitches of the fly, and then picking up to cast again. This frenetic, machinelike fishing is exhausting, and it's much better to watch ahead of the boat, pick one spot, and then to fish it carefully with a cast or two. You'll be forsaking other likely looking spots in the process, but it's almost always more productive to fish one spot carefully than to fish half a dozen in haphazard fashion.

Other things being equal, the most accurate caster on a float trip will catch the most and often the largest fish. Accuracy in this case means being able to consistently place a fly within a couple of inches of any target from 40 to 50 feet away. Although this is sometimes necessary to hit the narrow feeding lane of a rising trout, such accuracy more often means simply that your fly will remain in a productive spot for a second or two longer than if your cast were a few inches short. On popular float-fishing rivers such as the Madison or Big Horn, there may be as many as two hundred or even more drift boats and rafts covering the same few miles of river in the same day. If you can cast accurately to within an inch or two of likely spots—which many fishermen can't do—you'll have an advantage simply because you'll be covering fish that many other fishermen haven't reached. While this sort of ability comes mostly from long practice, matching your tackle to the needs of your fishing is at least half the battle and is an area in which many trout fishermen—especially those new to float fishing—are needlessly deficient.

Fly casting from a MacKenzie-style drift boat.

As usual, your tackle needs are generally dictated by fly size. What's ususual for many people is that some of the most productive float-fishing flies for trout are either heavy or air resistant or both, which makes them hard to cast accurately. While a #2 Marabou Muddler streamer may feel light in your hand when dry, it soaks up considerable water when fished and thus becomes very heavy in the air. The large stonefly nymphs and sculpin imitations popular on western waters are usually tied with plenty of lead wire to keep them near the bottom where they work best, and that weight makes them likewise difficult to cast. While it's possible to cast such flies with the four-, five- or six-weight lines most trout fishermen are accustomed to using, this requires both enormous skill and very high line speeds; in other words, it's a lot of work. Fly lines of greater mass will carry such flies more easily in casting, which means a seven- or eight-weight is a better choice. If fishing with such flies all day, my own choice is a 9-foot eight-weight rod with a moderate progressive action that allows good loop control and relatively slow line speeds with a weight-forward floating line and with larger flies. This rig seems to allow the greatest accuracy with the least work on my part and is similar in theory to that commonly suggested for bass fly-fishing, in which a slow-actioned rod is used with a line of large mass for casting big, air-resistant bass bugs.

Leaders are another problem. Most commercial versions are inadequate for use with large flies, having soft, gentle tapers that won't transfer enough energy on the cast. Among other things, this means the supple braided leaders you might prefer for fishing little drys on slow spring creeks are the worst possible choice in this case. The easiest route for use with your seven- or eight-weight floating line is the addition of a very stiff butt section. You'll have to experiment to get this right, but start with nylon of about .030 diameter and work up or down from there as needed. Then either build or add a ready-made leader with a steep taper down to a .010 to .012 tippet about 18 inches long for an overall length of about 9 feet or so. You must be able to throw a perfectly straight line with positive and accurate turnover at the end of every cast, and heavy flies will simply cause supple leaders to collapse backward instead of straigtening on the water.

My tippet-size suggestions are in the 10- to 12-pound-test range, which may sound heavy to those not accustomed to larger fly sizes. Not only are such tippets needed to straighten the cast, they may allow for some margin of error in your knot tying that will inevitably weaken your leader in the first place. Not too much error, however. Your straight-line casting means your fly is being fished on a relatively tight line with little if any slack. When a big brown trout piles out from under a logjam to hammer your streamer, the force of the strike can be enormous. Even with 10-pound-test tippets, you'll break off such fish on the strike if you aren't careful to set the hook deliberately and not with an instinctive, violent yank.

While some float trips entail the use of large flies all day long, it's more common to use such flies part of the time and to fish with small drys or nymphs when a hatch and rising trout are encountered. The ideal solution, circumstances permitting, is to carry two fully rigged rods—a heavy setup rigged for large flies and your usual four-, five-, or six-weight rig for smaller ones. Your extra rod or rods should be stowed in the boat *with rod tips pointing to the rear*, regardless of the type of watercraft you're using. A rearward-pointing rod will slide off brush and sticks encountered when the boat drifts near the bank. Rods pointing forward will

have their tips caught in bankside obstructions and will often snap if the boat's moving so fast that it can't be stopped in time. Many drift boats and other craft have rod racks installed under the inside gunnels to protect rods by keeping them entirely within the boat—an ideal solution.

If you're only going to take one rod, take the heavy one. This will allow you to fish both large and small flies, which the lighter one will not, or at least not as easily. You'll probably want to change your entire leader in changing from large flies to small, rather than just going to a smaller tippet size. Since you've already attached a stiff, monofilament butt section to your seven- or eight-weight line, just snip off the short, fast taper you used for large flies. Then use a blood knot to add a conventional and supple small-fly leader tapered to whatever tippet size your fly requires—5X for size 14 or 16 flies, for example. The leader-changing process shouldn't take more than a couple of minutes and is well worth the effort in that it allows soft, slack-tippet landings of small flies instead of slapping them on the water as would be apt to be the case if you retained your original short, fast taper.

Many drift-boat guides I've met seem to favor large, floppy hats and heavy shirts. Aside from other practical considerations such as warmth and preventing sunburn, this clothing is worn in self-defense against a client's errant casting. Guides are understandably touchy about being hit in the head or neck (or anywhere else) by your sharp-hooked fly, so pay attention. There are certain ways of casting that will reduce the risk to both your guide and to yourself and that also increase the likelihood of a successful cast.

Assume for the moment a right-handed caster fishing standing up in the bow of a drift boat, in which case the guide will be seated at the oars 3 or 4 feet behind the caster. The guide will usually be running the boat parallel to and near the more productive of two riverbanks, which will usually change as the main current shifts from one side of the river to the other. In the first case, fishing the left bank as one looks downstream, things are easy. A conventional forward cast has the airborne line out over the water and mostly to the front of the boat, so you can cast to the bank and slightly ahead of the boat without difficulty.

When the main current and your guide switch to the opposite, or right-hand, bank, things get more complicated. Now a right-handed, conventional cast will bring the line and fly between the caster and the guide, or even directly over the guide's head if—as you should be—you're aiming slightly downstream of the boat. Any kind of backhanded casting stroke would solve the problem, but that's hard to accomplish in any case and most especially so with larger line and fly sizes.

Here's a trick Phil Wright taught me years ago on the Big Hole that has since made for many happy guides and correspondingly better fishing. While continuing to use a conventional forehanded casting stroke, cant the rod over your head to the left at about 45 degrees. Your casting arm will be held fairly high in this method, allowing the tipped-over rod to clear your head. With an 8- or 9-foot rod, the line will again be traveling on your left side instead of whistling past the guide's ear. This also allows the addition of some body English to the cast as you bend back a little with the backcast and forward a little with the forward cast, which quite literally reinforces the rigid wrist you maintain for the sake of getting a tight and accurate casting loop. I use this method all the time when fishing large, heavy flies in this situation, which allows the guide to concen-

trate more on finding fish and less on ducking. With smaller flies that I'm most confident of controlling in the air, I may sometimes continue to use a conventional cast but with the casting arc tilted toward the water, allowing a high backcast that gives the guide and myself plenty of clearance.

It's common on many float trips for there to be one fly fisherman in the front of the boat, a guide in the middle at the oars, and a second angler in the back. Most instructions are given for the angler in front; the fisherman in the back of the boat may be angling's most neglected character, both in print and in practice. For one thing, the guide is facing forward—downstream, in this case—so the bow caster in front of the guide usually gets the benefit of most of the guide's coaching. The guide will notice you, however, and perhaps roughly if you're fishing from the stern and hit him with your fly. The casting suggestions made previously for the bow angler are exactly reversed for the fisherman in the stern: For a right-handed caster, use a conventional overhead cast when fishing the right bank (looking downstream), which will keep the line and fly out over the water and not over the guide. When fishing the left bank, use a conventional casting stroke, but cant the rod to your left so the line again travels over the water and not between you and the guide.

Most fishermen feel as if they're playing second fiddle when fishing from the backseat—wives or children are often relegated to this spot, for example—because the bow fishermen inevitably gets first crack at a promising-looking spot along the bank. There are some ways in which the rearmost angler can catch just as many fish as the bow caster—and often larger ones—but you'll have to pay close attention to the fishing.

As the boat travels downstream, it's impossible for the bow caster to cover every good-looking spot because of the boat's speed. So the first rule for backseat fishermen is to watch and then to cast where the bow person doesn't. Second, although the bow caster may be trying the better spots, only a few of these will produce fish, many of which may swirl or splash at the fly without hitting it. Pay attention! Having seen this happen to the bow caster, as the boat moves foward this spot becomes all your own, and for once you *know* it holds a fish. You may be able to hit this spot with a couple of casts while your partner in front can only watch. For this reason, it's a good idea for the bow and stern anglers to be using different fly patterns unless a particular fly happens to be red-hot at a particular time. The now-agitated trout that refused the bow person's fly might readily accept yours as long as it's sufficiently different.

Life in the back of the boat can be a great choice. Since fishing from this spot isn't supposed to be as productive as the bow, you'll feel less pressure to perform and can more easily just set your rod down and enjoy the ride, if that's your inclination. When it comes to making a stop along the bank, the bow person or the guide will almost always be the ones having to jump out into the brush and muck to secure the boat; you won't have to move until you've got a dry and easy spot for getting out, and, of course, you'll be first in the boat instead of having to shove and then jump when it's time to head on downstream. Finally, since there's often a friendly competition going between casters in the front and back, you can have the immense satisfaction of catching fish that the bow person has missed, one of which is usually worth at least two trout taken any other way.

Most of this discussion has centered on guided float trips in drift boats or rafts on larger, usually fast-moving rivers. Canoeists, especially, often fish quieter waters or pick their way along the edges of faster rivers, in either case usually without a guide. The major problem in this case is stopping or slowing the drifting canoe sufficiently to allow fishing a particular spot.

When trout fishing from a canoe on slow-moving brushy streams as most commonly found in the Northeast and upper Midwest, I usually drift down the left bank (when facing downstream). As a right-handed caster, this allows me a conventional overhead or sidearm cast down and across stream, the same sort of cast that I'd use if wading. Instead of an anchor, I use a big spring-loaded clamp—a large, car-battery clamp off an old pair of jumper cables is one example—attached to a short rope that's tied to my seat. I can then grab a branch or bush, attach the clamp, and thus hold the canoe still while I fish. Releasing the clamp allows me to drift farther downstream without the tangles, muck, weeds, and water disturbance entailed by an anchor.

If you must use an anchor, be careful of your choice. Mushroom-shaped or grappling-hook-type anchors are fine if the river bottom is sand or fine gravel. On rocky bottoms, they will be impossible to retrieve as you dangle downstream in the current, which may be strong enough to completely prevent you from moving upstream of the anchor to free it. In this case, a round or pear-shaped metal ball will tangle less often, but still may become jammed in a rocky crevice. Freeing an anchor can become serious work in a hurry, which is why I seldom use one. On some rivers of relatively even depth and slow current, of which Michigan's Au Sable is a good example, it's common practice to drag a length of heavy chain to slow a drifting boat, although I've often wondered whether or not the links clattering noisily along the bottom scare trout.

I most often use a canoe as a means of getting from place to place on large rivers, rather than directly as a fishing vehicle. Like green grass and fences, larger trout always seem to be rising on the opposite side of any given river, which may be unreachable by wading or without a long walk. A canoe, in this case, is a handy way of getting from one side to the other and, if you're lucky, getting away from all the other fishermen on the near shore. Just make sure you figure out *first* how you're going to get back. Having made the crossing, you may have to pull the canoe for some distance upstream along the bank before trying to return, depending on the current's speed and the length of your crossing.

At some point during a day's float, you or your guide will likely beach the boat so you can get out and fish a potentially productive area more thoughoughly by wading. On heavily floated and fished rivers where there's lots of boat traffic, this can be an important opportunity to do something different.

By the second October that Vern Gallup, Jim Ellett, and I spent several days floating and fishing Montana's productive Big Horn, word had gotten out about the fantastic fishing of the year before. For many years, that river, which flows through a Crow Indian reservation, had been closed to fishing, its numerous brown and rainbow trout unmolested by anglers. It was finally opened by court order to drift fishing, and the fishing was then—and sometimes still is—extraordinary in this fertile tailwater.

On this particular afternoon, the river was crowded with fishermen in drift boats and rafts, and there was considerable jockeying

and competition for choice spots along the river. We had pulled out on a gravel bar adjacent to a long, deep and wide run, and were eating lunch and watching the other boats go by. Many of the fishermen had been set up by their guides with floating strike indicators on their leaders, which held their small nymphs suspended a few feet below the surface as the boats drifted slowly along. It's an especially productive method on this and other slow-moving trout rivers, which—until a fish hits—is also about as interesting as watching grass grow. Most of their indicators had been set shallow for fishing the riffles above and below our deep run, and their guides didn't bother to re-rig for the deeper water of the moment, knowing another shallow riffle was just downstream.

Ellett waded upstream of our gravel bar and starting firing a big marabou on a fast-sinking, shooting-head line into the deep water between the boats. His line bellied deep in the currents, far deeper than the drifting anglers were fishing. In short order he was grinning widely and holding a bucking rod as a rainbow cartweeled next to the nearest boat. He released the fish, and promptly hooked a brown trout in the same fashion.

Finally he hooked a larger fish that didn't come in quite so quickly, and he waved at me to wade up with his camera. I stood in front of him to take a photo as he cradled the trout—a rainbow of about 4 pounds—and then he waved me quickly to one side.

"But the light's no good from this side," I protested while moving over.

"To hell with the light." He grinned. "I want to make sure the boys in the boats get a good look at the fish!"

26
Small Streams

Just as the railroad bums used to sing of a Big Rock Candy Mountain with its eternal springs of lemonade, so trout fishermen dream of No-Name Brook. The brook always flows somewhere in a shadowed ravine or sunlit meadow. Here the water is always cool and clear; never high and muddy, and never low and hot. There are always wildflowers along the bank or carpeting the meadow, and green moss thickly covers the rocks and ledges, perhaps with a bed of watercress where a cold spring quietly drips. You'll see songbirds, of course; probably bright little warblers darting on golden wings from bushes to snatch mayflies in the air, or perhaps a water ouzel with its quick white wink, slipping out of a rapid and onto a rock with its beak full of caddis larvae collected underwater. Unlike many such brooks, No-Name has no blackflies or mosquitoes in its little valley; rattlesnakes, leeches, and other things that bite, claw, or scratch have been likewise mysteriously banished. The wind isn't the reason, I know, because in this valley the wind never blows.

There are trout in No-Name's small pools, fish that have lived here undisturbed for generations. If the brook happens to be in the West, the trout may be little rainbows that still bear purple, heart-shaped parr marks along their sides, like valentines under the sparkling surface of the stream. Or perhaps they're cutthroats, all butter yellow and purple and black spotted and carrying the colors of the meadow on their sides. In the East, the trout will ideally be brook trout with bright fins and spots the color of brookside violets. There might also be a small brown trout or two or three, hiding shyly in the shadows. In any case, when hooked, a trout will invariably leap in a graceful arc, its image indelible against a background of curving ferns and tumbling water.

You may have caught a dozen trout in No-Name Brook. Or only two. Or none. It doesn't seem to really matter as the brook slips into evening shadow and you head for home. On the way, you pick wild raspberries where the berries are abundant along the stream, their tall canes strangely lacking thorns. An old fence line marks the only dry path through the alder swamp near the road. When you finish stowing your gear in the car, it's almost dark, and when you look back toward the woods, the path has become invisible in the shadows. As if it had never existed.

Ah, romance! Somehow small streams seem to have much of it, and big rivers very little. Both fishing writers and writers who happen to fish have been extolling the lyrical virtues of smaller brooks and streams since Hector was a pup, which is a very long time. It's been several centuries, for example, since British poet John Donne gave little brooks what may still be their ultimate romantic image:

Come live with me, and be my love,
And we will some new pleasures prove
Of golden sands, and crystal brooks,
With silken lines, and silver hooks.

A large river, which might also have golden sands and crystal-clear water, simply won't fit within Donne's image because—unlike a brook—it offers no intimacy. Tradition, color, scenery, wildlife, more and larger trout, fly hatches, excitement, adventure; a river may offer all or most of these things, but intimacy, never. And that's *the* thing about small streams that over the centuries has transformed them into the idyllic essence of a trout-fisherman's eternally optimistic soul.

There are other reasons, too, foremost among which is a short-pants tradition that holds small streams central to a trout fisherman's genealogy. Like rivers, trout fishermen begin with brooks and streams, exploring their banks as small boys on warm summer days and testing their trout with worms and crickets before growing up to ply their dry flies on the world's distant waters. Or so our tradition maintains. There's thus

an emotional attachment to small streams, one dictated by pervasive tradition and one that trout fishermen invariably adopt regardless of whether or not they experienced such fishing as children. Since the mid-1960s, increasing numbers of people have been taking up trout fishing as adults, usually with the help of a friend or a fly-fishing school. Instruction often takes place at a casting pond or on a larger river; small streams are usually too small for a class of a dozen students, and basic casting practice is best taken in a wide-open area. So while our graduate might readily adopt a reverential attitude toward smaller waters—an attitude that is, after all, basic equipment—actually fishing such waters can pose some new and unique problems.

Small streams for this discussion are those less than 20 feet wide, and often much smaller. They are of two basic types, and a single stream may encompass both water types as its topography changes from one area to the next. There are tumbling, mountain streams and brooks of fairly steep gradient that typically assume a stair-step pattern of waterfalls, riffles, and rapids interspersed more or less regularly with pools and flat runs as the water progresses down its slope. Other small streams are of the meadow variety, which may or may not actually flow through a meadow, but which are characterized by a low gradient and a series of ess-shaped, meandering bends. I'll call these types mountain streams and meadow streams as a matter of convenience, with the understanding that mountain streams also occur in areas of low hills and that meadow streams encompass certain small, spring creeks as well as slow flowages through swamps instead of meadows.

Most such streams in trout country stay relatively cool all summer, usually being in areas of cold headwater sources, heavily shaded, or at relatively high altitudes. From a thermal standpoint, they are often ideal trout habitat unless the water is so cold as to inhibit growth. Unfortunately, activities such as logging or livestock grazing sometimes reduce or eliminate trees and bushes along the stream, reducing the number of shaded areas and causing a dramatic temperature increase in addition to other problems such as increased flows of mud and silt into the stream. Anything that artificially slows the water has a similar effect; beaver dams are notorious for warming headwater streams, although such dams have the beneficial effect of collecting and concentrating nutrients in their slower flows and may temporarily improve the fishing as a result. It's common in many areas for riparian homeowners to remove streamside vegetation for a better view of their stream and to sometimes build stream-fed ponds as part of their landscaping. I wince every time I see this happening for I know that the effect of a single house may be small, but becomes significant when multiplied by dozens of houses along a small country creek where homeowners are unwittingly killing the object of their affection.

Other things, such as water temperature and chemistry, being equal, meadow streams are usually more productive of trout and other aquatic life than mountain streams. During times of heavy rainfall or melting snow, the higher flows of mountain streams are usually constrained to a single channel that's both narrow and steep, which means the erosive effects of flooding are enormous. Aquatic plants and insect larvae are crushed and washed away in large numbers, juvenile trout and other fish are killed or widely dispersed, and the stream channel itself is dramatically altered. Meadow streams typically have more stable flows and are less subject to erosion when flooded. In the event of high

water, the shallow gradient of meadow water means the flood extends up and over the stream banks, covering the adjacent low-lying ground rather than having its erosive force concentrated only in the stream channel. There are thus usually more survivors within the aquatic community—including trout—when water levels return to normal.

Trout in small streams are usually easily spooked, which most often means an approach from below is best, with the fisherman casting upstream to likely spots from a position of downstream concealment. Dry flies will be the easiest patterns to fish with in such cases, and—since in the absence of a hatch most small-stream trout aren't especially selective—just about any small, drab pattern will do the job. Most casts will be short, meaning 25 feet or less, and will often have to be accomplished through narrow, brushy alleys above the stream. All of the foregoing helps to lend definition to small-stream tackle.

First, there's sneaking up on the trout. Your clothing should be drab and generally matching in tone the woodland or open area that provides your background. Many small streams are sufficiently shallow to require no more than hip-length wading boots; others will be occasionally deeper, for which you'll want chest waders. In either case, many of your approaches to the lower ends of pools will be made on your hands and knees, which makes some sort of knee pads especially helpful. I use a buckle-on kind commonly sold in gardening stores. As usual, the basic rules of stalking trout apply, which means watching carefully first to check the actual or probable locations of fish. Your movements should be low and very slow. Actually wading in the small pool you're fishing will probably ruin it, so stay below the pool or low on the bank.

I'm partial to longer graphite rods for lighter line weights—meaning rods of 8 to 9 feet, taking line weights of five or less—even for small-stream fishing, because the long reach allowed by such rods is helpful in so many different ways. But on many small streams, especially those with lots of brush and bushes, there simply isn't room for waving a long stick, so a shorter rod is appropriate. Rods of 6 to 7 feet will give you many more opportunities for conventional casting in tight quarters, and sooner or later most experienced trout fishermen wind up buying such a rod specifically for small-stream work.

A short rod in this case offers several advantages beyond the obvious one of greater maneuverability in tight spots. You should be able to throw tight, fast loops with such a rod at distances of 15 to 40 feet, which will enable greater accuracy. Often you'll be aiming for a deep pocket the size of a lunch pail at the head of a tiny pool, and the advantages of being able to drop your fly on a dime will quickly become apparent. Higher line speeds will also allow you to shock the cast slightly by stopping it abruptly, recoiling the leader tippet to provide a little slack near the fly when it lands. This is especially important because other types of slack-line casting may be impossible in the narrow confines of a little creek.

Your short-line casting may be enhanced by the use of a line that's one size heavier than that for which the rod is rated. The slight additional weight will bend the rod more easily in casting a short line, helping to speed up and tighten your casting loops at distances of less than 30 feet. Leaders for use on tumbling, pocket-water streams can be short; 9 feet is usually plenty, and 7 or 8 feet may be better, in any case designed with a steep taper for positive turnover in casting. This is a compromise, by the way, because you'll probably encounter a few exceptionally long pools requiring a cast of 40 to 50 feet, in which case your short leader is a disadvantage. Sometimes this can be overcome

by adding a longer (3 to 4 feet) tippet section, although a perfectionist will change the entire leader for a longer, more supple version to fish such a pool with best results.

Open meadow waters place fewer constraints on your casting, which makes longer rods a much better choice. The added length will give you more clearance above grasses and brush to your rear while casting from your knees, which you'll be doing often. Such things as flipping loops of slack line to avoid dragging the fly on the water, reaching around corners, and even dapping a fly over the edge of a bank while lying on your stomach are all common to meadow-water fishing and are most easily done with rods of 8 to 9 or more feet instead of shorter ones. If a choice has to be made, as in the case of a stream that flows through a short meadow before tumbling through a woodland, I wind up taking the short rod for the sake of its versatility. Inevitably, though, at several points during a small-stream day, I wind up wishing for the rod I didn't bring. One answer, of course, is to take two rods, but this is so awkward in practice as to be no answer at all.

Finding trout in small streams is easy— almost—because there are fewer places to look. The deep pockets where water tumbles over a falls or ledge are obvious spots, as are the little fast-water chutes at the heads of miniature pools. If the pools are a little larger, say 10 to 20 feet long, the trout's location becomes more of a problem. While there is almost always one or more trout at the head or deepest portion of the pool, the largest fish will often hold at the pool's lower, or downstream, end and in very shallow water. This is particularly true if there's any overhead cover such as a low-hanging bush nearby, and is especially true of larger brown trout.

Such a fish is a problem because it's usually motionless and hard to see unless it happens to take something from the surface, in which case you'll probably notice its movement. Because you haven't seen the fish, it's usually the one you spook when sneaking up to the pool's tail and planning a cast to deeper water at the upper end. This, of course, scares the rest of the trout, and all the time you spent crawling slowly up on hands and knees is wasted. I have many times gotten to within peeking distance of a small quiet pool and then watched in frustration as a broad wake headed out of the tail shallows toward the shelter of an upstream stump.

There are a couple of things you can do in this instance. The first is to *always* assume that at least one trout is holding in the tail shallows of any pool, which is true more often than not. This means you'll be sneaking up on and carefully fishing the tail of the pool first, forgetting for the time being the better-looking water near the pool's upper end. Second, if and when you do spook this fish, make a point of remembering exactly where it was holding in the stream. It will be there tomorrow, and it or another like it will be in the same spot next year, assuming a similar water level and that floods don't alter the streambed in the interim. If your upstream approach proved unworkable, you can later sneak around and cast downstream to the fish, or perhaps the configuration of the stream bank will allow you to hide behind a bush or rock and cast to the fish from one side or the other.

Meadow streams can be even more difficult in this regard. As the creek meanders through its many curves, there is below each curve a relatively long stretch of water along one bank that's usually deeper than the rest of the pool (except where the water first enters the pool, which is almost always its deepest point). This may only be a few feet long if the stream is a couple of feet wide, but may be 20 or 30 feet long if the stream is a dozen feet wide or more. Trout often hold in single file along such a bank, each one a few feet behind the other. Scare one, and you'll scare them all. It's a tough problem, especially so because the slowly moving water is often clear, unruffled, and only a foot or so deep.

Again, the best answer is usually fishing carefully upstream from the opposite bank. Wading is out of the question, at least in terms of not scaring the fish. This is the kind of situation in which observations made before fishing are really essential. Over half an hour of watching, I might see each trout rise once or twice as they feed intermittently on small terrestrial insects. I can note the position of each rise with respect to some object on the bank, remembering that there's a trout located 2 feet above a particular grass clump and 2 feet this side of the far bank, for example, and marking in my mind the location of several fish in similar fashion. If the trout are actively feeding on a hatch of mayflies or other insects, all of the foregoing is of course more obvious.

Waiting and watching enable the formulation of a plan for catching each fish in turn, working slowly upstream from one fish to the next, and playing fish very gently as they're hooked to avoid spooking the others. This also involves deciding ahead of time on the best positions from which to cast. In looking over the bank from which I'll be fishing, I may see a depression in the ground that offers a great hiding spot or a bush behind which I can hide. Spooking a fish or bungling a cast when fishing a larger river may be of little consequence just because there will be other trout available not far away. In small-stream fishing, however, there's less room for everything—including our own mistakes—and this is part of its appeal.

All of this crawling around and sneaking up below trout is a lot of work, of course, so sometimes I do what I do and not what I say; namely, fish downstream by standing up and wading. This can be successful to the extent that the little stream's water is broken and tumbling, the rough character of which helps hide me from the fish. Wading and fishing downstream is the worst possible tactic in calm, meadow waters, where the noise of your wading will scare fish, as will the clouds of silt that you stir up with your feet. There are some creeks I fish, however, that are so brushy and narrow that they're impossible to fish except by standing in midstream and floating a small nymph downstream on a long line. This works well enough, as long as I'm able to extend 40 or 50 feet of line down in the current ahead of my own position and then take time and care in wading slowly downstream. It is a lazy way of fishing, which sometimes feels just right.

Although trout of small streams are usually small themselves, there are sometimes surprises. Larger trout, meaning trout of 2 or 3 pounds and sometimes much more, are most often encountered in small streams in conjunction with a spawning migration. This does not mean a mass of huge fish converging on a little creek, an idea that many people associate with runs of salmon, but most often a few individual large trout that have made their way upstream from a larger river that may be many miles back downstream along our little tributary. The biggest brown trout I've ever seen in eastern waters—with one exception—have been fish of 10 pounds or more I've discovered in little creeks barely 10 feet wide in late fall, discoveries that have always taken place while I'm equipped with a shotgun and grouse-hunting gear and with nary a fly rod in sight. The same is often true of rainbows in small creeks during March and April as that fish's spring spawning time approaches, and many northwestern trout fishermen have more than once had the shock of discovering a pair of immense steelhead in their favorite little

trout pool if that particular stream offers unimpeded access to the ocean.

Large trout may also be resident in small streams, and this is most true of meadow waters. These streams, by virtue of their relatively stable flows, can offer more food and shelter to larger trout than steeper, tumbling creeks. The meadow-meandering, little Gibbon River in Yellowstone Park has become a well-known example, one that offers brown trout in excess of 20 inches and seemingly out of all proportion to the small size of the creek. But if any particular meadow stream holds any brown trout, the chances are very good that it also holds a few very large ones year round. These fish will be secretive and very hard to find, especially during the daylight hours. The slow current of such streams often means a muddy bottom, which is in part the sort of habitat used by several species of large, burrowing mayfly nymphs. Almost all of these species hatch in late evening during June or early July in various parts of the country, and this is the best possible time for locating the largest browns in any reach of meadow water, trout that seldom rise to hatches of lesser insects.

The largest resident trout I've ever seen come from a small stream was a tragedy. Concrete bridge abutments next to small streams tend to be undercut by the current over time and become a favorite lair of larger brown trout. There was such a spot near my northern Vermont home of many years ago where a stream that averaged perhaps 20 feet wide curled against the side of an old bridge before passing under the road and downstream. This particular river held naturalized populations of brooks, browns, and rainbows, few of which ever exceeded a foot in length. The best I'd been able to do in several years of trying here was an 18-inch brown taken from a late-summer pool after dark on a bass bug.

My night-fishing career on this stream ended when the beaver drove me from the river. For part of one summer, I made a practice of fishing at night in the summertime, standing still in a long, quiet pool, casting big drys into the distant blackness, and waiting tensely for a strike. It was spooky and usually very quiet. On one such evening there was an enormous crash in the water a few feet behind me, shattering my nerves completely and sending me scrambling out of the water. Beaver. The curious animals kept swimming around me in the dark and then slapping their tails on the water in alarm after deciding I didn't belong in their pool. There were just as many beaver in this stream as there were pools, so after a few nights I gave up. On the last such night, however, I tried the old abutment after dark, swinging a big Muddler through the blackness and hoping for a ferocious yank on the line. There was a tremendous splashing under the bridge, and I—being several times burned and more than twice shy—decided it was another beaver, pulled in my line, and left. I was wrong.

About a week later, I noticed one of the neighborhood kids dangling a fishing line over the bridge. The kid had a big treble-hooked lure tied to his line, and I stopped to ask him what he was doing.

"Aw, just tryin' to snag a few suckers. We'll put 'em under the tomato plants," he said. I wished him luck and left.

About an hour later the kid pulled into my barnyard with a huge brown trout dangling from the handlebars of his bicycle. The fish's tail dragged on the ground. By my tape, it measured 31 inches, and it pulled 6½ pounds on the kitchen scale. A trout of that length in good condition would weigh almost twice as much, but this was a big-headed, skinny, long snake of a fish as black as the hole in which it had lived for who knows how many years. I was aghast. Then suspicious. I looked, and there was a gaping wound in the fish's side where it had been snagged by the kid's hook.

"I came so you could take a picture of me and the fish," he pleaded. So I took the picture, developed the film, and gave the kid a print, which promptly appeared in the local paper. I should have given the kid hell for snagging a trout, and then a long lecture on sportsmanship. I should have caught that fish myself, for that matter, and caught it fairly. But I didn't do any of those things. It's bugged me ever since, and I've often wondered over the years if that magnificent trout was ultimately buried under a tomato plant.

27
Some Thoughts on Fly Tying

At least once each winter I'm overcome by feelings of virtue, and so decide to clean, organize, and sort all my fly-tying materials. This takes considerable time, not because of all the related paraphernalia, but because of the memories and ideas such activity brings to mind.

A clump of soft, black-dyed marabou takes me instantly to a little tundra creek in southwestern Alaska. The stream was about 30 feet wide, meandering slowly amid clumps of scrub birches and open meadow before entering a big lake. It was late autumn; a time when a unique strain of big rainbow trout enter this particular creek, holding in its quiet flows for about three weeks before returning to the lake. From where I knelt on the bank at the inside of a bend, I could see the water's surface hump slightly as a trout sometimes moved near the far bank.

I tied a black-marabou leech pattern about 3 inches long—one of several I'd made the previous winter—to the heavy leader, and soaked the fly in the water nearby, getting ready to cast. Finally I dropped the fly against the far bank and started twitching the rod tip to work the feathers in the current. Suddenly there was a huge wake behind the fly, so big and so frightening that I was shocked into stillness, unable to pull the fly away from the fish as I sometimes inadvertently do when really excited. The fish took in a broad swirl, was hooked, and promptly headed downstream toward the lake at full speed. The chase covered several hundred yards as the fish plowed down the little creek and as I ran along the bank, trying to keep up and to recover line on the reel.

Finally we stopped in a large backwater. The water was deep near the bank, and there were no shallows in which I could trap the trout. Twice I had it near enough to reach for its head, and twice my hand slipped away, unable to span the trout's broad back. Then the trout began to roll, turning, splashing, and flopping in the water near my feet. The hook pulled out, and I watched, feeling utterly drained, as the trout swam freely downstream. It was longer than a yardstick, I guessed, and almost 20 pounds.

I put the marabou back in a plastic bag and tossed it into a box with a sigh. It may be a long, long time before I see another trout such as that one, I thought, and then picked up a dark-gray rooster cape from another box and started searching for its envelope. Sunlight was reflecting off the snow outside, illuminating the feathers in my hand. As I looked more closely, the individual fibers on each feather seemed to glow with tints of gray and bronze and silver. There was a vague sheen over the many feathers of this particular neck that promised stiffness of fiber, the kind that makes the very best dry flies. Its colors reminded me of something I'd read long ago by the late John Atherton, an artist and angler who once lived in nearby Arlington, Vermont, and for years fished the Battenkill as I do even now.

In his 1951 book *The Fly and the Fish*, Atherton used his perceptions as an artist to bring the word "impressionism" to American fly tying. This connection is commonly known, but what he actually wrote is not, and it's very important:

> If you will look closely at a live dun [mayfly] . . . you will observe that his coloring is "impressionistic." It is built up of many tiny variations of tone such as we find in the paintings of Renoir, Monet and others of the impressionistic school of art.

Atherton then proceeds with a practical definition that should be just as important among flytiers now as it was when first written more than forty years ago:

> As an artist, realizing how the intelligent use of color can give life to a picture, I feel that anglers are prone to neglect the possibility of using more living color in their flies. If an artist were to thoroughly mix certain colors to obtain a gray and then apply it to the canvas, the gray would be devoid of any lifelike quality. But, if he should apply the same colors to the canvas without mixing them beforehand, the result would have a great deal more vibration, light and life. At close range, the effect would be one of a mixture of colors. But at a slight distance, they would appear close to the color and value of his original mixed gray, except that it would be alive and not dead.

One of Atherton's fly-tying answers consisted of blending furs of various colors to achieve that impressionistic effect in the bodies of his nymphs, drys, and wets. This is easily done in a variety of ways; I use a small electric blender to combine various furs in dry form (adding no water to the blender). While a few of the original fly patterns described in his book remain popular—most notably the Atherton Medium Nymph—these days they are very rarely tied with the subtle color blends he originally used.

The question of color is extremely important, but is to a large degree taken for granted by trout fishermen in buying or tying their flies. That trout can see and react to colors has been well established by numerous studies and is beyond dispute. The color-sensitive cone cells in a trout's retina retract as darkness approaches, leaving the trout to rely on its black-and-white-(and gray)-sensitive rod cells in very dim light and darkness. This produces a response to dry flies under certain conditions that is remarkable, has been widely noted, but is worth repeating because of the questions it raises.

I have often cast repeatedly over a rising trout during an evening rise, only to have the fly consistently refused. This is relatively commonplace when trout are being selective, and something about the artificial fly of the moment isn't quite right. As the evening grows later, the ambient light of day gradually dims. At some point in this interval of increasing darkness, the trout will probably take the same fly it has been refusing for the past hour or so. I have long since satisfied myself that this response is because of the fish's reduced color perception in the growing darkness and not because of some other fault of fly pattern, drag, or a mismatched hatch. Often I persist in using a refused but still plausible (to me) fly pattern in such situations for lack of a better answer and firm in my belief that the fish will soon take as darkness falls. This, to me at least, has become incontrovertible proof that color makes a difference.

So far, so good. Knowing that trout can see colors, we quite logically use a blend of yellow and tan furs or synthetic fibers to imitate a mayfly species that has a yellow body. Much of the time this works adequately, but not always. We are left with a very large question. While we know that colors can be seen, we still have little idea as to how they are perceived by trout.

I suspect the ringer in this whole business is the trout's demonstrated ability to see the ultraviolet portion of the spectrum *in addition to* those longer wavelengths and colors of light that are visible to humans. The trout's ultraviolet sensitivity has been known for some time in the scientific community and certainly isn't radical news, but it's never been adequately related to our many theories of artificial-fly dressing. Well, simple, you say. Just shine a black light or other ultraviolet source over your fly-tying materials to see what they look like with that addition.

Not so simple. Certain synthetic materials—especially those with optical brighteners added in their manufacture—will fluoresce under ultraviolet light. But what a human sees in this case is the visible-spectrum response of such materials to ultraviolet and not the ultraviolet light itself, the wavelengths of which are simply below our sensitivity levels. The apparent color of the objects we view is the sum of the colors or light wavelengths they reflect that are within our range of color sensitivity. The trout's perception of such sums will also include ultraviolet, which as with other wavelengths will be reflected to varying degrees by different materials, becoming part of the sum color visible to the fish. The fish's perceptual sum includes ultraviolet. Ours does not. We both see a color, but apparently we and the trout do not see the same color at the same time.

Thinking about this has given me a headache more than once, for reasons readily apparent to any trout fisherman of some experience. The whole idea throws many imitative concepts into a cocked hat because we can quite literally no longer see what we're doing, at least from the trout's viewpoint. But perhaps I can suggest a partial answer or at least a possible explanation as to why many trout flies seem to work in spite of themselves.

I was idly flipping through one of my youngest son's books the other day—a picture book of insects for young people, rich with color photographs—when I saw a picture of a gray butterfly. With a second look and troubling to read the caption, it turned out not to be a gray butterfly, but a vividly colored tropical species that had been photographed under ultraviolet light. Eureka! The discussion on this particular page centered on the behavioral function of bright colors in butterflies as linked to their apparent ability to perceive ultraviolet light. Can it be, I wondered, that ultraviolet serves to mute a trout's color perception rather than enabling it to differentiate among colors better than we can? Now there's a question—a good one—for which I don't have an answer. If true, which it may or may not be, it could be part of the reason why flies that are sometimes obviously off-color work very well. And further, why some flies that seem to have a color that's right on sometimes work very poorly.

Why a selectively feeding trout happens to accept or reject a particular fly is the Great Mystery of trout fishing. It has been studied casually by anglers for centuries and much less casually by laboratory scientists for decades. Such few and partial answers as have been developed, most of which have been explored previously in this book, have produced more questions than solutions. One large question about which many fishermen wonder is how a trout can be sometimes so fussy over the body color of a particular dry fly while apparently ignoring the large and blatantly obvious hook extending from the rear of the fly. The answer is both obvious and complex and is partly suggested in the writings of both G. E. M. Skues and Atherton: The trout—most of them, at least—don't *care* about the hook.

Now I didn't say that to be silly. Of course trout don't care about the hook. If they did, fly fishermen would never catch anything. This reminds me of my old friend Gardner Grant's explanation of why an Atlantic salmon rises to an artificial fly, which is always a puzzle because such sea-run salmon aren't feeding in the streams where they're being caught. Grant put the question to me one afternoon as we shared some water along the upper Beaverkill, and I knew even as he asked that I'd been had. Such things had happened before, however, and I knew the pain would be only temporary, so I responded.

"Okay, Gardner. I'll bite. Why does the salmon rise to the fly?"

"Because he likes it!" This struck me as being quite funny, especially because it's so obviously true. Generations of anglers have searched without complete success for a more definitive answer, and Grant, erudite angler that he is, has gone through more than his share of complex theories. So when I say the trout doesn't care about the hook, there must obviously be more to the question than just that.

I have likened a trout's selectivity as to a particular fly to a single jigsaw piece missing from the center of an otherwise completed and large puzzle. The trout looks for all those attributes of a fly—the single jigsaw piece—that make it fit. The trout does not look for those attributes that are extraneous, such as a hook, and have no relation to the fish's visual matching of a new item with the known—in the trout's experience—characteristics and behavior of a particular insect.

Likewise, when you are trying to complete a jigsaw puzzle, you'll hunt around for the piece that has the obvious configuration and color to match the blank space. Anything of any other shape on the table—a coffee cup, paper clip, matchbook—is rejected so quickly it's almost not even seen. Something that's close in shape and color to the missing piece may rate a quick second look—which is the same thing as a trout's false rise and rejection of a fly—but then is quickly passed over. By this analogy, perhaps, we may together have discovered why trout ignore the very hooks that to us seem so obvious.

Sooner or later most trout fishermen start to tie their own flies. I happen to have started at about age ten and am still at it. Once a few basic skills are mastered, the inventive angler—all anglers are inventive, regardless of their experience—will inevitably try making flies that might be better than the old standards for his or her particular water. Sometimes such efforts work; sometimes they don't. When such attempts are successful, the personal satisfaction is enormous: You've arrived. Just remember to learn and tie some standard patterns first, thereby gaining the knowledge and experience to better pursue your own inclinations.

This is not a fly-tying book *per se*, although I've included several color plates of both new and old flies together with their pattern descriptions as a matter of reference. I'll use the rest of this chapter to provide a series of close-up photos of my own fingers at the tying vise, giving very basic directions for tying a Gold-Ribbed Hare's Ear Nymph, which you can fish with some confidence in any of America's trout streams. This will provide those people who happen to have this book and no others with the ability to at least do something. But the following instructions are rudimentary, at best. Not long ago I wrote a simple, short, and inexpensive book aimed at raw beginners to the fly-tying game called *John Merwin's Fly-Tying Guide* that's still in print, so you may want to check it. Going further among the many books available on fly tying, my favorites are three by Eric Leiser, a longtime friend who is the only one among many fishing authors to have written three separate books on the three most important topics in fly tying: materials, tying techniques, and a catalog of popular fly patterns.

Fly-tying tools are both few and simple and are widely available from fly shops and mail-order catalogs. As usual, you get what you pay for, and better quality tools are substantially easier to use and last longer than tools of lesser quality and price. If you happen to buy one of the many fly-tying kits available, most of which include tools, get one of the more expensive ones, which invariably include tools of better quality.

Here, then, in captioned photographs is one method for tying this country's most popular nymph pattern.

I'm using a light wire Mustad 94840 hook for this pattern, because I don't want it to sink deeply when fished. Mustad models 3906B and 9671 are also commonly used; both are heavier wire.

Secure hook in vise and hold 6/0 black-nylon tying thread against hook as shown. Free end of thread is held between left thumb and index finger; fly-tying bobbin—a thread-winding device—is in right hand.

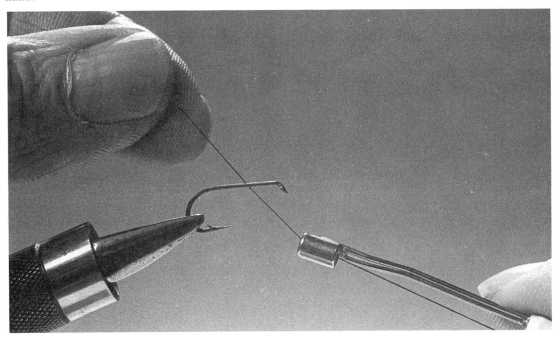

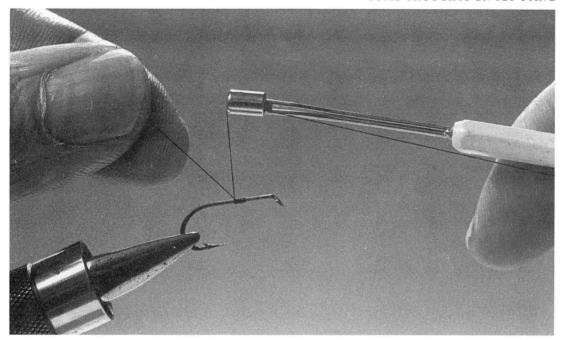

Wind thread clockwise (away from your body) on top of itself to secure thread to hook shank. After a few turns, trim excess free end.

Select four or five mottled woodduck flank fibers for tails, measuring their length against hook shank. I like tails that are slightly less than one shank length.

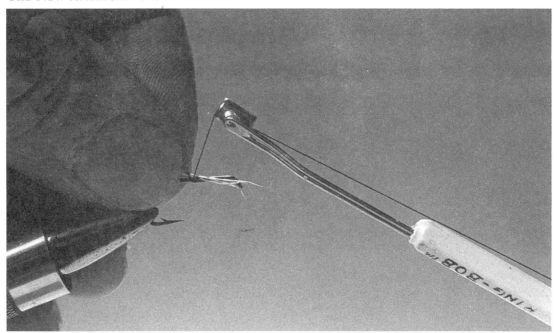

Holding fiber butts against near side of hook, overwrap with a few turns of thread. The winding action will roll the fibers from the near side to the top of the hook shank where they belong.

Holding fibers firmly with left hand, wind thread to rear of shank. At that point, make one turn of thread behind and under tail fibers to elevate and spread them. Then wind thread back to middle of shank, where fine, oval, gold-tinsel ribbing should be attached.

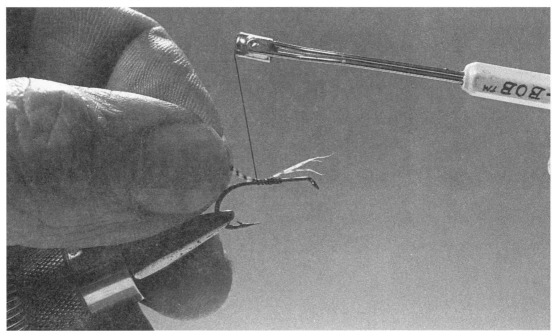

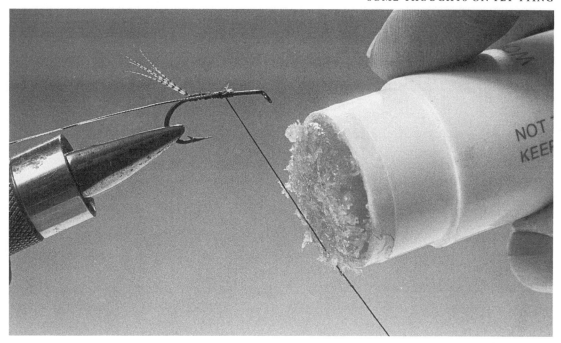

Coat thread with tacky dubbing wax, sold by fly shops for this purpose, by rubbing gently along thread. A little wax goes a long way; don't use huge gobs.

Pluck some soft fur from a hare's mask and hold loosely against waxed thread with right index finger.

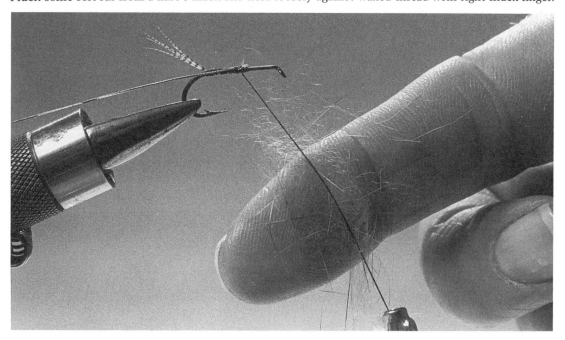

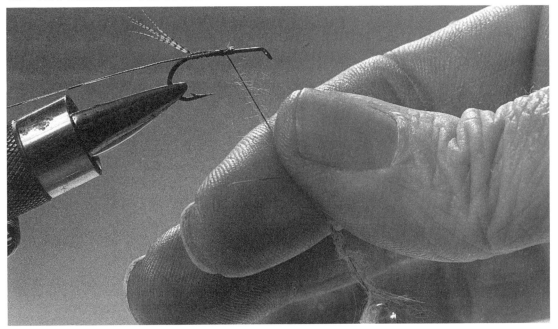

Use your thumb and index finger to roll fur onto thread, making a loose yarn. Do not roll your thumb and finger back and forth, but twist in one direction only.

Fur yarn or dubbing has been wound over rear two-thirds of hook shank, also binding the tinsel ribbing back to the rear of the hook. Note the neatly tapered body shape. A section of gray, mallard-wing quill will be used for the nymph's wingcase.

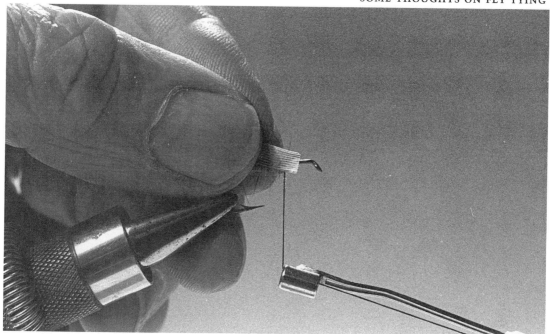

As with the tails, holding the duck-quill section at the side of the hook will cause it to roll to the top (where it belongs) when overwrapped with tying thread.

Wingcase has been tied in and dubbed body completed forward to just behind the hook eye. Remember to leave room for a small head; crowding the hook eye with tying materials at this point is a common error you should avoid.

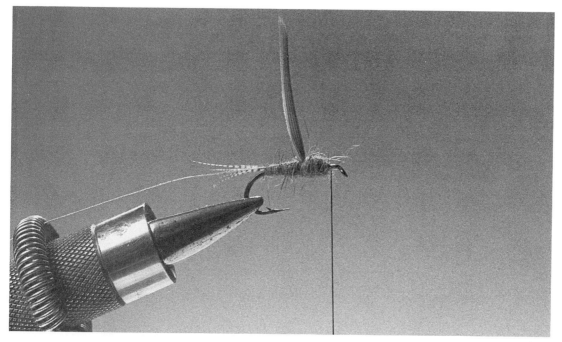

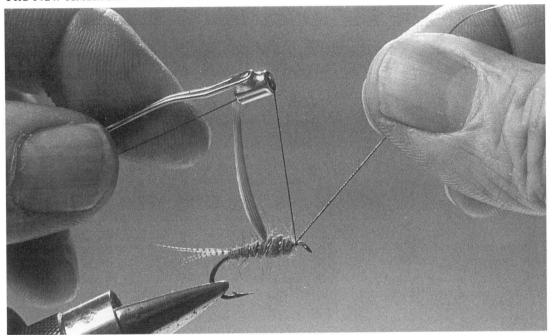

Gold ribbing has been brought forward. (I use three spiraled turns behind the wingcase and two in front.) Holding the ribbing in your right hand, use your left to make three turns of thread to fasten the ribbing; then trim the excess.

Use right hand to pull wingcase down and forward over body, securing with thread wraps. Trim excess.

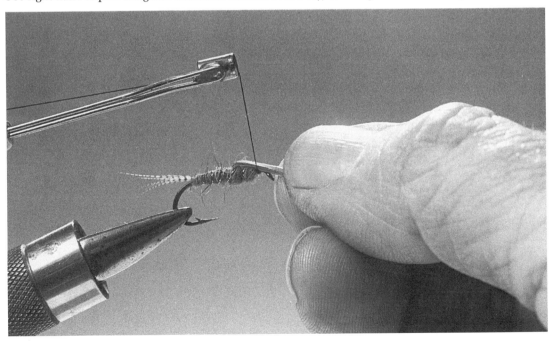

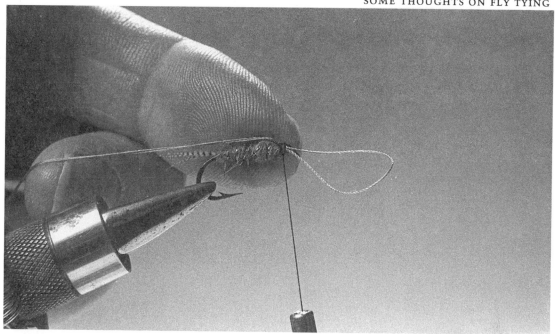

Now make a whip-finish knot, which is the most secure way to complete your fly. (In the picture, I've tied in a short loop of thread at the fly's head and am pushing my left index finger against the fly's head to keep everything in place for a moment.)

Keep your left index finger on fly's head while pulling a few inches of thread from the bobbin. Cut the thread and put its free end through the loop.

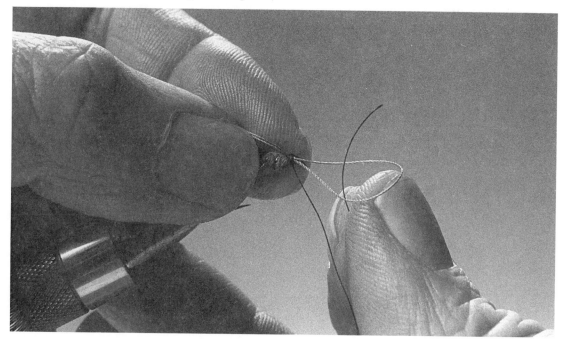

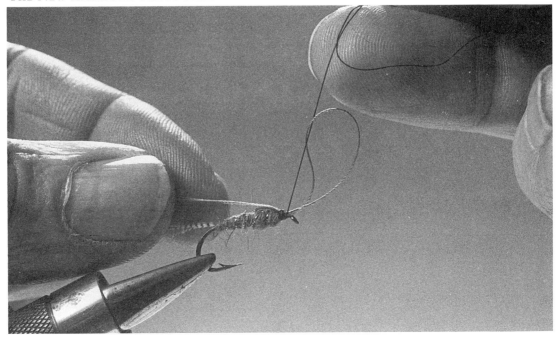

Now you can put tension on the free end of the tying thread with your right hand and remove your left index finger from the fly's head.

Pull on the thread loop with your left hand, which will pull the tying thread to the rear and under the thread wraps that held the loop in the first place. Trim excess.

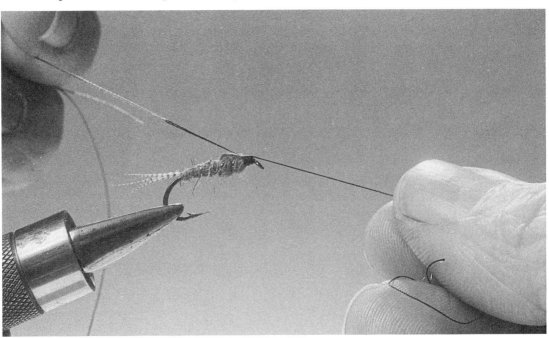

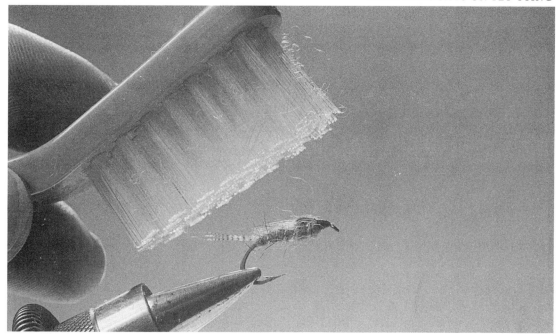

Brush the nymph's fur body gently with a toothbrush or other small brush. The backlighting in this photo shows how the fur roughened in brushing gives a soft, lifelike aura to the fly.

The finished nymph. The roughened fur simulates legs, so the hackle fibers used for some patterns aren't essential here.

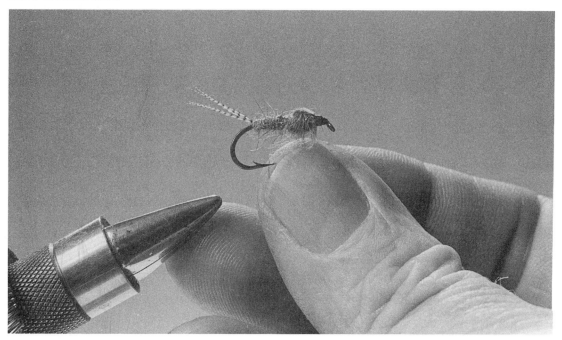

28
The New Compleat Angler

In searching for a particular time within the past few decades that could mark a transition or watershed in modern trout fishing, I've settled on the 1970s and more specifically on 1972. This was the year in which the late Joe Brooks' classic book *Trout Fishing* appeared. It was the last in a line of widely popular general works on fly-fishing for trout, a collection that also included A. J. McClane's 1953 *The Practical Fly Fisherman* and Ray Bergman's 1938 *Trout.* By the early 1970s we as trout fishermen were becoming specialists instead of generalists, with books such as Carl Richards and Doug Swisher's 1971 *Selective Trout* and Ernest Schwiebert's monumental 1973 *Nymphs* leading the way. Even though I'm fond of suggesting that much of what we regard as new in trout fishing is merely the rediscovery of ideas or techniques that have been kicking around for centuries, it's quite true that the changes in our sport over the past twenty years have been astounding and widespread. Many of those changes have been detailed throughout this book, and—having come near the end—it's time to both recapitulate and to touch on a few areas not yet explored.

The first American graphite fly rods were introduced in 1973 and quickly came to dominate our trout fishing. Most such rods were lighter and faster actioned than their earlier bamboo or fiberglass counterparts, and trout fishermen were soon casting farther and with less effort. Partly because of the new graphite rods and partly because of a market-share battle among manufacturers, fly-line types began to undergo an incredible diversification at about the same time, and their present variety is extraordinary. One fly-line company, for example, now manufactures more than four hundred different fly lines, which, based on my own survey of their manufacturing history, is almost a tenfold increase over twenty years.

Our flies have changed, too. The 1970s saw explosive growth for several large-scale wholesalers of trout flies, those manufacturers who had finally been able to produce millions of trout flies of excellent quality while at the same time utilizing the lower costs of foreign labor. Retail fly shops around the country now often get most of their trout flies from one or a handful of distributors, with the result that our fly patterns have become homogenized, often with the unfortunate loss of regional variations that had evolved over decades of use on particular streams.

Many trout fishermen began fishing with a greater variety of trout flies, as well. Although the concept of emerger patterns is an old one, fly patterns imitating emerging mayflies, caddis, and midges began to become widely popular during the 1970s and are even more so today. The number of popular nymph patterns has also grown much more during the same period than at any other time, and there are also many more dry flies that are imitative of specific insect species—

both in terms of fly pattern and in terms of design. During this same interval—1972 to the present—fly design has gradually replaced pattern as the primary concept involved in imitating a wide variety of insects and other trout foods. No-hackles, parachutes, comparaduns, and thorax-style dry flies are all *designs* that began their popularity in the 1970s, any one of which can be and is applied to a variety of specific fly patterns. Interestingly, and at the same time, there's been a general reduction in the number of different, widely sold streamer flies, with Zonker, Woolly Bugger, and Muddler designs generally replacing dozens of different streamer patterns that were popular during the 1950s and 1960s.

Our leaders are stronger, thanks to radical improvements in the chemistry of nylon and nylon alloys. The strength of fine-diameter leader material has effectively doubled over the past twenty years. During the early 1970s, for example, 5X (.006 inch) material was commonly rated at a 2.5-pound breaking strain, a figure that's since become almost 5 pounds for certain monofilaments of the same diameter. This trend is almost certain to continue with ongoing advances in nylon chemistry, and I look for 5X material testing at 8 or even more pounds within my lifetime, with corollary increases in the strengths of other diameters. All of this means that more fly fishermen are able to fish smaller flies with greater confidence on leaders as fine as 8X (.003 inch) that have a breaking strength of almost 2 pounds. Twenty years ago, such fishing was regarded as a stunt; now it's commonplace.

Neoprene waders are now widely used and available in a variety of brands, while in 1972 the first pairs were barely off the drawing board. Other fishing garments and accessory items have likewise improved, mostly in terms of their construction quality, and we've seen high-tech fabrics such as Gore-Tex, Ultrex, Supplex, and a host of others added to the fisherman's wardrobe. Cotton is no longer a staple, nor is wool.

Trout fishermen are also better read. Not necessarily because they read more, but because there's more for them to read. Of all the changes in trout fishing during the past twenty years, the growth of various fly-fishing media has probably been the most significant. In 1972 there was one nationally circulated, commercial magazine devoted to fly-fishing: *Fly Fisherman*, which was begun in St. Louis by Don Zahner in 1969 and which he soon moved to Vermont, where I became involved for a number of years as an editor. Twenty years later, there are four different such magazines, each published by a different company and all with respectable circulations although *Fly Fisherman* is still by far the largest.[1] These four magazines have a combined circulation of more than 250,000 copies per issue (not allowing for duplication of subscribers), which is almost ten times the readership of *Fly Fisherman* during the early 1970s.

This growth in periodicals has enabled a couple of things; specifically, a new immediacy in the marketing of fly-fishing products, and the rapid exchange of fishing information on a national scale. The numbers of fly-fishing products, manufacturers, and retailers have grown enormously in this interval, mostly because the growing fly-fishing media allowed almost instantaneous exposure of products and ideas to a national audience comprised exclusively of fly fishermen. Twenty years ago, you might only have discovered a new fly pattern or a special reel by traveling from northern California to fish in New York or vice versa, in which case the discovery would have been yours alone when you brought it home. Today this sort of knowledge becomes nationally known in a matter of weeks, and your discoveries are instantaneously shared with hundreds of thousands of other trout fisherman.

The growth of trout-fishing periodicals also coincided with the growth of the computer industry and its increased application in assorted marketing fields. This in turn has allowed numerous surveys, all concerned with defining a mythical "average" trout fisherman. That means you.

If you happen to be an American fisherman, you're one of 30,742,212 people who purchased a recreational fishing license in this country during 1991, according to figures compiled by the U.S. Fish and Wildlife Service.[2] Not all of your 30 million fellow anglers fly fish for trout, of course. I've been asked hundreds of times over the past twenty years just how many people within that 30-million group are bona fide, serious fly fishermen, and, of course, I don't know the answer. Nobody does. The question often comes up when fly-fishing industry folks are visiting among themselves, and the number I hear most often is a million, meaning dedicated fly fishermen—most of whom are trout fishing—as opposed to those who fly fish only occasionally or rarely.

To narrow your identity down still further, I'll turn to some marketing surveys that *Fly Fisherman* began conducting when I was there during the 1970s. The most recent survey I've seen happens to have been made in 1983 and covered the approximately 140,000 readers held by the magazine at that time. By that data, you are forty-five years old and male (only 1 percent of those surveyed were female). Your average annual income (in 1983) was a little more than $60,000; you have at least some college education; and your home (in 1983) has an (average) value of a little more than $135,000. You probably have been fly-fishing for more than six years with your two graphite rods and four fly reels, which you use between twenty and thirty times a season. This information is a

little outdated, but I doubt very much that it's changed substantially in the interim.

Don't be bothered if your personal profile doesn't happen to fit this demographic data; there's nothing wrong with you. The 1980s were a time when various national media discovered trout fishing and it became known as something of a yuppie sport. Part of this trend began when former President Jimmy Carter took up fly-fishing for trout while in office, embracing the sport with the typically overwhelming zeal of the adult convert; hook, line, and no sinker. In any case, fly-fishing made its way into the background of numerous television commercials and magazine ads, and numerous old-line trout fishermen complained bitterly for several years about inept yuppies in designer fly vests cluttering up their favorite pools.

This image was ephemeral and apparently at least partly wrong. Leon Chandler recently retired after fifty years with Cortland Line Company, a major maker of fly lines, and has had his finger on trout fishing's demographic pulse for as long as anyone. I asked Chandler not long ago about fly-fishing's growth during the 1980s and whether or not young stockbrokers and attorneys were overwhelming the sport. He smiled and told me that in spite of the latter's high visibility, as far as he could tell the greatest increase in numbers of fly fishermen was coming from the vast ranks of blue-collar workers who might fish just as intently, but more quietly. It's an assessment with which I agree.

There has been rapid growth in other angling media, as well, which has paralleled the growth of its periodicals. The numbers of trout-fishing books, already substantial before 1972, grew enormously in subsequent years, and, for the most part, became more and more specialized. Over the past twenty years there have been, for example, several titles devoted solely to caddisflies and several more that have covered only stoneflies, all from the trout-fisherman's perspective. There have been numerous recent books dealing only with nymph fishing, and an even greater number about fishing with dry flies. I won't bother with a litany of titles—many of the better ones are listed in the Bibliography—but the point is that the available trout-fishing knowledge in book form has become enormous and often highly technical. Usually such specialization has been a practical consideration, being the only way to really explore a particular topic in a book of manageable length. Any one of the chapters in this particular book, for example, could easily be expanded into a rather large book of its own, although in some cases that might be more than you need—or want—to know.

Finally, there are videotapes, which are also a recent development. These are terrific learning tools. You can now sit in your easy chair, for example, with your VCR remote control in one hand and your fly-rod butt in the other, while getting casting instruction from a professional. When you need to study a particular point, you just freeze the picture on the screen or rewind the tape to watch a sequence over again. Such tapes have found their best application in teaching techniques of fly casting and fly tying and are not about to replace books. There would be little point, for example, in presenting the tying of hundreds of fly patterns on videotape, most of which are tied using the same basic skills. Books, of course, are more portable than VCRs, are well endowed with an appealing tradition and sense of permanence, and most importantly can offer more information per unit cost than any one- or two-hour videotape could possibly achieve.

Catch-and-release fishing for trout and other gamefishes came of age during the 1970s and 1980s and is now widely practiced, either by special regulation, personal inclination, or both. Many trout fishermen regard the concept as a new one, but the oldest reference I've found in print appears in the well-known *Treatise on Fishing with An Angle*, which was written in England sometime before the year 1450:

> Also, you must not be too greedy in catching your said game[fish], as in taking too much at one time, a thing which can easily happen if you do in every point as this present treatise shows you.[3]

The reasoning, of course, is that catching and removing from the stream as many trout as possible reduces the numbers of trout available to be caught, thereby reducing your future sport. It's like cutting off your nose to spite your proverbial face.

The idea of releasing alive more fish than you kill found its foremost modern proponent in the late Lee Wulff, who in his 1938 *Handbook of Freshwater Fishing* said that "a gamefish is too valuable to be caught only once."[4] In subsequent years Wulff was a vocal, persistent, and often pugnacious advocate of that view, doing whatever he felt he had to do to get that message across to both anglers and to fisheries-management agencies. By the time he died in 1991 at age eighty-six, he had the distinct satisfaction of seeing catch-and-release angling become widespread, not only for trout but also for almost all other gamefish in both fresh and salt water.

Unfortunately, during the 1970s and 1980s a relatively small—but very vocal—proportion of fly fishermen took the position that killing *any* trout was bad, and further that catch-and-release or no-kill regulations were the panacea for every troubled trout stream nationwide. This position was often strongly taken and with no practical basis beyond a deeply felt moral conviction. The intolerant image this position projected to non-fly-fisherman eventually rubbed off on all those who fly fish for trout, regardless of how they felt as individuals. In the eyes of many, fly-fishing for trout became synonymous with a bunch of catch-and-release kooks who wanted to keep anyone and everyone from killing and eating trout. At the moment, we as trout fisherman are faced with something of a backlash in this regard, and not just from within the angling public. Not long ago, for example, I happened to overhear a fisheries biologist, employed by his state to inventory, monitor, and improve its fishing, say that he'd gone out of his way to avoid "having to deal with those college boys," meaning the fly-fishing crowd. I almost asked him where he got *his* degree. This obviously should not be taken as being representative of all fisheries professionals, but it does happen; it's ugly; and it's partly our fault.

The relative merits of catch-and-release regulations have been debated exhaustively among fisheries managers, anglers, and regulatory authorities since the early 1970s after the significant success of such regulations in certain areas of Yellowstone Park. The results are inconclusive. Anglers would like to believe there can be a general consensus, a formula that can be universally applied, but I don't think that's possible. For one thing, if a stream is so unproductive as to naturally produce very few trout bigger than a foot long, then a regulation designed to protect trout over 14 inches makes little

sense; there are too few to protect in the first place. If a stream is capable of producing larger trout but is fished so lightly that overall trout mortality caused by angling is insignificant, then a catch-and-release regulation may also be superfluous.

If, however, a stream or river is capable of supporting good numbers of trout, some of them large, and if it can be shown that angling pressure is dramatically reducing the numbers of medium- to large-size trout, then a catch-and-release regulation is probably appropriate. Many such situations nationwide are governed by reduced catch limits or special, so-called "slot" limits that require only fish within a certain size range to be released. In such cases, fisheries managers usually carry out sophisticated statistical analyses based on trout-population samples taken over a period of years to determine an allowable kill rate. At this point, my own view diverges from that of many managers, because in the situation I just described I believe the best kill rate is none. Not two trout, and not three trout under 12 inches long. None.

My own view as a fishermen is rather immediate. Trout that are killed today won't be available for me to catch tomorrow or next week. Professional managers tell me that their regulations conform to the carrying capacity of the stream, meaning the number of trout in a range of sizes that the stream can support over time. They tell me that some of these fish will be taken by natural predators or will die over the winter anyway, so they might as well be harvested during the fishing season. Fine, I answer. Then have no-kill all season except for the last week, when we can have a free-for-all. In that case, the trout I catch and release in April I can catch again in August, and perhaps even again in September, before somebody finally whacks it on the head or it dies of old age in February.

A biologist with no data is naked; the

more data one has, the more comfortable one becomes. It's the nature of the beast, and rightly so, I guess, because there has to be some basis for the decision-making process. Because I believe things are often better accomplished by consensus than by confrontation, I tend to temper my own feelings about catch-and-release when I occasionally get involved in such debates locally or regionally. Fortunately, such modern trends in the management of trout fisheries as habitat improvement—and management by watershed according to the needs of a specific stream and its users, rather than blanketing regulations by region—are making such debates increasingly productive.

I can't remember ever being so angry. I stormed through the door at the Angler's Nook on the lower Battenkill and started sputtering at George Schlotter, who as usual was hunkered over the fly-tying vise in a corner of his shop.

"Now what's the matter?" he asked, and then turned back to his ninety-first #12 Adams of the afternoon.

"George, you would not believe this . . . this . . . this guy! What he did to me!" I was really beside myself. This happens seldom, so George knew enough to pay attention.

"Yeah? So what happened?" George took off his glasses and set them on the bench, ready to listen.

"I was standing in the Spring Hole, where I'd been working over this pretty good brown trout along the bank for about half an hour. Finally the fish quit rising, so I just stood still to wait him out for a while; you know how I do.

"Anyway, this guy gets out of his car, walks up the bank, crosses the big riffle above the pool I was fishing, and then sits down and watches me for a few minutes. Then he gets up and starts wading down along edge right where the fish were rising. So I said to him, 'There's a fish there I'm trying to catch!' He quits walking and sits down again.

"Next thing you know, I look up, and the guy's wading across the river right toward me. He wades right up next to me—so help me—and asks me how the fishing is. So I tell him it was pretty good until he walked through the damn middle of it.

" 'Oh, that doesn't bother 'em,' he says. 'I've fished here for twenty-five years, and my buddies and I always catch lots of fish. See? There's one now!'

"Right then, George, a little brookie slapped over by the bushes. I ask him why doesn't he go away and leave me alone. The whole rest of the river is just about empty of fishermen, and he can go anywhere he wants. By now he sees I'm getting ticked off, and he looks at me like I'm a little odd.

"So he wades out of the pool behind me. I watched him cross the highway bridge down below. Then he started to walk back up the opposite bank. And then . . . then . . ." I lost the sentence in a sputter.

George nodded while I took a deep breath. "So then what happened?" he asked.

"So then!" I said. "Then the sonuvabitch waded back into the pool across from me and started casting about 40 feet away! George, I mean I went ballistic! After twenty-five years the guy should have some idea of manners! George, the rest of the river was empty! I called him names, George; I really did, and you know I don't do that. And then to hell with it. I left." With that I wrenched open the door of George's little refrigerator, grabbed a can of cold soda, and seriously considered biting off its top.

George stared out the window toward the trees, and we were both silent for several minutes. "You know," he finally said, "there's not much left of The Old Code anymore. It's too bad."

The Old Code. Although I usually react to its transgressors more mildly than in the instance I just described—usually by leaving quietly—it's become increasingly apparent to me in recent years that many fishermen, especially newer ones, just have no idea that any such thing exists. The term refers to those lessons in stream etiquette that were part of every trout-fishing book George and I read as kids, but which have been strangely absent from most such books published after the 1970s.

I think what's happened is that in certain very popular catch-and-release areas fly fishermen have become accustomed to fishing within 20 or 30 feet of one another. There are plenty of fish, so there's no need to move around. In such cases, a third angler wading in to fish between two others 50 feet apart has become accepted—or at least tolerated—practice. This happens often in the catch-and-release stretches of New York's Beaverkill, and I've also seen it happen on Idaho's Henrys Fork of the Snake River, especially during popular periods of major hatches.

Unfortunately, the Great Mistake comes when such fishermen assume this behavior to be an acceptable norm everywhere, which is not true. Nor should it be true. On many rivers where the trout are wilder in nature and of greater shyness, such trespassing on another angler's space ruins the fishing for all. Then too, many fishermen—myself included—like to fish in relative solitude and without chatting with anglers on either side about the merits of a particular rod or fly pattern. Don't assume—as many seem to— that just because you enjoy this sort of social angling that everyone else must enjoy it. I often drive an extra 10 miles to find an empty pool or riffle and am always disappointed if another angler later decides to join me. Even resentful if that fisherman has other, obvious choices, but marches in regardless. Here are a few suggestions.

When an angler working downstream meets another working upstream, the angler fishing upstream should be given the right of way. The person fishing down should get quietly out of the river well above the other fisherman and walk well around him or her before getting in the river once again and continuing to fish down. I've had some fishermen observe this nicely, only to walk splashing in the water behind me. Do whatever it is you have to do to avoid spoiling the other fellow's chances. Walk through poison ivy. Risk your waders in crossing a barbed-wire fence. I would.

If a pool or a riffle is occupied by one or more fishermen, stay out of it. There are almost always other options that can be found with a little exploring along the same river. You may also sometimes see a fisherman standing or sitting and watching a pool or run. Most probably the fishermen is intent on a particular fish or spot and is merely resting it. But not always, so it's sometimes worth your while to ask if he or she minds if you fish there. Just remember to honor the answer with a smile and a wave regardless of whether it's yes or no.

Finally, if there is absolutely no other spot nearby to fish and you feel compelled to enter a pool or riffle that's already occupied, ask first. This means before you step in the water.

"I'm sorry, but there's not much room around this evening. Do you mind if I walk in below (or above) you?" Such thoughtfulness is rare these days, and thus even more appreciated when it occurs.

I have trouble with endings, which is where we are at the moment. Certain editors— both within my own family and without— have told me that I sometimes end a piece of writing too abruptly. I think that comes from having said my piece and feeling that's that. I'm not fond of flourishes, and I'm terrible at cocktail parties. There will be some little blue-winged olives on the river tomorrow afternoon at about three o'clock. So I'm going fishing. And I hope you are, too.

So long.

1. They are *Fly Fishermen, Fly Rod & Reel* (which I started in 1979 after leaving *Fly Fisherman*), *The American Angler*, and *Flyfishing*. There's now also a trade publication for the fly-fishing industry, *Fly-Tackle Dealer*, which I started during 1980–81, and two well-known organizational publications—*Trout* and *The Fly Fisher*, which are published by Trout Unlimited and The Federation of Fly Fishers respectively.

2. Source: Sport Fishing Institute *Bulletin* No. 436, July 1992.

3. As cited in McDonald (1972).

4. Most commonly now repeated with the addition of the word "good," as "A good gamefish is too valuable to be caught only once." Wulff added that word later; it didn't appear in the original text. I think the earlier version is better because *any* gamefish is certain to be good in someone's view.

APPENDIX A
Metric Equivalents

I have followed the English system of measurement in this book in order to avoid having hundreds of double-number sets providing metric equivalents. The following conversions should allow anyone who wishes to calculate the metric equivalent of any English dimension of length, area, weight, or temperature cited in the text. Temperature is the most important and is given in greater detail.

Temperature

Degrees centigrade (C) can be calculated from degrees Fahrenheit (F.) by the formula $C = 0.56(F - 32)$. Degrees Fahrenheit can be calculated from degrees centigrade by $F = 1.8C + 32$. The following table will be helpful.

C°	F°	C°	F°
0	32.0	16	60.8
1	33.8	17	62.6
2	35.6	18	64.4
3	37.4	19	66.2
4	39.2	20	68.0
5	41.0	21	69.8
6	42.8	22	71.6
7	44.6	23	73.4
8	46.4	24	75.2
9	48.2	25	77.0
10	50.0	26	78.8
11	51.8	27	80.6
12	53.6	28	82.4
13	55.4	29	84.2
14	57.2	30	86.0
15	59.0		

Distance/Length

One meter = 39.370 inches
One inch = 2.540 centimeters
One foot = 0.305 meter
One yard = 0.914 meter
One centimeter = 0.394 inch
One meter = 1.094 yards

Because technical publications often give dimensions of fish and other organisms only in millimeters, the following chart may be helpful.

INCHES	MILLIMETERS	INCHES	MILLIMETERS
1	25	11	279
2	51	12	305
3	76	13	330
4	102	14	356
5	127	15	381
6	152	16	406
7	178	17	432
8	203	18	457
9	229	19	483
10	254	20	508

Area

One square mile = 2.59 square kilometers

Weight

One pound = 454 grams
One kilogram = 2.205 pounds

APPENDIX B
Knots

Following are brief, illustrated descriptions of the trout fisherman's basic knots. For a complete review of this topic with detailed directions, see *Practical Fishing Knots II*, by Lefty Kreh and Mark Sosin.

Arbor Knot

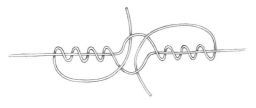

Used for attaching fly-line backing to reel spool.

Blood Knot

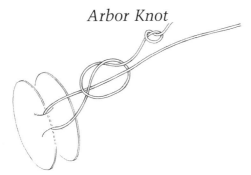

Used for joining strands of monofilament of similar diameter, as you would in making your own leaders. The difference in diameter of the two strands should not be greater than .002 inch for best results. The Double Surgeon's Knot that follows is easier to tie and more useful in joining fine-diameter strands of tippet material.

Double Surgeon's Knot

Most often used for joining strands of fine-diameter tippet, although entire leaders can be made with this knot. The two sections to be joined are overlapped by 3 or 4 inches. The free ends are then formed into a loop and passed through the loop twice before tightening. Lubricate with saliva and then tighten firmly and evenly. Uneven tightening weakens this knot dramatically.

Nail Knot

This knot is commonly used to join a leader butt to the end of a fly line. You'll need a small-diameter tube, such as a common cocktail straw. The drawings of this particular knot appear courtesy of Berkley and Company.

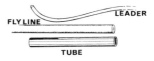

1. Overlap the tube, fly-line end, and leader butt.

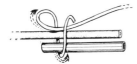

2. Start winding the rear of the leader butt clockwise over itself, the fly line, and the tube.

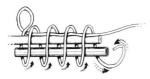

3. After making four complete wraps, insert the end of the leader butt in the tube as shown.

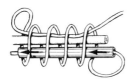

4. While holding the entire assembly between the thumb and index finger of one hand, feed the leader butt all the way through the tube.

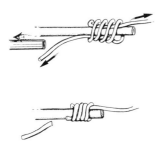

5. Keep holding the knot firmly with thumb and index finger while using your other hand to remove the tube and to then tighten the left and right sides of the leader. After the knot is partly tight, use pliers to get a firm grip on the leader's tag end (that which will be trimmed away) so the knot can be drawn even more tightly. Trim excess leader butt and fly-line tip. There are several other ways of tying this knot. What I've shown is the easiest for beginners, although not the fastest method. See Kreh and Sosin (1991).

Perfection Loop

This is an old knot that was used in making loops at the ends of gut leaders. It's still useful for adding a loop to the end of your nylon leader butt for making any sort of loop-to-loop connection. Having made a Perfection Loop, you can also tie the end of your fly line to it with a simple square knot. This latter is a down-and-dirty method that's sufficiently strong but awkward and bulky, so it's almost never shown in fishing books. It's also very fast and easy, and I've seen many of the pros use this method when they're in a real hurry, so don't be embarrassed when you use it as a last resort. Just remember to replace it later with a stronger, more compact Nail Knot.

1. Make a loop about an inch in diameter by passing the leader butt behind itself.

2. Make a second, slightly smaller loop in front of the first while again passing the leader butt behind itself as shown. The entire assembly can be held by pinching the intersection of the loops and leader butt with the thumb and index finger of one hand.

3. Pass the leader-butt end horizontally between the two loops. Then pass the front loop through the rear loop, pulling on the front loop as you do

so as to tighten the knot. Remember to lubricate the knot with saliva as it's drawn tight. Trim the excess leader butt.

Turle Knot

Over many years, I've come to use this knot and its variations for attaching almost all my trout flies—large and small—to leaders of various sizes. The only exceptions are very large flies made on ringed-eye hooks, in which case I use what's now called a Trilene Knot. See Kreh and Sosin (1991). The Turle Knot offers the advantage of a straight connection to hooks with up- or down-turned eyes, a feature lacking in alternative knots.

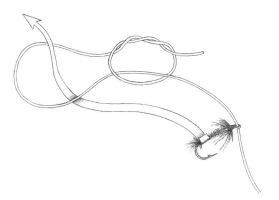

1. Thread leader tippet through hook eye with free end extending about a foot beyond the fly. Make a slipping loop by tying the tippet around itself with an overhand knot, which uses *two* turns as shown. Pass the fly through the loop and tighten the knot in one of two ways as shown in the following.

2. In the case of up- or down-eyed hooks, the knot is seated around the fly's head and behind the hook eye as shown. If the knot is well lubricated with saliva and drawn up gently, you'll avoid the curlicue effect created in the tippet by such commonly used knots as the Improved Clinch.

3. Many years ago I started using the same knot for flies tied on the miniature ringed-eye hooks, such as Mustad's 94859, that I often use in size 20 and smaller. In this case, however, the knot is seated in front of the ringed eye and not behind it. At first this was a happy accident that was basically a messed-up Turle Knot. It worked so well that I've used it for more than fifteen years with small flies because this knotting method helps me to avoid the aggravating curling effect that other knots produce when used with ultra-fine tippets and small hooks. I've recently seen this same knot called a "Swirl Knot" by Swisher and Richards in their book *Emergers*, which was the first description of this variation I'd seen in print. It's still a Turle Knot, however, so I've kept that name.

APPENDIX C
Fly Patterns

The fly patterns described match those shown in the accompanying color plates. Unless otherwise noted, all illustrated flies were tied by my friends Barry and Cathy Beck of Benton, Pennsylvania, to the specifications given here. The Becks are well known among experienced trout fishermen in this country as being among the best and most experienced American flytiers. Having examples of their work in these pages is a privilege for which I'm grateful.

In most cases, the selection of fly patterns for the color plates was made on the basis of variety in pattern design rather than on the importance of the patterns themselves. The plate and pattern descriptions of emergers, for example, show a variety of modern approaches to the same imitative problem. Any one of these approaches can be adapted to a variety of specific patterns.

Novice flytiers might use a book such as my own inexpensive *John Merwin's Fly-Tying Guide* for basic instruction. More advanced tiers will find all the methods needed for tying the flies mentioned in this book described in Eric Leiser's comprehensive *Book of Fly Patterns* and in various works by Ernest Schwiebert.

PLATE I
Classic Streamer Flies

Black Ghost

HOOK: Mustad 9575, sizes 2–10
THREAD: Black nylon, 6/0
TAIL: Yellow hackle fibers
BODY: Black floss (sometimes wool)
RIBBING: Flat silver tinsel
WING: Four white saddle hackles
HACKLE: Yellow hackle fibers as beard
CHEEK: Jungle cock (optional)

COMMENT: The fly in the accompanying photograph was tied by the late Herb Welch of Maine, who originated this pattern more than fifty years ago.

Colonel Bates

HOOK: Mustad 9575, sizes 2–10
THREAD: Black nylon, 6/0
TAIL: Red-dyed goose-quill fibers
BODY: Flat silver tinsel
WING: Two long yellow saddle hackles, topped by two slightly shorter white saddles
HACKLE: Brown hackle fibers as beard
CHEEK: Mallard flank feathers under jungle cock (optional)

COMMENT: The fly shown was originated and tied by the late Carrie Stevens and named after the late Joe Bates, who wrote extensively about streamer flies. The ring of red thread in the head was a Stevens' signature, which has often been copied by subsequent tiers.

Edson Tiger Dark

HOOK: Mustad 9575, sizes 2–10
THREAD: Yellow nylon, 6/0
TAG: Flat gold tinsel
TAIL: Yellow hackle fibers or golden-pheasant crest
BODY: Yellow chenille, tied slim
WING: Brown bucktail dyed yellow (sometimes red fox squirrel tail)
HACKLE: Red hackle fibers as beard
CHEEK: Circle of gold foil; jungle cock (optional) in later versions
HEAD: Yellow thread

COMMENT: The illustrated fly was tied by the late Bill Edson of Maine, who originated the pattern.

Edson Tiger Light

HOOK: Mustad 9575, sizes 2–10
THREAD: Yellow nylon, 6/0
TAG: Flat gold tinsel
TAIL: Barred woodduck flank fibers
BODY: Peacock herl, tied slim
WING: Dyed-yellow bucktail, with the tip of a dyed-red hackle feather tied flat on top at head and extending one-quarter shank length to the rear
CHEEK: Circle of gold foil; jungle cock (optional) in later versions
HEAD: Yellow thread
COMMENT: The fly illustrated was tied by the late Bill Edson. An important characteristic of the Edson bucktails is a wing that extends only a little past the hook bend, which reduces tangles when casting.

Gray Ghost

HOOK: Mustad 9575, sizes 2–10
THREAD: Black nylon, 6/0
TAIL: None
BODY: Orange floss, tied slim
RIBBING: Flat silver tinsel
WING: Below hook shank: four or five peacock-herl strands under white bucktail, as shown; above hook shank: golden-pheasant crest curving downward, under four long, slim medium-dun saddle hackles (A topping of peacock-herl strands is sometimes added but doesn't show in the original pattern illustrated.)
SHOULDER: Silver-pheasant body feathers
CHEEK: Jungle cock
COMMENT: The most famous streamer fly of all time. The fly illustrated was tied by its originator, the late Carrie Stevens of Upper Dam, Maine.

Supervisor

HOOK: Mustad 9575, sizes 2–10
THREAD: Black nylon, 6/0
TAIL: Red wool yarn, short
BODY: Flat silver tinsel
WING: White bucktail (sparse) under two pale-blue-dyed saddle hackles under two pale-green saddles tied slightly shorter, all topped by three or four strands of peacock herl
HACKLE: White hackle fibers as beard

CHEEK: Jungle cock
COMMENT: The illustrated fly was tied by the late Joe Bates, who wrote widely about streamer flies during his lifetime.

Warden's Worry

HOOK: Mustad 9575, sizes 2–10
THREAD: Black nylon, 6/0
TAIL: Red-dyed goose-quill section
BODY: Yellow/orange dubbing fur
RIBBING: Oval gold tinsel
WING: Brown bucktail
HACKLE: Yellow hackle fibers as beard
COMMENT: A simple and still-effective bucktail pattern. The illustrated fly was dressed by Gardner Percy.

Welch Rarebit

HOOK: Mustad 9575, sizes 2–10
THREAD: Black nylon, 6/0
TAIL: Red-dyed hackle fibers under peacock sword fibers
BODY: Flat silver tinsel
RIBBING: Oval silver tinsel
WING: Four white saddle hackles, topped with five or six peacock-herl strands
HACKLE: Blue saddle-hackle fibers under slightly shorter guinea-fowl fibers
CHEEK: Jungle cock
COMMENT: Another classic Maine pattern, shown as tied by the late Herb Welch, its originator.

PLATE II
Modern Streamer Flies

Badger Matuka

HOOK: Mustad 9575, sizes 2–10
THREAD: Brown nylon, 6/0
TAIL: None
BODY: Pale cream wool yarn or fur dubbing, with a small amount of red dubbing or wool behind head
RIBBING: Fine oval gold tinsel
WING: Four golden-badger hackles, tied Matuka style
HACKLE: Golden badger
COMMENT: Other color combinations are also ef-

fective; notably an olive body with olive-dyed grizzly hackle as a wing, also black and black.

Black-Nosed Dace

HOOK: Mustad 9575, sizes 2–10
THREAD: Black nylon, 6/0
TAIL: Short section of red wool yarn
BODY: Flat or embossed silver tinsel
WING: White bucktail under black-dyed bucktail under brown bucktail; equal parts of each
COMMENT: The late Art Flick's famous pattern, within which I've substituted bucktail for the polar-bear and black-bear hair Flick originally prescribed but which is now more difficult to obtain.

Black-Striped Minow

HOOK: Mustad 9575, sizes 2–10
THREAD: Brown nylon, size 6/0
TAIL: Section of white-tipped woodduck flank feather
BODY: Flat silver tinsel
WING: White bucktail under brown bucktail, both tied sparse; one golden-badger hackle on each side
HACKLE: Orange hackle fibers tied as beard
CHEEK: Jungle cock or equivalent
COMMENT: A longtime personal favorite, originally described in the 1950 book *Taking Larger Trout*, by the late Larry Koller.

Light Spruce

HOOK: Mustad 9575, sizes 2–10
THREAD: Black nylon, 6/0
TAIL: Six peacock sword fibers
BODY: Rear half: red floss; forward half: peacock herl
WING: Four golden- or silver-badger saddle hackles
HACKLE: Hackle to match wing wound as a collar
COMMENT: One of the oldest western U.S. streamer patterns. The equally popular Dark Spruce is essentially the same pattern but made with dark furnace hackle.

Mickey Finn

HOOK: Mustad 9575, sizes 2–10
THREAD: Black nylon, 6/0
TAIL: None

BODY: Flat silver tinsel
RIBBING: Oval silver tinsel
WING: Yellow-dyed bucktail under red-dyed bucktail under yellow-dyed bucktail
COMMENT: Popularized by the late John Alden Knight about fifty years ago. The lower bunches of yellow and red bucktail fibers should each account for about one quarter of the total wing, with the upper bunch of yellow making up the remaining half.

Mini-Muddler

HOOK: Mustad 3906B, sizes 4–14
COMMENT: Other than hook style and size, this is exactly the same pattern as the conventional Muddler described previously. The fly assumes a stouter profile when dressed as a reduced version on a wet-fly hook and is extraordinarily effective, probably because it is generally imitative of a variety of swimming nymphs and most especially those of various dragonfly genera.

Muddler Minnow

HOOK: Mustad 79580, sizes 2–10
THREAD: Brown nylon, 6/0
TAIL: Brown-mottled turkey quill
BODY: Flat gold tinsel
WING: Sparse gray-squirrel tail fibers under brown-mottled turkey quill
HACKLE/HEAD: Light-brown deerhair, spun and trimmed
COMMENT: Originated by Dan Gapen in the 1930s, this is probably the world's most popular modern trout fly. Commercial versions suffer greatly from overdressing; sparse ties work best.

Soft-Hackle Streamer

HOOK: Mustad 3906, sizes 2–8
THREAD: Nylon, color to contrast with wing, 6/0
TAIL: A few strands of Flashabou or Krystal Flash
BODY: None
WING: Blood marabou palmered as hackle over hook shank, finished with a turn or two of mallard flank at the head (Popular colors include black, yellow, olive-and-black, and white.)
COMMENT: Originated by Boston-area tier Jack Gartside, this pattern is easy to make, wonder-

fully effective, and its wing seldom tangles on the hook point. This is a new pattern rapidly growing in popularity.

Thunder Creek Silver Shiner

HOOK: Partridge Thunder Creek or other streamer hook with ringed (meaning straight) eye, sizes 1/0–10
THREAD: White nylon, 6/0
BODY: Flat or (preferably) embossed silver tinsel
WING: Brown bucktail on top, white bucktail on the bottom; tied Thunder Creek style
HEAD: Finished with clear epoxy glue; eye painted cream with black pupil
COMMENT: A very effective style seldom found in commercial catalogs, because it's relatively difficult to make. See Keith Fulsher's 1973 book *Tying and Fishing the Thunder Creek Series.*

Whitlock Sculpin

HOOK: Mustad 36890, sizes 3/0–10
THREAD: Brown nylon, 6/0
TAIL: None
BODY: Tan wool yarn or dubbing over wraps of lead wire; short section of red wool at head
RIBBING: Oval gold tinsel
WING: Four grizzly saddle hackles dyed brown and tied Matuka style
PECTORAL FINS: Prairie-chicken body feathers, one each side; or substitute other short, wide feathers that give a mottled appearance
HEAD: Deerhair spun and trimmed to shape, leaving a collar of untrimmed hair as hackle; colors should be mixed to give a dark, mottled effect. Trim head to broad wedge shape to match natural sculpins.
COMMENT: The best-known modern sculpin imitation as designed by Dave Whitlock of Arkansas. Colors are often varied. A good big-fish fly, so don't be bashful about trying ultralarge sizes.

Woolly Bugger

HOOK: Mustad 79580, sizes 2–12
THREAD: Black nylon, 6/0
TAIL: Black marabou, as long as hook shank
BODY: Dark-olive chenille, sized to match hook size

HACKLE: Black saddle hackle palmered forward over body
COMMENT: Sometimes made with a few flashy filaments such as Flashabou or Krystal Flash added to the tail. Other color combinations are also effective, notably all black, all white, or all yellow.

Wool Sculpin

HOOK: Mustad 9672 or 79580, sizes 1/0–8
THREAD: Brown Monocord, 3/0
TAIL: None
BODY: Olive wool yarn or dubbing; in weighted version, over lead-wire wraps
RIBBING: Gold wire
WING: Strip of light-olive rabbit fur, tied down Matuka style
PECTORAL FINS: Sage grouse feathers dyed olive, one each side
HEAD: Bunches of olive, gray, and brown wool spun and trimmed into sculpin-shaped head, with a few wool fibers left trailing as a hackle collar
COMMENT: Originated (as far as I can tell) by Craig Mathews of West Yellowstone, Montana, and described in the 1987 book *Fly Patterns of Yellowstone,* which he coauthored with John Juracek. Wool as a head absorbs more water and sinks more readily than deerhair. Try other color combinations; I like to fish an unweighted white or tan version near the surface.

Yellow Marabou Muddler

HOOK: Mustad 79580, sizes 2–10
THREAD: Gray nylon, 6/0
TAIL: Red hackle fibers
BODY: Flat gold tinsel
WING: Yellow marabou with a topping of six to eight strands peacock herl
HEAD: Natural tan deerhair spun and trimmed to shape, a few of the rearward hairs left untrimmed as a hackle collar
COMMENT: A favorite big-trout fly, especially in larger sizes. Also try white wing/silver body or black wing/silver body. Sometimes tied weighted with lead wire under tinsel.

Zonker

HOOK: Mustad 9575 (turned-down eye) or 9674 (ringed eye), sizes 2–10
THREAD: Black nylon, 6/0
TAIL: None
BODY: Silver tubing (braided Mylar or equivalent), pulled over a shaped underbody made of metallic adhesive tape; rear of body and wing attached above hook bend with a band of red tying thread
WING: Strip of natural brown rabbit fur
HACKLE: Grizzly, tied as a wet-fly collar
COMMENT: A widely used streamer style that became popular in the 1970s. Black, white, or yellow are other popular colors.

PLATE III
Traditional Wet Flies

Black Gnat

HOOK: Mustad 3906B, sizes 6–18
THREAD: Black nylon, 6/0
TAIL: None
BODY: Black fur dubbing
WING: Slate-gray duck-quill sections
HACKLE: Black hen hackle
COMMENT: Sometimes tied with a red hackle-fiber tail and a black chenille body.

Black Spider

HOOK: Mustad 3906B, sizes 14–20
THREAD: Black nylon, 6/0
BODY: Reddish-brown fur dubbing, tied slim
HACKLE: Starling or other dark-gray/black soft hackle, tied long
COMMENT: One of W. C. Stewart's nineteenth-century soft-hackled classics.

Blue-Winged Olive

HOOK: Mustad 3906B, sizes 12–18
THREAD: Black nylon, 6/0
TAIL: Medium-dun hackle fibers
BODY: Medium-olive fur dubbing
WING: Slate-gray duck-quill sections
HACKLE: Medium dun
COMMENT: Often effective in smaller sizes as an imitation of various *Baetis* mayfly spinners that lay their eggs underwater, subsequently drifting with the current.

Breadcrust

HOOK: Mustad 3906B, sizes 8–18
THREAD: Brown nylon, 6/0
TAIL: None
BODY: Orange dubbing, wool, or floss
RIBBING: Reddish-brown quill stem, preferably wide and with wraps closely spaced
HACKLE: Grizzly hen hackle
COMMENT: Too often tied with a narrow rib and thus showing too much orange.

Dun Spider

HOOK: Mustad 3906B, sizes 14–20
THREAD: Gray nylon, 6/0
BODY: Natural gray muskrat-fur dubbing, tied slim
HACKLE: Any soft, medium-dun hackle
COMMENT: The second of Stewart's classic wet flies.

Leadwing Coachman

HOOK: Mustad 3906B, sizes 6–18
THREAD: Black nylon, 6/0
TAG: Fine gold tinsel
TAIL: None
BODY: Peacock herl
WING: Slate-gray duck-quill sections
HACKLE: Medium-brown hen hackle
COMMENT: One of the most basic of all winged wet-fly patterns; especially effective in smaller sizes.

Light Cahill

HOOK: Mustad 3906B, sizes 6–18
THREAD: Yellow nylon, 6/0
TAIL: Mottled woodduck flank fibers
BODY: Cream fur dubbing
WING: Mottled woodduck flank fibers
HACKLE: Cream hen hackle

March Brown

HOOK: Mustad 3906B, sizes 6–18
THREAD: Brown nylon, 6/0
TAIL: Mottled woodduck flank fibers
BODY: Hare's mask dubbing
RIBBING: Yellow cotton thread
HACKLE: Brown-mottled grouse or hen
WING: Brown-mottled turkey-quill sections

Partridge and Green

HOOK: Mustad 3906B, sizes 12–18
THREAD: Black nylon, 6/0
TAIL: None
BODY: Medium-green floss
HACKLE: Mottled gray partridge, tied sparse
COMMENT: As with most other flies in this series, works best in smaller sizes.

Picket Pin

HOOK: Mustad 9672, sizes 6–16
THREAD: Black nylon, 6/0
TAIL: Brown hackle fibers
BODY: Peacock herl
RIBBING: Soft, brown hen hackle palmered forward over body
WING: Gray-squirrel tail fibers
HEAD: Peacock herl
COMMENT: A traditional tie that's a very effective imitation of many small, early-season dark stoneflies.

Red Spider

HOOK: Mustad 3906B, sizes 14–20
THREAD: Yellow nylon, 6/0
BODY: Yellow dubbing fur or floss, tied slim
HACKLE: Brown-mottled woodcock shoulder feather, or hen hackle of a similar color, tied long and sparse
COMMENT: The third of Stewart's spider series. Stewart did not specify a body in his patterns, only giving hackle type and thread color, so I've interpolated the patterns into modern terms from his nineteenth-century descriptions.

Royal Coachman

HOOK: Mustad 3906B, sizes 6–18
THREAD: Black nylon, 6/0
TAIL: Golden-pheasant tippet fibers
BODY: Rear one third: peacock herl; middle one third: red floss; forward one third: peacock herl
WING: White duck-quill sections
HACKLE: Soft, brown hen hackle
COMMENT: The also-effective Coachman wet fly omits the red floss, having a body of peacock herl only.

PLATE IV
Traditional Dry Flies

Adams

HOOK: Mustad 94840, sizes 8–20
THREAD: Black nylon, 6/0
TAIL: Brown and grizzly hackle fibers, mixed
BODY: Medium-gray muskrat dubbing fur
WING: Grizzly hen-hackle tips
HACKLE: Brown and grizzly, mixed
COMMENT: Without a doubt, our most popular dry fly. Hen-hackle tips are specified instead of grizzly rooster-hackle tips because the hen hackles offer a slightly broader and more effective wing profile.

Badger Spider

HOOK: Mustad 94840, sizes 12–20
THREAD: Black nylon, 6/0
TAIL: Silver-badger hackle fibers, twice normal length
BODY: Fine, flat gold tinsel
HACKLE: Silver badger, two sizes larger than normal for hook size
COMMENT: Most purveyors of dry-fly hackle have very limited supplies of silver badger, so these highly effective flies are absent from most catalogs. Most custom tiers can tie these for you, however, or will sell you a few hackles so you can make your own.

Cream Variant

HOOK: Mustad 94840, sizes 10–16
THREAD: Yellow nylon, 6/0

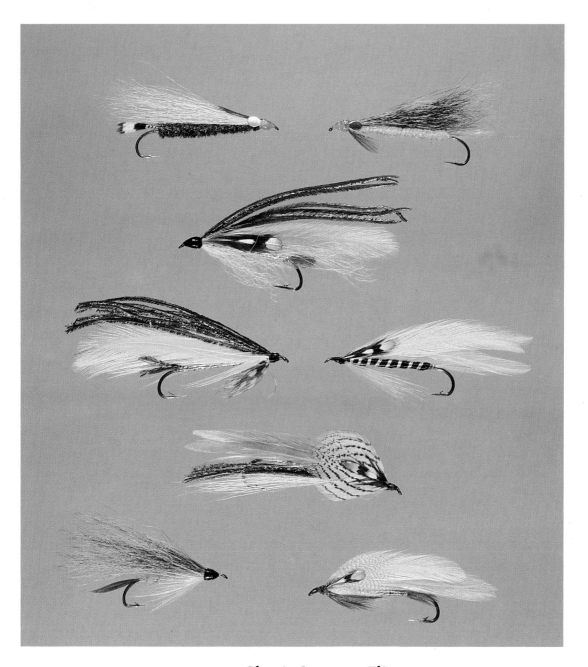

PLATE I: Classic Streamer Flies

(From the top, left to right) *Row 1:* Edson Tiger Light, Edson Tiger Dark. *Row 2:* Supervisor. *Row 3:* Welch Rarebit, Black Ghost. *Row 4:* Gray Ghost. *Row 5:* Warden's Worry, Colonel Bates.

PLATE II: Modern Streamer Flies

(From the top, left to right) *Row 1:* Muddler Minnow, Black-Striped Minnow, Mini-Muddler. *Row 2:* Yellow Marabou Muddler, Woolly Bugger, Thunder Creek Silver Shiner. *Row 3:* Wool Sculpin, Black-Nosed Dace, Mickey Finn. *Row 4:* Whitlock Sculpin, Light Spruce, Badger Matuka. *Row 5:* Soft-Hackle Streamer, Zonker. *Tied by George Schlotter*

PLATE III: Traditional Wet Flies

(From the top, left to right) *Row 1:* March Brown, Royal Coachman, Leadwing Coachman. *Row 2:* Blue-Winged Olive, Black Gnat. *Row 3:* Picket Pin. *Row 4:* Light Cahill, Partridge and Green, Breadcrust. *Row 5:* Black Spider, Dun Spider, Red Spider. *Tied by Barry and Cathy Beck*

PLATE IV: Traditional Dry Flies

(From the top, left to right) *Row 1:* Red Quill, Hendrickson, Quill Gordon. *Row 2:* Light Cahill, Adams, Gray Fox. *Row 3:* Cream Variant, Badger Spider, Dun Variant. *Row 4:* White Wulff, Royal Wulff, Gray Wulff. *Tied by Barry and Cathy Beck*

PLATE V: Modern Dry Flies

(From the top, left to right) *Row 1:* Comparadun Hendrickson, Adams Parachute, Blue-Winged Olive Thorax. *Row 2:* Cut-Wing March Brown, Rusty Spinner, Green Drake Paradrake. *Row 3:* Fluttering Stonefly, Gray/Yellow No-Hackle. *Row 4:* Henryville Special, Elkhair Caddis, Delta-Wing Caddis, Flush-Floating Caddis. *Tied by Barry and Cathy Beck*

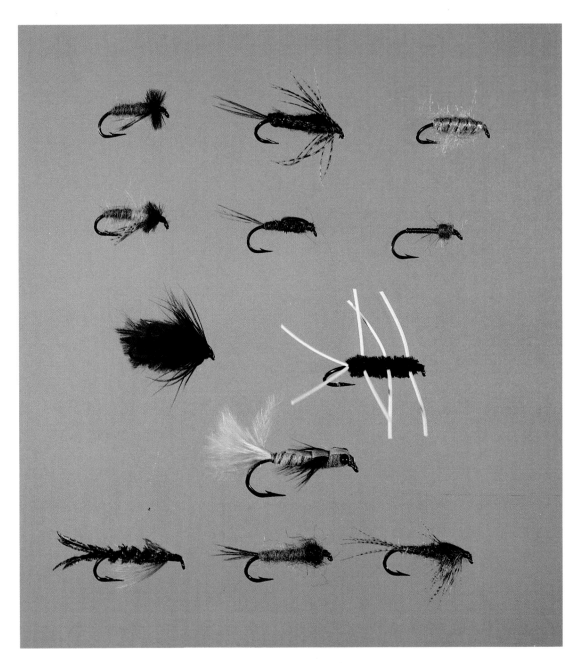

PLATE VI: Nymphs

(From the top, left to right) *Row 1:* Muskrat Nymph, Brown Drake Nymph, Scud. *Row 2:* Peeking Caddis Larva, Pheasant Tail Nymph, Brassie. *Row 3:* Assam Dragon, Girdle Bug. *Row 4:* Damselfly Nymph. *Row 5:* Zug Bug, Cranefly Larva, Hendrickson Nymph. *Tied by Barry and Cathy Beck*

PLATE VII: Emergers

(From the top, left to right) *Row 1:* Vermont Caddis, Hendrickson Turkey-Flat Emerger, Blue-Winged Olive Floating Nymph. *Row 2:* Sparkle Dun, Gray/Yellow No-Hackle Emerger, Sparkle Pupa. *Row 3:* Black Midge Pupa, Griffith's Gnat, Sparkle Pupa/Emergent. *Row 4:* Green Drake Emerger, Usual, Cream Halo Emerger. *Tied by Barry and Cathy Beck*

PLATE VIII: Terrestrials

(From the top, left to right) *Row 1:* Cinnamon Ant, Black Thread Ant, Black Fur Ant. *Row 2:* McMurray Ant, Jassid, Black Flying Ant. *Row 3:* Foam Beetle, Feather Beetle, Vernille Inchworm. *Row 4:* Jay/Dave's Hopper. *Row 5:* Letort Hopper, Letort Cricket. *Tied by Barry and Cathy Beck*

TAIL: Cream hackle fibers, twice normal length
BODY: Stripped quill from a large cream hackle feather
HACKLE: Cream, tied two sizes oversize
COMMENT: The traditional imitation of *Potomanthus* mayflies, but useful in various sizes when any cream-colored mayflies are on the water. Easily trimmed top and bottom at streamside to make a spent-wing pattern.

Dun Variant

HOOK: Mustad 94840, sizes 10–16
THREAD: Black nylon, 6/0
TAIL: Dark dun hackle fibers, twice normal length
BODY: Stripped quill from a large brown hackle feather
HACKLE: Dark dun, two sizes oversize
COMMENT: The late Art Flick's pattern. He especially favored the Gray Fox Variant, tied in similar style with a tail of golden-ginger hackle, and front hackle of dark ginger, golden ginger, and grizzly, mixed.

Gray Fox

HOOK: Mustad 94840, sizes 10–20
THREAD: Yellow nylon, 6/0
TAIL: Golden ginger hackle fibers
BODY: Beige dubbing fur (originally fox)
WING: Mottled mallard flank fibers
HACKLE: Golden ginger and grizzly, mixed
COMMENT: Like many standard dry patterns, this is useful in a wide range of sizes, although the natural mayfly that it was originally designed to imitate (*Stenonema ithaca*) occurs as a size 12 or 14.

Gray Wulff

HOOK: Mustad 94840, sizes 8–20
THREAD: Black nylon, 6/0
TAIL: Brown bucktail (or calftail) fibers
BODY: Gray wool yarn or muskrat dubbing
WING: Brown bucktail (or calftail)
HACKLE: Medium dun
COMMENT: The original Wulff dry, which Lee Wulff once told me he first tied during the winter of 1929–30 to imitate the large *Isonychia* mayfly duns found along upstate New York's Ausable River.

Hendrickson

HOOK: Mustad 94840, sizes 12–20
THREAD: Black nylon, 6/0
TAIL: Medium-dun hackle fibers
BODY: Fox belly fur dubbing, naturally urine stained to a pinkish cast; or any tannish-gray dubbing blend with a faint pink tint
WING: Mottled woodduck flank
HACKLE: Medium dun

Light Cahill

HOOK: Mustad 94840, sizes 8–20
THREAD: Cream nylon, 6/0
TAIL: Cream hackle fibers
BODY: Cream dubbing fur
WING: Mottled woodduck flank
HACKLE: Cream

Quill Gordon

HOOK: Mustad 94840, sizes 12–20
THREAD: Black nylon, 6/0
TAIL: Light-dun hackle fibers
BODY: Stripped peacock quill
WING: Mottled woodduck flank
HACKLE: Light dun

Red Quill

HOOK: Mustad 94840, sizes 8–20
THREAD: Black nylon, 6/0
TAIL: Medium-dun hackle fibers
BODY: Stripped quill from a brown (so-called red) hackle feather
WING: Brown-mottled woodduck flank
HACKLE: Medium dun
COMMENT: My favorite dry fly, as originated by Art Flick. Widely effective in smaller sizes.

Royal Wulff

HOOK: Mustad 94840, sizes 8–20
THREAD: Black nylon, 6/0
TAIL: White bucktail (or calftail) fibers; sometimes golden-pheasant tippet fibers instead
BODY: In thirds: peacock herl, red floss, peacock herl
WING: White bucktail (or calftail)
HACKLE: Medium brown

White Wulff

HOOK: Mustad 94840, sizes 8–20
THREAD: White nylon, 6/0
TAIL: White bucktail (or calftail) fibers
BODY: White wool yarn or dubbing
WING: White bucktail (or calftail)
HACKLE: Golden badger

PLATE V

Modern Dry Flies

Adams Parachute

HOOK: Mustad 94840, sizes 10–20
THREAD: Black nylon, 6/0
TAIL: Brown and grizzly hackle fibers, mixed
BODY: Gray muskrat dubbing fur
WING: Single upright clump of white calftail fibers
HACKLE: Brown and grizzly mixed, wound horizontally around base of wing
COMMENT: Parachute-style drys date back at least to the 1930s but have become popular only in recent years. Widely adaptable to a range of patterns, this style is especially valuable in smaller sizes because it doesn't obstruct the hook gap with tying materials. Many commercial versions are made with upright, white wings for better visibility; gray or any other subdued wing color is more effective.

Blue-Winged Olive Thorax

HOOK: Mustad 94840, sizes 12–24
THREAD: Black nylon, 6/0
TAIL: Dun hackle fibers, tied to splay horizontally
BODY: Medium-olive dubbing fur
WING: Single upright post of gray-dyed turkey-body feather (so-called turkey flat), set one-third shank length back from hook eye
HACKLE: Medium dun wound radially behind and in front of upright wing, leaving small fur-dubbing thorax exposed forward to hook eye (Hackle often trimmed at bottom to place fly flush on surface.)
COMMENT: Thorax-style drys were apparently originated by Vince Marinaro in the late 1940s, and by his design were a very high-floating fly. The style described here is one that evolved at Orvis Company, Manchester, Vermont. It's an effective style, but rather unlike Marinaro's original

version that shares the same name. Again, this style can be adapted to a variety of patterns.

Comparadun Hendrickson

HOOK: Mustad 94840, sizes 10–20
THREAD: Black nylon, 6/0
TAIL: Medium-dun hackle fibers, tied to splay horizontally
BODY: Tannish-gray fur dubbing
WING: Medium-gray deerhair set one-third shank length back from hook eye, tied upright and flaring over 180 degrees from one side of the hook to the other, simulating legs and wings at the same time
COMMENT: This outstandingly effective and simple dry-fly style was developed during the 1970s by Al Caucci and Bob Nastasi, patterned after the old Haystack series tied by Fran Betters along New York's Ausable years before. The same style is used in a wide variety of patterns.

Cut-Wing March Brown

HOOK: Mustad 94840, sizes 12–14
THREAD: Orange nylon, 6/0
TAIL: Three golden-pheasant tail fibers
BODY: Sandy-beige dubbing fur, tied extended
WING: Mottled tan/brown hen feathers, cut to shape
HACKLE: Brown and grizzly, mixed
COMMENT: Cut-wing dry flies, of which there are many versions and styles, seem to offer the ultimate in realism, but often more than is necessary to fool trout. This particular version is taken from Eric Leiser's excellent *Book of Fly Patterns*.

Delta-Wing Caddis

HOOK: Mustad 94840, sizes 8–20
THREAD: Black nylon, 6/0
TAIL: None
BODY: Medium-gray fur dubbing
WING: Two medium-dun hen-hackle tips, tied flat and extending outward from the hook shank at about 45 degrees on each side
HACKLE: Medium dun, trimmed away on bottom of fly
COMMENT: Larry Solomon's design, and very effective when trout are feeding on spent caddis-

flies. Vary colors and sizes to suit the needs of a particular time and place.

Elkhair Caddis

HOOK: Mustad 94840, sizes 10–20
THREAD: Brown nylon, 6/0
TAIL: None
BODY: Hare's mask dubbing fur
WING: Elkhair downwing style
HACKLE: Brown hackle palmered over body
HEAD: Trimmed elkhair butts
COMMENT: Al Troth's now-famous caddis dry, which has evolved into *the* adult-caddis imitation nationwide. Floats high and is easily twitched on the surface. Used in a variety of sizes and colors.

Flush-Floating Caddis

HOOK: Mustad 94840, sizes 10–20
THREAD: Black nylon, 6/0
TAIL: None
BODY: Medium-tan dubbing fur
WING: Three mottled-tan hen-hackle tips, tied downing in a tentlike configuration over the body (Hackle tips should first be thinly coated with vinyl cement for durability.)
HACKLE: Light dun, wound radially at head, then trimmed at bottom
COMMENT: Adapted from a style by Idaho's Rene Harrop that I published years ago in *Fly Rod & Reel* magazine, this answers the need for a flush-floating adult caddis imitation. Vary sizes and colors to suit. Excellent for fussy fish.

Fluttering Stonefly

HOOK: Mustad 94840, sizes 8–20
THREAD: Black nylon, 6/0
TAIL: None
BODY: Salmon (pale-orange/red) polypropylene yarn tied in at hook bend and extending one to two shank lengths to rear
WING: Gray elkhair, extending rearward same length as body
HACKLE: Brown, heavily palmered over hook shank
ANTENNAE: Two short sections of brown-dyed monofilament (optional)
COMMENT: Nevin Stephenson, a fly-fishing guide, first showed me this pattern along Montana's Big

Hole in the 1970s. The fly proved so effective that I quickly got him to describe it in a *Fly Fisherman* magazine article, after which the fly's popularity spread throughout the Rocky Mountain states. This large stonefly imitation is designed to be twitched on the surface. An excellent style in smaller sizes and other colors for stoneflies everywhere. Larger sizes and bigger fish may require a heavier-wire hook style.

Gray/Yellow No-Hackle

HOOK: Mustad 94840, sizes 16–24
THREAD: Yellow nylon, 6/0
TAIL: Pale-dun hackle fibers, tied to splay horizontally
BODY: Pale-yellow dubbing fur
WING: Pale-gray duck-quill sections
HACKLE: None
COMMENT: Exceptional style of mayfly imitation, popularized by Carl Richards and Doug Swisher in their 1971 *Selective Trout*. Especially good in smaller sizes and in a variety of colors to suit; e.g., Gray/Olive (Blue-Winged Olive).

Green Drake Paradrake

HOOK: Mustad 94840, sizes 10–12
THREAD: Yellow nylon, 6/0
TAIL: Moose body-hair fibers
BODY: Dyed-olive elkhair, tied extended
RIBBING: Yellow tying thread
WING: Dyed-gray elkhair or deerhair, single upright clump
HACKLE: Grizzly dyed yellowish olive
COMMENT: This specifically imitates the western Green Drake (*Ephemerella grandis*), but in other colors is an excellent imitative style for any of the larger mayfly species.

Henryville Special

HOOK: Mustad 94840, sizes 10–20
THREAD: Olive nylon, 6/0
TAIL: None
BODY: Olive floss
RIBBING: Grizzly hackle palmered over body
WING: A few fibers of mottled wodduck flank under paired mallard-quill sections tied downwing and flaring slightly outward
HACKLE: Brown

COMMENT: A venerable caddis imitation; vary colors to suit.

Rusty Spinner

HOOK: Mustad 94840, sizes 8–26
THREAD: Brown nylon, 6/0
TAIL: Pale-dun hackle fibers, tied long and splayed horizontally
BODY: Dark-reddish-rust fur dubbing
WING: Pale-gray polypropylene yarn fibers, tied sparse and spent
HACKLE: None
COMMENT: This has become *the* prototypical spent-mayfly or spinner imitation. Most often tied with white yarn wings, but pale gray is a much better choice, which I first suggested in my 1979 *Stillwater Trout* and have come to believe even more strongly over the years. Most commercial versions are overdressed, in which case I remove half or even more of the wing fibers streamside with scissors. Vary body color to suit; other important colors include olive, cream, white, black, gray, and bright green.

PLATE VI
Nymphs

Assam Dragon

HOOK: Mustad 9672, sizes 2–10
THREAD: Brown nylon, 6/0
TAIL: None
BODY: Wound with a narrow strip of natural brown seal fur still on the hide, combed to the rear while winding, usually over an underbody of lead wire
HACKLE: Brown-dyed grizzly, long fibered and soft
COMMENT: A general-purpose imitation of a dragonfly nymph developed by the late Charles Brooks. A little crude looking, but very effective.

Brassie

HOOK: Mustad 9671, sizes 12–20
THREAD: Black nylon, 6/0
TAIL: None
BODY: Close wraps of copper wire

HEAD: Gray muskrat fur dubbing
COMMENT: An especially good imitation of various midge larvae common to tailwater fisheries. Drifts deep on a light leader tippet.

Brown Drake Nymph

HOOK: Mustad 79580, sizes 10–12
THREAD: Brown nylon, 6/0
TAIL: Light-brown pheasant fibers
UNDERBODY: Brass wire tied at sides of hook shank, over which is wrapped light-brown floss; floss then mottled with dark-brown lacquer on top and sides and black underneath
OVERBODY: Clear, flat monofilament or clear Swannundaze
GILLS: Light-gray marabou bunched along sides of body and partly picked out after ribbing with fine gold wire
WINGCASE: Darkly brown-mottled feather tied down over thorax area
HACKLE: Brown-mottled pheasant fibers
COMMENT: Adapted from one of Ernie Schwiebert's patterns as described in his 1973 book *Nymphs*. Too complicated for wide commercial availability, this mayfly nymph imitation can be custom ordered, or you can make your own. It's an excellent style that I've used with great success in imitating the nymphs of larger burrowing mayfly species.

Cranefly Larva

HOOK: Mustad 79580, sizes 6–10
THREAD: Black nylon, 6/0
TAIL: Four to six pheasant-tail fiber tips, tied short
BODY: Dyed-olive-gold rabbit fur, dubbed roughly, usually over lead-wire wraps
THORAX: Brown rabbit, roughly dubbed
COMMENT: These larvae are common to almost all trout streams and are taken readily by trout. The overall effect in tying should be a cigar-shaped nymph with very short tails and a head slightly darker than the body.

Damselfly Nymph

HOOK: Mustad 9672, sizes 6–10
THREAD: Olive nylon, 6/0

TAIL: Three to four soft, pale-green ostrich herl tips or small tuft of marabou fibers

BODY: Pale-yellowish-green fur dubbing, tied slim

RIBBING: Fine gold wire

WINGPADS: Any small pale-olive-dyed feather, tied down at head and cut short

HACKLE: Pale-olive-dyed mottled partridge

EYES: Small nylon beads made by melting the ends of short sections of monofilament

COMMENT: Adapted from a Dave Whitlock pattern as described in Migel and Wright (1979). Damselfly nymphs are known to be important in trout ponds but are also common to the slower, weedy reaches of many trout streams.

Girdle Bug

HOOK: Mustad 9672, sizes 2–10

THREAD: Black nylon, 6/0

TAIL: Two strands black or gray rubber hackle

BODY: Black chenille

LEGS: Black or gray rubber hackle, one or two strands tied in horizontally at increments of one-third body length, creating three sets of legs along the entire body

ANTENNAE: Two strands of black or gray rubber hackle

COMMENT: A crude, ugly, and devastatingly effective fly for larger trout, often tied heavily weighted with lead wire, in which case it casts like a brick. According to some versions I was shown in the early 1970s, the addition of palmered hackle over the body turns the fly into a Yuk Bug.

Hendrickson Nymph

HOOK: Mustad 9671, sizes 12–18

THREAD: Olive nylon, 6/0

TAIL: A few (meaning three to five) mottled wood-duck flank fibers

BODY: Blended dubbing comprised of tan fox, dark beaver, and claret-dyed seal's fur, with a resultant general gray-brown shade

RIBBING: Fine gold wire

WINGCASE: Gray duck-quill section

HACKLE: Brown-mottled grouse (or hen)

COMMENT: Art Flick's version, and the prototypical modern mayfly nymph.

Muskrat Nymph

HOOK: Mustad 9671, sizes 10–20

THREAD: Black nylon, 6/0

TAIL: None

BODY: Gray muskrat dubbing fur

HACKLE: Guinea-hen hackle, tied beard style

HEAD: Black ostrich herl

COMMENT: An old pattern usually attributed to Oregon tier Polly Rosborough; simple, effective, and perhaps most resembling a variety of midge and cranefly larvae.

Peeking Caddis Larva

HOOK: Mustad 3906, sizes 10–14

THREAD: Black nylon, 6/0

TAIL: None

REAR BODY: Hare's mask dubbing

FORWARD BODY: Chartreuse or bright-green fur dubbing, about one-quarter total body length

HACKLE: Brown partridge, short and sparse

HEAD: Black fur dubbing

COMMENT: In concept, a caddis larva partly protruding from its case. Sometimes made with a cream forward portion and usually tied weighted. This particular version is adapted from Mathews and Juracek (1987).

Pheasant-Tail Nymph

HOOK: Mustad 3906B, sizes 14–22

THREAD: Fine copper wire

TAIL: Four tips of fibers from center tail feather of male ringnecked pheasant

BODY: Same four pheasant fibers wrapped around wire and then wrapped forward to form body, thickening at thorax area

WINGCASE: Butts of pheasant fibers, pulled forward over thorax and tied down at hook eye

HACKLE: None

COMMENT: Frank Sawyer's original pattern. Other modern versions use tying thread with a wire ribbing and sometimes add hackle or legs. Effective whenever a small, dark nymph is called for, which is often.

Scud

HOOK: Mustad 3906, sizes 12–16
THREAD: Gray nylon, 6/0
TAIL: None
RIBBING: Fine gold wire
BODY: Pale-olive seal's fur dubbing
CARAPACE: Clear strip cut from polyethylene bag, pulled over top of body and bound with ribbing
LEGS: Dubbing fibers picked out along underside of body
COMMENT: Freshwater shrimp ("scuds") and sowbugs are a primary food of trout in the stable, weedy flows of many tailwaters and spring creeks.

Zug Bug

HOOK: Mustad 9671, sizes 10–18
THREAD: Black nylon, 6/0
TAIL: Three peacock sword fibers, tied short
BODY: Peacock herl
RIBBING: Fine oval silver tinsel
WINGCASE: Mottled mallard flank, cut short, square, and tied down at head only
HACKLE: Soft, brown hen hackle

PLATE VII

Emergers

Black Midge Pupa

HOOK: Mustad 94840, sizes 14–24
THREAD: Black nylon, 6/0
TAIL: White hackle fibers, tied very short
BODY: Black dubbing fur, tied slim
THORAX: Gray, fluffy fibers from base of a hackle feather, dubbed loosely
SPIRACLES: White hackle fibers, tied short
COMMENT: Useful in a wide range of body colors, including red, olive, cream, tan, and brown.

Blue-Winged Olive Floating Nymph

HOOK: Mustad 94833, sizes 16–26
THREAD: Olive nylon, 6/0
TAIL: Two to four medium-dun hackle fibers
BODY: Medium-olive dubbing fur
EMERGING WINGS: Ball of medium-gray dubbing on top of thorax area

HACKLE: Four or five medium-dun hackle fibers, set horizontally at each side of thorax
COMMENT: Adaptable to a wide range of smaller mayfly species, especially those in the *Baetis* genus. Excellent directions for tying this style are found in Arbona (1989).

Cream Halo Emerger

HOOK: Mustad 94833, sizes 10–26
THREAD: Nylon, 6/0, color to match body
TAIL: Cream marabou fibers, short and sparse
BODY: Cream seal dubbing (or synthetic substitute)
HALO: Short slip of thin, translucent packing foam, tied horizontally
SPIKE: Fluorescent orange (or other color) deerhair tied short and forward over hook eye
COMMENT: A slight variation of a new Gary LaFontaine pattern, as described in his thought-provoking 1990 book *The Dry Fly*. Adaptable to a wide range of colors and dependent on the floatation and optical effects created by the foam "halo" that suspends the fly vertically at the surface. A neat trick.

Gray/Yellow No-Hackle Emerger

HOOK: Mustad 94833, sizes 10–26
THREAD: Yellow nylon, 6/0
TAIL: Tan hackle tip, reversed and tied in to resemble nymphal shuck
BODY: Pale-yellow dubbing fur
WINGS: Gray duck-quill sections, tied no-hackle style
COMMENT: Adaptable to a range of colors. Developed by Carl Richards and Doug Swisher. See Swisher and Richards (1992), plus their earlier works.

Green Drake Emerger

HOOK: Mustad 94831, sizes 10–12
THREAD: Olive nylon, 6/0
TAIL: Three or four moose body-hair fibers
BODY: Olive fur dubbing
RIBBING: Yellow thread or floss
HACKLE: Grizzly dyed yellow olive
COMMENT: While this pattern is specifically imitative of an emerging western Green Drake, this

simple, hackled style can be adapted well to any mayflies of the widespread *Ephemerella* genus. Alter materials, colors, and sizes to suit. See Arbona (1989) for specific tying instructions.

Griffith's Gnat

HOOK: Mustad 94840 or 94859, sizes 16–28
THREAD: Black nylon, 6/0
TAIL: None
BODY: Peacock herl
RIBBING: Undersize grizzly hackle palmered over body
COMMENT: Works especially well as an emerging midge imitation. The design concept here is as important as the specific pattern, so alter both body and hackle colors to suit your needs.

Hendrickson Turkey-Flat Emerger

HOOK: Mustad 94840, size 14
THREAD: Gray nylon, 6/0
TAIL: Medium-dun hackle fibers, tied splayed horizontally
BODY: Reddish-brown fur dubbing
WING: Medium-dun turkey-flat fibers about one-half body length
HACKLE: Medium-dun hackle fibers, sparse, as beard
COMMENT: Developed by veteran Pennsylvania tier Barry Beck, a simple emerger style readily adaptable to a wide range of mayfly species.

Sparkle Dun

HOOK: Mustad 94840 or 94859, sizes 14–24
THREAD: Nylon, 6/0, to match body color
TAIL: Any pale, translucent synthetic yarn, a few fibers tied to trail one-half to a full shank length past hook bend in imitation of shed nymphal shuck
BODY: Fur dubbing, color to match a particular mayfly hatch
WING: Dun-dyed deerhair, upright and splayed comparadun style
COMMENT: A simpler version of the older Swisher/Richards stillborn-dun concept, highly effective and popularized in the writings of Craig Mathews and John Juracek. See Mathews and Juracek (1987).

Sparkle Pupa

HOOK: Mustad 94840, sizes 12–16
THREAD: Pale-olive nylon, 6/0
TAIL: None
UNDERBODY: Green Antron yarn and cream dubbing fur, blended in equal proportions and dubbed over lead-wire wraps
OVERBODY: Pale-green Antron yarn pulled loosely over and around underbody in a distinct "bubble" shape
HACKLE: Mottled wodduck fibers, sparse and long, along sides of fly
HEAD: Dubbed brown marabou or fur
COMMENT: Adapted from Gary LaFontaine's series of caddis-pupa imitations as described in his wonderful 1981 book *Caddisflies*. This style has evolved into *the* pupal imitation nationwide. Vary colors and sizes to suit.

Sparkle Pupa/Emergent

HOOK: Mustad 94840, sizes 12–16
THREAD: Black nylon, 6/0
TAIL: None
UNDERBODY: Green Antron yarn and cream dubbing fur, blended in equal proportions and dubbed
OVERBODY: Pale-green Antron yarn fibers; a few left trailing as a pupal shuck, the balance pulled loosely over and around the underbody
WING: Tan-mottled deerhair tips, tied downwing and short
HEAD: Brown dubbing, fur, or marabou
COMMENT: Another LaFontaine pattern that's become a new standard for emerging caddis imitations. Vary colors and sizes to suit.

Vermont Caddis

HOOK: Mustad 94840, sizes 12–20
THREAD: Olive nylon, 6/0
TAIL: None
BODY: Dyed-olive hare's mask dubbing fur
HACKLE: Brown and grizzly, mixed, one size smaller than normal for hook size
COMMENT: A pattern that evolved along the lower Battenkill in upstate New York during the 1970s. Fished without any added floatant, the fly hangs vertically in the surface tension like an emerging caddis. Also used in other body colors, most often tan.

Usual

HOOK: Mustad 94840, sizes 12–18
THREAD: Cream nylon, 6/0
TAIL: Guard hairs from the footpad area of a snow-shoe-rabbit's foot
BODY: Pale underfur from rabbit's foot, dubbed roughly
WING: Snowshoe-rabbit's-foot guard hairs, tied upright and splayed comparadun style
COMMENT: Originated by Fran Betters along upstate New York's Ausable, this awkward-looking fly is an exceptional mayfly-emerger pattern that's since been adapted by many tiers in a range of sizes and body colors.

PLATE VIII
Terrestrials

Black Flying Ant

HOOK: Mustad 94840 or 94859, sizes 10–26
THREAD: Black nylon, 6/0
BODY: Two ovoid balls of black dubbing fur
WING: Two pale-dun hen-hackle tips, both tied to splay horizontally from the same side of the fly near the head
HACKLE: Black, tied sparse at waist and trimmed away at bottom of fly
COMMENT: Placing both wings on one side of the fly gives the appearance of a natural lying on its side, which is how flying ants most commonly drift on the surface. The wings of these insects are attached near the head and not at the waist, which is a fault found in most commercial imitations.

Black Fur Ant

HOOK: Mustad 94840 or 94859, sizes 10–28
THREAD: Black nylon, 6/0
BODY: Two distinct lumps of black dubbing fur at either end of hook shank to give hourglass profile
HACKLE: Black, tied sparse between fur lumps

Black Thread Ant

HOOK: Mustad 94840 or 94859, sizes 10–20
THREAD: Black nylon, 6/0
BODY: Two distinct tapered bulges built of thread wraps at either end of hook shank, lacquered to a high gloss
HACKLE: Black, tied sparse between body lumps
COMMENT: The difference between dubbed and lacquered bodies on ant imitations is dramatic, with the latter being more effective in larger sizes.

Cinnamon Ant

HOOK: Mustad 94840 or 94859, sizes 10–28
THREAD: Brown nylon, 6/0
BODY: Cinnamon dubbing fur
HACKLE: Dark ginger, tied sparse

Feather Beetle

HOOK: Mustad 94840 or 94859, sizes 16–26
THREAD: Black nylon, 6/0
TAIL: None
HACKLE: Black or dark dun, palmered over body and trimmed top and bottom
BODY: Peacock herl, any dark dubbing fur, or dark ostrich herl
WING: Black or dark dun body feather from any of a variety of birds, lacquered and trimmed to ovoid shape, tied flat
COMMENT: Most effective in smaller sizes.

Foam Beetle

HOOK: Mustad 94840, sizes 12–18
THREAD: Black nylon, 6/0
TAIL: None
BODY: Black, thin synthetic foam over-wrapped with tying thread
SHELLBACK: Black foam pulled forward over body
LEGS: A few fibers of dyed-black elkhair or deerhair, tied horizontally near head
HEAD: Trimmed end of foam strip
COMMENT: Simple and unsinkable. Adapted from Mathews and Juracek (1987).

Jassid

HOOK: Mustad 94840 or 94859, sizes 16–26
THREAD: Black nylon, 6/0
BODY/HACKLE: Black, palmered over hook shank and trimmed top and bottom
WING: One jungle-cock nail feather, tied flat
COMMENT: The late Vince Marinaro's superb pattern, often tied now with small lacquered feathers other than scarce jungle cock. The original is still the best.

Jay/Dave's Hopper

HOOK: Mustad 9671, sizes 8–12
THREAD: Brown nylon, 6/0
TAIL: Dyed-red calftail fibers, short
BODY: Yellow yarn, with a short loop of yarn extending past hook bend
RIBBING: Brown hackle, palmered over body, then trimmed short
UNDERWING: Yellow-dyed calftail or deerhair fibers
OVERWING: Section of brown-mottled turkey quill, lacquered and cupped over sides
LEGS: Sections of ringneck-pheasant tail fibers, knotted for legs
HEAD/COLLAR: Deerhair, spun and trimmed Muddler style
COMMENT: The currently popular grasshopper imitation among many commercial tiers. Developed by Dave Whitlock and modified by Jay Buchner, hence the name.

Letort Cricket

HOOK: Mustad 9671, sizes 12–16
THREAD: Black nylon, 6/0
BODY: Black fur dubbing
WING: Black quill section (e.g., black-dyed goose)
COLLAR/HEAD: Dyed-black deerhair, spun and trimmed as per Letort Hopper

Letort Hopper

HOOK: Mustad 9671, sizes 8–16
THREAD: Tan nylon, 6/0
TAIL: None
BODY: Yellow dubbing fur
WING: Brown-mottled turkey-quill section
HEAD/COLLAR: Tan or gray deerhair, spun and trimmed Muddler style, with flaring fibers cut away from the fly's underside
COMMENT: A great combination of simplicity and effectiveness, especially in smaller sizes.

McMurray Ant

HOOK: Mustad 94840, sizes 12–22
THREAD: Black nylon, 6/0
BODY: Two small pods of black-lacquered balsa wood anchored at either end of a short monofilament section
HACKLE: Black, tied sparse at waist
COMMENT: Unsinkable and often—but not always—effective.

Vernille Inchworm

HOOK: Mustad 9671, sizes 12–16
THREAD: Yellow or chartreuse nylon, 6/0
BODY: Fluorescent-green or chartreuse chenille (sometimes marketed as "Vernille")
COMMENT: A sinking inchworm pattern from Barry Beck. Easy and effective.

Bibliography

Abercrombie, M., M. Hickman, M. Johnson, and M. Thain, eds. 1990. *The new Penguin dictionary of biology*. New York: Penguin.

Adron, J., P. Grant, and C. Cowey. 1973. A system for the quantitative study of the learning capacity of rainbow trout and its application to the study of food preferences and behaviour. *J. Fish. Biol.* 5:625–36.

Adron, J., and A. Mackie. 1978. Studies on the chemical nature of feeding stimulants for rainbow trout, *Salmo gairdneri* Richardson. *J. Fish. Biol.* 12:303–10.

Alexander, G. R. 1979. Predators of fish in coldwater streams. In *Predator-prey systems in fisheries management*. *See* Stroud 1979.

Ali, M., ed. 1975a. *Vision in fishes: New approaches in research*. New York: Plenum.

———. 1975b. Retinomotor responses. In *Vision in fishes*. *See* Ali 1975a.

Ali, M., and W. Muntz. 1975. Electroretinography as a tool for studying fish vision. In *Vision in fishes*. *See* Ali 1975a.

Ali, M., and H. Wagner. 1975. Distribution and development of retinomotor responses. In *Vision in fishes*. *See* Ali 1975a.

Allan, J. 1981. Determinants of diet of brook trout (*Salvelinus fontinalis*) in a mountain stream. *Can. J. Fish. Aquat. Sci.* 38:184–92.

———. 1982. The effects of reduction in trout density on the invertebrate community of a mountain stream. *Ecology* 63:1444–55.

———. 1984. Hypothesis testing in ecological studies of aquatic insects. In *The ecology of aquatic insects*. *See* Resh 1984a.

Allard, D. 1978. *Spencer Fullerton Baird and the U.S. Fish Commission*. New York: Arno.

Allen, D., and F. Munz. 1983. Visual pigment mixtures and scotopic spectral sensitivity in rainbow trout. In *Predators and prey in fishes*. *See* Noakes 1983.

Allen, K. 1951. *The Horokiwi Stream: A study of a trout population*. Fisheries Bulletin no. 10. Wellington, New Zealand: New Zealand Marine Dept.

Alstad, D. 1982. Current speed and filtration rate link caddisfly phylogeny and distributional patterns on a stream gradient. *Science* 216:533–34.

Anderson, N., and R. Wisseman. 1987. Recovery of the Trichoptera fauna near Mt. St. Helens five years after the 1980 eruption. In *Proceedings of the fifth international symposium on Trichoptera*. *See* Bournaud 1987.

Arbona, F. 1989. *Mayflies, the angler, and the trout*. New York: Lyons and Burford.

Armour, C., D. Duff, and W. Elmore. 1991. The effects of livestock grazing on riparian and stream ecosystems. *Fisheries* 16(1):7–11.

Atema, J. 1980. Chemical senses, chemical signals, and feeding behavior in fishes. In *Fish behavior and its use in the capture and culture of fishes*. *See* Bardach 1980.

Atema, J., R. Fay, A. Popper, and W. Tavolga, eds. 1988. *Sensory biology of aquatic animals*. New York: Springer-Verlag.

Atherton, J. 1951. *The fly and the fish*. New York: Macmillan.

Avery, E. 1983. *Population dynamics of wild trout and associated sport fisheries in two northern Wisconsin streams*. Technical Bulletin no. 141. Madison: Wisconsin Department of Natural Resources.

Bachman, R. 1983. Brown trout don't always do what they're supposed to. *Trout* 24(2):20–25.

———. 1984. Foraging behavior of free-ranging wild and hatchery brown trout in a stream. *Trans. Am. Fish. Soc.* 113:1–32.

Bainbridge, R., G. Evans, and O. Rackham, eds. 1966. *Light as an ecological factor*. New York: John Wiley & Sons.

Balon, E., ed. 1980. *The charrs.* The Hague: D. W. Junk.

Baltz, D., and P. Moyle. 1984. Segregation by species and size class of rainbow trout and Sacramento sucker in three California streams. *Environmental biology of fishes.* 10:101–10.

Baltz, D., et al. 1987. Influence of temperature on microhabitat choice of fishes in a California stream. *Trans. Am. Fish. Soc.* 116:12–20.

Baltz, D., B. Vondracek, L. Brown, and P. Moyle. 1991. Seasonal changes in microhabitat selection by rainbow trout in a small stream. *Trans. Am. Fish. Soc.* 120:166–76.

Bardach, J., and J. Todd. 1970. Chemical communication in fish. In *Advances in chemoreception.* Vol. 1. *See* Johnson, J., 1970.

Bardach, J., J. Magnuson, R. May, and J. Reinhart, eds. 1980. *Fish behavior and its use in the capture and culture of fishes.* Manila: International Center for Living Aquatic Resources Management.

Barton, D., and S. Smith. 1984. Insects of extremely small and extremely large aquatic habitats. In *The ecology of aquatic insects. See* Resh 1984a.

Behnke, R. 1970. The application of cytogenetic and biochemical systematics to phylogenetic problems in the family Salmonidae. *Trans. Amer. Fish. Soc.* 99(1):237–48.

———. 1972. The systematics of salmonid fishes of recently glaciated lakes. *J. Fish. Res. Bd. Canada* 29:639–71.

———. 1983a. The McCloud River rainbow trout. *Trout* (Spring):35–38.

———. 1983b. Westslope cutthroat trout. *Trout* (Autumn):35–39.

———. 1986a. Redband trout. *Trout* (Autumn):34–39.

———. 1986b. Brown trout. *Trout* (Winter):42–47.

———. 1987a. How a trout sees. *Trout* (Summer:32–39.

———. 1987b. Brook trout. *Trout* (Summer):42–46.

———. 1988. Phylogeny and classification of cutthroat trout. In *Status and management of interior stocks of cutthroat trout. See* Gresswell 1988a.

———. 1990a. The family tree: Origins of trout and salmon. *Trout* (Spring):37–40.

———. 1990b. Livingston Stone, J. B. Campbell, and the origins of hatchery rainbow trout. *The American Fly Fisher* 16(3):20–22.

———. 1991. From hatcheries to habitat? Look again. *Trout* (Autumn):55–58.

Benke, A. 1984. Secondary production of aquatic insects. In *The ecology of aquatic insects. See* Resh 1984a.

Bergin, J. 1990. An evaluation of five strains of brown trout. In *Brown trout workshop. See* Borawa 1990a.

Bergman, R. 1938. *Trout.* New York: Penn.

Billingsley, C., and B. Haase. 1990. Effects of catch-and-release regulations on an urban wild brown trout fishery. In *Brown trout workshop. See* Borawa 1990a.

Binns, N., and F. Eiserman. 1979. Quantification of fluvial trout habitat in Wyoming. *Trans. Am. Fish. Soc.* 108:215–28.

Binns, N., and M. Oberholtzer. 1990. Restoring sediment-damaged trout habitat in Hog Park Creek, Wyoming. In *Brown trout workshop. See* Borawa 1990a.

Blaxter, J. 1975. Fish vision and applied research. In *Vision in fishes. See* Ali 1975a.

———. 1980. Vision and the feeding of fishes. In *Fish behavior and its use in the capture and culture of fishes. See* Bardach 1980.

———. 1988. Sensory performance, behavior, and ecology of fish. In *Sensory biology of aquatic animals. See* Atema 1988.

Bleckmann, H. 1988. Prey identification and prey localization in surface-feeding fish and fishing spiders. In *Sensory biology of aquatic animals. See* Atema 1988.

Borawa, J., ed. 1990a. *Brown trout workshop: Biology and management.* Asheville, N.C.: Southern Division, American Fisheries Society. (Mailing address: Brown Trout Workshop, Rte. 1, Box 1638, Clarkesville, GA 30523)

———. 1990b. Field evaluation of domestic versus half-wild brown trout fingerling stockings. In *Brown trout workshop. See* Borawa 1990a.

Borger, G. 1979. *Nymphing.* Harrisburg, Pa.: Stackpole.

Bournaud, M., and H. Tachet, eds. 1987. *Proceedings of the fifth international symposium on Trichoptera.* The Hague: D. W. Junk.

Boyle, R., and R. A. Boyle. 1983. *Acid rain.* New York: Nick Lyons Books.

Brittain, J. 1982. Biology of mayflies. *Ann. Rev. Entomol.* 27:119–48.

Brooks, C. 1976. *Nymph fishing for larger trout.* New York: Nick Lyons Books.

Brooks, J. 1972. *Trout fishing.* New York: Outdoor Life.

Brown, A., R. Oldham, and A. Warlow. 1980. Chironomid larvae and pupae in the diet of brown trout (*S. trutta*) and rainbow trout (*S. gairdneri*) in Rutland Water, Leicestershire. In *Chironomidae. See* Murray ed., 1980.

Brown, J. 1991. *A treasury of reels.* Manchester, Vt.: American Museum of Fly Fishing.

Bryan, J. 1973. Feeding history, parental stock, and food selection in rainbow trout (*Salmo gairdneri*). *Aquaculture* 11:159–72.

Bryan, J., and P. Larkin. 1972. Food specialization by individual trout. *J. Fish. Res. Bd. Canada* 29:1615–24.

Burger, C., and L. Gwartney. 1986. A radio tagging study of Naknek Drainage rainbow trout. Anchorage: U.S. National Park Service.

Burks, B. 1953. *The mayflies, or Ephemeroptera, of Illinois.* Illinois Natural History Survey Bulletin 26.

Butler, M. 1980. Emergence phenologies of some Arctic Alaskan Chironomidae. In *Chironomidae. See* Murray 1980.

———. 1984. Life histories of aquatic insects. In *The ecology of aquatic insects. See* Resh 1984a.

Bynum, W., E. Browne, and R. Porter, eds. 1985. *Dictionary of the history of science.* Princeton, N.J.: Princeton Univ. Press.

Calabi, S. 1979. Cold feet and curses. *Rod & Reel* 1(1):65–74.

Callicott, J. 1991. Conservation ethics and fishery management. *Fisheries* 16(2):22–28.

Cambell, R., D. Rimmer, and D. Scott. 1984. The effect of reduced discharge on the distribution of trout. In *Regulated rivers. See* Lillehammer 1984.

Camp, S. 1913. *Fishing with floating flies.* New York: Macmillan.

Campbell, F., and L. Maffei. 1974. Contrast and spatial frequency. *Scientific American* 231:106–14.

Carlander, K. 1969. *Handbook of freshwater fishery biology.* Iowa City: Univ. of Iowa Press.

Caucci, A., and R. Nastasi. 1975. *Hatches.* New York: Comparahatch.

Charnov, E., and W. Schaffer. 1973. The population consequences of natural selection: Cole's result revisited. *American Naturalist* 107:791–93.

Chaston, I. 1969. Seasonal activity and feeding pattern of brown trout in a Dartmoor stream in relation to availability of food. *J. Fish. Res. Bd. Canada* 26:2165–71.

Cianciara, S. 1980. Stages and physiological periods in the development of *Cloeon dipterum* L. (Baetidae). In *Advances in Ephemeroptera biology. See* Flannagan 1980.

Clapp, D., R. Clark, Jr., and J. Diana. 1990. Range, activity, and habitat of large, free-ranging brown trout in a Michigan stream. Unpublished manuscript.

Coble, D., et al. 1985. Comparative learning ability of selected fishes. *Can. J. Fish. Aquat. Sci.* 42:791–96.

Cole, L. 1954. The population consequences of life history phenomena. *Q. Rev. Biol.* 29:103–37.

Courtenay, W., Jr., and C. Kohler. 1986. Exotic fishes in North American fisheries management. In *Fish culture in fisheries management. See* Stroud 1986.

Cummins, K. 1979. The natural stream ecosystem. In *Ecology of regulated streams. See* Ward 1979a.

Cummins, K., and J. Wuycheck. 1971. *Caloric equivalents for investigations in ecological energetics.* Stuttgart: International Association of Theoretical and Applied Limnology. Communication no. 18.

Darnell, R., and R. Meierotto. 1962. Determination of feeding chronology in fishes. *Trans. Amer. Fish. Soc.* 92:313–20.

Davies, B., and K. Walker, eds. 1986. *The ecology of river systems.* The Hague: D. W. Junk.

Daxboeck, C., and G. Holeton. 1978. Oxygen receptors in rainbow trout, *Salmo gairdneri. Can. J. Zool.* 56:1254–59.

DeWald, L., and M. Wilzbach. 1992. Interactions between native brook trout and hatchery brown trout: Effects on habitat use, feeding, and growth. *Trans. Am. Fish. Soc.* 121(3):287–96.

Dodds, G., and F. Hisaw. 1924. Ecological studies of aquatic insects. *Ecology* 5:137–48, 262–71.

———. 1925. Ecological studies of aquatic insects. *Ecology* 6:123–37, 380–90.

Dunbrack, R., and L. Dill. 1983. A model of size-dependent surface feeding in a stream-dwelling salmonid. In *Predators and prey in fishes. See* Noakes 1983.

Dwyer, W., and B. Rosenlund. 1988. Role of fish culture in the reestablishment of greenback cutthroat trout. In *Status and management of interior stocks of cutthroat trout. See* Gresswell 1988a.

Easter, S., Jr. 1975. Retinal specialisations for aquatic vision: Theory and facts. In *Vision in fishes. See* Ali 1975a.

Edmunds, G., Jr., S. Jensen, and L. Berner. 1976. *The mayflies of North and Central America.* Minneapolis: Univ. of Minnesota Press.

Edmunds, G., Jr., and C. Edmunds. 1980. Predation, climate, and emergence and mating of mayflies. In *Advances in Ephemeroptera biology. See* Flannagan 1980.

Edmunds, G., Jr., and W. McCafferty. 1988. The mayfly subimago. *Ann. Rev. Entomol.* 33:509–30.

Edwards, C. 1972. Nature and origins of pollution of aquatic systems by pesticides. In *Pesticides in aquatic environments. See* Kahn 1972.

Elliot, J. 1968. The daily activity patterns of mayfly nymphs. *J. of Zool.* 155:201–21.

Ellis, R., and H. Gowing. 1957. Relationship between food supply and condition of wild brown trout in a Michigan stream. *Limnology and Oceanography* 2(4):299–308.

Engerbretson, D. 1982. Fly-rod actions. *Rod & Reel* 4(2):38–45.

Fausch, K. 1984. Profitable stream positions for salmonids relating specific growth rate to net energy gain. *Can. J. of Zool.* 62:441–51.

Fausch, K., and R. White. 1981. Competition between brook trout and brown trout for positions in a Michigan stream. *Can. J. Fish. Aquat. Sci.* 38:1220–27.

Fay, R. 1978. Sound detection and sensory coding by the auditory systems of fishes. In *The behavior of fish and other aquatic animals. See* Mostofsky 1978.

Feldmeth, C., and T. Jenkins, Jr. 1973. An estimate of energy expenditure by rainbow trout (*Salmo gairdneri*) in a small mountain stream. *J. Fish. Res. Bd. Canada* 30:1755–59.

Fenner, J. 1990. Angling optics: The fish, fisher and fly. *Trout* 31(2):81–95.

Ferguson, A., and F. Mason. 1981. Allozyme evidence for reproductively isolated sympatric populations of brown trout, *Salmo trutta* L., in Lough Melvin, Ireland. *J. Fish Biol.* 18:629–42.

Ferguson, D., and N. Ferguson. 1991. Voodoo fish management. Trout Unlimited *Action Line* (Spring).

Fernald, R. 1988. Aquatic adaptations in fish eyes. In *Sensory biology of aquatic animals. See* Atema 1988.

Flannagan, J., and K. Marshall, eds. 1980. *Advances in Ephemeroptera biology.* New York: Plenum.

Flick, A. 1947. *Streamside guide to naturals and their imitations.* New York: Putnam.

Flick, W. 1971. New trout for old waters. *The* [New York] *Conservationist* (June/July):18–21.

———. 1991. Brook trout. In *Trout. See* Stoltz 1991.

Fontaine, T., and S. Bartell, eds. 1983. *Dynamics of lotic ecosystems.* Ann Arbor, Mich.: Ann Arbor Sci. Pub.

Ford, A. 1964. *John James Audubon.* Norman, Okla.: Univ. of Oklahoma Press.

Friesen, M., J. Flannagan, and P. Laufersweiler. 1980. Diel emergence patterns of some mayflies (Ephemeroptera) of the Roseau River (Manitoba, Canada). In *Advances in Ephemeroptera biology. See* Flannagan 1980.

Galand, G., and B. Liege. 1975. Réponses visuelles unitaires chez la truite. In *Vision in fishes. See* Ali 1975a.

Gibson, G. 1829. Trout Fishing in Cumberland County, Pa. *American Turf Register and Sporting Magazine* (September):28.

Ginetz, R., and P. Larkin. 1973. Choice of colors of food items by rainbow trout (*Salmo gairdneri*). *J. Fish. Res. Bd. Canada* 30:229–34.

Gingrich, A. 1974. *The fishing in print.* New York: Winchester.

Goodspeed, C. 1939. *Angling in America.* New York: Houghton Mifflin.

Graff, D. 1986. The politics of wild trout. *Trout* 27(1):12–19.

Grayton, B., and F. Beamish. 1977. Effects of feeding frequency on food intake, growth, and body composition of rainbow trout (*Salmo gairdneri*). *Aquaculture* 11:159–72.

Gregory, M. 1978. Fly lines. *Fly Fisherman* 9(2):52–58.

Gresswell, R. E., ed. 1988. *Status and management of interior stocks of cutthroat trout.* American Fisheries Society Symposium 4. Bethesda, Md.: American Fisheries Society.

Greswell, R., and J. Varley. 1988. Effects of a century of human influence on the cutthroat trout of Yellowstone Lake. In *Status and management of interior stocks of cutthroat trout. See* Gresswell 1988.

Griffith, J. 1972. Comparative behavior and habitat utilization of brook trout and cutthroat trout in small streams in northern Idaho. *J. Fish. Res. Bd. Canada* 29:265–73.

———. 1974. Utilization of invertebrate drift by brook trout and cutthroat trout in small streams in Idaho. *Trans. Am. Fish. Soc.* 103:440–47.

Gullefors, B. 1987. Changes in flight direction of caddis flies when meeting changes in the environment. In *Proceedings of the fifth international symposium on Trichoptera. See* Bournaud 1987.

Gyselman, E. 1980. The mechanisms that maintain population stability of selected species of Ephemeroptera in a temperate stream. In *Advances in Ephemeroptera biology. See* Flannagan 1980.

Hairston, N., Jr., K. Li, and S. Easter, Jr. 1982. Fish vision and the detection of planktonic prey. *Science* 218:1240–42.

Halford, F. [1889] 1973. *Dry-fly fishing in theory and practice.* Reprint. Reading, England: Barry Shurlock.

Hannan, H. 1979. Chemical modifications in reservoir-regulated streams. In *Ecology of regulated streams. See* Ward 1979a.

Hara, J. 1986. Role of olfaction in fish behavior. In *The behavior of teleost fishes. See* Pritcher 1986.

Harmon, R., and J. Cline. 1980. At the edge of the window. *Rod & Reel* 1(7):41–45.

Hartzler, J., R. Bachman, D. Baylor, R. Butler, and K. Erbsbak. 1990. Effects of siltation and temperature on brown trout (*Salmo trutta*) in the Paint Branch watershed. In *Brown trout workshop. See* Borawa. 1990a.

Hassler, T., M. Coleman, and B. Nielson. 1986. Hatcheries and wild trout management. In *Fish culture in fisheries management. See* Stroud 1986.

Healey, M. 1984. Fish predation on aquatic insects. In *The ecology of aquatic insects. See* Resh 1984a.

Hearn, W. 1987. Interspecific competition and habitat segregation among stream-dwelling trout and salmon: A review. *Fisheries* 12(5):24–31.

Hegge, O., Dervo, B., and J. Skurdal. 1991. Age and size at sexual maturity of heavily exploited arctic char and brown trout in Lake Atnsjo, southeastern Norway. *Trans. Am. Fish. Soc.* 120:141–49.

Helfman, G. 1981a. The advantage to fishes of hovering in shade. *Copeia* 392–99.

———. 1981b. Twilight activities and temporal structure in a freshwater fish community. *Can. J. Fish. Aquat. Sci.* 38:1405–20.

Hewitt, E. [1926] 1930. *Telling on the trout.* 2d ed. New York: Scribners.

———. 1948. *A trout and salmon fisherman for seventy-five years.* New York: Scribners.

Hoffman, C., et al. 1946. *Field studies on the effect of DDT on aquatic insects.* Publication E-702, U.S. Dept. of Agriculture, Bureau of Entomology and Plant Quarantine. Washington, D.C.

Holden, P. 1979. Ecology of riverine fishes in regulated stream systems, with emphasis on the Colorado River. In *Ecology of regulated streams. See* Ward 1979a.

Hölldobler, B., and E. Wilson. 1990. *The ants.* Cambridge, Mass.: Harvard Univ. Belknap Press.

Hopkins, A. 1938. Bioclimatics—a science of life and climate relations. U.S. Dept. Ag. Misc. Publ. 280. Washington, D.C.: U.S. Dept. of Agriculture.

Hopp, R., and B. Blair. 1973. Plant phenology in eastern and central North America: Development of networks and preliminary results. Univ. of Vt. Ag. Exp. Sta. Bulletin 677. Burlington, Vt.: Univ. of Vermont.

Hubbs, C. 1964. History of ichthyology in the United States after 1850. *Copeia* 42–60.

Hudy, M. 1990. Brown trout population structures in White River tailwaters currently managed under no special regulations. In *Brown trout workshop. See* Borawa 1990a.

Hunt, R. 1984. *Annual production by brook trout in Lawrence Creek during eleven successive years.* Technical Bulletin 82. Madison: Wisconsin Dept. of Natural Resources.

———. 1990. Habitat development techniques used to improve brown trout fisheries in Wisconsin. In *Brown trout workshop. See* Borawa 1990a.

Hutchinson, G. 1981. Thoughts on aquatic insects. *BioScience* 31:495–500.

Hynes, H. 1970. *The ecology of running waters.* Toronto: Univ. of Toronto Press.

———. 1984a. The relationships between the taxonomy and ecology of aquatic insects. In *The ecology of aquatic insects. See* Resh 1984a.

———. 1984b. Aquatic insects and mankind. In *The ecology of aquatic insects. See* Resh 1984a.

———. 1984c. Running waters and mankind. In *The ecology of aquatic insects. See* Resh 1984a.

Jackson, B. 1992. Sinking-tip and sinking lines. *Fly Rod & Reel* 14(1):38–41, 86–88.

Jasper, H., and J. Raynauld. 1975. The retina as a model of the brain. In *Vision in fishes. See* Ali 1975a.

Jenkins, T. 1969a. Social structure, position choice, and distribution of two trout species (*Salmo trutta* and *Salmo gairdneri*) resident in mountain streams. *Anim. Behav. Monogr.* 2(2):57–123.

———. 1969b. Observations on color changes of brown and rainbow trout in stream habitats, with description of an unusual color pattern in brown trout. *Trans. Am. Fish. Soc.* 3:517–19.

Johnson, J., et al., eds. 1970. *Advances in chemoreception. Vol. 1.* New York: Appleton-Century-Crofts.

Johnson, P. 1984. *The scientific angler.* New York: Scribners.

Jones, R. 1990. A review of regulations and angler catch characteristics on selected Yellowstone National Park brown trout streams. In *Brown trout workshop. See* Borawa 1990a.

Jordan, D. 1891. Report of the explorations in Colorado and Utah during the summer of 1889, with an account of the fishes found in each of the river basins examined. *U.S. Fish Commission Bulletin 1891.* Washington, D.C.: U.S. Fish Commission.

Juracek, J., and C. Mathews. 1992. *Fishing Yellowstone hatches.* New York: Nick Lyons Books.

Kahn, M., ed. 1972. *Pesticides in aquatic environments.* New York: Plenum.

Kahn, M., J. Lech, and J. Menn, eds. 1979. *Pesticide and xenobiotic metabolism in aquatic organisms.* Washington, D.C.: American Chemical Society.

Kamil, A. 1988. Behavioral ecology and sensory biology. In *Sensory biology of aquatic animals. See* Atema 1988.

Kaya, C. 1976. *Reproductive biology of trout in a thermally enriched environment: the Firehole River of Yellowstone National Park.* RLO-2228-T2-2, 2d ann. prog. rpt. U.S. Energy Research and Development Administration. Washington, D.C.

Kaya, C., L. Kaeding, and D. Burkhalter. 1977. Use of a cold-water refuge by rainbow and brown trout in a geothermally heated stream. *Prog. Fish Cult.* 39(1):37–39.

Kendra, W. 1991. Quality of salmonid hatchery effluents during a summer low-flow season. *Trans. Am. Fish. Soc.* 120:43–51.

Kennedy, H. 1967. *Seasonal abundance of aquatic invertebrates and their utilization by hatchery-reared rainbow trout.* Technical Paper no. 12, Bureau of Sport Fisheries and Wildlife, U.S. Dept. of Interior. Washington, D.C.

Kerfoot, W., and A. Sih, eds. 1987. *Predation: Direct and indirect impact on aquatic communities.* Hanover, N.H.: Univ. Press of New England.

Kincaid, H., and C. Berry, Jr. 1986. Trout broodstocks used in management of national fisheries. In *Fish culture in fisheries management. See* Stroud 1986.

King, W. ed. 1975. *Wild Trout Management.* Vienna, Va.: Trout Unlimited.

Koeman, J., and J. Strik, eds. 1975. *Sublethal effects of toxic chemicals in aquatic animals.* New York: Elsevier Scientific.

Kondolf, G., G. Cada, M. Sale, and T. Felando. Distribution and stability of potential salmonid spawning gravels in steep boulder-bed streams of the eastern Sierra Nevada. *Trans. Am. Fish. Soc.* 120:177–86.

Kozel, S., W. Hubert, and M. Parsons. 1990. Relations of habitat features to brown trout abundance in unimpacted drainages on the Medicine Bow National Forest, Wyoming. In *Brown trout workshop. See* Borawa 1990a.

Kreh, L. and M. Sosin. 1991. *Practical Fishing Knots II.* New York: Lyons and Burford.

Krueger, C., A. Gharret, T. Dehring, and F. Allendorf. Genetic aspects of fisheries rehabilitation programs. *Can. J. Fish. Aquat. Sci.* 38:1877–81.

Kureck, A. 1980. Circadian eclosion rhythm in *Chironomous thummi*; ecological adjustment to different temperature levels and the role of temperature cycles. In *Chironomidae. See* Murray 1980.

Kwain, W., and H. MacCrimmon. 1967. The behaviour and bottom colour selection of the rainbow trout, *Salmo gairdneri* Richardson, exposed to different light intensities. *Anim. Behav.* 15:75–78.

LaFontaine, G. 1981. *Caddisflies.* New York: Nick Lyons Books.

———. 1990. *The dry fly.* Helena, Mont.: Greycliff.

Lamberti, G., and J. Moore. 1984. Aquatic insects as primary consumers. In *The ecology of aquatic insects. See* Resh 1984a.

Larson, G., and S. Moore. 1985. Encroachment of exotic rainbow trout into stream populations of native brook trout in the southern Appalachian Mountains. *Trans. Am. Fish. Soc.* 144:195–203.

Legendre, P., C. Schreck, and R. Behnke. 1972. Taximetric analysis of selected groups of western North American *Salmo* with respect to phylogenetic differences. *Systematic Zoology* 28:292–307.

Leisenring, J. 1941. *The art of tying the wet fly.* New York: Dodd Mead.

Leisenring, J., and Hidy, V. 1971. *The art of tying the wet fly and fishing the flymph.* New York: Crown.

Leiser, E. 1973. *Fly tying materials.* New York: Crown.

———. 1977. *The complete book of fly tying.* New York: Knopf.

———. 1987. *The book of fly patterns.* New York: Knopf.

Lillehammer, A., and S. Saltveit, eds. 1984. *Regulated rivers.* Oslo: Oslo Univ. Press.

Lord, R. 1946. The Vermont test water study: 1935 to 1945 inclusive. Fisheries Research Bulletin no. 2. Montpelier, Vt.: Vermont Fish and Game Service.

Lorson, R., and M. Marcinko. 1990. Age and growth statistics comparing brown trout scales and otoliths. In *Brown trout workshop. See* Borawa 1990a.

Lowe, R. 1979. Phytobenthic ecology and regulated streams. In *Ecology of regulated streams. See* Ward 1979a.

Lythgoe, J. 1966. Visual pigments and underwater vision. In *Light as an ecological factor. See* Bainbridge 1966.

———. 1975. The structure and phylogeny of iridescent corneas in fishes. *In Vision in fishes. See* Ali 1975a.

———. 1988. Light and vision in the aquatic environment. In *Sensory biology of aquatic animals. See* Atema 1988.

McCafferty, W. 1981. *Aquatic Entomology.* Boston: Science Books International.

McClane, A. 1953. *The Practical fly fisherman.* Englewood Cliffs, N.J.: Prentice-Hall.

———. 1974. *McClane's new standard fishing encyclopedia.* New York: Holt, Rinehart and Winston.

MacCrimmon, H. 1971. World distribution of rainbow trout. *J. Fish. Res. Bd. Canada* 28:663–704.

MacCrimmon, H., and J. Campbell. 1969. World Distribution of Brook Trout. *J. Fish. Res. Bd. Canada* 26:1699–1725.

MacCrimmon, H., T. Marshall, and B. Gots. 1970a. World distribution of brown trout. *J. Fish. Res. Bd. Canada* 27:811–18.

———. 1970b. World distribution of brown trout, *Salmo trutta;* further observations. *J. Fish. Res. Bd. Canada* 27:811–18.

MacCrimmon, H., B. Gots, and M. Morse. 1990. Stream habitat effects on reproduction success and juvenile production on brown trout. In *Brown trout workshop. See* Borawa 1990a.

———. 1972. *Quill Gordon.* New York: Knopf.

McDonald, J. 1947. *The complete fly fisherman:*

The notes and letters of Theodore Gordon. New York: Scribners.

———. 1963. *The Origins of Angling.* New York: Doubleday.

McFadden, J. 1961. A population study of the brook trout, *Salvelinus fontinalis.* Wildlife Monographs 7.

———. 1976. The trout and the trophy. *Fly Fisherman* 8(1):18–23.

McFadden, J., and E. Copper. 1962. An ecological comparison of six populations of brown trout. *Trans. Am. Fish. Soc.* 91:53–62.

McFarland, W., and E. Loew. 1983. Wave-produced changes in underwater light and their relations to vision. In *Predators and prey in fishes. See* Noakes 1983.

Marcinko, M., R. Lorson, and R. Snyder. 1990. Changes in wild brown trout standing stocks after termination of stocking. In *Brown trout workshop. See* Borawa 1990a.

Marinaro, V. 1950. *A modern dry-fly code.* New York: Putnam.

———. 1976. *In the ring of the rise.* New York: Crown.

Marnell, L. 1986. Impacts of hatchery stocks on wild fish populations. In *Fish culture in fisheries management. See* Stroud 1986.

Martin, D. 1987. *Fly-tying methods.* New York: Nick Lyons Books.

Matsumura, F., G. Bush, and T. Misato, eds. 1972. *Environmental toxicology of pesticides.* New York: Academic Press.

Menzie, C. 1972. Effects of pesticides on fish and wildlife. In *Environmental toxicology of pesticides. See* Matsumura 1972.

Merritt, R., and K. Cummins, eds. 1984. *An introduction to the aquatic insects of North America.* 2nd ed. Dubuque, Ia.: Kendall/Hunt.

Merritt, R., K. Cummins, and T. Burton. 1984. The role of aquatic insects in the processing and cycling of nutrients. In *The ecology of aquatic insects. See* Resh 1984a.

Merwin, J. 1977. Mr. Hewitt's window box. *Fly Fisherman* 7(3):98–100.

———, ed. 1979. *Stillwater trout.* New York: Nick Lyons Books.

———, ed. 1987. *McClane's angling world.* New York: Dutton.

———, ed. 1988. *The compleat McClane.* New York: Dutton.

———, ed. 1989. *The compleat Lee Wulff.* New York: Dutton.

———. 1990a. *John Merwin's fly-tying guide.* New York: Viking Penguin.

———, ed. 1990b. *The compleat Schwiebert.* New York: Dutton.

———. 1991. *Streamer-fly fishing.* New York: Lyons and Burford.

Migel, J., and L. Wright. 1979. *The masters on the nymph.* New York: Nick Lyons Books.

Minshall, G. 1984. Aquatic insect-substratum relationships. In *The ecology of aquatic insects. See* Resh 1984a.

Mitchell, S. 1814. *Report . . . On the fishes of New York.* New York: D. Carlisle.

Morris, D., and M. Booker. 1980. An assessment of the importance of the Chironomidae (Diptera) in biological surveillance. In *Chironomidae. See* Murray 1980.

Morton, W. 1980. Charr or char: A history of the English name for members of the salmonid genus *Salvelinus.* In *The charrs. See* Balon 1980.

Mosser, E., and W. Buchman. 1980. The dynamics of a fly cast. *The Flyfisher* (Fall):5–9.

Mostofsky, D., ed. 1978. *The behavior of fish and other aquatic animals.* New York: Academic Press.

Moyle, P. 1969. Comparative behavior of young brook trout of domestic and wild origin. *Prog. Fish Cult.* 31:51–56.

———. 1976. *Inland fishes of California.* Berkeley: Univ. of California Press.

Moyle, P., H. Li, and B. Barton. 1986. The Frankenstein effect: Impact of introduced fishes on native fishes in North America. In *Fish culture in fisheries management. See* Stroud 1986.

Moyle, P., and J. Cech, Jr. 1988. *Fishes: An introduction to ichthyology.* 2d ed. Englewood Cliffs, N.J.: Prentice-Hall.

Muntz, W. 1975. Visual pigments and the environment. In *Vision in fishes. See* Ali 1975a.

Murdoch, W., and J. Bence. 1987. General predators and unstable prey populations. In *Predation: Direct and indirect impact on aquatic communities. See* Kerfoot 1987.

Murray, D., ed. 1980. *Chironomidae. Ecology, sys-*

tematics, cytology and physiology. New York: Pergamon.

Myers, G. 1964. A brief sketch of the history of ichthyology in America to the year 1850. *Copeia* 33–41.

Myrberg, A., Jr. 1980. Sensory mediation of social recognition processes in fishes. In *Fish behavior and its use in the capture and culture of fishes. See* Bardach 1980.

Nakatsugawa, T., and P. Nelson. 1972. Studies of insecticide detoxification in invertebrates; an enzymological approach to the problem of biological magnification. In *Environmental toxicology of pesticides. See* Matsumura 1972.

Needham, P. 1938. *Trout streams*. Ithaca, N.Y.: Comstock.

Newbury, R. Hydrologic determinants of aquatic insect habitats. In *The ecology of aquatic insects. See* Resh 1984a.

Noakes, D., D. Lindquist, G. Helfman, and J. Ward, eds. 1983. *Predators and prey in fishes*. The Hague: D. W. Junk.

Northmore, D., F. Volkmann, and D. Yager. 1978. Vision in fishes: Color and pattern. In *The behavior of fish and other aquatic animals. See* Mostofsky 1978.

O'Brien, W. 1987. Planktivory by freshwater fish: Thrust and parry in the Pelagia. In *Predation: Direct and indirect impact on aquatic communities. See* Kerfoot 1987.

Parker, N. 1986. Physical and biological factors influencing growth and survival of stocked fish. In *Fish culture in fisheries management. See* Stroud 1986.

Peckarsky, B. 1984. Predator-prey interactions among aquatic insects. In *The ecology of aquatic insects. See* Resh 1984a.

Peckarsky, B., P. Fraissinet, M. Penton, and D. Conklin, Jr. 1990. *Freshwater macroinvertebrates of northeastern North America*. Ithaca, N.Y.: Cornell Univ. Press.

Peters, J., L. Arvy, and W. Peters. 1980. Pictet and Eaton: The first mayfly specialists. In *Advances in Ephemeroptera biology. See* Flannagan 1980.

Phillips, D. 1982. Different strokes. *Rod & Reel* 4(1):12–17.

Pickering, A., et al., eds. 1981. *Stress and fish*. London: Academic Press.

Pinder, L. 1980. Spatial distribution of Chiron-

omidae in an English chalk stream. In *Chironomidae. See* Murray 1980.

———. 1986. Biology of freshwater Chironomidae. *Ann. Rev. Entomol.* 31:1–24.

Pobst, D. 1982. When your fly rod fits. *Rod & Reel* 4(1):28–31.

———. 1990. *Trout stream insects*. 1990. New York: Lyons and Burford.

Potter, B., and B. Barton. 1986. Stocking goals and criteria for restoration and enhancement of cold-water fisheries. In *Fish culture in fisheries management. See* Stroud 1986.

Power, G. 1980. The brook charr, *Salvelinus fontinalis*. In *The charrs. See* Balon 1980.

Pritcher, T., ed. 1986. *The behavior of teleost fishes*. Baltimore: Johns Hopkins Univ. Press.

Raymond, S. 1980. *Kamloops*. Portland, Oreg.: Frank Amato Publications.

Reid, G. 1961. *Ecology of inland waters and estuaries*. New York: Reinhold.

Reiger, G., ed. 1975. *Fishing with McClane*. Englewood Cliffs, N.J.: Prentice Hall.

Resh, V., and D. Rosenberg, eds. 1984a. *The ecology of aquatic insects*. New York: Praeger.

———. 1984b. The growth of aquatic insect ecology. In *The ecology of aquatic insects. See* Resh 1984a.

Richardson, J. 1987. Patterns of geographic variation in adult flight phenology of some Nearctic Trichoptera. In *Proceedings of the fifth international symposium on Trichoptera. See* Bournaud 1987.

Ringler, N. 1975. The mechanism of selective predation in drift-feeding brown trout (*Salmo trutta*). Ph. D. diss. Ann Arbor, Mich.: Univ. of Michigan.

———. 1983. Variation in foraging tactics of fishes. In *Predators and prey in fishes. See* Noakes 1983.

Ringler, N., and D. Brodowski. 1983. Functional responses of brown trout (*Salmo trutta* L.) to invertebrate drift. *Journal of Freshwater Ecology* 2(1):45–57.

Ritz, C. 1959. *A fly fisher's life*. New York: Henry Holt.

Robins, C., et al. 1991. *Common and scientific names of fishes from the United States and Canada*. Bethesda, Md.: American Fisheries Society.

Rogers, P., and M. Cox. 1988. Underwater sound

as a biological stimulus. In *Sensory biology of aquatic animals.* See Atema 1988.

Rosen, M., and N. Cornford. 1971. Fluid friction of fish slimes. *Nature* 234:49–51.

Rudd, R., and S. Herman. 1972. Ecosystemic transferal of pesticides residues in an aquatic environment. In *Environmental toxicology of pesticides.* See Matsumura 1972.

Russell, R. 1977. Rainbow trout life history studies in Lower Talarik Creek—Kvichak Drainage. Study G-II-E. Anchorage: Alaska Department of Fish and Game.

Ruttner, F. 1963. *Fundamentals of limnology.* 3d ed. Toronto: Univ. of Toronto Press.

Savolainen, E. 1978. Swarming in Emphermeroptera: The mechanism of swarming and the effects of illumination and weather. *Ann. Zool. Fenn.* 15:17–52.

Scarola, J. 1987. *Freshwater fishes of New Hampshire.* Concord, N.H.: New Hampshire Fish and Game Dept..

Schreck, C. 1981. Stress and compensation in teleostean fishes: Response to social and physical factors. In *Stress and fish.* See Pickering 1981.

Schreck, C., and P. Moyle, eds. 1990. *Methods for fish biology.* Bethesda, Md.: American Fisheries Society.

Schullery, P. 1987. *American fly fishing: A history:* New York: Nick Lyons Books.

Schwassmann, H. 1975. Refractive state, accommodation, and resolving power of the fish eye. In *Vision in fishes.* See Ali 1975a.

Schwiebert, E. 1955. *Matching the hatch.* New York: Macmillan.

———. 1973. *Nymphs.* New York: Winchester.

———. 1978. *Trout.* New York: Dutton.

———. 1979. The evolution of the nymph. In *The masters on the nymph.* See Migel 1979.

Scrimshaw, S., and W. Kerfoot. 1987. Chemical defenses of freshwater organisms: Beetles and bugs. In *Predation: Direct and indirect impact on aquatic communities.* See Kerfoot 1987.

Sheldon, A. 1984. Colonization dynamics of aquatic insects. In *The ecology of aquatic insects.* See Resh 1984a.

Shirvell, C., and R. Dungey. 1983. Microhabitats chosen by brown trout for feeding and spawning in rivers. *Trans. Am. Fish. Soc.* 112:355–67.

Sigler, W., and J. Sigler. 1990. *Recreational fisheries: Management, theory, and application.* Reno, Nev.: Univ. of Nevada Press.

Sih, A. 1987. Predators and prey lifestyles: An evolutionary and ecological overview. In *Predation: Direct and indirect impact on aquatic communities.* See Kerfoot 1987.

Simon, R. 1986. Improving strains and species genetically for higher production, faster growth, and increased survival. In *Fish culture in fisheries management.* See Stroud 1986.

Simons, D. 1979. Effects of stream regulation on channel morphology. In *Ecology of regulated streams.* See Ward 1979a.

Sivak, J. 1975. Accommodative mechanisms in aquatic vertebrates. In *Vision in fishes.* See Ali, 1975a.

Skues, G. 1910. *Minor tactics of the chalk stream.* London: A. & C. Black.

———. 1921. *The way of a trout with a fly.* London: A. & C. Black.

———. 1949. *The way of a trout with a fly.* 4th ed. London: A. &. C. Black.

———. [1932] 1976. *The chalk stream angler.* Winchester, England: Barry Shurlock. Reprint. Original title *Side-lines, side-lights, & reflections.*

Slobodkin, L. 1964. *Growth and regulation of animal populations.* New York: Holt, Rinehart and Winston.

Smith, G., and R. Stearley. 1989. The classification and scientific names of rainbow and cutthroat trouts. *Fisheries* 14(1):4–10.

Solem, J., and T. Bongard. 1987. Flight patterns of three species of lotic caddisflies. In *Proceedings of the fifth international symposium on Trichoptera.* See Bournaud 1987.

Solomon, D., and R. Templeton. 1976. Movements of brown trout in a chalk stream. *J. Fish Biol.* 9:411–23.

Spieth, H. 1938. Studies on the biology of Ephemeroptera, I. Coloration and its relationship to seasonal emergence. *Canadian Entomologist* 70:210–18.

Stalnaker, C. 1979. The use of habitat structure preferenda for establishing flow regimes necessary for maintenance of fish habitat. In *Ecology of regulated streams.* See Ward 1979a.

Stanford, J., and J. Ward. 1984. The effects of regulation on the limnology of the Gunnison

River: A North American case history. In *Regulated rivers. See* Lillehammer 1984.

———. 1986a. Fish of the Colorado system. In *The ecology of river systems. See* Davies 1986.

———. 1986b. Reservoirs of the Colorado system. In *The ecology of river systems. See* Davies 1986.

———. 1986c. The Colorado River system. In *The ecology of river systems. See* Davies 1986.

Stewart, W. 1857. *The practical angler.* 3d ed. Edinburgh: A. & C. Black.

Stoltz, J., and J. Schnell, eds. 1991. *Trout.* Harrisburg, Pa.: Stackpole.

Strong, D., D. Simberloff, L. Abele, and A. Thistle. 1984. *Ecological communities: Conceptual issues and the evidence.* Princeton, N.J.: Princeton Univ. Press.

Stroud, R., ed. 1979. *Predator-prey systems in fisheries management.* Washington, D.C.: Sport Fishing Institute.

———. ed. 1986. *Fish culture in fisheries management.* Bethesda, Md.: American Fisheries Society.

Stuber, R., B. Rosenlund, and J. Bennett. 1988. Greenback cutthroat trout recovery program: Management overview. In *Status and management of interior stocks of cutthroat trout. See* Gresswell 1988.

Sweeney, B. 1978. Bioenergetic and developmental response of a mayfly to thermal variation. *Limnology and Oceanography* 23:461–77.

———. 1984. Factors influencing life-history patterns of aquatic insects. In *The ecology of aquatic insects. See* Resh 1984a.

Sweeney, B., and R. Vannote. 1978. Size variation and the distribution of hemimetabolous aquatic insects: Two thermal equilibrium hypotheses. *Science* 200:444–46.

———. 1981. *Ephemerella* mayflies of White Clay Creek: Bioenergetic and ecological relationships among six coexisting species. *Ecology* 62(5):1353–69.

Swisher, D., and C. Richards. 1971. *Selective trout.* New York: Nick Lyons Books.

———. 1975. *Fly fishing strategy.* New York: Nick Lyons Books.

———. 1992. *Emergers.* New York: Nick Lyons Books.

Thorn, W. 1990. Effects of habitat improvement and a special regulation on a wild brown trout population. In *Brown trout workshop. See* Borawa 1990a.

Tippetts, W., and P. Moyle. 1978. Epibenthic feeding by rainbow trout (*Salmo gairdneri*) in the McCloud River, California. *J. Anim. Ecol.* 47:549–59.

Trautman, M. 1957. *The fishes of Ohio.* Columbus, Ohio: Ohio State Univ. Press.

Trotter, P. 1987. *Cutthroat: Native trout of the West.* Boulder, Colo.: Colorado State Univ. Press.

Trotter, P., and P. Bisson. 1988. History and discovery of the cutthroat trout. In *Status and management of interior stocks of cutthroat trout. See* Gresswell 1988a.

Vannote, R., et al. 1980. The river continuum concept. *Can. J. Fish. Aquat. Sci.* 37:130–37.

Vannote, R., and B. Sweeney. 1980. Geographic analysis of thermal equilibria: A conceptual model for evaluating the effect of natural and modified thermal regimes on aquatic insect communities. *American Naturalist* 115(5):667–95.

Varley, J., and R. Gresswell. 1988. Ecology, status, and management of the Yellowstone cutthroat trout. In *Status and management of interior stocks of cutthroat trout. See* Gresswell 1988.

Vincent, R. 1975. Effect of stocking catchable trout on wild trout populations. In *Wild trout management. See* King 1975.

Vincent, R., and W. Miller. 1969. Altitudinal distribution of brown trout and other fishes in a headwater tributary of the South Platte River. *Ecology* 50(3):464–66.

Von Behr, L. 1882. Five American Salmonidae in Germany. *U.S. Fish Commission Bulletin: 1882.* Washington, D.C.: U.S. Fish Commission.

Ward, J. 1975. Bottom fauna-substrate relationships in a northern Colorado trout stream: 1945 and 1974. *Ecology* 56:1429–34.

———. 1984. Ecological perspectives in the management of aquatic insect habitat. In *The ecology of aquatic insects. See* Resh 1984a.

———. 1987. Trichoptera of regulated Rocky Mountain streams. In *Proceedings of the fifth international symposium on Trichoptera. See* Bournaud 1987.

Ward, J., and J. Sanford, 1979a. eds. *Ecology of regulated streams.* New York: Plenum.

———. 1979b. Ecological factors controlling stream zoobenthos with emphasis on thermal modification of regulated streams. In *Ecology of regulated streams. See* Ward 1979a.

———. 1984. The regulated stream as a testing ground for ecological theory. In *Regulated rivers. See* Lillehammer 1984.

Ward, J., and L. Berner. 1980. Abundance and altitudinal distribution of Ephemeroptera in a Rocky Mountain stream. In *Advances in Ephemeroptera biology. See* Flannagan 1980.

Ward, J., H. Zimmerman, and L. Cline. 1986. Lotic zoobenthos of the Colorado system. In *The ecology of river systems. See* Davies 1986.

Ware, D. 1971. Predation by rainbow trout: The effect of experience. *J. Fish. Res. Bd. Canada* 28:1847–52.

———. 1972. Predation by rainbow trout: The influence of hunger, prey density, and prey size. *J. Fish. Res. Bd. Canada* 29:1193–1201.

———. 1973. Risk of epibenthic prey to predation by rainbow trout (*Salmo gairdneri*). *J. Fish. Res. Bd. Canada* 30:787–97.

Waters, T. 1983. Replacement of brook trout by brown trout over 15 years in a Minnesota stream: Production and abundance. *Trans. Am. Fish. Soc.* 142:137–46.

Webb, P., and D. Weihs. 1983. *Fish biomechanics.* New York: Praeger.

Webster, D., and W. Flick. 1981. Performance of indigenous, exotic, and hybrid strains of brook trout in waters of the Adirondack Mountains, New York. *Can. J. Fish. Aquat. Sci.* 38:1701–7.

Weithman, A. 1986. Economic benefits and costs associated with stocking fish. In *Fish culture in fisheries management. See* Stroud 1986.

Welch, P. 1952. *Limnology.* 2d ed. New York: McGraw-Hill.

Wesche, T., C. Goertler, and C. Frye. 1990a. Contribution of riparian vegetation to trout cover in small streams. In *Brown trout workshop. See* Borawa 1990a.

———. 1990b. Modified habitat suitability index model for brown trout in southeastern Wyoming. In *Brown trout workshop. See* Borawa 1990a.

Wiederholm, T. 1984. Responses of aquatic insects to environmental pollution. In *The ecology of aquatic insects. See* Resh 1984a.

Wiggins, G. 1977. *Larvae of North American caddisfly genera.* Toronto: Univ. of Toronto Press.

Wilcox, R. 1988. Surface-wave reception in invertebrates and vertebrates. In *Sensory biology of aquatic animals. See* Atema 1988.

Wiley, M., and S. Kohler. 1984. Behavioral adaptations of aquatic insects. In *The ecology of aquatic insects. See* Resh 1984a.

Willers, W. 1991. *Trout biology.* 2d ed. New York: Lyons and Burford.

Williams. D. 1980. Applied aspects of mayfly biology. In *Advances in Ephemeroptera biology. See* Flannagan 1980.

———. 1984. The hyporheic zone as a habitat for aquatic insects and associated arthropods. In *The ecology of aquatic insects. See* Resh 1984a.

Wilson, R. 1980. Classifying rivers using Chironomid pupal exuviae. In *Chironomidae. See* Murray 1980.

Wood, C., J. Turner, and M. Graham. 1983. Why do fish die after severe exercise? *J. Fish Biol.* 22:189–201.

Woodward, D., A. Farag, E. Little, B. Steadman, and R. Yancik. 1991. Sensitivity of greenback cutthroat trout to acidic pH and elevated aluminum. *Trans. Am. Fish. Soc.* 120:34–42.

Wright, L. 1972. *Fishing the dry fly as a living insect.* New York: Dutton.

Wydoski, R. 1986. Informational needs to improve stocking as a cold-water fisheries management tool. In *Fish culture in fisheries management. See* Stroud 1986.

Wynne, M., and L. Lickett. 1990. Evaluation of the Shuler Creek Renovation Project—preliminary findings. In *Brown trout workshop. See* Borawa 1990a.

Zimmerman, H., and J. Ward. 1984. A survey of regulated streams in the Rocky Mountains of Colorado, U.S.A. In *Regulated rivers. See* Lillehammer 1984.

Zimmerman, M., and T. Wissing. 1980. The nutritional dynamics of the burrowing mayfly, *Hexagenia limbata.* In *Advances in Ephemeroptera biology. See* Flannagan 1980.

Index